Walking

New England

Walking Places in
New England

by Vicki Shearer

out there press
asheville, north carolina
www.outtherepress.com

Walking Places in New England

© 2001 Victoria Shearer

Out There Press
PO Box 1173
Asheville, NC 28802
www.outtherepress.com

Maps by Simply Maps

Library of Congress Control Number: 2001089195
ISBN: 1-893695-04-2

The author and publisher have made every effort to ensure the accuracy of the information contained in this book. Nevertheless, they can not be held liable for any loss, damage, injury, or inconvenience sustained by any person using this book. Readers should keep in mind that walks in wilderness areas of county, state, and national parks have some risk. Please be careful.

Cover photograph: The Freedom Trail Foundation
Cover design: James Bannon

Manufactured in the United States

10 9 8 7 6 5 4 3 2 1

Table of Contents

Acknowledgments

Creating Walking Places in New England was a labor of love. The project had a two-year gestation— four months of background research, six months on the road . . . and on the trails . . . and on the sidewalks. . . and up the rocky paths, and more than a year writing. But even with the protracted birth of this book, I simply can't hang up my walking shoes. I'm hooked for life, I guess.

I've said it before and I'll say it again . . . I get by with a little help from my friends. My undying gratitude goes to all those wonderful people in New England—my new friends—who helped make this massive endeavor possible, probable, and passionately enjoyable. Thank you to the tourist councils, chambers of commerce, government agencies, publicists, innkeepers, restaurateurs—too numerous to mention by name lest I forget someone—for keeping me fed, rested, and headed in the right direction and for sharing your secret favorite walking places in New England.

And thank you to my walking companions, you brave souls who volunteered to accompany me on portions of my adventure. You were all great sports, even when I didn't program time for lunch and pushed you beyond your endurance. Even when you weren't walking with me in person, you supported me in spirit, all the way. First and foremost, thanks to my husband Bob, who hit the trails with me for weeks in Vermont, New Hampshire, and Maine and on junkets to Nantucket, Cape Ann, and Boston. Thanks for your love and companionship, your undying patience through this all-consuming project, and for picking up the slack I dropped in our daily lives. I love you.

Thanks to my two dearest friends, Suzanne Tobey and Vivienne Afshari. Suzanne, who accompanied me on walks in Litchfield Hills, central Connecticut, and western Massachusetts dropped her arch at Chesterfield Gorge and needed medical attention for months. Vivienne joined me in Maine and we trekked the trails of the south coast, consumed as much lobster as we could possibly pack in, and spent way too much time in Kennebunkport looking for Barbara Bush. Thanks also to my cousin, LuAnn Smith, who came all the way from Fort Lauderdale to explore Block Island and the Connecticut coast with me. We hadn't spent time together since we were kids, but with long hours on the trails, we caught up on 30 years and became best buddies once again.

Special thanks also to Peggie Hunter and Glen Faria, who went way beyond the scope of professional duties to share their expertise of New England and help me organize my walking schedule. In the process, I made two new friends. You are the best! And a sincere note of gratitude must go to Jim Bannon of Out There Press for sharing his vision and inviting me on board.

And finally, to our forefathers— thanks for finding this place, New England. I was thrilled to discover it too!

VHS

Preface

"I have met with but one or two persons in the course of my life who understood the art of Walking, that is, of taking walks—who had a genius, so to speak, for sauntering . . . I think that I cannot preserve my health and spirits unless I spend four hours a day at least . . . sauntering through the woods and over the hills and fields, absolutely free from all worldly engagements. . . . But the walking of which I speak has nothing in it akin to taking exercise . . . but is itself the enterprise and adventure of the day. . . There is in fact a sort of harmony discoverable between the capabilities of the landscape within a circle of ten miles' radius, or the limits of an afternoon walk, and the threescore years and ten of human life. It will never become quite familiar to you. . . . For every walk is a sort of crusade . . . not a solitary phenomenon, never to happen again, but . . . it would happen forever and ever . . . and cheer and reassure the latest child that walked there . . . more glorious still."

Henry David Thoreau
Walking, 1862

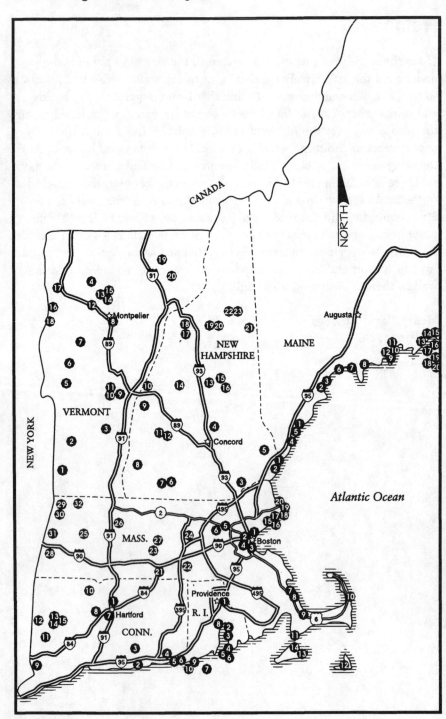

Connecticut

1. Yale University
2. Old Saybrook Point
3. Essex Village
4. Connecticut College Arboretum
5. Mystic Seaport
6. Historic Stonington Borough
7. Historic Wethersfield
8. Amistead Trail
9. Weir Farm
10. People's State Forest
11. Mine Hill Preserve
12. Bull's Covered Bridge River Walk
13. White Flower Farm
14. Historic Litchfield
15. Trail of the Senses

Maine

1. Kennebunkport
2. Historic Portland
3. Back Bay Cove Loop
4. Marginal Way
5. Wells Estuarine Reserve
6. Historic Brunswick
7. Bath Architectural Walking Tour
8. Salt Bay Preserve Heritage Trail
9. Rockland Breakwater
10. Camden Village Center
11. Camden Hills State Park
12. Merryspring Horticultural Nature Park
13. Fort Knox State Historic Site Park
14. Castine History Tour
15. Blue Hill
16. Edgar M. Tennis Preserve
17. Barred Island Preserve
18. Settlement Quarry
19. Acadia National Park
20. Bar Harbor

Massachusetts

1. Freedom Trail
2. Black Heritage Trail
3. Back Bay
4. Cambridge and Harvard University
5. Lexington and Concord
6. Walden Pond
7. Historic Plymouth
8. Plymouth Plantation
9. Heritage Plantation
10. Cape Cod National Seashore
11. Shining Sea Bikepath
12. Historic Nantucket
13. Historic Edgartown
14. Oak Bluffs Camp
15. Historic Salem
16. Historic Marblehead
17. Sedgwick Gardens
18. Gloucester
19. Village of Rockport
20. Halibut State Park
21. Old Sturbridge Village
22. Purgatory Chasm State Reservation
23. Rockhouse Reservation
24. Tower Hill Botanic Gardens
25. Chesterfield Gorge
26. Old Deerfield
27. Doane's Falls Reservation
28. Stockbridge
29. Williams College
30. Mount Greylock State Reservation
31. Hancock Shaker Village
32. Natural Bridge State Park

New Hampshire

1. Portsmouth Harbor Trail
2. Seacoast Science Center
3. America's Stonehenge
4. Canterbury Shaker Village
5. Evelyn Browne Trail
6. Miller State Park
7. Rhododendron State Park
8. Chesterfield Gorge
9. Saint Gaudens
10. Dartmouth College
11. The Fells Historic Site
12. Mount Sunapee Lake Solitude Trail
13. Science Center of New Hampshire
14. Paradise Point Nature Center
15. West Rattlesnake Bridle Path Trail
16. Loon Center/Markus Sanctuary
17. Lost River Gorge
18. Franconia Notch State Park
19. Round the Lake Trail
20. Crawford Notch State Park
21. Sabbaday Falls
22. Lost Pond Trail
23. Thompson's Falls Trail

Rhode Island

1. Providence
2. Blithewald Mansion and Gardens
3. Green Animals Toplary Garden
4. Historic Newport
5. Bellevue Avenue Mansion Walk
6. Cliff Walk
7. Block Island Greenway Trails
8. Village of Wickford
9. East Beach
10. Napatree Point

Vermont

1. Historic Old Bennington
2. Equinox Preservation Trust
3. Grafton Ponds Trails
4. White Rocks Ice Beds Trail
5. Silver Lake Trail
6. Robert Frost Interpretive Trail
7. Texas Falls Nature Trail
8. Montpelier Architectural Tour
9. Quechee Gorge Trail
10. Woodstock Village
11. Vermont Raptor Center
12. Little River State Park
13. Trapp Family Chapel Trail
14. Stowe Recreation Path
15. Weissner Woods
16. Shelburne Museum
17. Burlington Waterfront Bikepath
18. Vermont Wildflower Farm
19. Willoughby State Forest
20. Darling State Park

Introduction

New England

A Yankee atmosphere pervades all of New England, rendering its borders almost inconsequential and setting the region distinctively apart from the rest of the United States. The six states that comprise New England—Connecticut, Rhode Island, Massachusetts, Vermont, New Hampshire, and Maine— form a colorful patchwork of mountains, forests, seacoast, historic sites, and uninhabited wilderness. Like a Currier and Ives print, New England of yesteryear still remains. Small farms separated by stone fences pepper the landscape, linked by narrow, winding roads and covered bridges that lead to small villages filled with quaint houses. New England's central Yankee character, based on a Puritan work ethic, frugality, moral conscience, and a proud independent streak, developed from its common historical and geographical evolution.

Historical Evolution

Long before the Pilgrims set foot on Plymouth Rock, English sea captain John Smith outlined the Northeast coast from Cape Cod to Maine and subsequently showed his map to the English royal family, who dubbed the area New England. As the Pilgrims and Puritans established colonies throughout New England, they brought with them simple tastes, strong principles, and firm religious beliefs. First settling in Massachusetts—Plymouth in 1620, Boston in 1630—Puritan colonies grew to more than 80,000 by 1700. But the Puritans granted no religious freedoms to doubters or those of other faiths, so many left Massachusetts Bay Colony to form self-governing settlements elsewhere. Offshoot colonies grew up in Connecticut, Rhode Island and New Hampshire, numbering 50,000 colonists by 1700.

The colonists enjoyed good relations with the Indians for 50 years after the Pilgrims landed, but the white man's perpetual seizure of native lands caused resentments to grow, and bloody battles with the settlers began. In the wars that followed between the French and the British, the Indians sided with the French. When the British got control of Canada in 1763, effectively ending the French and Indian Wars, Indian harassment of New England ended.

Initially, the colonists existed on subsistence farming. Farms were small because soil was so rocky and difficult to till. The townships were about six miles square, with houses built around a common green, near the church and town meeting hall. Privately owned fields surrounded the village. The village green, replicated in hundreds of towns in all six states, is perhaps the most quintessentially recognizable icon in all of New England.

By the 18th century, discouraged by the hard climate and bad soil, New Englanders utilized other resources, such as lumber from bountiful forests, natural harbors for shipping goods, abundant fish from the ocean, and rivers for generating power. They concentrated on building up commerce, to minimize their dependence on English goods, and started a thriving sea trade with Europe, Africa, and the West Indies. England didn't pay much attention to the colonies up to this time, considering them small and inconsequential, but once the wealth of the colonies began to grow, the Mother Country decided to take a bigger cut of the pie and placed new restrictions upon them.

This was the turning point in our history. Taxes and restrictions grew and grew, until it reached a boiling point with the Stamp Act of 1765, which placed duties on newspapers, licenses, legal documents, etc. The act was repealed a year later because colonists protested so much. Then in 1767, England levied the Townshend Acts, which placed taxes on tea, paints, paper, and glass. Protests turned violent in March 1770— the Boston Massacre— when a crowd threw snowballs at British troops in Boston. The troops, in turn, fired into the crowd, killing a handful of colonists and enraging all others.

England repealed all of the Townshend Acts except that on tea, but resentments continued to grow. Finally, disguised as Indians, Samuel Adams and the Sons of Liberty boarded English ships in Boston Harbor and dumped 342 chests of East India tea overboard. King George III responded by closing Boston Harbor. Colonists retaliated by calling a meeting of the First Continental Congress in September 1774 to plan a boycott of British imports. Shots were fired at Lexington and Concord and the Revolutionary War began.

The rest, as they say, is history, and much of the Revolution was played out in New England, where it began. Massive stone monuments immortalize the Battle of Bunker Hill (1775) and the Battle of Bennington in Vermont (1777). Wethersfield, the first settlement in Connecticut, also lays claim to an important Revolutionary encounter. Here, George Washington held a meeting with Count de Rochambeau, who commanded the French forces in America. This meeting led to the end of the Revolution because the colonists and the French subsequently combined forces and defeated the British at Yorktown, in Virginia.

The Revolutionary War depressed commerce for a time, but by the turn of the 18th century, a class of wealthy merchants prospered due to trade with China, Russia, and the East Indies. And a golden era of whaling, centered in Nantucket and New Bedford, Massachusetts, lasted until oil was discovered in Pennsylvania in 1859.

From 1840 to 1860, Yankee clipper ships were built in New England. Known for their speed, the clippers, nonetheless, were expensive to build, required a large crew, and could carry only a small cargo. Steamships replaced the Yankee clippers in the last third of the century, when the shipping industry began to require larger ships. New England's smaller ports, such as Salem, Providence, and Newport declined, while Boston grew in importance. The emergence of the steamship and the transcontinental railway, which broadened the domestic market, led to the gradual demise of shipbuilding in New England.

Factories developed in Massachusetts, Rhode Island, and Connecticut in the mid-19th century. Company mill towns sprang up all over New England. By 1860 New England produced 75 percent of all cotton goods in the U.S. A shortage of labor led to the arrival of thousands of English and Irish immigrants to man the textile mills. Manufacturing expanded to the production of guns, clocks, sewing machines, shoes, and more. Some of the more famous products bore brand names still recognizable today, such as Colt (revolvers), Goodyear (tires), and Rogers (silver plate). New England notables such as Samuel Morse (telegraph) and Alexander Graham Bell (telephone) invented other technological improvements.

Financing became big business in the 19th century, as New England financed much of the development in the rest of the country. Yankees believed the New England colonies to be the first permanent civilization in America, feeling they reached maturity while the rest of America was still growing. Only when steelmaking became key to industrial growth did New England fall behind the rest of the nation.

In the 1920s, the death knell tolled for the New England textile industry. Synthetics were introduced in the South, and stubborn Yankees refused to produce the fabric. Mills were closed in New England and reopened in southern states, which, with the advantage of a cheaper labor source, were able to produce the popular goods at a lower cost. Abandoned textile mills can still be seen in many New England cities.

New England's economy rebounded after World War II, with the advent of the electronic age, and continues to thrive into the 21st century computer-driven era. New England cherishes and preserves its common history with a Yankee determination rarely matched by other regions of the United States.

Geographical Evolution

At the end of the last Ice Age, giant chunks of ice littered the landscape of the Northeast, eventually melting to form hollows that became ponds. Over time, the ponds became shallower, turning to marshland, then dried out completely. Filled with silt, these hollows eventually supported plants, forests, and wild creatures, breathing life into the New England landscape.

New England was united— and divided from the rest of the country—by six geographic phenomena. First, the region was relatively secluded, bordered on the south and east by saltwater ocean, on the north by forest, and in the west by mountains. The area remained homogeneously populated until the 19th century, when the first wave of immigrants began infiltrating the Yankee stronghold.

Second, glaciers had scoured most of the soil from the bedrock of New England, making farming endeavors a hardscrabble existence. A third factor, which also contributed to the difficulty of farming the region, was the harsh New England climate. Settlers were often battered by nor'easters, severe storms caused when warm southern air mixed with cool northern masses. The storms were named nor'easters because, from the land, the spinning winds appeared to be coming from the northeast.

Fourth, New England is tied together by its 6,000-mile coastline, which extends from Passamaquoddy Bay in northern Maine to Greenwich, Connecticut on Long Island Sound. As difficult as it was for settlers to farm the land of New England, the sea turned out to be a lucrative gold mine. The icy Labrador Current runs south in the Atlantic Ocean over banks, or shallow underwater shelves, which allows the water to become warmer. The warm water fosters the growth of plankton, which, in turn, attracts a rich bounty of fish, such as cod, mackerel, flounder, and shellfish. This treasure trove led to the development of the New England fishing industry. Georges Bank is the largest and most well known such underwater shelf off the New England coast.

Mountains comprise the fifth geographic feature uniting New England, ranging higher in the northern states and tapering to the foothills of Connecticut. The White Mountains of New Hampshire rank as the highest in New England, topped by Mount Washington, at 6,288 feet, the tallest peak in the Northeast. The Green Mountains of Vermont, the Berkshires of Massachusetts, and Litchfield Hills of Connecticut dominate the western region of New England, between the Connecticut River Valley and the New York border.

Finally, the Connecticut River, New England's longest river, flows south between New Hampshire and Vermont for 407 miles, then bisects the state of Connecticut. Beginning in three small New Hampshire lakes near the Canadian border, the Connecticut River empties into the Long Island Sound at Saybrook. The river was navigable as far north as Hartford, Connecticut, which became a deepwater port and evolved into the insurance center of New England. The insurance industry had its beginnings in Hartford, where underwriters would share the risk of the ship owner for a percentage of the profits.

The Connecticut River Valley is the most fertile area of New England. Glaciers created a huge dam in the river, near present-day Middletown, Connecticut, forming a giant lake. The dam broke, the lake washed away, and rich soil remained. Tobacco, vegetable, and dairy farms flourished in the valley all the way up to Hanover and Lebanon, New Hampshire.

New England has been blessed with a richly diverse historical and physical landscape. This bounty unites New England like nowhere else in the United States. So tie up your walking shoes and join me on an exploratory trek through New England.

How to Use This Book

Historic and compact, New England begs to be explored on foot. The six states, encompassing just over 66,000 square miles, are chock-a-block with regional treasures, some well known, others coveted Yankee secrets. This book, *Walking Places in New England*, offers 121 easy-to-moderate walks, designed for "real" people, those of us with curious minds, but, perhaps, limited athletic abilities.

Most walks in this book are easy. Easy walks will have many flat or gentle sections and only a few steep pitches. Moderate walks are actually hikes in natural areas that climb fairly continuously uphill with occasional rest sections. You'll encounter some steep pitches and a vertical climb between 700 and 1500 feet. If you're not in good physical condition, plan a half to full day for round trip and allow for frequent rest stops. For all walks, bring plenty of bottled water, insect repellent, and sunscreen. And you'll probably want to take your camera—New England is very pictur esque—and a small pair of binoculars.

These one-to-five mile treks encompass five categories of pedestrian discoveries: parks, preserves, and forests; gardens and arboretums; historic districts and classic universities; quaint and picturesque villages; and one-of-a-kind, only-in-New England adventures. In addition, I've included 37 rainy day indoor rambles, just in case Mother Nature doesn't cooperate with the weather.

Parks, Preserves, and Forests
The six New England states are blessed with myriad state parks and reservations, private preserves, national forests, national historic sites, and the second most visited national park in the United States, Maine's Acadia National Park. The natural area walks you'll find in this book are more than "just a pleasant walk in the woods." Each one nets a special encounter—a spectacular waterfall, an interesting rock formation, a glimpse at historical ruins, a walk near the sea, or an astounding panoramic view.

Gardens and Arboretums
No doubt about it, Yankees have green thumbs. Garden walks in this book encompass floral fantasies that include flower farms, botanical gardens, a

college arboretum, topiary gardens, and formal gardens planted on the sweeping acreage of magnificent historic mansions.

Historic Districts and Classic Universities
New England was the birthplace of our nation, and Boston is the diamond in the region's bejeweled crown. This book will take you to our other gems—historic towns and cities founded by our forefathers—and document your walks through history. You'll also be introduced to historic universities, such as Yale, Harvard, Dartmouth, and Williams College.

Quaint and Picturesque Villages
New England can probably boast of more quaint, picturesque villages than any other part of the United States. Most often designed around the quintessential New England village green—complete with a white steepled church, an imposing town hall, a vintage tavern, and an ancient cemetery—the villages are as enticing as they are historic.

One-of-a-Kind, Only-in-New England Adventures
These are the best discoveries of all, the on-foot adventures that defy classification. You'll find outdoor living history museums, granite and marble quarries, science centers, breakwaters and beaches, an underground army fort, even America's answer to Stonehenge.

Rainy Day Options
If the weather isn't fine, or you are simply ready to get out of the sun, indoor explorations on foot will keep you diverted. Choose from museums, casinos, historic house tours, and factory tours, plus a potpourri of unusual shopping excursions.

FINDING YOUR WAY
The book is divided into six sections, one for each state—Connecticut, Rhode Island, Massachusetts, Vermont, New Hampshire, and Maine. Walks in each state are organized by region. After the region's introduction, you'll find a shaded box that includes "Information" and "Getting There," which provides you with the logistics of getting to the area and contact numbers for additional information. A shaded box precedes each detailed walk as well, highlighting the practical information you will need to know before embarking on your on-foot adventure. "Information" gives you local information sources; "Getting There" supplies you with exact driving directions to the walk's location; "First Steps" tells you where to

first secure a map and/or guided brochure before directing you the walk's starting point.

Lodging and Restaurants

Inns and taverns were important social institutions in the 18th century. Travelers and locals gathered to exchange news. Country inns were also important because drovers enroute to Boston market could only travel a few miles each day with their livestock and needed a place to bed down. After exploring New England on foot, you, too, will need a bed, sustenance, and libation. *Walking Places in New England* is designed so that you can choose a home base and explore all the walks of a state's region like the spokes of wheel. To that end, at the conclusion of walks for each region of each state, I have included 10 lodging choices and 10 restaurant recommendations. New England is renowned for classic historic bed and breakfasts and inns, and our lauded Yankee cuisine ranges from sweeping seafood offerings to cozy country dinners. All recommendations are the result of either my own personal visit to the establishment, or that of a trusted friend or colleague.

Price Code for Lodging

Listings rate lodging choices according to a dollar sign ($) price code, based on the cost of a standard room, per night, double occupancy. Rates are based on high season, which is usually June through October and during some winter months in ski mountain areas. Most recommended bed and breakfasts and inns offer a complimentary breakfast—either a simple continental breakfast or a sumptuous full breakfast that sometimes includes three courses and is often served by candlelight. Some establishments also serve complimentary tea and pastries around 4pm or offer a cocktail hour with complimentary appetizers. Inquire about these amenities when you make your reservation. Advance reservations for lodging in New England are a must, especially in high season, on holidays, and during the autumn leaf season. Most recommended lodgings have websites, which enable you to book online.

$	$80 to $139
$$	$140 to $199
$$$	$200 to $259
$$$$	$260 and higher

Price Code for Restaurants

Listings rate restaurant choices according to a dollar sign ($) price code, based on the cost of dinner for two, without starters, dessert, alcoholic beverages, taxes, or tip.

$ Less than $25
$$ $25 to $40
$$$ $40 to $55
$$$$ More than $55

New England Websites

For more lodging and restaurant choices in New England, log onto these websites:

www.newenglandinns.com
www.travelassist.com
www.innbook.com
www.bedsbreakfastsandinns.com
www.bbonline.com
www.newengland.com
www.mass-vacation.com
www.visitnh.gov
www.ctbound.org
www.bnb-link.com
www.visitvt.com
www.1-800-vermont.com
www.vtguides.com
www.visitmaine.com
www.visitrhodeisland.com

Connecticut

Introduction

The third smallest state in the U.S. (5,009 square miles), Connecticut is also one of the nation's most prosperous. Dissatisfied with the religious intolerance of the Massachusetts Bay Colony, colonists formed Connecticut's first English settlement in Wethersfield in 1635, followed by settlements in Windsor and Hartford (now the state capital). The three banded together in 1639, forming the Hartford Colony (later called the Connecticut Colony) and adopted the Fundamental Orders of Connecticut, which are often cited as the basis of America's Constitution. Connecticut is nicknamed "The Constitution State."

The name Connecticut is an adaptation of the Indian word "quinnehtukqut," which means "long river place." The Connecticut, Thames, and Housatonic Rivers dissect the state, eventually emptying into Long Island Sound. Devotedly patriotic during the American Revolution, Connecticut supplied nearly half of George Washington's troops in the New York battles of 1776.

Colonists found most of Connecticut's rocky soil unsuitable for farming, turning, instead to the sea for their livelihood. Whaling and shipbuilding flourished along the coast, where Connecticut's oldest established towns line the 253-mile shoreline. Manufacturing developed early in Connecticut, which has always been one of the most industrialized New England states. The Industrial Revolution from 1768 to 1800 created a booming economy in Connecticut, which became a state in 1788. From cameras to clocks, silver to submarines, firearms to fire irons, mills to munitions, Connecticut's industry set the standard for the nation. The state lays claim to the invention of many American staples, including the hamburger, sewing machine, lollipop, pay telephone, Polaroid camera, steel fish hook, and the helicopter.

Connecticut occupies the southern edge of an eroded, uplifted area called the New England peneplain. The land slopes to the northwest from the Atlantic coast of Long Island Sound to the steep foothills of Litchfield Hills, a beautiful, bucolic area considered by many as the last outpost in Connecticut. Much of southern Connecticut is now a bedroom community of New York City, sustaining Connecticut's motto, "He who transplanted still sustains." Some city centers in the state have declined over the centuries, their empty mills and warehouses ghostly reminders of

Connecticut's manufacturing glory days.

While the white or "charter oak" rates as the state tree of Connecticut and the prevalent mountain laurel, its state flower, Yankee traders are said to have contributed to the state's alternate nickname, the Nutmeg State. These peddlers sold wooden nutmegs in days of yore, passing them off to the unsuspecting as the real thing.

Coastal Connecticut

Linked to the sea by its extensive shoreline on Long Island Sound, Connecticut's coastal towns and villages harbor a bounty of beauty and a rich maritime history. Sitting at the very doorstep of America's beginnings, the picturesque hamlets along the coast and at the mouth of the Connecticut and Housatonic Rivers set the stage for many an historical drama. The contemporary villages along Connecticut's coast have preserved and celebrated their copious colonial treasures, a time warp that begs to be explored on foot.

Regional Information

Southeastern Connecticut Tourism District (Connecticut's Mystic & More!), 470 Bank St., New London, CT 06320; 860/444-2206; 800/863-6569; www.mysticmore.com.

Chamber of Commerce of Southeastern Connecticut, 105 Huntington St., New London, CT 06320; 860/443-8332.

Connecticut River Valley & Shoreline Visitors Council, 393 Main St., Middletown, CT 06457; 800/486-3346, www.cttourism.org.

Mystic Chamber of Commerce, 28 Cottrell St., Mystic, CT 06355; 860/572-9578.

Mystic Coast & Country, 183 Providence-New London Turnpike, North Stonington, CT 06359; 860/599-8812; 800/mycoast; www.mycoast.com.

Connecticut Office of Tourism, 505 Hudson St., Hartford, CT 06106; 860/270-8080; www.state.ct.us/tourism.

Getting There

By Rail: Amtrak runs between New York City's Penn Station and Boston with stops at New Haven, Old Saybrook, New London, and Mystic.

By Air: Groton New London Airport (860/445-8549) offers connections on Action Airline and U.S. Air Express. Tweed-New Haven Airport (203/946-8285) serves Continental and US Air Express. T.F. Green Airport (401/737-4000) in Warwick, RI, offers flights on most major airlines.

By Automobile: Take I-95 up the coast of Long Island Sound.

Yale University and Historic New Haven

A group of Puritans arrived in Quinnipiac Harbor in 1638, settling on the shores of a small river that ran through present-day George Street. They named the village New Haven in 1640. The far-sighted colonists laid out the village green as a common place to gather and do business and as a location for future public buildings. Plans for establishing a college in New Haven began as early as 1648, but it was not until 1701, when 10 Bradford Congregational ministers got together to find a more orthodox, conservative alternative to Harvard that the Collegiate School was formed. This school was relocated from Bradford to Saybrook in 1707 and then lured to New Haven in 1716, with the promise of generous funding and land grants. The school was named after the second major benefactor, Elihu Yale, whom trustees hoped would continue to give copiously to the school. Though Mr. Yale died before he even learned of the honor, Yale continued to prosper and grow into the fine academic institution it remains today.

Information

Greater New Haven Convention and Visitors Bureau, 59 Elm St., New Haven, CT 06510; 203/777-8550; 800/332-stay; www.newhavencvb.org. Yale University Visitor Information Center, 149 Elm St., New Haven, CT 06510; 203/ 432-2300.

Getting There

By Rail: Metro North New Haven Line from New York City's Grand Central Terminal (212/532-4900, 800/638-7646) or Amtrak Boston-to-Washington line to Union Station, New Haven (800 /872-7245). Bus available from train station to New Haven Green.
By Auto: Take I-95 or I-84 to I-91, exit 3 (Trumbull St.). Turn left on Prospect St. (becomes College St.), to Elm St., and turn left to New Haven Green.

First Steps

Stop at the Yale University Visitor Information Center (1), across from the north side of the New Haven Green, and pick up a map of Yale University and New Haven Green and also the History of Grove Street Cemetery brochure/map. Free tours, guided by Yale students, leave the Visitors Center Mon. through Fri., between 10:30am and 2pm, and Sat. and Sun. at 1:30pm. Alternately, you can obtain a free audiocassette and recorder from the Visitor Center for a self-guided tour. First take either the student-led or self-guided tour of the campus. Then continue your walk at New Haven Green and the Grove Street Cemetery as discussed below. Plan to spend the day on this three-fold exploration.

Yale University and Historic New Haven. Begin your exploration from the Yale University Visitor Center (1) with the one-hour walking tour of Yale University with a student guide, who will provide a background of Yale's history and fine collegiate architecture. You will proceed down College Street, walking through the portals of Phelps Gate archway into the Old Campus (2). Since 1933, undergraduates have lived in dormitories that surround the Old Campus, which are called the 12 residential colleges. A unique concept among American universities, each residential college is a separate entity designed to give the students who dwell within a sense of belonging to a small group within the larger, more formidable whole. The students remain in their respective residential college for three of their four years.

Among the distinctive buildings you'll see on this tour is Connecticut Hall (3), the oldest building at Yale, c.1750. It is the only remaining structure from Yale's Old Brick Row. Famous Yale graduates who lived here include Eli Whitney, Noah Webster, President William Taft, and Nathan Hale, America's first spy. James Gamble Rogers, who based his designs on details of Oxford and Cambridge, developed the architecture of Branford College (4), American Collegiate Gothic. In an effort to make the building look authentically old, Rogers devised empty statue niches, purposefully broken window panes, and dripped acid on the exterior's mixture of brick and limestone.

Of particular interest on the Yale campus is the Beinecke Rare Book and Manuscript Library (5), designed in 1961. Its walls are built of more than a hundred sheets of paper-thin, translucent marble. The library houses a 1455 Gutenberg Bible. Yale is also loaded with fine museums, including Yale University Art Gallery (1111 Chapel St.), Peabody Museum of Natural History (170 Whitney St.), Yale Center for British Art (1080 Chapel St.) and the Collection of Musical Instruments (15 Hillhouse Ave.).

After you tour the campus of Yale University and return to the Visitor Information Center, cross to New Haven Green (6), which is bordered by College, Chapel, Church, and Elm Streets. The Green was laid out in

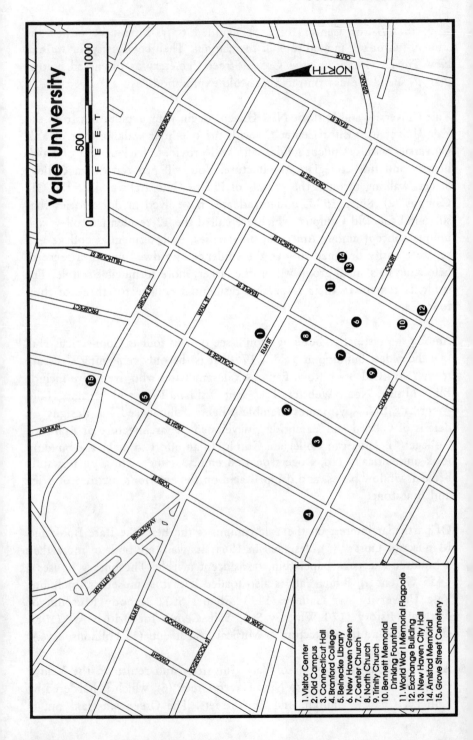

Yale University

FEET
0 — 500 — 1000

NORTH

1. Visitor Center
2. Old Campus
3. Connecticut Hall
4. Branford College
5. Beinecke Library
6. New Haven Green
7. Center Church
8. North Church
9. Trinity Church
10. Bennett Memorial Drinking Fountain
11. World War I Memorial Flagpole
12. Exchange Building
13. New Haven City Hall
14. Amistad Memorial
15. Grove Street Cemetery

1638, one of nine squares of what is called America's first planned city. Three churches grace the center of the Upper Green.

Center Church (7)—the first and only church in New Haven for 100 years—was founded in 1639. The present meeting house was constructed in 1814, atop the former old burial ground. (It is believed that more than 10,000 bodies are buried here. The last burial occurred in 1812. About 10 years later, the old markers were removed and taken to the new burial ground, Grove Street Cemetery. The land was filled without disturbing the graves.) Go to the lower basement level of the church to see the historic crypt, which has tombstones dating back to 1687. Among those buried here is Benedict Arnold's first wife, Margaret, who died in 1775. (The crypt is open Wed., Fri., and Sat., from 11am to 1pm or by appointment, 203/787-0121.) Be sure to stop in the sanctuary to see the beautiful Tiffany window over the pulpit, which contains 2,320 separate pieces of glass.

United Congregational Church, or North Church, (8) was formed in 1812 by uniting two separate factions that had left the ecclesiastical confines of Center Church. Both United and Center churches are good examples of the Federal style of architecture. Trinity Church (9) is the first Gothic Revival church in America, c.1813. Its design was fashioned after that of St. Martin-in-the-Fields in London.

Marking the Lower Green is the Bennett Memorial Drinking Fountain (10), placed on the busy corner of Church and Chapel Streets in 1907, as a reminder that horses once dominated the streets surrounding the Green. The fountain provided water for both humans and animals. Also on the Lower Green is the World War One Memorial Flagpole (11), a memorial to New Haven soldiers killed in battle.

Architecturally significant buildings bordering the Green include the Exchange Building (12), c.1832, an imposing commercial building now housing Bank of Boston Connecticut, and the New Haven City Hall (13), a High Victorian Gothic built in 1861. The Amistad Memorial (14), sculpted in 1992 by Ed Hamilton, sits on the site of the former New Haven Jail, where the Africans of the Amistad were detained before their trials in Hartford and New Haven. Each side of the three-sided, 14-foot, bronze-relief statue depicts a part of the life of Joseph Cinque (a.k.a. Sengbe Pich), the African leader.

After exploring New Haven Green, walk down Elm Street to High Street. Turn right and proceed to the Grove Street Cemetery (15), established in 1796. Walk through the Egyptian-Revival stone entrance and explore the "avenues" of this fascinating ancient cemetery, the first chartered burial ground in the United States to use family plots. Among those buried here are: Eli Whitney, inventor of the cotton gin (Cedar Avenue); Noah Webster, author of the first American dictionary (Cedar Avenue); Roger Sherman, statesman and signer of the Articles of Association, Declaration of Independence, Articles of Confederation, and the Constitution (Maple Avenue); and Eli Whitney Blake, inventor of the stone crusher, whose brother invented the corkscrew (Linden Avenue).

As you head back to where you began at the Visitor Center, stop at the imposing Woolsey Hall, c.1901, which is now the home of the New Haven Symphony Orchestra.

Old Saybrook Point

Native Americans—first the peaceful Algonquin-Nehantics then the warring Pequots—settled at the mouth of the Connecticut River, naming it Pashbeshauke (place at the river's mouth). The river was called Quonitocutt, or Long Tidal River. Adrian Block, the Dutch navigator, discovered the area in 1614, and by 1623 the Dutch West Indies Company started a trading post here and changed the name to Kievit's Hoeck. The English arrived in 1635, renaming the settlement Saybrook for the two original grantees, Lord Saye and Lord Brook. The Dutch and English skirmished over the area, but the English prevailed. The town grew up around its first military fortification, Fort Saybrook. The English settlement of Saybrook encompassed the seven present day towns known as Chester, Deep River, Essex, Lyme, Old Lyme, Westbrook, and Old Saybrook. One by one these settlements incorporated as separate villages. This town officially became Old Saybrook in 1947. Two-thirds of this enchanting seaside village's boundaries are water.

Information

Old Saybrook Chamber of Commerce, Box 625, 146 Main St., Old Saybrook, CT 06475; 860/388-3266; www.oldsaybrookct.com.
Old Saybrook Historical Society, 350 Main St., P.O. Box 4, Old Saybrook, CT 06475.

Getting There
Take I-95 to exit 67, Rte. 1 south, to Rte. 154 south (Main St.).

First Steps
Stop at the Chamber office for a map of Old Saybrook.

Old Saybrook Point. Begin your 4.3-mile walk at Fort Saybrook Monument Park (1) at the end of Main Street. The first people to occupy this site were the Algonquin Nehantic Indians, who had a village of 1600 on this site more than 400 years ago. In 1635 the English built Fort Saybrook as a first-line defense against the Dutch, who also wanted to colonize the area. The English repelled the Dutch and fought off the marauding Pequots in ensuing years. The original fort burned in 1647, and a simpler replacement was built on the adjacent "New Fort Hill." The second fort saw action against the Dutch and again during the Revolutionary War and the War of 1812 against the British. Valley Railroad obtained the land here in 1870, in order to lay track to Saybrook Point. Fort Hill was leveled and a causeway with railroad trestle was built to Fenwick.

Walk across this causeway, now Bridge Street (2). On your right is South Cove, which is peppered with white swans, languidly gliding around the tranquil pond. On your left is the Connecticut River. After you cross the inlet, turn left on Nibang Avenue into the private, picturesque Borough of Fenwick, which was named after the first governor of the Saybrook colony, Colonel George Fenwick. Turn right on Fenwick Avenue, past the Fenwick Golf Course, to the dead end, which is a private beach (3). From here you'll be able to garner a great view of Saybrook Point Lighthouse. Retrace your steps to Agawam Avenue and turn right. This tony area is filled with big, rambling turn-of-the-last-century beach "cottages." On your right you'll see such a house, which sits directly on the water backed with a bucolic pond. This is the home of movie actress Katharine Hepburn (4). At the fork, jog left on Neponset Avenue, then right on Sequassen Avenue, where you'll walk on a narrow private road (foot traffic welcome) through a marsh meadow of sea oats (5). Look up, you'll see many osprey nests. The coastline here is beautiful, and you can see Plum Island to your left.

The road terminates amid a small community of private homes and the Lynde Point Lighthouse (6), which originally was a wooden structure

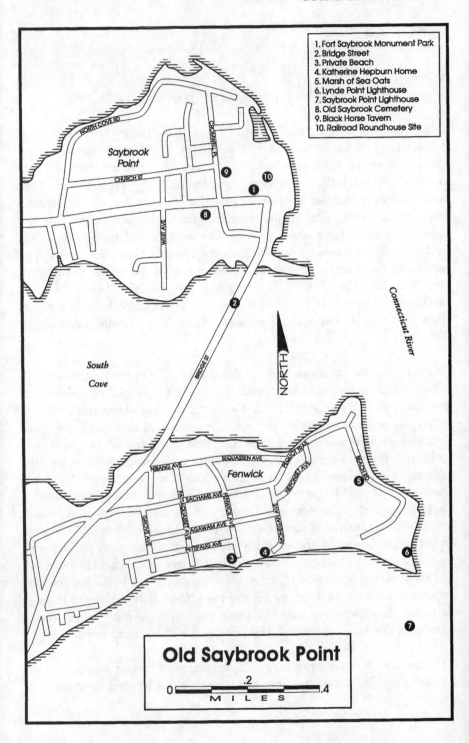

1. Fort Saybrook Monument Park
2. Bridge Street
3. Private Beach
4. Katherine Hepburn Home
5. Marsh of Sea Oats
6. Lynde Point Lighthouse
7. Saybrook Point Lighthouse
8. Old Saybrook Cemetery
9. Black Horse Tavern
10. Railroad Roundhouse Site

Old Saybrook Point

0 ——— .2 ——— .4
MILES

erected in 1803 to mark the entrance to the Connecticut River and the Old Saybrook Harbor. This "inner light" was replaced by the present structure in 1838. At the far end of the Old Saybrook Point is the "outer light," Saybrook Point Lighthouse (7), built in 1886 at the river's mouth. The only easement access to the "outer light" is across private land. (You must seek permission from homeowners before trespassing here.) This lighthouse features a Fresnel lens and a rotating beacon visible for 14 miles.

Retrace your steps through the marsh meadow bordering Sequassen Avenue and return to the causeway via Nibang Avenue.

> **Yankee Accents**
>
> Though joined by common history and geography, New England Yankees do not speak with one tongue. Here are a few hints to help you translate the subtle regional differences.
>
> • Maine, New Hampshire and eastern Vermont: Clipped pronunciation makes words such as coat, home, and stone, sound like cut, hum, and stun.
>
> • Rhode Island, eastern Connecticut, and eastern Massachusetts: Immortalized by the Kennedy dynasty, this accent drops the "r" in words such carve, park, and barn, rendering them calf, pack, and bahn.
>
> • Speech in western Connecticut and Massachusetts has held onto the elusive "r," but fractures the "u," making butcher sound like bootcher.
>
> • Vermont, which was colonized by settlers from Connecticut, has accents from both parts of the state—barn may still be bahrn, but on will become awn. Listen closely and remember to say, "Excuse me, what did you say?"

Swans dominate the cove on your right; the golf course is on your left. Cross back over the Bridge Street causeway and turn left on Main Street to the Old Saybrook Cemetery (8). Here are buried the Pratts and the Fenwicks, early residents of Old Saybrook. You'll see a stone commemorating the first site of Yale University, which was founded in 1701 as the Collegiate School. The school moved to New Haven in 1716, as Yale College. One of the 17 colleges of the present-day Yale University is named Saybrook College.

Turn right on North Cove Road, past the Town Boat Landing to Cromwell Place. This was part of the original Saybrook settlement, and many of the historic homes are dated. Look for the former Black Horse Tavern (9) on your left (historical marker on private residence), which was a general store, inn, tavern and post office in the early 1700s. When you get back to Main Street, turn left and return to Fort Saybrook Monument Park. Near the parking area you'll find the former site of the railroad roundhouse (10). A boardwalk at the edge of a brackish pond marsh affords a good bird watching opportunity.

Essex Village

Nestled on the west bank of the Connecticut River, Essex was settled as part of the Saybrook colony in 1646. Native Americans called the area Potopaug—a "point of land between two coves." By the middle of the 1700s, this was a bustling seafaring community. Shipbuilding began in 1773, and America's first warship, the *Oliver Cromwell*, was completed here in 1775. The British attacked the waterfront in the War of 1812, burning 28 ships at anchor. The village broke away from Saybrook and incorporated in 1852, renaming itself after the English county of Essex. Transatlantic trade flourished in the 19th century, and shipbuilding continued until 1931, when use of wooden ships declined and the railroad replaced steamship traffic.

Information
Essex Historical Society/Hill Academy, 22 Prospect St., Essex, CT 06426; 860/767-0681; www.Essexct.com.
Connecticut River Museum, 67 Main St., Essex, CT 06426; 860-767-8269.

Getting There
Take I-95 to exit 69, then Rte. 9 north to exit 3, West Ave., to Main St.

First Steps
Pick up "A Walking Map of Essex" at the Griswold Inn on Main Street.

Essex Village. The Connecticut River Museum and the Essex Historical Society has put together a mapped 1.5-mile walk of picturesque Essex. The tour guides you past 46 historically significant buildings in the village. Begin your walk at the Connecticut River Museum at Steamboat Dock. The first wharf was built on this site in 1656. The museum is housed in an 1878 warehouse that served vessels traveling between Hartford and New York until 1931. The museum features permanent and changing exhibits of nautical artifacts illustrating the maritime history of the Connecticut River Valley. A replica of our country's first submarine, *Turtle*, used in the Revolutionary War, is also on display here.

From Steamboat Dock, go to the cul-de-sac circle, where you'll see several 18th-century buildings once occupied by the Hayden Chandlery, a witch hazel distiller and the tavern/inn of Uriah and Ann Hayden. Head up

Main Street, where the walking tour brochure will illuminate the low-down on the early Essex residents who lived and worked in the historical structures, most of which were built in the 1700s. Today, most of these buildings house interesting shops, cafes, and boutiques. The Griswold Inn, built by Sala Griswold in 1776, was the first three-story building constructed in the lower Connecticut River Valley. The Gris is the backbone and heart of Main Street (see Lodging and Food and Drink).

At the top of Main Street at Essex Square, walk up the hill to the First Congregational Church of Essex, built in 1852. Across the street, a former Methodist church has been converted into a dramatic private residence. Around the corner on Prospect Street you'll find two of the village's other churches, Our Lady of Sorrows Catholic Church and The First Baptist Church. First Baptist, built in 1845 in the Egyptian-Revival style, features a sanctuary painted in colonial colors and stained-glass windows highlighting Noah's Ark, Doves, and the Anchor of Faith. The building was once lit with whale oil lamps.

Walk back to Main Street. The Essex Historical Society is housed in the Hill's Academy one-room brick schoolhouse, c. 1832. Continue up Main Street, noting the historic buildings. Stop at the Pratt House Museum (open weekends, June 1 to Oct. 1, 1 to 4pm). Built in the early 1700s by John Pratt Jr., grandson of one of Essex's original settlers, and added onto by subsequent generations, the house and barn are now a museum run by the Essex Historical Society. The museum showcases furnishings from the 17th through the 19th centuries, plus permanent collections of tools, ivory products, iron works, and an authentically restored herb garden.

The walking route takes you past the Town Hall, built in 1895, then leads you down Grove Street to the Grove Street Cemetery, where many of the 19th-century Essex movers-and-shakers now reside. Turn right on North Main Street, where the historic residences date to the 1800s. Stop at Riverview Cemetery to see the interesting 18th-century gravestones, which feature winged skulls, faces with wings, urns, and willow carvings. You will pass the site of the second ropewalk, which ran from the hill of North Main Street, between Bushnell and Pratt Streets, down to the shipyards and operated until the turn of the last century. (The first ropewalk—Grover L'Hommedieu Ropewalk—started at the top of Main Street, at Essex Square, and extended to the Jared Hayden House at #43.

The Historical Society feels it was torn down about 1814.) A ropewalk was a long, covered walk where ropes were manufactured.

Walk down Pratt Street. The historic homes here belonged to Essex seafarers and date from 1800 through the 1860s. The street ends at the wharf and the Essex Island Marina. The pretty harbor is filled with sailboats. Turn right on Ferry Street to Main and retrace your steps back to Steamboat Dock.

Connecticut College Arboretum, New London

Connecticut College established this 20-acre arboretum in 1931. Species of trees and shrubs native to eastern North America and southern New England grow profusely within its boundaries. A 2-mile walking trail with two optional loops winds throughout the property. No admission is charged here.

Information
Connecticut College Arboretum, Williams St., New London, CT 06320; 860-439-5020.

Getting There
Take I-95 to Rte. 32 north (exit 83S/84N). Turn into Connecticut College. After the guardhouse, turn right and follow signs for "all other buildings." Turn left and exit through gates of campus onto Williams Street. The arboretum is across the road.

First Steps
Pick up a "Self-Guided Tour" brochure at the kiosk just inside the gates of Connecticut College Arboretum.

Connecticut College Arboretum. The clearly marked cedar-chip paths of the arboretum's main trail (brown posts with white numbers and arrows) visit nine botanical stations, all of which are extensively detailed in the self-guided walking tour brochure. The first habitat the trail traverses is a forested wetland, where at least some amount of water lurks year round. Red maples are prevalent here, and the ground is covered for much of the spring and summer with skunk cabbage. Station two is a stand of tulip trees, part of the magnolia family that was planted in 1936.

The path to station three skirts the Arboretum Marsh Pond. Dominating this station is the Gries Memorial Native Conifer Collection, featuring hemlocks, red cedars, bald cypresses and a variety of pines. Flanking the conifer area is a wildflower meadow, particularly colorful in late summer. Beyond lies the Edgerton and Stengel Wildflower Garden, accessed by a wooden boardwalk. This wooded garden peaks in early May. A dam at station four has created the 3-foot-deep pond. Water lilies pepper its shallow areas.

Station five is a deciduous woodland area filled with mountain laurel and oak, maple and hickory trees. Here you have the option of following the Sphagnum-Heath Bog Loop (5A) around the backside of the habitat. Moss and sedges form the center of the bog, surrounded by cranberries and high-bush blueberries. The trail proceeds to station six alongside granite ledges. Granite was quarried here during the early 1900s. The hillside has been planted with hickory trees.

Here you can take another optional loop to the Bolleswood Natural Area, which is littered with granite outcroppings. Because it was not good land for agriculture, some old-growth forest remains. Eastern hemlocks are the most commonly encountered conifers in these forests, but at least 100 of these centuries-old trees were destroyed in the 1938 hurricane.

Buck Lodge, a stone structure given by the Buck family to the Arboretum in 1937, station seven, is used for community educational and recreational gatherings. Follow the trail to the edge of the pond and the outdoor theater, a hemlock and arborvitae adorned amphitheater also donated by the Bucks. Station nine is the holly collection, followed by the viburnum collection and the honeysuckle, heath, and azalea gardens.

Something is always blooming at the Connecticut College Arboretum from May through August. In autumn the botanical collections transform the preserve into a fairyland of colored leaves.

Mystic Seaport

Dedicated to the preservation of America's maritime past, Mystic Seaport houses the largest collection of boats—nearly 500 vessels—and maritime photography in the world. Mystic Seaport includes a re-created

19th-century seaport village on 17 waterfront acres on the Mystic River that showcases historic homes, trade shops, and tall ships, as well as exhibit galleries and a working shipyard, all illustrating early America's relationship with the sea. Mystic Seaport once was a shipyard owned by the Greenman brothers—George, Clark, and Thomas. In the mid-1800s, the brothers launched almost 100 vessels from this site. Several buildings are original to the site, but most of the historic structures were brought from Mystic or other locations in New England.

Information
Mystic Seaport, 75 Greenmanville Ave., Mystic, CT 06355; 888 /9SEAPORT, www.mysticseaport.org

Getting There
Take I-95 to exit 90. Continue south on Rte. 27 for 1 mile to the entrance. The Mystic Trolley makes pickups at most hotels, Mystic Seaport, and Mystic Chamber of Commerce daily, from the end of May to mid Oct.

First Steps
Pick up a map and guide when you pay your admission fee. An audio tour is available if so desired.

Mystic Seaport. Begin your tour of Mystic Seaport at the *L.A. Dunton* (1), a 123-foot Gloucester fishing schooner built in 1921 in Essex, Mass. Seasonal demonstrations aboard this round-bow fishing vessel include raising anchor, salting cod, and operating the dory. Commonly used in New England in the 1920s, this is the last surviving schooner of its kind. Explore the decks below, where you can still smell the cod. Next visit the *Sabino* (2), which was built in Maine in 1908. The 57-foot *Sabino*, a National Historic Landmark, is one of the last coal-fired steamboats in the U.S. to still carry passengers. She'll take you on a 30-minute river cruise from May to mid-October. Moored nearby is the *Florence* (3), a 1926 Mystic-built dragger.

Continue past the Village Green to the Thomas Oyster House (4), a good representation of a traditional 19th-century oyster shop. The shop was built in 1874 in New Haven, which was then the largest oyster distribution center of New England. Across the road, the Mystic River Scale Model (5) shows Mystic as it was in the glory years of 1850 to 1870. The

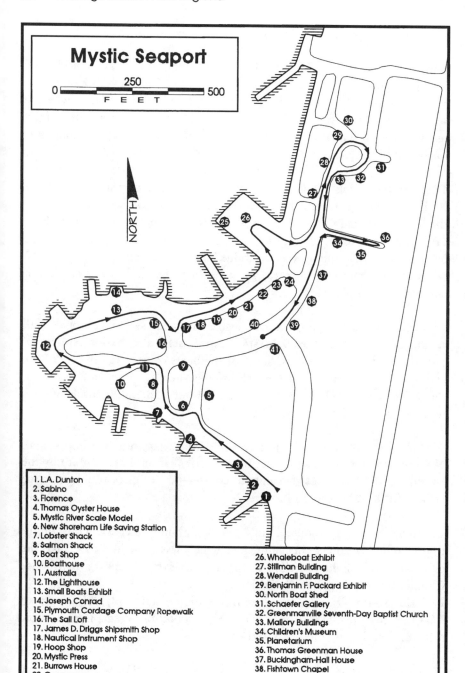

Mystic Seaport

0   250   500
F E E T

NORTH

1. L.A. Dunton
2. Sabino
3. Florence
4. Thomas Oyster House
5. Mystic River Scale Model
6. New Shoreham Life Saving Station
7. Lobster Shack
8. Salmon Shack
9. Boat Shop
10. Boathouse
11. Australia
12. The Lighthouse
13. Small Boats Exhibit
14. Joseph Conrad
15. Plymouth Cordage Company Ropewalk
16. The Sail Loft
17. James D. Driggs Shipsmith Shop
18. Nautical Instrument Shop
19. Hoop Shop
20. Mystic Press
21. Burrows House
22. Cooperage
23. Mystic Bank
24. Sputer Tavern
25. Charles W. Morgan

26. Whaleboat Exhibit
27. Stillman Building
28. Wendall Building
29. Benjamin F. Packard Exhibit
30. North Boat Shed
31. Schaefer Gallery
32. Greenmanville Seventh-Day Baptist Church
33. Mallory Buildings
34. Children's Museum
35. Planetarium
36. Thomas Greenman House
37. Buckingham-Hall House
38. Fishtown Chapel
39. Geo. H. Stone General Store
40. Shipcarver's Shop
41. Sailor's Reading Room
42. Village Green

village sported more than 250 buildings and five shipyards in those days.

The U.S. Life Saving Service was begun by Congressional law in 1874 and incorporated into the U.S. Coast Guard in 1915. The New Shoreham Life Saving Station (6), c.1874, was brought here from Block Island, where it was in active service in Old Harbor for 16 years. The building faces inland, as it did on Block Island, and the boat room displays original gear for breeches buoy and surfboat rescues.

The Lobster Shack (7) is a reproduction of those commonly found in Noank, Conn., in the late 1800s. Most authentic shacks were destroyed in the 1938 hurricane. The Salmon Shack (8) was moved to Mystic from Lincolnville, Maine, in 1969. Isaac Ames began the salmon fishing business in 1837 and it was continued by his descendents until 1947, when salmon became too scarce for a profit to be made. Original fishing equipment is displayed.

Classes at the Boat Shop (9) teach construction and use of traditional small sailing crafts and rowboats. Mystic Seaport staff also builds replicas of historically significant vessels. Some of the boats constructed in workshops end up in the Boathouse (10), which offers visitors the opportunity to rent them for self-guided shore excursions. Motor and sailing tours with a licensed captain also are offered here.

The schooner *Australia* (11), a two-masted vessel built in Long Island, N.Y., served as a blockade runner in the Civil War until her capture by the Union navy. She later became a coaster—a freight-carrying sailing vessel—in the Chesapeake Bay area.

Continue on to Lighthouse Point. The Lighthouse (12) is a copy of the Brant Point Lighthouse in Nantucket, which was built in 1746. Like the original, whose light is visible for 10 miles, Mystic Seaport's lighthouse contains a "fourth-order Fresnel lens."
Pass the Youth Training Building (no exhibits, staff only) to the Small Boats Exhibit (13). Here you'll find a huge collection of small crafts, from skiffs and dories to workboats and yachts.

The *Joseph Conrad* (14), a full-rigged sail-training ship with a 111-foot metal hull, was built in 1882 in Copenhagen. Retired from the Danish merchant service in 1934 and then used as a private yacht, she has been permanently moored at Mystic Seaport since 1947. This floating exhibit is also used as a dormitory for Mystic Seaport's educational programs.

Walk to the Plymouth Cordage Company Ropewalk (15), built in 1824 in Plymouth, Mass., where it made rope for whalers and other vessels. The ropewalk was a level area staked with pegged posts on which the hemp or manila ropes were hung after they were spun or woven. Rope-making machinery is set up just as it would have functioned during production days in the mid-1800s.

The Sail Loft (16), nearby, was operated by Charles Mallory, a successful 19th-century Mystic sail-maker. The exhibit includes the tools of the trade. Also in this building is the Rigging Loft, which displays tools of Captain William J. White, a rigger from New London. Here, too, you'll see the Ship Chandlery, the boat-shopping emporium of its day, which offered all the supplies required for months at sea.

Accurate interpretations of 19th-century trades are demonstrated in the trade shops that line the main street of the seaport. The goods produced here are used on the grounds of Mystic Seaport. James D. Driggs Shipsmith Shop (17) manufactured ironwork for the whaling industry in the 19th century in New Bedford, Mass. The Nautical Instrument Store (18) displays navigation equipment. The Hoop Shop (19) illustrates the production of mast hoops (kept a ship's sails attached to the base of the mast in the 1800s). The Smith family, hoopmakers from Canterbury, Conn., used the equipment displayed here until the 1930s.

The Mystic Press (20) represents a hand-set print shop of the late 1800s, displaying the tools and technology of the times. The 19th-century Burrows House (21), once situated on the Mystic River shores in Groton, is furnished as the home of a sea-faring family. The production of buckets and pails is demonstrated at the Cooperage (22), and the Mystic Bank (23), first opened in 1833 in what is now Old Mystic, was dismantled stone by stone and reassembled in Mystic Seaport. You can still get a 5-cent beer at Schaefer's Spouter Tavern (24)—served in a shot glass!—as well as sandwiches and stews.

The centerpiece of Mystic Seaport is undoubtedly the *Charles W. Morgan* (25), a wooden whaling ship built in 1841 and restored to the "rig of a double-topsail bark," which she had from the 1880s until she was retired as a whaler in 1921. The *Morgan*, which sailed 37 separate voyages, is the world's last surviving whaling ship. She is docked at Chubb's Wharf, a granite wharf modeled after those in New Bedford, Mass. Here you'll see sail-setting and furling demonstrations and a reenactment of a whale hunt. Go down below and explore the cramped crew's quarters of the blubber room. Piles of barrels surround the *Morgan*, just as they would have on a 19th-century wharf. The nearby Whaleboat Exhibit (26) features a fully equipped whaleboat that contains gear typical of such ventures in the 1880s.

Leaving Chubb's Wharf, proceed to the Stillman Building (27), once a part of the Greenman brothers' 1862 textile factory and now a formal museum housing exhibits highlighting America's relationship with the sea. The Wendall Building (28), which still sits on its original site, exhibits ships' carvings and figureheads, the three-dimensional carved figures placed on the bow of a vessel, usually illustrating the name of the ship. Sometimes seamen removed their ship's figurehead, for fear of the superstition that if the carving ever broke off, bad luck would follow the ship and its crew.

The *Benjamin F. Packard* Exhibit (29) displays the restoration of the aft cabin of the 244-foot downeaster clipper ship that carried cargo from the U.S., around Cape Horn to Pacific ports in the late 19th century. Ornate woodwork and appointments from the scuttled ship were rebuilt into this building, which was another of the Greenman brothers' mills in the mid 1800s. Small, beautifully restored boats are displayed in the North Boat Shed (30), nearby. Vintage photos depict these same boats in their turn-of-the-last-century splendor.

Walk to the Schaefer Gallery (31), where you'll see changing exhibits of ship models, maritime artifacts, prints, and paintings. Don't miss the spectacular scrimshaw exhibit. More than one million books, charts, maps, journals, and pieces of manuscript material are stored here. Visit the Greenmanville Seventh-Day Baptist Church (32), built in 1851 near the present location of Mystic Seaport's south gate. The tower clock was added in 1857, on permanent loan from Yale University.

Exhibits in the Mallory Buildings (33) illustrate the 160-year shipping and shipbuilding business the Mallory maritime dynasty established during the 19th and early 20th centuries. Proceed to the Children's Museum (34), which is full of "Please touch" areas—hand's-on exhibits around the theme "It's a Sailor's Life for Me." Kids can swab the deck and dress up in nautical gear. The Planetarium (35) showcases exhibits on celestial navigation and holds daily shows illustrating the night sky. The Thomas Greenman House (36), built in 1842, is the only one of the Greenman brothers' houses open to the public. Still on its original site, the house is furnished as the mid-Victorian home of a well-to-do family.

Retrace your steps to the four-way crossing and stop at the Buckingham-Hall House (37), where open-hearth cooking is demonstrated. Built in 1760s (the kitchen dates to the 1690s) in Old Saybrook, this pre-Revolutionary structure was once the home of Reverend Thomas Buckingham, one of the founders of the Collegiate School (1701), which later became Yale University.

Six of the 12 benches in Fishtown Chapel (38), c.1889, are original; the rest came from other period churches in the area. Boardman School, c.1768, was a Preston, Conn. classroom for six generations. George H. Stone, a retired North Stonington merchant, stocked the shelves of the general store exhibit—Geo. H. Stone General Store (39)—with his own authentic memorabilia. H.R. & W. Bringhurst Drugstore displays the collection of the Bringhurst family, who operated an apothecary in Delaware from the late 1800s to the early 20th century. A period doctor's office adjoins the pharmacy. The Shipcarver's Shop (40) demonstrates ornamental carving, a lost art once widely crafted in the production of ships' figureheads.

At the Seamen's Friend Society Sailor's Reading Room (41), you can often find a role player—a costumed staff member charged with an issue of the day. The role player stays in character at all times, sometimes moving around the village. If the role player does leave the reading room, signage indicates where he/she will be located.

Try to time your return to the Village Green (42) so that you don't miss the chantey singing or the "breeches buoy sea-to-land rescue drill." From 1871-1915, members of the Life Saving Station, precursor to the Coast Guard, practiced this drill, so that they could complete a rescue in under 5 minutes. Reenactments take place daily in the summer and on weekends in fall, weather permitting.

Before ending your exploration of Mystic Seaport, be sure to visit the H.B. duPont Preservation Shipyard, where the nearly lost art of wooden shipbuilding still endures and where the re-created ship *Amistad* was built.

Historic Stonington Borough

William and Anna Cheseborough formed the first settlement in Stonington Borough in 1649 on a peninsula jutting into Long Island Sound known as the Point. The settlement grew and the name was changed several more times—Southertown, Mystic, and finally Stonington in 1666. Long an agriculture and maritime community, Stonington withstood British onslaughts in both the Revolutionary War and the War of 1812. Portuguese from the Azores settled here to harvest whales, seals, and fish from the sea. With the advent of the railroad and steamship in 1837, agriculture, mills, and even tourism flourished here. Stonington Borough prospered in the 19th century as a railway and steamship terminus. Today, the sleepy fishing village is a picturesque haven of well-preserved historic houses and vessel-filled harbors.

Information
The Stonington Historical Society, Stonington Free Library, Wadawanuck Square, Stonington, CT 06378; 860-535-1131.

Getting There
Take I-95 to exit 91. From the north, turn right at bottom of ramp; from the south, turn left under the underpass. After 1/3 mile, turn left at the fork onto Pequot Trail and continue for 1.5 mile. Go straight through the light, crossing Rte. 1, for 0.8 mile further. At the four-way stop, turn left on Trumbull Ave. Turn right over the viaduct and bear left into Stonington Borough.

First Steps
Park on the street across from the Stonington Free Library on Water Street at Wadawanuck Square. Stop in the library for a map of Stonington Borough.

Historic Stonington Borough. Begin your walk of the borough at the corner of Water and Broad Streets at the Ephraim Williams House (1), c.1840. This late Federal-period home features an intricate hip roof with a chimney at all four corners. Corinthian-style columns support the pediment above the front entrance. In the middle of the block at 170 Water Street sits the Widow Luke Palmer's House (2), c.1847, a distinguished Georgian with Ionic columns.

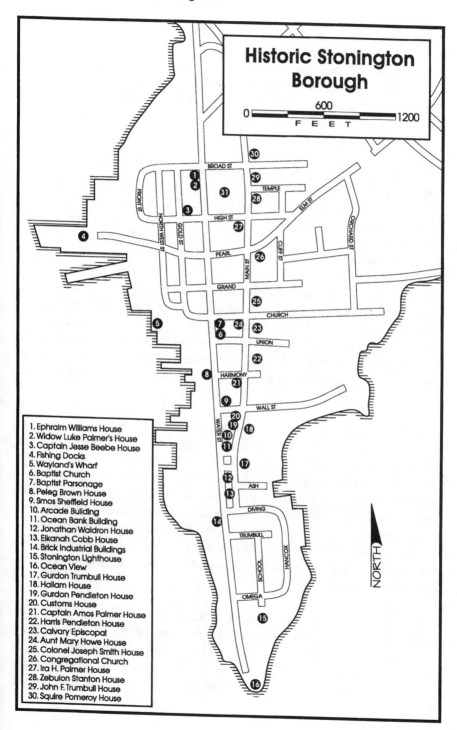

Historic Stonington Borough

0   600   1200
F E E T

BROAD ST
TEMPLE
FRONT ST
NORTH WEST ST
GOLD ST
HIGH ST
ELM ST
ORCHARD ST
PEARL
MAIN ST
CLIFF ST
GRAND
CHURCH
UNION
HARMONY
WALL ST
WATER ST
ASH
DIVING
TRUMBULL
SCHOOL
HANCOX
OMEGA

NORTH

1. Ephraim Williams House
2. Widow Luke Palmer's House
3. Captain Jesse Beebe House
4. Fishing Docks
5. Wayland's Wharf
6. Baptist Church
7. Baptist Parsonage
8. Peleg Brown House
9. Smos Sheffield House
10. Arcade Building
11. Ocean Bank Building
12. Jonathan Waldron House
13. Elkanah Cobb House
14. Brick Industrial Buildings
15. Stonington Lighthouse
16. Ocean View
17. Gurdon Trumbull House
18. Hallam House
19. Gurdon Pendleton House
20. Customs House
21. Captain Amos Palmer House
22. Harris Pendleton House
23. Calvary Episcopal
24. Aunt Mary Howe House
25. Colonel Joseph Smith House
26. Congregational Church
27. Ira H. Palmer House
28. Zebulon Stanton House
29. John F. Trumbull House
30. Squire Pomeroy House

Turn right on High Street. Mid-block, the Captain Jesse Beebe House (3), c.1785, a gambrel-roofed saltbox, is turned sideways to the street. Beebe was captain of a packet that hauled cargo between Stonington and New York. Follow High Street to the fishing docks (4), from which Stonington's still-active fishing fleet sets off daily. Picturesque to the max, the vessels of Connecticut's only dragging fleet paper the docks, and the harbor beyond is peppered with sailing schooners.

From the docks, go up Pearl Street and turn right on Water Street and, opposite Union Street, find a little blue sign that says, "Borough Right of Way," with an arrow pointing to the right. Walk through brick arches to Wayland's Wharf (5), the public pier. Here you'll discover a small gazebo for sitting plus an endless view of the sailboat-filled harbor and the jetty. Retrace your steps back to Water Street and turn right.

On the corner of Water and Union Streets sits the former Baptist Church (6), c.1889, which originally had turrets and was carved and embellished with festoons. The Charles Fullers bought the structure in 1959 and remodeled it as an Indonesian-inspired private home. The former Baptist parsonage next door (7), c.1890, was built in a vertical style known as Carpenter Gothic, featuring high-pitched rooflines, towers and pinnacle porches.

On Water Street, south of Harmony, you'll see the Peleg Brown House (8), c.1786, a late-Colonial-style home belonging to the shipowner/merchant, whose daughter married Captain Nathaniel Palmer in 1798. Palmer—whose Victorian mansion on Palmer Street is now maintained as a museum (open Tues. through Sun., 10am to 4pm; tours on the hour until 3pm; admission charged) by the Historical Society—discovered Antarctica when he was 21 years old. Look for the Amos Sheffield House (9), c.1765, at the corner of Wall and Water Streets. Historians believe this early-Georgian-style residence was raised so that a basement could be inserted underneath.

The Arcade Building (10), c.1830, a Greek-Revival building with an eight-column façade, was Stonington's first "shop center." In the 1920s it operated as a fish market. The stately Ocean Bank Building (11), c.1851, on Cannon Square, is also Greek Revival. The two cannons in the center of the Square were used to defend Stonington against the invading British in 1783.

Walk further down Water Street to the Jonathon Waldron House (12), c.1783, and the Elkanah Cobb House (13), c.1769, which both sustained much damage in the British attack of 1814 because they were situated so close to the end of Long Point. Across the street you'll see a complex of abandoned brick industrial buildings (14). Over the centuries, horseshoe nails, firearms, silk thread, machine gun mounts, and finally plastics were manufactured here.

Look down Trumbull Street to see some interesting early row houses, then continue on to the end of the point and the Stonington Lighthouse (15), c.1823. A museum operated by the Historical Society since 1927 (open daily 10am to 5pm, July and August; closed Mon. in the other months; admission charged), six rooms of exhibits depict the lives and times of Stonington's fishermen, merchants, shipbuilders, traders, and craftsmen. Walk down to the tip of the Point, where you'll be rewarded with a phenomenal oceanic panorama that includes glimpses of Mystic, Conn., and Watch Hill, R.I.

Retrace your steps to Cannon Square. Turn right on Main Street. The Gurdon Trumbull House (17), c.1840, is typical of the late Federal period, when merchants could afford more spacious homes. A cupola crowns its hip roof. The original parlor of the Georgian-style Hallam House (18), c.1844, overlooked the street but changed several years later to look over picturesque Narragansett Bay instead. Across the street overlooking Cannon Square is the dignified Gurdon Pendleton House (19), c.1848, a late Federal-period structure owned by the proprietor of the Ocean Bank. The Customs House (20), c.1820, just south of Wall Street, was built as the original Ocean Bank. Converted to a government facility between 1873 and 1913, the building housed agents who collected duties placed on imports of whale oil and seal skins. It is now a private residence.

The Captain Amos Palmer House (21), c.1787, at the corner of Main and Wall Streets, hoards a colorful history. The height and position of this house made it a target of the British attack of 1814, and the residence was hit many times. Legend has it that one shot narrowly missed Captain Palmer, who became enraged. When the ball cooled, he took it down the street to the militia battery and sought permission to return it to the British. He did so with a direct hit. Famous residents who lived in this house in subsequent years include James McNeill Whistler and the family of Stephen Vincent Benet.

Continue along Main Street. The brick for the Harris Pendleton House (22), c.1850, was brought to Stonington as ballast in a sailing ship. Note that the color of the bricks has a pinkish cast, rather than the dark red of that made in New England. Pristinely maintained former sea captains' houses line both sides of this street, punctuated here and there by a vintage church, such as the Calvary Episcopal (23), c.1847. Illustrative of a style known as American Church Gothic, this structure was designed by Richard Upjohn, who also designed Trinity Church in New York City.

The Aunt Mary Howe House (24), c.1790, sits across from the church. Originally owned by a spinster locally known as Aunt Mary, it is a long, low structure that for a time was used as a bakery and then the town library. Rare in New England is the double-hipped roof of the Colonel Joseph Smith House (25), c.1800, a handsome Georgian structure with graceful pillars surmounted by a pediment and a leaded fanlight.

The property of the old Congregational Church (26), c.1834, borders the right-of-way for the former Stonington railroad that went to the steamboat wharf. The tracks ran behind a picket fence at the right of the building. Now a unified Baptist and Congregational group, the church is known as United Church of Stonington. Peek inside, the interiors of this structure are very pretty.

The Ira H. Palmer House (27), c.1847, at the corner of Main and High Streets combines Greek-Revival and Victorian-inspired architectural themes in a style known as Transitional. Wadawanuck Square showcases other grand seafarers' mansions, which were generally built by wealthy residents that made their fortunes in the railroad, shipping, and finance industries in the middle of the 19th century. The Zebulon Stanton House (28), c.1776, an early Georgian with simple Ionic pilasters, was the home of a silversmith who added a "silver-shop wing." The John F. Trumbull House (29), c.1860, illustrates the French Second Empire design, featuring a mansard roof, dormer windows, and an ornamental porch over the front door. The Squire Pomeroy House (30), c.1855, is an imposing Federal-style granite structure with a hip roof.

End your tour at the Stonington Library in the middle of Wadawanuck Square. Standing on the site of a former grand hotel, the library opened in 1900 and houses a fascinating collection of volumes on historical Stonington Borough.

Rainy Day Options

The story of the Mashantucket Pequot Tribal Nation comes to life in the 308,000-square-foot, $135 million complex, opened in August 1998 as the **Mashantucket Pequot Museum**. This interactive museum utilizes state-of-the art technology to tell the tribe's story. The Pequot Village is one of the best aspects of this museum. You will receive a personal, portable, digital audio system that leads you through the re-creation of a 16th-century coastal Pequot village. The life-size diorama, whose figures were cast from Native American models, emits the sights, sounds and a narrative history of the times. Rather than being heavy handed and preachy, the presentation is informative, entertaining and long overdue to be told. Open daily, 10am to 7pm, Memorial weekend through Labor Day; closed Tues. other months; admission charged. *(From I-95, exit 92, follow Rte. 2 to Rte. 214. Follow signs for Mashantucket Pequot Museum, 110 Pequot Trail. Contact: 800/411-9671; 860/396-6800; www.mashantucket.com)*

At the turn of the last century, artists fled New York and Boston each summer, flocking to Old Lyme and Florence Griswold's boarding house to sketch and paint the rural landscape. Mimicking the works of the French Impressionists, this art colony formed the bedrock of the American Impressionist movement. An Old Lyme historic landmark with 11 acres of gardens, Miss Florence's stately old Georgian-style house, built in 1817, is now the **Florence Griswold Museum**, which showcases the Lyme Art Colony collection of paintings, sculpture, and photographs, as well as the dining room caricature murals. The illustrative panels, which reveal the personalities of the artists as well as tales of their times together, were painted as a gift to Miss Florence. Open Tues. through Sat., 10am to 5pm, Sun. 1 to 5pm, Apr. through Dec.; from Jan. through May, open Wed. through Sun., 1pm to 5pm; guided tours are offered on the half hour; admission charged. *(From I-95, exit 70, take Rte. 1 to 96 Lyme St. Contact: 860/434-5542, www.flogris.org).*

If a rainy day keeps you from the great outdoors, consider exploring your luck in one of Coastal Connecticut's gaming casinos. Besides every option to test Lady Luck, you'll find food and entertainment galore at **Foxwoods Resort Casino** *(From I-95, exit 92, take Rte. 2 west and follow the signs. Contact: 860/312-3000; 800/200-2882; www.foxwoods.com)* and **Mohegan Sun** *(From I-95 exit 84, Rte 32 north to I-395 north. Take exit*

79A, Rte 2A east to Mohegan Sun Blvd. in Uncasville. Contact: 888 /226-7711; www.mohegansun.com). Foxwoods is operated under the auspices of the Mashantucket Pequot tribe; Mohegan Sun is affiliated with the Mohegans. Admittedly more Las Vegas than New England, these glitzy gaming oases pack 'em in by the busload.

Lodging

For more lodging ideas, check out www.yourtravel-hq.com/htlindex or consult the New England-wide accommodations websites and reservation services that are listed in "How to Use This Book."

Intricate oak millwork and antique accents help create the classy ambiance at **Three Chimney's Inn** ($$, 1201 Chapel St., New Haven, 203 /789-1201, 800/443-1554, www.ultranet.com/~chimney3). But it's the thoughtful details that make an overnight stay here a personal delight. A welcome basket includes a giant chocolate chip cookie, apple, and thermos of hot water; an adult-beverage honor bar supplements complimentary tea, sherry, and port in the parlor; and a third-floor pantry can be raided for free late-night snacks. Just like at home!

Once broken-down and overgrown in brambles, **Deacon Timothy Pratt Bed and Breakfast** ($$, 325 Main St., Old Saybrook, 860/395-1229, www.oldsaybrook.com/Pratt) now is restored to its 1746 glory. The common areas and three guest rooms showcase post-and-beam construction, hand-carved pegs, and hand-hewn beams. Owner Shelley Nobile found hidden treasures during the renovation: a beehive oven in the kitchen, wood-burning fireplaces in nearly every room, and corncob insulation in the attic.

Sporting a spa, pool, fitness center, marina, and sweeping vistas of the Connecticut River and Long Island Sound, **Saybrook Point Inn** ($$+, 2 Bridge St. Old Saybrook, 860/395-2000, www.saybrook.com) offers it all. Guest rooms were totally redecorated in 1999. Many have gas fireplaces. For a romantic getaway, book the Lighthouse Suite out on the dock; the yacht-filled marina is picturesque to the max.

The Old Lyme Inn ($$, 85 Lyme St., Old Lyme, 860/434-2600, 800/434-5352, www.oldlymeinn.com) exudes the casual yet elegant atmosphere of an English country house. Five rooms are upstairs in the c.1850 farmhouse; eight more in a more recently built North Wing. All feature comfy beds—some 4-poster—antique reproduction furnishings, and modern amenities. Food in the taproom and restaurant is topnotch (see Food and Drink.)

The heart, soul, and spirit of Essex since 1776, the **Griswold Inn** ($$, 36 Main St., Essex, 860/767-1776; www.griswoldinn.com), steeps in its copious history. More than a bed and a hot meal, the Gris is pure colonial country. Rooms are spartan but comfortable, spread among a number of vintage dwellings along the former horse-path thoroughfare. But the pulse of the town beats in the popular 1778 taproom, where lively banjo music and sea shanty sing-alongs perform to standing-room-only twice weekly.

The Inn at Chester ($$, 318 West Main St., Chester, 860/526-9541; www.innatchester.com), a former farmhouse built by John Parmelee in 1778, was a private home until 1982, when it was turned into an inn. Furniture in the 41 guest rooms are colonial reproductions built by Eldred Wheeler. Chockablock with vintage antique memorabilia, the inn is a charming country getaway also renowned for its fine cuisine (see Food and Drink).

Randall's Ordinary ($$+, Rte. 2, North Stonington, CT 06359, 860/599-4640, www.randallsordinary.com) welcomes guests to John Randall's original farmhouse and three-story barn building, built in 1685, for a remarkable return to the 17th-century. Carefully preserved to period authenticity—wide-planked yellow-pine floors and exposed pegged beams—the rooms are furnished simply with antiques and canopy beds. The 21st century intrudes only when deemed necessary for creature comforts. Dinner here is special (see Food and Drink).

Offering accommodations in two early 1800s houses, **Antiques and Accommodations** ($$+, 32 Main St., North Stonington, 860/535-1736, 800/554-7829, www.visitmystic.com/antiques) sprinkles cherished antique furniture and collections throughout all the bed chambers and common rooms. A barn full of antiques bears witness to the owners' more than 25 trips to England; you can browse a bit and go home with an old treasure. Situated in the historic district along the Lieutenant River, **Bee and Thistle Inn** ($+, 100 Lyme St., Old Lyme, CT, 860/622-434-1667, 800 /622-4946; www.beeandthistleinn.com) features English gardens and gracious amenities amid a 1756 classic colonial.

Norwich Inn & Spa ($$$$, 607 West Thames St., Rte. 32, Norwich, 860/886-2401; www.) is an historic Georgian that combines the amenities of a fine inn with the rejuvenating pampering of a first-class spa.

Food and Drink

For more dining options, consult www.restaurants.com.

Said to be the birthplace of America's first hamburger in 1900, **Louis' Lunch** ($, 263 Crown St., New Haven, 203/752-1444) is an institution in New Haven. The burgers are still broiled vertically in the original cast iron grill and served between two slices of toast. And don't even try to add mustard or ketchup as a garnish, you'll get yelled at—only cheese, tomato, and onion will do.

An 1855 colonial overlooking Milford Green, **Rainbow Gardens Inn** ($$, 117 North Broad St., Milford, 203/878-2500) serves up imaginative pastas, salads, and dinner entrees that reflect globally inspired fusion. The dining room is homey, heirloom photos add to the familial atmosphere, and miniature birdhouses are everywhere—at least 25 are nailed to a tree in the front yard.

A spirited selection of noodles and "un-noodles" are the specialties at **Noodles** ($+, 286 Main St., Old Saybrook, 860/388-6224), an intimate storefront eatery on Old Saybrook's main thoroughfare. Fast, fun, and reasonably priced, all menu items also are available for takeout.

Started by Johnny Adinolfo in 1957 and now owned by Bob Hansen, **Johnny Ad's Restaurant** ($, 910 Boston Post Rd., Old Saybrook, 860/388-4032) is a local favorite Johnny Ad's, a legend in Old Saybrook, is a side-of-the-road seafood "shack" ubiquitous along Connecticut's Long Island Sound. Come here for great Rhode Island clam chowder, fried clams or lobster rolls.

The Old Lyme Inn ($$$$, 85 Lyme St., Old Lyme, 860/434-2600, 800/434-5352, www.oldlymeinn.com) offers two dining options, both memorable. The cozy taproom, which showcases a Victorian bar from an old tavern in Pittsburgh, serves an extensive array of tasty dishes, plus a less expensive, light fare menu. The Empire Room—elegant with high ceilings, floor-to-ceiling pier mirror, star-studded red wallpaper, and massive maritime mural—provides innovative interpretations of traditional New England cuisine.

Each dining room of the **Griswold Inn** ($$+, 36 Main St., Essex, 860/767-1776)—Covered Bridge, Steamboat, Library, and Gun Room—presents its own vision of Essex's historic past, displaying one of the most important maritime art and antique firearms collections in America. Cuisine at the Gris is pure country, including the famous 1776 sausages. The Sunday Hunt Breakfast is modeled after the English breakfasts the British demanded during their brief occupation of Essex.

Quintessentially maritime, **Black Seal Seafood Grille** ($-$$, 15c Main St., Essex, 860/767-0233) is a popular pub/eatery decked out with high ceilings, nautical decor, ship models, oars, boat hulls, and nautical photos. The food runs to standard but tasty tavern fare plus a good selection of fresh local seafood.

The rustic dining room at **The Inn at Chester** ($$$, 318 West Main St., Chester, 860/526-9541) is a former Connecticut barn that was disassembled and rebuilt at the inn, board by board, with the weathered boards facing inside. The New American cuisine served within is equally as inventive. Breads and pastries are made on-premises, and chocolate lovers must try this award-winning selection—a chocolate cigar served with a chocolate matchbook full of, you guessed it, chocolate matches.

Lobster just doesn't get any better than this! **Abbotts' Lobster in-the-Rough** ($-$$,117 Pearl St., Noank 860/536-7719) perches at the edge of Stonington Harbor in the quaint coastal village of Noank. Open daily from early May through Labor Day and weekends until Columbus Day, Abbot's steamed lobster is legendary. Eat at picnic tables on the pier and drink in the nautical atmosphere as the boats chug through the harbor. (If you want to drink alcoholic beverages, however, BYOB.)

All the food is great at the **Mooring Restaurant** ($$, Mystic Hilton, 20 Coogan Blvd., Mystic, 860/572-0731, www.hilton.com), but especially innovative is the "Thin's In" menu by Diane Rubin. Special lunch and dinner entrees are prepared daily following the parameters of Ms.

Rubin's successful weight loss program. So, it looks like you can have your cake and eat it too!

From the street, this might look like a run-of-the-mill cafe, but cuisine at **Water Street Cafe** ($-$$, 142 Water St., Stonington, 860/535-2122) is special. Upscale but not uppity, this casual bistro combines the freshest of the seaport's offerings in imaginative combinations. Daily blackboard specials may entice you away from the menu, and don't miss the exquisite crème brûlée if it is offered as a chef's special.

Nothing is ordinary about dinner at **Randall's Ordinary** ($$$$, Rte. 2, North Stonington, CT 06359, 860/599-4640, www.randallsord inary.com). Authentic 18th-century recipes, using antique vegetables, fresh from the kitchen garden, are prepared over an open hearth. You are paying for the colonial ambiance as well as the cuisine, but this historical tasting should not be missed. Randall's was a stop on the Underground Railroad; a hatch to the hideout is in the hearth-room. For a less pricey option, come for breakfast or lunch.

Central and Western Connecticut

Sometimes called "the last green valley between Boston and Washington," central and western Connecticut is an undulating landscape rich with woodlands, streams, and quaint colonial villages. The land slopes northwestward to its highest elevation in Litchfield Hills, an area peppered with horse farms and well-preserved historic homes.

Regional Information
Litchfield Hills Visitors Bureau, P.O. Box 968, Litchfield, CT 06759; 860/567-4506; www.litchfieldhills.com.
Greater Hartford Tourism District, 234 Murphy Rd., Hartford, CT 06114; 860/244-8181, 800/793-4480; www.enjoyhartford.com.
State of Connecticut Department of Environmental Protection Bureau of Outdoor Recreation State Parks Division, 79 Elm St., Hartford, CT 06106; 860/424-3200; www.dep.state.ct.us.

Getting There
By Air: Bradley International Airport in Windsor Locks is served by express shuttles by most major airlines (888/624-1533).
By Automobile: I-95 east to I-91 north, connects with I-84, which enters Connecticut from New York State and runs northeast.

Historic Wethersfield

Wetherfield has always had its roots in the soil, for its very fertility has proved to be its prosperity. Sitting on a protected cove of the Connecticut River, Wethersfield, which was settled in 1634, was an important river port. Vessels took crops of red onions to market. Later, the Charles C. Hart Seed Company and Comstock, Ferre & Company became successful seed companies, which flourish to this day. Much of the village is an historic district, with more than 200 homes built before 1850.

Information
Wethersfield Historical Society, 150 Main St., Wethersfield, CT 06109; 203/529-7656, 888/653-9384 (24-hour information hotline).
Wetherfield Visitor's Center, Main St., Wethersfield, CT 06109; 203/529-7161, www.wethersfieldct.com

Getting There
Take I-91 to exit 26 and follow the signs to Keeney Cultural Center on Main St.

First Steps
Park at the Wetherfield Museum/Keeney Cultural Center and get a map of the village from the Visitor's Center. (Open Apr. 1 through Dec. 15, Thurs. through Sat.—10am to 4pm, Sun.—1 to 4pm.) This is the perfect stroll on an autumn afternoon. From the last day in September to the third week of October, the "Scarecrows of Main Street" competition transforms the main thoroughfare. You can explore the tiny village in an hour, visiting historic houses and spotting some of the most inventive scarecrows around. Admission is charged at Webb-Deane-Stevens Museum, Hurlbut-Dunham House, Buttolph-Williams House, Captain James Francis House, and the Museum of the Wethersfield Historical Society. Inquire at the Visitor's Center for hours of operation and tickets.

Historic Wethersfield. Begin your 2-mile exploration of historic Wethersfield at the Wethersfield Museum (1), 200 Main St., where you'll find exhibits on regional crafts, furniture, and memorabilia of the Connecticut River Valley displayed. Visit the Hurlbut-Dunham House (2) next door, 212 Main St., a magnificent brick mansion that combines elements of both Georgian and Victorian styling. The house is elegantly furnished to reflect opulent lifestyles of several different eras. Then cross

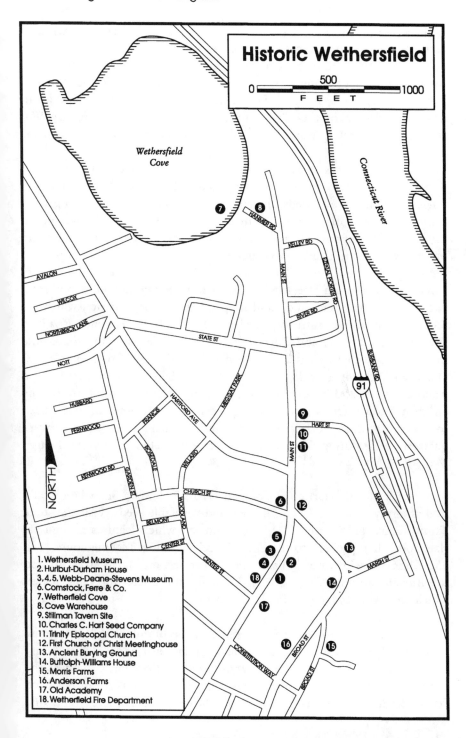

Historic Wethersfield

0 — 500 — 1000

FEET

Wethersfield Cove

Connecticut River

NORTH

1. Wethersfield Museum
2. Hurlbut-Durham House
3, 4, 5. Webb-Deane-Stevens Museum
6. Comstock, Ferre & Co.
7. Wetherfield Cove
8. Cove Warehouse
9. Stillman Tavern Site
10. Charles C. Hart Seed Company
11. Trinity Episcopal Church
12. First Church of Christ Meetinghouse
13. Ancient Burying Ground
14. Buttolph-Williams House
15. Morris Farms
16. Anderson Farms
17. Old Academy
18. Wetherfield Fire Department

Main Street to the Webb-Deane-Stevens Museum, 211 Main St., which is actually composed of three well-preserved 18th-century houses. The collections of furniture and decorative arts reflect the lives of the homes' owners, merchant Joseph Webb (3), diplomat Silas Deane (4) and leatherworker Issac Stevens (5). George Washington once slept in an upstairs bedroom of the Webb House and planned Revolutionary War strategy in the parlor. Murals here tell the story of the battle of Yorktown.

Follow Main Street's brick sidewalk to Comstock, Ferre & Co. (6), 263 Main St., a well-known seed company founded in 1820. Though they no longer grow their own seeds, the company still operates as a retail garden center and seed distributing company, at which bulk seed is sold to growers and other retail customers. Look around, you may find some unusual varieties to plant in your garden.

Continue down Main Street, which is lined with majestic old maple trees, walking past the homes and retail shops of the historic district, which are identified by dated historical markers. Turn left on Hanmer Road to Wetherfield Cove (7) and Cove Warehouse (8). This was the site of the maritime trade that flourished between 1650 and 1830. Cross Main Street and head back to the village center. At 320 Main Street (9) you'll see a beautiful gray and mauve Victorian with a slate mansard roof. The Stillman Tavern, famous as a hostelry during the revolutionary war, used to stand on this spot. Washington and Rochambeau's retinue were quartered here during the Yorktown conference held at the Webb House, May 19 to May 24, 1781.

Stop at Charles C. Hart Seed Company (10), 304 Main St., where you'll find an array of unusual herb, flower, and vegetable seeds. Visit the stone Trinity Episcopal Church (11), 300 Main St., which features an unusual slate roof, then proceed to the First Church of Christ Meetinghouse (12), 250 Main St., which was built in 1761. Turn left on Marsh Street to find the Ancient Burying Ground (13). Look for the interesting table plates, which date from the mid to the late 1700s.

Cross Marsh Street to Broad Street and visit the Buttolph-Williams House (14), 249 Broad St. The house was built at the turn of the 18th century and is furnished to reflect life in Wethersfield at that time. This was the setting for Elizabeth George Speare's 1958 book, *The Witch of Blackbird Pond*. Broad Street splits around Broad Street Green, where you'll find

Morris Farms (15) on one side and Anderson Farms (16) on the other. These farms are fun to visit after the fall harvest, when they are loaded with pumpkins, apples, and cider.

Turn right on Constitution Way, then right on Main Street and visit the Old Academy (17), 150 Main St., Wethersfield's former schoolhouse, built in 1804. The building now houses the offices of the Wethersfield Historical Society. Cross to the Wetherfield Fire Department (18), 171 Main St., chartered by the Connecticut General Assembly on May 12, 1803. This is the oldest volunteer fire department in New England in continuous existence and one of the oldest in the U.S. End your tour of historic Wethersfield back at the Keeney Cultural Center.

Farmington Freedom Trail

Farmington was an important stop on the Underground Railroad—the secret route to help fugitive slaves flee north—beginning in 1840. "Conductors," citizens of Farmington who were sympathetic to the cause, guided these "passengers" out of town in the dark of the night. The abolitionists sheltered the former slaves in their homes, the "stations" of the "railroad." Legend portends so many slaves passed through Farmington that the city could be nicknamed Grand Central Station.

In 1839, 53 Mendi tribesmen who were abducted from Africa and transported as cargo left Havana aboard the Spanish slave ship *Amistad*. They revolted, took control of the ship, killed most of the Spanish crew, and set a course for Africa. The two remaining crew instead steered the ship northward and ended up in Long Island Sound. The U.S. navy seized the ship, and the Africans were imprisoned in the New Haven jail. A series of trials began, culminating at the U.S. Supreme court, where former President John Quincy Adams convinced the courts to free the Africans in February 1841.

In March of that year, 38 of the Mendi were sent to Farmington to live while money was raised to return the liberated slaves to Africa. The group stayed in Farmington, farming and studying, for nine months. One died in the village and is buried in Riverside Cemetery. The Freedom Trail was authorized by the Connecticut General Assembly in 1995.

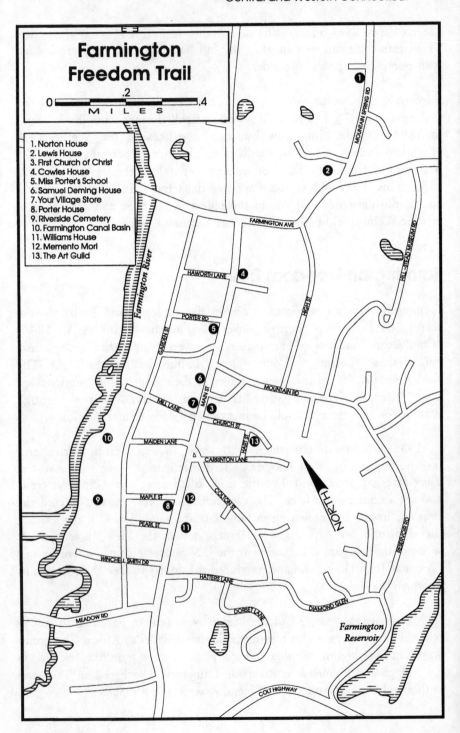

Farmington Freedom Trail

0   .2   .4
M I L E S

1. Norton House
2. Lewis House
3. First Church of Christ
4. Cowles House
5. Miss Porter's School
6. Samuel Deming House
7. Your Village Store
8. Porter House
9. Riverside Cemetery
10. Farmington Canal Basin
11. Williams House
12. Memento Mori
13. The Art Guild

Information
Farmington Historical Society, Main St., Farmington, CT 06034; 860/678-1645.

Getting There
Take I-84 to Rte. 4, to Rte. 10 south.

First Steps
Pick up a Freedom Trail guide at the Farmington Library, which is behind the First Church of Christ Congregational Church. Each location on the Freedom Trail is marked with a granite pillar bearing a square brass plaque that says "Freedom Trail" and is etched with the image of a coach lantern with rays of light and a single star. Guided tours of the Farmington Freedom Trail sites are offered by the Farmington Historical Society by appointment.

Farmington Freedom Trail. Most of the Farmington Freedom Trail, which includes Underground Railroad safe houses and sites connected to the *Amistad* case, is easily accessible by foot, although most of the structures are private homes and cannot be explored. First, drive by the two stops away from the busy Main Street thoroughfare. John T. Norton was an Amistad supporter, who lived in a grand home at 11 Mountain Spring Rd.—Norton House (1)—with his family. Elijah Lewis hid fugitives from slavery in a space at the base of the chimney at Lewis House (2), 1 Mountain Spring Rd.

Park at the Farmington Library, entrance on Church St. As you follow the prescribed 1.5-mile Freedom Trail route, you'll walk past many historically dated vintage buildings, which were not associated with *Amistad* or the Underground Railroad, but nevertheless are well preserved and interesting architectural specimens. Main Street, Rte. 10, is a very busy road, lined with towering trees. Cross with caution.

Referring to your "Farmington Freedom Trail" guide for historical details, walk to the First Church of Christ (3) at 75 Main St, which was founded in 1652. Many abolitionists were members here and welcomed the *Amistad* Africans to worship alongside them. The steeple of this white clapboard church is particularly beautiful. Turn right on Main Street to Cowles House (4), number 27. Mary Ann and Horace Cowles hid fugitive slaves here, a stop on the Underground Railroad.

Cross Main Street and reverse direction. Proceed to the Georgian-style brick building, 60 Main Street. This is Miss Porter's School (5), founded as a girls' school in 1843 by Sarah Porter, eldest daughter of abolitionist Rev. Noah Porter. Further on is the Samuel Deming House (6), 66 Main St., a white clapboard colonial, c. 1770, that also served as a stop on the Underground Railroad. Turn right on Mill Lane to Your Village Store (7), which was a general store run by Samuel Deming in the mid 1800s. The Africans from the *Amistad* attended classes in a room on the second floor.

Retrace your steps and continue down Main Street. Porter House (8), 116 Main St., was owned by Rev. Noah Porter. Minister of First Church of Christ from 1806 to 1866, Porter was a firm abolitionist. The Porters provided a home for Marghru, a young girl from the Amistad. Take a short detour down Maple Street to Garden Street and the Riverside Cemetery (9), where the body of Foone, the lone *Amistad* African who died in Farmington, is buried. It is believed he drowned in the Farmington Canal basin (10), nearby. The Africans farmed the land across from the cemetery for a time.

Return to Main Street via Pearl Street. Carefully cross Main to Williams House (11), 127 Main St. Austin Williams lived in this white Georgian-style structure, which features an unusual iron porch. Williams built a dormitory for the African men from the *Amistad*, later housing his horses and carriages there and harboring fugitive slaves in the basement beneath.

Looping back down Main Street, stop at Memento Mori (12), an old graveyard that rests behind wooden arches, pillars, and gate, surrounded by hundred-foot-tall pines. Revolutionary gravestones date back to the early 1700s. As you proceed down Main Street, notice that the homes are set back from the road and quite grand.

Turn right on Carrington Lane, then left on Hart Street to the last stop on the Farmington Freedom Trail, the Art Guild (13), at the corner of Hart and Church Streets. Here women of the First Church of Christ met, in 1841, to sew clothing for the Africans. This was the site of many rowdy abolitionist, and anti-abolitionist, meetings. Return to the Farmington Library to end your tour.

Weir Farm National Historic Site

Enamored with the bucolic Connecticut landscape, J. Alden Weir purchased a 153-acre Branchville Road farm in 1882 for $10 and a painting. This fortuitous turn of events netted the inspiration for hundreds of paintings and drawings from Weir and other talented turn-of-the-last-century American Impressionist artists. The artists took brushes, canvases, and paints into the countryside, drawing the beauty of the scenic landscape.

Information
Weir Farm National Historic Site, 735 Nod Hill Rd., Wilton, CT 06897; 203/834-1896; www.nps.gov/wefa.

Getting There
From I-95 or the Merritt Parkway, take Rte. 7 north. Turn left on Rte. 102. Go 0.3 mile then turn left on Old Branchville Rd. Turn at first left to 735 Nod Hill Rd.

First Steps
Stop at the Burlingham House Visitor Center across from the parking area. Watch the short video on the life of artist J. Alden Weir, then, for a nominal fee, purchase the Weir Farm Historic Painting Sites Trail Guide. Note that although the grounds are open daily from dawn to dusk, the Visitor Center is open only Wed. through Sun. Ranger-led tours of the studios of J. Alden Weir and sculptor Mahonri Young are scheduled at intervals.

Weir Farm. One of only two national historic sites devoted to the life and times of an American artist (see Saint-Gaudens National Historic Site in the New Hampshire chapter), Weir Farm chronicles the nearly four decades of Weir's artistic endeavors. Color photos of Weir's paintings, which correspond with the exact vistas he encountered from the locations a hundred years ago, document the self-guided tour of Weir's painting sites. The landscapes have changed over time, of course, but the representations are unmistakable. The sensation of intruding upon Weir's private reflective moments is eerily unsettling, but the scenery is, indeed, beautiful.

Allow about an hour for touring the 12 painting sites, especially if you enjoy studying the paintings and the landscape in detail. Then, if your time allows, explore the walking trails of the 60-acre farm or those on the adjoining 29-acre Nod Hill Refuge, which is owned by the town of Ridgefield, or the 110-acre Weir Preserve, owned by the Nature Conservancy. Entrances to the refuge and preserve are on Pelham Lane and Nod Hill Road.

People's State Forest, Riverton

Peoples State Forest is like the forest primeval—an old-growth forest of towering white pines, some more than 200 years old. Strangler vines climb barren tree trunks, gurgling streams weave a mosaic tapestry around lichen-covered boulders, and ferns punctuate the pine needle carpet that embroiders the dense forest floor. A favorite haunt of Native Americans, the 3,000 acres of People's State Forest sprawl along the east bank of the West Branch of the Farmington River. Six intersecting walking trails are clearly blazed; the walking trail brochure describes and maps the trail alternates.

Information
State of Connecticut Department of Environmental Protection Bureau of Outdoor Recreation, State Parks Division, 79 Elm St., Harford, CT 96106-5127; 860/424-3200.

Getting There
Take I-95, Rte. 15 (Merritt Parkway), or I-84 east to Rte. 8 north. Then take Rte. 44 east to Rte. 318, to Pleasant Valley. Cross the river and proceed north on East River Road. Fork right on Greenwoods Rd. to the Nature Museum parking area.

First Steps
Hiking maps are available from the kiosk at the Nature Museum headquarters on Greenwoods Road.

People's State Forest. The Agnes Bowen Trail (orange blaze; 2.5 miles) and the Robert Ross Trail (blue blaze; 2 miles) both begin at the Nature Museum. They fork east and west after about a quarter mile, eventually connecting with two yellow blazed trails to form a big loop. This long loop, though strenuous, covers an interesting range of terrain. The Charles Pack Trail (yellow blaze; 1.9 miles) hooks into the Agnes Bowen Trail at about the halfway point and stops at the upper end of Greenwoods Road. After a short distance on the paved road, the trail continues, now called the Jessie Gerard Trail (yellow blaze; 1.3 miles). It intersects with Robert Ross Trail just beyond the site of an ancient Indian soapstone quarry.

The Agnes Bowen Trail, a former 1930s ski trail, skirts Beaver Brook Swamp. Mossy rocks pepper the path, beneath a canopy of feathery pines. Charles Pack Trail crosses Beaver Brook via a rather primitive footbridge: Two sturdy logs, planed off but mossy, must be navigated over the stream—tight-rope style. An old cellar hole, remains of an old colonial home, is visible from this trail. A fork of the Jessie Gerard Trail traverses an old Indian settlement known as Barkhamsted Lighthouse and leads to the Chaugham Lookouts, where the vista is spectacular. If you are particularly fit and adventuresome, ascend to the lookouts more directly, by climbing the alternate route —299 stone steps.

Lyme Disease

When walking in wooded and grassy areas of New England, take the necessary precautions against Lyme disease. Lyme disease is an illness spread by the bite of a bacteria-carrying deer tick. Called a deer tick because it often feeds on deer or the white-footed mouse, the tick is about the size of a poppy seed and often goes unnoticed. Usually it is the baby tick—called a nymph—that feeds on people.

Deer ticks are found on grass or bushes and will crawl onto the lower part of your body, such as your ankles. Once on your body, they will crawl to other areas and attach themselves. When walking in the natural areas of New England, take these precautions: Wear a hat, a long-sleeve shirt tucked into your pants, long pants tucked into your socks, and closed-toe shoes. Liberally apply insect repellent with a high deet factor.

After your walk, inspect yourself for possible deer ticks, each of which will resemble a small black freckle or mole. Pay special attention to your back, groin, hairline, and under your arms. To make sure no ticks are secreted in your clothing, put your clothes in a dryer for 30 minutes, which will kill them.

Early signs of Lyme disease include a rash-like patch that resembles a bull's-eye, which usually, but not always, forms around the bite. Headache, fatigue, fever, and flu symptoms often occur within a few days of the bite. When discovered in late stages, Lyme disease often presents itself with joint pain and swelling. Left untreated, Lyme disease can cause arthritis, heart problems, and nervous system disorders. Contact a physician if you notice any possible symptom of Lyme disease. Diagnosis can be determined by a simple blood test. For more information, contact the Massachusetts Department of Public Health Bureau of Communicable Disease Control, 617/983-6800.

A separate trail, unconnected with the aforementioned loop, leads from Greenwoods Road to its terminus on a town road near Rte. 81. This trail, the Elliott Bronson Trail (red blaze; 1.5 miles), crosses a 60-foot cliff in the southern part of Peoples State Forest, which nets a great view of the surrounding countryside.

Mine Hill Preserve, Roxbury

Listed on the National Register of Historic Places, Mine Hill Preserve encompasses a 19th-century iron-ore mine, Shepaug Spathic Iron and Steel Company, and a once prolific granite quarry.

Information
Litchfield Hills Travel Council, P.O. Box 968, Litchfield, CT 06759-0968; 860/567-4506; www.litchfieldhills.com.

Getting There
From I-95 or Rte. 15 (Merritt Parkway), or I-84, take Rte. 7 north, to Rte. 67 east to Roxbury. In Roxbury, take Rte. 67 for 2.3 miles north of Roxbury Town Hall and turn right onto Mine Hill Rd., after crossing the Shepaug River. Proceed on the dirt road a short distance. Parking area is uphill on the right.

First Steps
Visit the website of Litchfield Hills Travel Council, where you can find the complete Litchfield Hills Touring Guide. This wonderful, comprehensive guide details 19 excursions in the Litchfield Hills area by car, foot, boat, or bicycle. Alternately, call Litchfield Hills Travel Council at the number above to secure a copy of the brochure brochure or stop at the Visitors Booth on Litchfield Green, which is open from June through mid-Oct. This walk is 3.5 miles (blue blaze) over easy to moderate terrain. Allow 2.5 to 3 hours to explore the area.

Mill Hill Preserve. From the parking lot, cross the footbridge and take the elevated Donkey Path, so named because donkeys once hauled ore-filled carts from the mines to the furnaces along iron rails imbedded in this path. On the right you can see the backsides of two huge fieldstone roasting ovens down below, which you will explore later in this walk.

Shepaug Spathic Iron and Steel Company created a honeycomb of mine tunnels here between 1865 and 1868. A cool rush of subterranean air greets you at the visible, grated openings of the two tunnels you will encounter. As you continue along the trail, notice a small pond. The company dammed Mineral Brook to obtain a good water source for the ironworks. After you've walked a short distance from the second tunnel, begin to look for the first of four mine shafts. The bright orange safety cages covering the shafts are easily identifiable.

Continue following the blue-blazed path, which begins a serpentine climb through an obstacle course of boulders. The path leads to a long-abandoned granite quarry. Shepaug Spathic Iron and Steel Company quarried this local granite to build two ore roasters, a blast furnace, a steel puddling furnace, and a rolling mill—the remains of which you'll encounter on this walk. Eight abandoned quarries pepper Mine Hill Preserve, and you'll notice huge granite slabs imbedded with blasting cable littering the landscape like moon stones. Though the iron mine ceased operation in the late 1870s, gray granite was quarried here until 1961. The granite was used in the construction of the Brooklyn Bridge, Grand Central Terminal, and East River Drive in New York City.

At a fork in the trail, when the blue blazes lead to the left, detour about 1,500 feet up the path to view the sheer face of an exposed granite wall. The dramatic cliff of stone is worth the trip. Retrace your steps and follow the blue blazes through a gate and along the dirt road that borders the meadow. The road becomes shady with pines as you approach the Shepaug River.

Take a sharp right following the blazes up the path to the ruins of the furnace site. Raw ore was heated in the roasting ovens (which you first viewed from the Donkey Path), in preparation for smelting. At the nearby blast furnace, said to be the most extensive and well-preserved in the state, the roasted ore was smelted to form iron. Ore and charcoal were loaded into the top of the furnace. Molted iron was tapped from the bottom of the furnace and cast into bars known as pigs. The impurities in the ore then were drawn off as slag.

From the furnace site, the path leads to some puzzling foundations, thought to be the remains of a puddling furnace and rolling mill, which converted the pig iron into steel. The precise function of these structures is not currently known. Once a bustling industrial site, the former furnace site is now a tranquil, faintly haunted hermitage alive with birds, butterflies, woodland flowers, and wild strawberries.

Bull's Covered Bridge River Walk, Kent

Be sure to bring a lunch with you before you set off on your walk, because the gigantic boulders bordering the gorge and waterfall at Bull's Covered Bridge make a phenomenally scenic picnic table. From the parking area, walk back over the third bridge toward the covered bridge. Take the short scenic Bull's Bridge Scenic Trail Loop to a large boulder that perches over the water, nearly under the bridge, and tuck into your repast. Four covered bridges spanned the Housatonic River at this spot since 1760, all named after the builder of the first bridge, Isaac Bull. The bridge was needed to carry ore and charcoal across the river for Bull's Ironworks. Legend portends that George Washington's horse fell into Bull's Bridge Falls in 1781. The current bridge was constructed in 1842.

Information
Litchfield Hills Travel Council, P.O. Box 968, Litchfield, CT 06759-0968; 860/567-4506; www.litchfieldhills.com.

Getting There
From I-95 or Rte. 15 (Merritt Parkway), or I-84, take Rte. 7 north to Bull's Bridge Road and turn left. Cross the bridge, go through the covered bridge, pass a parking area on your right, then cross the third bridge. Hiker parking is on the left.

First Steps
Visit the website of Litchfield Hill Travel Council, where you can find the complete Litchfield Hills Touring Guide. This wonderful, comprehensive guide details 19 excursions in the Litchfield Hills area by car, foot, boat, or bicycle. Alternately, call Litchfield Hills Travel Council at the number above to secure a copy of the brochure or stop at the Visitors Booth on Litchfield Green, which is open from June through mid-Oct. Allow 2 to 2.5 hours for this 4-mile roundtrip walk. The first mile is over easy terrain. The second mile (optional) is a moderate climb up Ten Mile Hill. Part of the Appalachian Trail, this path is marked with white blazes.

Bull's Covered Bridge River Walk. From the hiker parking area and scenic outlook, fork left to the trailhead for the river walk. Blazes are blue to begin with and then change to white, as the path becomes part of the Appalachian Trail. Follow the white blazes and keep the river on your left. The elevated path through a dense forest of hardwoods and hemlocks shadows the river, which pulses downstream in a mass of rapids and eddies. The juxtaposition of the cool, canopied forest path, with the river teeming far below, creates a scenic extravaganza not readily encountered, even in richly endowed New England.

At the junction of the Housatonic and Ten Mile Rivers, the waters merge mystifyingly at the Ten Mile River Gorge. Cross the Ned Anderson Memorial Bridge over the gorge, a dizzying panorama of rapids and rocks. The trail jogs right, then left for a bit, along Ten Mile River, then abruptly cuts left uphill. This is the point you should turn around and retrace your steps if you want an easy 2-mile hike. But if you are fit and still raring to go for another 2 miles, take the steep, steady incline to the top of Ten Mile Hill (trail is strewn with roots and boulders and is tricky to navigate, especially in bad weather). At the crest of the hill, you'll once again see both white and blue blazes. Follow the white blazes to the summit for a spectacular view over Litchfield Hills.

Retrace your steps back to Bull's Covered Bridge. The Housatonic River is now on your right and the views from the reverse perspective compose an entirely different panorama. The beauty of this walk will feed your soul.

White Flower Farm, Litchfield

White Flower Farm was started, almost by accident, by two New York writers. William Harris and Jane Grant purchased a house and just over an acre of land in the 1930s with the intent of being weekend gardeners. Soon their love of the land took them all over the U.S. and abroad in search of unusual plants. This obsession eventually led them to start their own nursery, which they called White Flower Farm, after an all-white garden they had planted in front of their home.

Information
White Flower Farm, Rte. 63, Litchfield CT, 06759-0050; 860/567-8789; 800/503-9624; www.whiteflowerfarm.com.

Getting There
From I-95, Rte. 15 (Merritt Parkway), or I-84, take Rte. 8 north, to Rte. 118 west, to Rte. 202 west into Litchfield. From Litchfield Center, take Rte. 63 for 3.3 miles south.

First Steps
Stop at the Visitors Information Center for a free self-guided walking tour brochure.

White Flower Farm. This nursery is named for the white border of flowers William Harris and Jane Grant planted in front of their house (now a private residence), today referred to as the Moon Garden. The Moon Garden is an all-white garden, whose flowers are said to gleam in the moonlight. You can see the garden at station-two of the walking tour.

The self-guided tour of 10 plant stations winds around a number of outbuildings, the greenhouse production area, and formally planted gardens, including a lovely rose arbor, conifer garden, and shrub garden at station-one. The propagation beds are particularly interesting. You will not be able to walk around in this area, but you are welcome to peek inside. Plants offered in the annual Garden Book Catalog are developed here.

Station-seven is a large garden called the Ericaceous border. Plants here belong to the heath family, such as rhododendrons, azaleas, heaths and heathers, mountain laurels, and blueberries. The garden is a study in color and texture in all seasons. The very unusual shrubs that comprise station-eight are known as tree peonies, a coveted plant in China for more than 1,500 years and brought here by Williams and Grant in the 1950s. Each tree showcases more than 50 saucer-sized blooms in late May and early June.

Display gardens border the south lawn, station-nine on your tour. These are perennial gardens that have featured the best of White Flower Farm floral species for almost fifty years. Plants bloom in succession from spring until fall, but peak viewing is usually in June and July. The plants are labeled with both common and botanical names.

Opened in 1949, White Flower Farm is the largest mail-order nursery in New England. Staffed with knowledgeable "garden advisors," this nursery makes a great wandering place for flower lovers and plant aficionados alike. You may not be able to leave station-ten—the White Flower Farm retail store—empty-handed.

Historic Litchfield

John Marsh of Hartford explored the western part of Connecticut in 1715, paying the Potatuck Indians 15 pounds for an area then called Bantam. First settled in 1720, Litchfield developed as a stop on the inland stage route from New York to the towns of New England. Later it served as a supply depot for the Continental Army during the Revolution, and an occasional holding place for Loyalist prisoners. (George Washington reportedly lodged here after a meeting in Hartford in 1780.) By 1810 Litchfield was the fourth largest town in Connecticut. But with the advent of the railroad and large-scale waterpower industries—both of which by-passed Litchfield—the town declined in population for more than a century. Today, Litchfield is considered one of the prettiest towns in New England.

Information
Litchfield Historical Society, On-The-Green, Litchfield, CT 06759, 860/567-4501. Litchfield Hills Travel Council, P.O. Box 968, Litchfield, CT 06759-0968; 860/567-4506; www.litchfieldhills.com.

Getting There
From I-95, Rte. 15 (Merritt Parkway), or I-84, take Rte. 8 north, to Rte. 118 west, to Rte. 202 west to Litchfield Green.

First Steps
Stop at the Litchfield Historical Society Museum and purchase a copy of "My Country," a 48-page booklet that includes the history of Litchfield and a detailed walk of North Street, South Street, and Litchfield Green, an area designated as a National Historic Landmark District in 1967.

Historic Litchfield. This 2.75-mile walk through Litchfield center acquaints you with more than 75 historically significant buildings. As you follow the Litchfield Historical Society's detailed walking tour of North Street, South Street, and Litchfield Green, you'll find that a large portion of vintage 18th-century Colonial-Revival architecture remains unaltered and well preserved to this day, mainly as private dwellings. Ethan Allen, Aaron Burr, John C. Calhoun, Harriet Beecher Stowe, Benjamin Tallmadge, and Oliver Wolcott, signer of Declaration of Independence, all lived or studied in Litchfield. Several of the historic buildings are open to public: Litchfield Historical Museum and Research Library, Tapping Reeve House and Law School, and Oliver Wolcott Library.

Litchfield Historical Society Museum is located in the Noyes Memorial Building, the main portion of which was built in the Beaux Arts style in 1901 by John A. Vanderpoel in memory of his grandmother, Julia Tallmadge Noyes. The Litchfield Historical Society was founded in 1856. The numerous galleries of the society's museum feature exhibits that relay Litchfield's rich history (The museum is open Tues. through Sat., 11am to 5pm, and Sun. 1 to 5pm, from mid-May to mid-Nov.; admission fee.)

Tapping Reeve started the first law school in the United States in Litchfield in 1773 in the family parlor at 82 South Street. As classes grew, a separate law school, known as Litchfield Law School, was built on the property. More than 1,500 lawyers graduated from this school in the 60 years it operated, including two U.S. vice presidents and more than 100 members of Congress. (Tapping Reeve House is open Tues. through Sat., 11am to 5pm, and Sun., 1 to 5pm, from mid-Apr. through late Nov.)

The Wolcott House, c.1799, adjoins the Oliver Wolcott Library, a modern structure on South Street. The house—built by Elijah Wadsworth and lived in by Oliver Wolcott Jr, Secretary of the Treasury under George Washington and Governor of Connecticut from 1817 to 1827—features an elegant second floor ballroom.

Charming and pristine, the village of Litchfield is a picture postcard of quintessential New England.

White Memorial Foundation

More than 35 miles of interconnecting trails on 4,000 acres of land in the foothills of the Berkshire Mountains comprise this privately owned wildlife sanctuary. The 23 trails vary widely, traversing hills and rocks, forests and marshes, skirting rivers, brooks, and ponds. Easiest, most accessible, and perhaps most interesting are the short Trail of the Senses

(1.25 mile) and the Interpretive Nature Trail (0.5 mile).

Information
White Memorial Foundation and Conservation Center, 71 Whitehall Rd., Litchfield, CT 06759-0368; 860/567-0857.

Getting There
From I-95, Rte. 15 (Merritt Parkway) or I-84, take Rte. 8 north to Rte. 118 west, to Rte. 202 west to Litchfield. From the center of Litchfield, follow Rte. 202 west for 2.5 miles. Entrance is on the left.

First Steps
Follow Whitehall Rd. to the Visitor Center to get a trail map and the "Interpretive Trail Guide."

White Memorial Foundation. Begin the Trail of the Senses at the Mott-Van Winkle Environment Center. Here you'll see the tiny wooden houses of the Connecticut Bluebird Restoration Project, as well as some of their feathery satisfied tenants. The Trail of the Senses promises a "sensory encounter with the natural world." Sixteen interpretive signs point out things to see, feel, smell, and imagine. This is a terrific trail for families with young children. The trail winds through an old Christmas tree plantation, a field, and a mature forest. Plants are labeled for easy identification. The trail passes three enormous trees—white pine, red oak, and red maple—around which you are invited to wrap your arms. Some signs are translated in Braille, such as the one that suggests you listen for the oven bird calling, "teacher, teacher, teacher," or a small warbler calling "cheese, cheese, Limberger cheese."

To find the Interpretive Trail, head down the road past the Museum. A signpost points to the nature trail. The trail guide describes the various trees, ponds, plants, and animal habitats here in detail. Beginning with New England's famed sugar maple, the tree from which maple syrup is made each spring, the picturesque trail leads to 17 nature stations.

You'll find a wolf tree, so called because it takes up so much space it acts much like a predator, choking out the younger trees beneath. Most of the evergreens along the path are white pines, easy to spot if you remember that their needles grow in bundles of five and that there are five letters in the word white. You'll learn to tell an interrupted fern from a sensitive fern and a cinnamon fern (its green leaves are "interrupted" by several pairs of brown ones).

The marsh wetlands, full of grasses and sedges, net sightings of geese, red-winged blackbirds, and blue herons. At the Bantam River the trail cuts left into an old-growth forest of white pines that is more than 200 years old. Here you'll learn about soil mixing and obscure animal habitats. After crossing a boardwalk over a marshy area, you will enter a grove of Eastern hemlocks, which thrive in the shady conditions caused by their 100-foot-tall pine brethren.

The trail emerges from the forest onto an old horse and buggy path, which passes through a good birding area. Look for the large glacial erratic, an errant rock deposited during the last ice age. Return to the museum, where you'll find a fascinating bird sanctuary, a nectar garden for hummingbirds, and the exhibits that describe what you'll see on the other trails in the White Memorial Foundation wildlife refuge.

Rainy Day Options

Upon her death in 1972, Edith Morton Chase gave her Litchfield estate to the state of Connecticut. Now called **Topsmead State Forest Park**, the stately Tudor is open for guided tours on the second and fourth weekends of the month, June through October, and the formal gardens and hiking trails are open to the public year round. Free admittance. *(From CT Rte. 118, turn right on E. Litchfield Rd. Proceed to first right and turn onto Buell Rd. After 1/8 mile turn right on Chase Rd. Parking lot is on the right. Tel. 860/567-5694.)*

Susan Wakeen, America's most awarded baby doll artist, has been creating dolls in Connecticut since 1982. The **Susan Wakeen Doll Company**, in Litchfield, features a tiny showroom, Create-A-Doll Kingdom, that is chock-a-block with baby doll parts, so you can design your own. Showroom is open Mon. through Sat., 10am to 5pm; Sun., 10am to 4pm. "Birthing a baby" must be done in person or via the Susan Wakeen Doll Company website: www.susanwakeendolls.com. *(Take Rte. 202 west (Bantam Rd.) from Litchfield Center to 425 Bantam Rd. Doll factory is on the left across from the Litchfield Inn. Tel. 860/567-9790.)*

Glebe House Museum and the Gertrude Jekyll Garden, in Woodbury, is the 18th-century family farm (glebe) of Reverend John Marshall, Woodbury's first Episcopal priest. Horticultural designer and writer Gertude Jekyll designed the small formal garden when the glebe was restored in 1923 and opened to the public in 1925, Glebe House Museum is open Apr. through Nov., Wed. through Sun., 1 to 4pm. Fee for admission. *(From I-84, take exit 15 and turn east on Rte. 6 for 5 miles. Turn left at the stoplight on Rte. 317 in Woodbury. About 0.25 mile down, follow the fork to the left. Glebe House is across from the next stop sign. Tel.: 203/263-2855.)*

Lodging

For more lodging ideas, check out www.yourtravel-hq.com/htlindex or consult the New England-wide accommodations websites and reservation services that are listed in "How to Use This Book."

Exuding the understated charm of an elegant old manor house, **Simsbury 1820 House** ($$, 731 Hopmeadow St., Simsbury; 860/658-7658, www.Simsbury1820House.com) passes the pillow test with an A+. The mahogany four-poster beds are awash with down comforters and scads of down pillows, inviting guests to sink into oblivion. The 34 guest rooms are adorned with Chinese porcelains and turn-of-the-last-century antique prints.

The Litchfield Inn ($+, Rte. 202, Litchfield, 860/567-5358, 800-499-3444 www.litchfieldinnct.com), a modern reproduction of an old-time country inn, makes a special statement with its eight theme rooms. Each is decorated to the nines following a campy theme such as the "Irish Room of Mami O'Rourke" (the owner's grandmother, who was referred to in the old song "East Side, West Side.") The other 30 rooms offer equally modern amenities and creature comforts in a more traditional fashion.

Toll Gate Hill ($+, Rte. 202, 1 Tollgate Rd, Litchfield, 860/567-4545), a pre-Revolutionary War tavern and inn, has been carefully restored, preserving 18th-century paneling, wide floorboards, corner cupboards, and colonial ambiance. Several vintage rooms are still over the former Captain William Bull Tavern, built in 1745 (see Food and Drink). Others are located in The Schoolhouse and Captain W. Bull House nearby. Like a classy old woman who rejects a facelift, instead reveling in the well-earned lines of character, the **Old Riverton Inn** ($, 486 East River Rd., Riverton, 860/379-8678, 800/379-8678; www.newenglandinns.com /inns/riverton) clings steadfast to its 1796 beginnings. Rooms still have original wide-plank wood floors, layered in paint; floors slope toward the hearth; and the plaster ceiling is pockmarked. Rooms are clean, comfortable, and inexpensive.

The Manor House ($+, 69 Maple Ave., Norfolk; 860/542-5690; www.manorhouse-norfolk.com) is an 1898 Victorian Tudor estate deemed "Connecticut's Most Romantic Hideaway" by The *Discerning Traveler*.

Under Mountain Inn ($$+, 482 Undermountain Rd., Rte. 41, Salisbury; 860/435-0242) provides a taste of old England in an 18th-century farmhouse. Travel and Leisure stated: "This is the country getaway we all wish we had."

The Boulders ($$+, East Shore Rd., Rte 45, New Preston, 860/868-0541, 800/552-6853; www.bouldersinn.com), an 1895 Victorian mansion, nestles at the foot of Pinnacle Mountain overlooking Lake Waramaug.

Built in 1894, the **Mayflower Inn** ($$$$, 118 Woodbury Rd., Rte. 47, Washington, 860/868-9466; www.mayflowerinn.com) sits amid 30 rolling acres. This Relais & Chateaux property is appointed with 18th- and 19th-century antiques, Tabriz rugs, and canopy beds.

The Farmington Inn ($$+, 827 Farmington Ave., Farmington, 860 /677-2821) gives each guest a unique bedtime story as a remembrance of their stay. This inn, located in the heart of the historic village, also welcomes pets.

Called "a great getaway" by Zagat, the **West Lane Inn** ($+, 22 West Lane, Ridgefield, 203/438-7323; www.westlaneinn.com) combines the gracious hospitality of a small manor house with the amenities of a modern hotel.

Food and Drink

For more options consult www.restaurants.com.

Small, intimate and cozy, **1820 Cafe** ($+, 731 Hopmeadow St., Simsbury, 860/658-7658, www.Simsbury1820House.com) nestles in the sub-level of Simsbury 1820 House. Green- and red-tartan plaid fabric adorns the walls; brick and stone foundations lay exposed, lighting is low and indirect; and hunt prints abound. The menu is small but innovative, portions adequate without being skimpy or overwhelming.

Village Pizza & Grinders ($, 233 Old Main St., Old Wethersfield, 860/563-1513) offers classic Italian grinders and pastas, Greek charbroils, ubiquitous salads, calzones, and all-American burgers. But the specialty here are the gourmet pizzas—no less than 21 different kinds. Portions are generous. It is impossible to leave here hungry.

The Bistro East Restaurant at the Litchfield Inn ($$, Rte. 202, Litchfield, 860/567-5358; www.litchfieldinnct.com) offers hearty country New England fare, prepared with the innovative twist of New American cuisine. The spacious hearth room sets a rustic scenario.

Toll Gate Hill ($$, Rte. 202, 1 Tollgate Rd, Litchfield, 860/567-4545) takes New England country cooking to a new plateau. The dimly lit paneled dining room of the former 1745 Captain William Bull Tavern oozes with a colonial charm that is surpassed only by the creativity of the award-winning cuisine.

A cozy colonial ambiance and simple but exceedingly tasty country fare distinguish the **Old Riverton Inn** ($+, Rte. 20, Riverton, 860/379-8678, 800/379-8678; www.newenglandinns.com/inns/riverton). Overlooking the west branch of the Farmington River, this 1796 inn was once a stagecoach stop between Albany and Hartford. Generous portions still attract diners for miles around.

Upscale and innovative, **West Street Grill** ($+, 43 West Street, Litchfield, 860/567-1374) justifiably has earned its reputation as the trend-setting restaurant of Litchfield (three stars awarded by the New York Times). Updated classics reflect specialties from all over the globe.

The Birches Inn serves New American cuisine and a sparkling vista of Lake Waramaug (233 West Shore Rd., New Preston, 860/868-0541, 800/552-6853; www.bouldersinn.com). It won the *Wine Spectator*'s "Award of Excellence."

Piccolo Arancio ($$+, 819 Farmington Ave., Farmington 86-/674-1224) delivers classic Italian cuisine amid the historic roots of the Farmington Freedom Trail. From antipasto to secondi, the dishes are authentically Old World.

Voted the "best new restaurant in 1997" by *Connecticut Magazine*, **Adrienne** ($$+, 218 Kent Rd., Rte. 7, New Milford, 860/354-6001) offers tantalizing American cuisine in the elegant surroundings of an 18th-century home.

The Pantry (Titus Square, Washington Depot, 860/868-0258) specializes in imported and domestic gourmet specialty foods and serves continental breakfast, lunch, picnic boxes, afternoon tea, and great take-out foods. Called "delicious and worth a detour" by Zagat's.

Rhode Island

Introduction

Measuring a scant 48 miles long and 37 miles wide, Rhode Island, the smallest state in the U.S., sports more than 400 miles of coastline on the shores of the Atlantic Ocean. Two legends portend how "little Rhody" got its name: Some believe the name is an adaptation of "roodt eylandt" or red island, a descriptive phrase used by an early Dutch navigator. More widely accepted is the story that, in 1524, Giovanni da Verrazano, a Florentine, named the large island at the mouth of Narragansett Bay Rhode Island because it reminded him of the Greek isle of Rhodes. This island is now called Aquidneck Island, more commonly known as Newport, the summer playground of the wealthy in the mid-18th century. Along with nearby Conanicut Island (Jamestown), Newport guards the entrance to Narragansett Bay.

Roger Williams, who left the Massachusetts Colony in search of religious and political freedom, founded the first permanent white settlement in Rhode Island at Providence in 1636 on land purchased from the Narragansett Indians. Providence, now the capital of Rhode Island, is 28 miles from the sea at the head of Narragansett Bay. Farming and sea trade were the early vocations in the colony.

Providence and Newport became two of the busiest ports in America, their wealth built upon a trade triangle whereby they traded rum for slaves with Africa and slaves for molasses and sugar in the West Indies. For a time the two cities rivaled New York, Boston, and Philadelphia in wealth and culture. In spite of its trade policies, Rhode Island was the first colony to ban slavery. It was also the first colony to declare independence from England—May 4, 1776—but the last of the 13 colonies to ratify the United States Constitution, demanding a Bill of Rights before they would sign. Rhode Island became a state in 1790.

Considered the birthplace of the American factory—Samuel Slater's cotton mill in 1790—Rhode Island used its trading wealth to establish a solid manufacturing base during the Industrial Revolution. The American jewelry industry began in Providence in 1824 by Nehemiah and Seril Dodge, and Jabez Gorham established a silversmith factory. Jewelry manufacture is the most important industry in Rhode Island to this day.

Famous Rhode Islanders include composer George Cohan; Nathaniel Greene, second in command to George Washington; and Oliver Perry, hero of the Battle of Lake Erie.

Regional Information
Rhode Island Tourism Division, 1 West Exchange St., Providence; 401/222-2601; www.VisitRhodeIsland.com.
The Rhode Island Welcome Center, I-95 north, between exits 2 and 3; 401/539-3031; www.visitrhodeisland.com.

Getting There
By Air: Most major carriers to T.F. Green Airport, Warwick, RI.
By Rail: Amtrak to Providence Station, 100 Gaspee St., Providence; 401/727-7388; 800-USA-RAIL; www.amtrak.com.
By Automobile: I-95 and I-195.
By Bus: Bonanza Bus lines service to and from Boston every hour, 1 Bonanza Way, Providence, (exit 25, I-95); 401/751-8800.

Historic Benefit Street and Waterfront, Providence

Roger Williams fled Massachusetts in 1636 because his Baptist beliefs were considered too extreme. He purchased land from the Narragansett Indians and established a colony that reflected his doctrine, separation of church and state. Naming the settlement for God's providence, which led him to this spot, he declared it a shelter for the persecuted of all religions. Unlike the typical layout of a New England settlement—a church surrounded by the village green—Providence was arranged along Towne Street (now Main Street), which followed the Great Salt River, its narrow plots extending up the steep hill that flanked the waterfront.

Main Street became so congested that Benefit Street was created in 1758. Each property owner was asked to give up a small parcel of land at the high end of their plot so that a new road could be built "for the common benefit of all." Running through the 18th-century residential community, Benefit Street—like Providence itself—continued to develop and prosper in the 19th century, becoming home to wealthy industrialists, sea captains, trade merchants and artisans. Benefit Street and the waterfront became seriously blighted by the middle of the 20th century with the decline of Providence's textile and jewelry industries, but the area has been

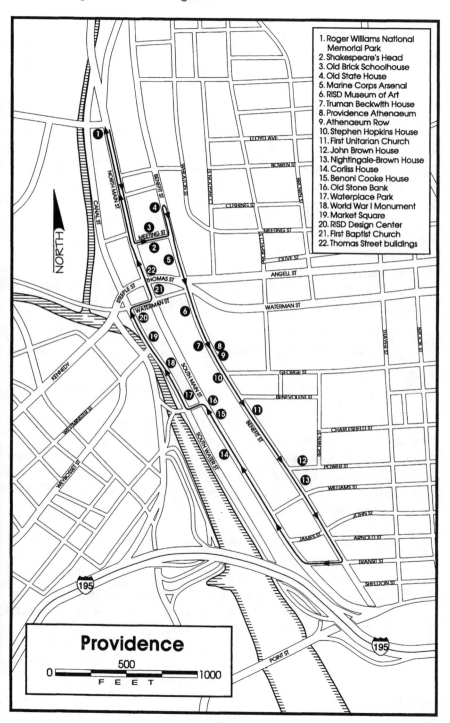

1. Roger Williams National Memorial Park
2. Shakespeare's Head
3. Old Brick Schoolhouse
4. Old State House
5. Marine Corps Arsenal
6. RISD Museum of Art
7. Truman Beckwith House
8. Providence Athenaeum
9. Athenaeum Row
10. Stephen Hopkins House
11. First Unitarian Church
12. John Brown House
13. Nightingale-Brown House
14. Corliss House
15. Benoni Cooke House
16. Old Stone Bank
17. Waterplace Park
18. World War I Monument
19. Market Square
20. RISD Design Center
21. First Baptist Church
22. Thomas Street buildings

Providence

0 — 500 — 1000

F E E T

reinvigorated, restored, and reincarnated thanks to historic preservation efforts that began in 1956. Brown University—third oldest college in New England—and Rhode Island School of Design occupy many of the buildings in this area.

Information
Providence Preservation Society, 21 Meeting St., Providence, RI 02903; 401/831-7440.
Rhode Island Historical Society, 110 Benevolent St., Providence, RI 02906-3152; 401/331-8575.
Providence/Warwick Convention & Visitors Bureau, Waterplace Park, One American Express Way, Providence; 401/751-1177; 800/233-1636; www.providencecvb.com.

Getting There
I-195 to South Main St., exit 2. Follow South Main to the Information Center at Roger Williams National Memorial Park on North Main St.

First Steps
Pick up a Banner Trail brochure, which has a good map of historic Providence, at the Information Center. This 3-mile loop will lead you down the Benefit Street Historic Mile and back along the waterfront.

Benefit Street and the Waterfront. Begin at Roger Williams National Memorial Park (1), which commemorates the spot where Roger Williams landed in 1636. A three-minute slide show recounts his life. From Roger Williams National Memorial Park, walk down North Main Street. (Waters from Narragansett Bay once came up to this point and were later filled in, much like Back Bay in Boston.)

Turn left on Meeting Street. The Providence Preservation Society is based in Shakespeare's Head, #21 (2), a three-story pre-Revolutionary structure, c.1772, once marked by a tall pole topped with a sign of Shakespeare's head. John Carter printed the colonial Providence Gazette here. (Inside, you can purchase a booklet describing all of the Benefit Street historic buildings. Refer to this booklet for details.)

Across the street at #24, the Old Brick Schoolhouse (3) was built in 1769 as a public school. It housed students from Brown University during the Revolution, when French troops took over the campus. Turn left at Benefit

Street, which is lined with converted gas lamps. The Old State House (4), #150, is a brick Georgian-style structure, c.1762. Here Rhode Island declared its independence from England on May 4, 1776, two months before the Declaration of Independence was even signed. Its architecture evolving over the centuries, the building served as a governmental seat until 1904.

Retrace your steps and continue along Benefit Street's brick sidewalks. The Marine Corps Arsenal (5) at #176 —an 1840 Victorian-Gothic building referred to as the old armory—features twin crenellated towers. Stop at #224, the Museum of Art, Rhode Island School of Design (6), which features more than 100,000 diverse works of art. Continue on to the Truman Beckwith House (7), on the corner of College Street, #42. Built for the wealthy cotton merchant and banker out of red brick with white pillars in 1827, it has housed the Brown University Handicraft Club since 1904.

New England Architecture

New England's quaint villages and city historic districts preserve a treasure trove of early American architecture. For common protection and comfort, colonial homes were built close together around a village green and near the settlement church, a meetinghouse that was usually white. Architectural designs from the mid-1600s to mid-1800s are generally classified as Colonial, Georgian, or Federal.

The earliest Colonial-style dwellings consisted of one room with a chimney and fireplace at one end topped by a half-story attic. Designed "to withstand wild animals, wild Indians, and cold winters," these dwellings were basic and unadorned. Colonists expanded their homes by adding other rooms with fireplaces as needed, leading to a recognizable rambling style often found in New England's historic villages. Many early Yankee farmhouses were attached under one roof all the way to the woodshed and the barn so that the farmer could get the kitchen stove started in the morning and feed the livestock without ever going out in the snows of the blustery New England winters.

As living in New England became easier and safer at the end of the 18th century, the Colonial style gave way to the more refined and gracious Georgian styling. Once the primary barrier against attackers, the front door became more decorative, often flanked by heavy pilasters. The Georgian style featured a central hallway; two chimneys; a nine-window, symmetrically arranged facade; clapboard exterior; and a hip or gambrel roof. Dentil work adorned cornices under the roofline.

At the end of the 1700s and well into the 1800s, a style known as Federal evolved in New England.

Reflecting the growing wealth of the times, the move was toward a handsomer, more sophisticated design. Rectangular and often three stories tall, Federalist homes had a fan light or a Palladian arched window above the doorway, side lights on each side of the door, and columns on either side of the front porch. Windows were six over six, with the third floor windows foreshortened. After 1800, brick was widely used for the exteriors of the houses.

With New England's booming economy in the mid 1800s came a variety of more intricate architectural styles. Greek Revival and Greek Revival Temple styles utilized simple, classic lines adorned with columns, pediments and oversized windows. Gothic Revival, or "gingerbread" style was typified by pointed arched windows and doors, steeply pitched roofs, and bargeboards under the eaves that were cut in intricate patterns. The Italianate style was distinguished by a low-pitched roof with overhanging eaves, symmetrical facade and "eyebrow" windows. The wooden siding of these buildings were often shallowly cut to imitate stone.

From the late 1800s to the first part of the 20th century, four more architectural styles emerged in New England. Dwellings designed in the Second Empire/Mansard style had mansard roofs, protruding dormers, and lavish ornamentation. Queen Anne featured towers and turrets, windows with stained glass, elaborate porches, and multicolored, shingled facades. The Shingle Style, asymmetrical, with low, broadly gabled or hipped roofs, stone chimneys, and large verandas, was a style popularly utilized by the wealthy for their coastal summer homes.

The Georgian Colonial Revival of the early 1900s combined features of many of the preceding periods, creating elaborate, multifaceted facades of grand proportions. For more information on New England's architectural styles, contact Sagadahoc Preservation Inc., Box 322, Bath ME 04530, 207/871-4099.

Across the street, the Providence Athenaeum (8), #251, a two-story granite Greek-Revival temple built in 1836, houses a collection of rare books and paintings. Edgar Allen Poe once frequented this membership library. Athenaeum Row (9), marked by five Ionic porticos, is the only Greek-Revival row house complex in Providence, built in 1845. The Stephen Hopkins House, 15 Hopkins Street, (10) was originally built in 1707 at the base of the hill and moved twice. Hopkins—a member of the Continental Congress, signer of the Declaration of Independence, 10-time governor of Rhode Island and chief justice of the Supreme Court—was the first chancellor of Brown University.

Designed by John Holden Greene in the Federal ecclesiastical style with Gothic accents, the First Unitarian Church (11), 301 Benefit Street, c.1816, features the largest bell ever cast at Paul Revere's foundry. The

John Brown House (12) was the first three-story mansion, c.1785, built on the hill above Benefit Street, now called College Hill. From here, John Brown, a prosperous merchant, could see his ships set sail for China in the harbor below. Now maintained as a museum by the Rhode Island Historical Society and open to the public, the house features period furnishings and reproductions of the original wallpaper. John Brown, the town's leading merchant, and his brothers Joseph, Nicholas and Moses played prominent roles in the development of Providence.

The 3.5-story clapboard Nightingale-Brown House (13) at #357 features a gable-on-hip roof and a five-bay facade. Built in 1791 by merchant Joseph Nightingale, one of five mansions on College Hill, the Federal-style building was purchased in 1814 by Nicholas Brown. The building now is part of Brown University. Walk down Benefit Street; turn right on Transit Street, then right on South Main Street, which once abutted the water-front. The shops and restaurants along this stretch are housed in restored warehouse buildings. The Corliss House (14) at #203 is the oldest surviving building, c.1750, on South Main Street. The Federal-style house at #110 was built in 1828 for Benoni Cooke (15), a sea captain and merchant.

Built in 1854 of granite in the Greek-Revival style by the Providence Institution for Savings, the Old Stone Bank (16) is topped with an ornate gold dome and features an American Renaissance interior. The building, 86 South Main Street, now houses the Brown University Haffenreffer Museum of Anthropology.

Cross South Main at Hemenway's restaurant, go through the Waterplace Park (17) to Providence River Park Walk along the river. The waterfront has enjoyed a renaissance in recent years. The park is peppered with sculptures, including one of Giovanni da Verazzano, first visitor to Rhode Island. Gondolas ferry visitors up and down the river. On some evenings, "water fires"—a light and music extravaganza—are lit in wood-filled metal brassieres that are mounted at intervals on granite foundations in the river.

Continue along the brick Canal Walk past the 108-foot granite World War I Monument (18). (On the columns of each Venetian-style bridge crossing the river, inlaid tile explanatory signs describe the historic significance of Providence's notable buildings.) At the Market Square site (19), the townspeople held the "Providence Tea Party in 1775," destroying bales of herbs in symbolic support of Boston's demonstration against the British. The Canal Walk leads past the Design Center of Rhode Island School of Design (20), whose three galleries display the works of RISD students and visiting graphic designers and photographers.

Turn right on Waterman Street, then left on North Main to # 75, the First Baptist Church (21). Designed by Joseph Brown and built in 1775, this was the third building used by the congregation founded by Roger Williams in 1638. This beautiful white building is regarded as the mother church of the American Baptist Church. The 185-foot steeple was constructed on nearby Steeple Street and then moved to its position atop the church.

Detour up Thomas Street to see a trio of buildings (22) that was the early home to Providence's costume jewelry industry. Seril Dodge built #10 and #11 in the Federal style in 1791, where his nephew developed the art of gold plating. Sydney Burleigh built the medieval-style stucco and exposed-timber building at #7 in 1885 for his Fleur-de-Lys arts and crafts studio. Backtrack down North Main Street to Roger Williams National Memorial Park.

Blithewold Mansion and Gardens

Wealthy Pennsylvania coal magnate Augustus Van Winkle purchased 33 acres overlooking Narragansett Bay and built Blithewold—early English for happy woodland—as a summer home in 1894. He died in a skeet-shooting accident in 1898, his widow remarried in 1901 and then the house burned to the ground in 1906. Not an auspicious beginning, this. The second Blithewold embodied better karma. Modeled after a 17th-century English stone manor, the house was designed to maximize vistas of Bristol Harbor. Extensive gardens were planted by Bessy Van Winkle McKee—an avid horticulturist—and then continued by her daughter and heir, Marjory Van Winkle Lyon.

Information
Blithewold Mansion & Gardens, 101 Ferry Rd., Bristol, RI 02809; 401/253-2707.

Getting There
From Providence take I-195 to exit 7. Follow Rte. 114 south for 13.5 miles through Barrington, Warren, and Bristol. Blithewold is on the right. From Newport take Rte. 114 north. Cross Mt. Hope Bridge, bear left at the fork onto Ferry Rd., Rte. 114. Blithewold is 1/8 mile on the left.

First Steps
Pick up a self-guided "Tree Tour" map when you pay your admission fee.

Blithewold Mansion and Gardens. Begin your exploration of Blithewold by touring the mansion. The Colonial-Revival interior of the 45-room, 20-bedroom, 9-bath home contains all the original furnishings of the Van Winkle/McKees, for only two generations of the family lived here. Marjorie bequeathed Blithewold to the Heritage Trust of Rhode Island after her death in 1976 at age 93, so that future generations could continue to enjoy the horticultural wonders of the gardens and arboretum. As an added bonus, you also get to see how she spent her summers, thanks to seasonal docent-guided tours of the mansion.

Wander the extensive grounds of Blithewold. Designed by John DeWolf of Brooklyn, New York, the property sports 2,000 mature trees and shrubs encompassing 200 exotic varieties. You'll find 90- to 100-foot-tall weeping beech and hemlocks; 13 giant sequoia trees; a 120-year-old weeping pagoda tree; and a ginkgo and bamboo grove planted in the 1930s. (The giant sequoia in front of Blithewold has been growing about one foot per year since it was planted in 1911.) The lawn itself is 10 square acres, flanked by clusters of trees known in horticultural circles as bosquets.

The cutting gardens are magnificent. Specialty gardens—rock, water, vegetable, rose—are tucked into woodland nooks and crannies. Volunteer gardeners help tend the plantings: the "rockettes" oversee the rock garden; "deadheaders" care for the cutting garden; "florabundas" cut back the rose garden. More than 50,000 bulbs burst into bloom between mid-April and mid-May.

A path leads from the mansion across the lawn to Bristol Harbor, along the waterfront, then through the specialty gardens and arboretum. The grounds are open year round, the mansion from April through October.

Green Animals Topiary Garden

In 1872 Thomas E. Brayton, treasurer of the Union Cotton Manufacturing Company in Fall River, Massachusetts, purchased a 7-acre estate overlooking Narragansett Bay as his summer "cottage." An earlier visit to the Azores ignited Brayton's interest in topiary—a dying art because it is so labor intensive—so he hired Joseph Carreiro, a Portuguese gardener, to design his gardens. Brayton's daughter Alice and Carreiro's son-in-law George Mendonca continued the topiary tradition upon their deaths.

Information
Green Animals, The Preservation Society of Newport County, 424 Bellevue Ave., Newport; 401/847-1000; www.NewportMansions.org.

Getting There
From Newport, take Rte 138 to Rte. 114 north. Turn left on Cory's Lane in Portsmouth. From Providence, take I-195 to exit 8, Rte. 114 south. Turn right on Cory's Lane.

First Steps
You'll receive a guide to the topiary gardens with your admission ticket. Green Animals is part of the Newport Preservation Society's multiple mansions ticket.

Green Animals Topiary Garden. The art of shaping shrubs into animal and geographic shapes by pruning and shearing began in Rome, circa 62 AD. It is commonly believed that the Romans originally introduced the art to England, where topiary became a popular craze between 1660 and 1774. Yew is traditionally planted for topiary in England, but it is very slow growing. Boxwood doesn't winter well at Rhode Island's latitude, so the Green Animals are planted with California privet—*Ligustrum ovalifolium*—a rapidly growing, hardy evergreen.

Green Animals Topiary Garden is a virtual leafy zoo. Walk through a maze of gigantic clipped animals and birds—giraffe, camel, rabbit, elephant and mama and baby teddy bears—who appear to cavort or lurk between topiary arches, spirals and geometric forms. The upper topiary lawn features a boar, bird, ostrich, reindeer, swan and even a horse with a rider.

Among the other plantings in the maze, you'll see fruit trees, a rose garden, annual beds, a gourd arbor, vegetable and berry gardens and a stand of 130-year-old beech trees. The Victorian-style Brayton House is open for tours and features the Preservation Society's antique toy collection.

Don't leave without finding "Spot the Dog" and the Rhode Island Red Rooster.

Historic Newport

Situated on the southernmost tip of Aquidneck Island, Newport has enjoyed a rich and colorful history. Founded in 1639 by the religiously persecuted from the Massachusetts Bay Colony, Newport attracted disaffected Jews from Portugal, Blacks from the West Indies and Quakers from the Netherlands in ensuing years as well, creating a multicultural community that prospered in the maritime trades by the beginning of the 18th century. During the Revolution, Newport hosted the French, who added their culture to the mix, influencing the cuisine and architecture of the area.

Newport never regained prominence as a seaport after the Revolution, instead attracting writers and artists to its picturesque shores. By the late 19th century Newport had metamorphosed into the summer playground of America's wealthiest industrialists and tycoons, who built mansions along the ocean and fostered the arts. Long regarded as the sailing capital of the world during the 1900s, Newport enters the 21st century as a vibrant resort community proudly displaying its multi-layered history and culture like a gilded crown.

Information
Newport County Convention and Visitors Bureau, 23 America's Cup Ave., Newport, RI 02840; 401/849-8048; 800/976-5122; www.GoNewport. com.
Newport Historical Society, 82 Touro St., Newport, RI 02840; 401/846-0813.

Getting There
Take I-95 to Rte. 4 south to Rte. 138 east, over the Jamestown and

Newport Bridges. Turn right on Farewell St., to America's Cup Avenue. Park at the Gateway Visitors Information Center on America's Cup Ave. You get a RIPTA all-day pass here, which enables you to ride a RIPTA bus anywhere in Newport.

First Steps
Pick up a map at the Visitors Bureau, 23 America's Cup Ave., before you begin your 4-mile historic loop of Newport. If you want a guided walking tour of Newport, contact one of these organizations: The Newport Historical Society, 401/846-0813; Newport on Foot, 401/846-5391; About Newport, 401/848-9744.

Historic Newport. Begin at the Visitors Bureau and walk up West Marlborough Street, crossing Thames Street to the picturesque St. Paul's United Methodist Church (1), c.1806, and the Jailhouse Inn (2). Now a bed-and-breakfast inn at 13 Marlborough Street, the building used to be a colonial jail in 1752. Continue on Marlborough to the White Horse Tavern (3), #26, the oldest operating tavern in America, which got its liquor license in 1673. Members of the colonial legislature gathered here for their annual meeting.

The oldest religious building in Newport, the Quaker Meetinghouse (4) at the corner of Farewell and Marlborough Streets, c.1699, was the home of Society of Friends until 1905. The Quakers made up the prominent religious group in early Newport and even in 1730 accounted for half of the religious population.

Turn right on Farewell, then right on Broadway to the Old Colony House (5). This was the seat of colonial government between 1739 and 1776, then the Rhode Island state house from 1776 to 1900, when a new state house was built in Providence. The brick structure is topped with a white cupola and a weathervane shaped like a whale. The Florence K. Murray Judicial Complex (6), the 1926 courthouse, dominates Washington Square. It faces Eisenhower Park, a small, leafy green dedicated to President Dwight D. Eisenhower, who spent time vacationing in Newport.

Head up Touro Street to #85, the Levi Gale House (7). The Greek-Revival structure, designed by Russell Warren in 1835 for lawyer Levi Gale, was moved from Washington Square to make room for the new county courthouse. Sephardic Jews from Spain and Portugal founded the Touro Synagogue (8), #72, in 1658. It is the oldest synagogue building in

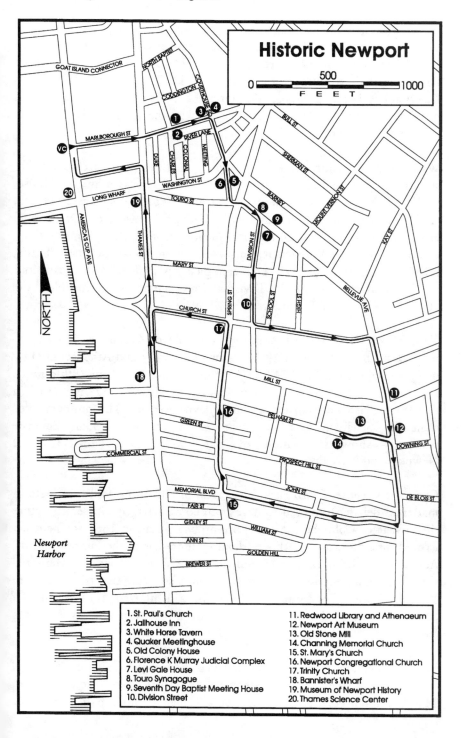

Historic Newport

1. St. Paul's Church
2. Jailhouse Inn
3. White Horse Tavern
4. Quaker Meetinghouse
5. Old Colony House
6. Florence K Murray Judicial Complex
7. Levi Gale House
8. Touro Synagogue
9. Seventh Day Baptist Meeting House
10. Division Street
11. Redwood Library and Athenaeum
12. Newport Art Museum
13. Old Stone Mill
14. Channing Memorial Church
15. St. Mary's Church
16. Newport Congregational Church
17. Trinity Church
18. Bannister's Wharf
19. Museum of Newport History
20. Thames Science Center

the United States. The synagogue was designed by Peter Harrison and built in 1763. The oldest torah in North America and a letter George Washington wrote in 1790 are displayed inside. Adjacent to the Newport Historical Society Museum and Library at 82 Touro Street, the Seventh Day Baptist Meeting House (9), circa 1729, is reportedly the oldest meetinghouse for that faith in America. Look at the William Claggett clock and the striking pulpit.

Walk down Division Street (10), which is filled with architecturally significant private homes. They include: #40, Lucas/Johnston House, c.1721, a high-style Georgian; #42, Capt. George Buckmaster House, c.1748, a blend of colonial and early Georgian; #46, Rev. Dr. Samuel Hopkins House, c.1758, an informal Georgian; #47, Peter Bours House, c.1760, a Colonial Vernacular; and #49, Union Congregational Church, c.1871,, a Gothic Revival. You can pick up a flyer that details the architectural features of the Division Street homes from the Newport Historical Society on Touro Street.

Turn left on Church Street, then right on Bellevue Avenue. Believed to be the oldest library in America, the Redwood Library and Athenaeum (11), #50, was constructed in 1747. It contains striking 18th- and 19th-century portraits. Founded in 1912, the Newport Art Museum (12) is housed in the 1864 Griswold Mansion at 76 Bellevue Avenue. The museum—designed by Richard Morris Hunt, who was the architect of many Bellevue mansions—showcases exhibits of contemporary and historical art of Newport and New England.

Cross the street to Touro Park. The origin of Old Stone Mill (13) is still a matter of debate. Rumored to have been constructed by Norsemen before the voyage of Columbus, it was more probably built in 1660 for Benedict Arnold, first governor of Rhode Island (grandfather of the famous traitor). Across from the park at 135 Pelham Street is the Channing Memorial Church (14), an imposing Gothic-style granite structure that is dedicated to William Ellory Channing (1780-1842), a Unitarian abolitionist. Of particular note in this church, c.1880, are a bronze plaque by Augustus Saint-Gaudens and beautiful stained-glass windows.

Walk up Pelham; turn right on Bellevue, then right again on Memorial Boulevard. On the corner of Memorial and Spring Street you'll find St. Mary's Church (15), c.1828, the oldest Roman Catholic parish in Rhode

Early Gravestone Symbols

One of the few remnants of colonial folk art, the headstones found on 17th and 18th century gravestones in New England's cemeteries provide a fascinating look back at the culture of the times. Carved from slate, the early stones most often featured a meaningful symbol and a brevity of words. When exploring the ancient graveyards, first you should notice that inscriptions always read, "Here lies the body of . . ." The wording reflects the religious beliefs of the colonists that the soul goes to heaven and only the body remains in the ground. What often looks like an elongated "f" in scripted epitaphs, is actually an "s" For instance, "Miff Conftance" is actually "Miss Constance." Also, the words "relict" or "consort" refer to one who has survived a spouse. It is not uncommon to find the graves of one husband and three subsequent wives, all buried in a row.

Early grave symbols had meanings and were usually carved to denote occupation of the deceased or to represent an otherworldly wish for the departed. Here—thanks to the Milford (Connecticut) Historical Society—are meanings for some of the more common symbols you may encounter on early gravestones in New England: anchors and ship—seafaring profession; bugles and horns—resurrection; crossed swords—military career; flying birds—flight of soul; hourglass—passing of time; shells—pilgrimage of life; trumpeters—heralds of the resurrection; arrows—morality; arches—victory in death; doves—purity of the soul; fruits—eternal plenty; willow—earthly sorrow; tree—life.

Island. Jacqueline Lee Bouvier and John F. Kennedy were married here on Sept. 12, 1953. Cross Memorial and walk down Spring Street. Renowned 19th-century painter John LaFarge decorated the interior of the 1835 Newport Congregational Church (16), which first gathered in 1695. The massive stone church features lovely stained glass windows. Spring Street features a panoply of historically dated colonial houses.

Trinity Church (17), in Queen Anne Square on Spring Street, was the first Anglican congregation in Newport, founded in 1698. The Episcopalian structure, which resembles Old North Church in Boston, was built in 1726 and features a three-tiered wineglass pulpit, an organ tested by Handel himself and Tiffany stained-glass windows. It is believed that Washington once worshiped here. Peek into the adjoining cemetery, then walk down Church Street.

Cross Thames Street and America's Cup Avenue and explore the Bannister's Wharf (18) shops and restaurants before heading down Thames to the Museum of Newport History (19), corner of Thames and Washington in the Brick Market. The museum combines interactive exhibits, paintings and videos to recreate the history of Newport. Continue down Thames to West Marlborough. Turn left and stop at the Thames Science Center (20), on America's Cup Avenue, to check out the exhibits before ending your tour at the Visitors Bureau.

Bellevue Avenue Mansion Walk

From the late 1800s through the turn-of-the-century, Newport glittered as the most prestigious gem on the East Coast. The summer resort getaway for America's most wealthy, who built gargantuan mansion "cottages" along the Atlantic Ocean on Bellevue Avenue, Newport witnessed an era where wealth and pedigree fostered social prominence, and wit and culture opened as many doors as money did. To frolic in this exclusive playground, one needed to flaunt a birthright of money and cachet. Intruders and imposters were ruthlessly excluded.

Information
The Preservation Society of Newport County, 424 Bellevue Ave., Newport, RI 02840; 401/847-1000; www.NewportMansions.org.

Getting There
Cross the Newport Bridge. Turn right on Farewell St., to America's Cup Ave. Turn left on Memorial Blvd., to Bellevue Ave. Turn right.

First Steps
Tickets for the Preservation Society mansion tours can be purchased at all properties or at the Museum Store at Bannister's Wharf. You may visit a single mansion or opt for a ticket for admittance at multiple properties—one, three, five, seven or ten. Guided tours are given at each of the mansions.

Bellevue Avenue Mansion Walk. Begin your 2.5-mile walk through the "Gilded Age" at the corner of Memorial Boulevard and Bellevue Avenue. Kingscote (1), a Gothic-Revival Victorian stick-style "cottage" built for George Noble Jones of Savannah in 1841, was the first such mansion in Newport. Small and intimate compared to the palaces built later along Bellevue, Kingscote was later purchased by China Trade merchant William Henry King. Five generations of his family occupied the mansion, which is furnished with King family collections.

The shingle-style Isaac Bell House (2) is undergoing restoration. Constructed in 1883, the mansion features an eclectic combination of architectural features—European, American and Japanese (open daily by appointment only). Pennsylvania coal magnate Edward J. Berwind had the stately Elms (3) built in 1901 as a copy of the chateau d'Asnieres,

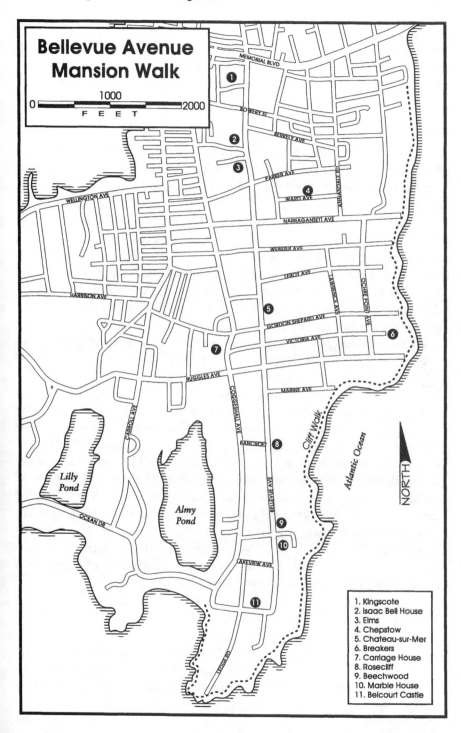

Bellevue Avenue Mansion Walk

0 — 1000 — 2000
FEET

MEMORIAL BLVD

BOWERY ST

BERKELEY AVE

PARKER AVE

WARD AVE

GREENOUGH AVE

NARRAGANSETT AVE

WEBSTER AVE

LEROY AVE

WELLINGTON AVE

HARRISON AVE

LAWRENCE AVE

OCHRE POINT AVE

GORDON SHEPARD AVE

VICTORIA AVE

RUGGLES AVE

MARINE AVE

CARROLL AVE

COGGESHALL AVE

BANCROFT

Cliff Walk

Atlantic Ocean

NORTH

Lilly Pond

Almy Pond

OCEAN DR

BELLEVUE AVE

LAKEVIEW AVE

LEDGE RD

1. Kingscote
2. Isaac Bell House
3. Elms
4. Chepstow
5. Chateau-sur-Mer
6. Breakers
7. Carriage House
8. Rosecliff
9. Beechwood
10. Marble House
11. Belcourt Castle

outside Paris. This limestone "cottage" featured the state-of-the-art technology of the times, including electricity. The grand staircase, with white marble steps and veined breccia molding, is particularly impressive, even by opulent Newport standards. And though the elms for which the mansion was named have succumbed to disease, the grounds here are exquisite.

In 1911, Mrs. Emily Morris Gallatin purchased Chepstow (4), an Italianate-style villa that was built in 1860. It showcases the collections of the New York Morris family, including landscape paintings by the Hudson River School artists (open daily during the summer). Perhaps the grandest mansion in Newport until the Vanderbilts came to town, Chateau-sur-Mer (5) was completed in 1852 as a retirement house for China Trade merchant William Shepard Wetmore. A granite fortress with unimpeded views of the ocean, the mansion is a mongrel, combining both early and late Victorian designs. Don't miss the Tree of Life, a painting on plaster that extends up three flights of the stairway's soffit to a bird-filled sky. The greenhouses, palm houses and grape arbors were removed in 1920 in an attempt at modernization, but the grounds still feature magnificent weeping and copper beech trees.

If you have time for only one mansion tour, make it the Breakers (6), which sits directly on the Atlantic at the end of Ochre Point Avenue. By far the grandest Newport Mansion, by any standard, the Breakers is the "cottage" of Cornelius Vanderbilt II. Opulent to the max, this 70-room Italian-Renaissance-style palace, completed in 1895, combines marble, gems, gilt and crystal with such turn-of-the-century luxuries as hot-and-cold running saltwater and freshwater taps. (Richard Morris Hunt designed this and many of the other Bellevue mansions.) The ocean view from the mosaic-decorated lower loggia will knock your socks off. The Breakers Stable and Carriage House (7)—one mile from the mansion, across Bellevue on Coggeshall Avenue—houses a collection of Vanderbilt memorabilia, carriages and the road coach *Venture*.

You'll detect a woman's touch at Rosecliff (8), which was built for Theresa "Tessie" Fair Oelrichs, a Nevada silver heiress. Modeled after the Grand Trianon, a baroque-style pavilion at Versailles, and completed in 1902, Rosecliff became Tessie's showcase for over-the-top summer entertaining. It is said that she "dressed like a queen, but ran her household like a tyrant." She loved to throw outrageous parties, once bringing in an entire circus. Scenes from both The Betsy (Sir Laurence Oliver, 1973) and The Great Gatsby (Robert Redford, 1976) were filmed at Rosecliff.

You'll be treated to a reenactment of Newport's Golden Age at Astor's Beechwood (9), the 1856 mansion of Caroline and William Backhouse Astor. Costumed interpreters stay in character, greet you as a personal guest and take you on a living history tour that introduces you to the servants, guests and even the Astors themselves. (This is not a Preservation Society house; separate admission is charged at the door.)

Sporting more than 500,000 cubic feet of marble—from America, Italy and Africa—Marble House (10) was the William Vanderbilts' architectural display of obscene wealth. Attempting to "one-up" their tony neighbors, the Vanderbilts demanded an authentically reproduced period building, both inside and out, and no expense was spared. Thus, the neoclassical design, inspired by the Petit Trianon at Versailles became a virtual "temple to the arts," featuring an ornate Louis XIV gold ballroom, Salon of Hercules dining room and a French-Gothic room designed to display the family collection of medieval art. Don't miss the restored Chinese teahouse where Alva Vanderbilt held a lavish Chinese costume ball in 1914.

Oliver Hazard Perry Belmont built the Louis XIII-style Belcourt Castle (11) in 1894. He later married Alva Vanderbilt after she divorced William K. Vanderbilt. Alva immediately set about renovating Belmont's "cottage" to suit her lavish tastes. The mansion is owned by the Tinney family, who opens it to the public for guided tours during much of the year (separate admission charge, call for times, 401/846-0669). Their considerable art and antique collections are on display.

Cliff Walk

Walkers have followed this 3.5-mile scenic path along the Atlantic Ocean since the 1700s. Before that, local deer and the foraging Narragansett tribe trampled this path.

Information
Cliff Walk—Friends of the Waterfront, www.gonewport.com.

Getting There

Take Memorial Boulevard to Easton's Beach. Parking is available at Easton's Beach and at meters on Memorial Boulevard. Most free, on-street parking is reserved for Newport residents.

First Steps

If you are planning to walk the entire length of the Cliff Walk, wear good walking shoes and bring plenty of water. There are no restrooms or concessions along the path. The last portion of the walk traverses rough terrain, with unfenced cliffs, 10 feet above the ocean.

Cliff Walk. Begin your stroll at Memorial Avenue at Easton's Beach and follow the paved walk along the wild-rose-flanked cliffs. You'll encounter the "40 steps" about 0.75 mile down the path, just past the mansions of Salve Regina University. The dramatic staircase leads down to a stone balcony that hangs over the sea. Built in the middle of the 19th century, the steps were used primarily by Irish domestics who worked in the mansions. They would gather here on weekends to sing and dance.

Now designated a National Recreation Trail, Cliff Walk leads past the sweeping oceanside lawns and gardens of the Breakers, Rosecliff, Astor's Beechwood, Marble House and Belcourt Castle. You'll encounter rugged terrain in the last 1.5 miles of the Cliff Walk, just after the second tunnel at Gail Rock. Hit by 12 hurricanes in the last century, this portion of the Cliff Walk is a mix of dirt path, broken pavement and rock boulders. Cliff Walk ends at the end of Bellevue Avenue at East Bailey's Beach, called Rejects' Beach by the locals, because it is at the end of the exclusive, private Bailey's Beach. One of the most extraordinary walks in New England, Cliff Walk offers unparalleled ocean vistas that should not be missed.

Block Island Greenway Trails

Block Island's original white settlers came from Boston in 1661 in search of intellectual and religious freedom from the oppressive dictates of the Massachusetts Bay Company. But the island's history began long before even navigator and fur trader Adriaen Block charted and named the island in 1614. The Narragansett Indians called the island Manisses, or Island of the Little God, because it had rich soil and its waters were teeming with fish and loaded with clams. They successfully fought off marauding Mohegans from Long Island, forcing them to their deaths off the 200-foot cliffs known today as Mohegan Bluffs. But the Narragansetts were unable to stop a white raiding party who seized the island and killed much of their tribe in 1636. The Native Americans lived peacefully with the first settlers, who arrived 25 years later, until they succumbed to the white men's diseases. The last Manisses Indian, Isaac Church, died in the late 19th century.

Block Island, isolated 12 miles off the Rhode Island coast, was plundered by French pirates in the late 1600s and early 1700s. Designated as New Shoreham by the Rhode Island General Assembly in 1672, Block Island settlers remained relatively defenseless during the American Revolution, so much so that George Washington ordered their livestock be moved to the mainland so the British couldn't capture them. By the War of 1812 the islanders declared neutrality, adopting a live-and-let-live attitude toward the British that is evident toward visitors to this day. Named one of the "last great places" in the Western Hemisphere by the Nature Conservancy, Block Island exudes a simple, casual, get-away-from-it-all ambiance that plays up its considerable gifts from Mother Nature without pretension.

Information
Block Island Chamber of Commerce, Drawer D, Water St., Block Island, RI 02807; 401/466-2982; 800/383-2474; www.blockislandinfo.com.
The Nature Conservancy, Ocean Ave., Block Island, RI 02807; 401/466-2129; www.tnc.org.

Getting There
By Ferry: Interstate Navigation Company offers service from Galilee State Pier in Point Judith, 401/783-4613 (1 hr., 10 min.), and from Providence (4 hrs.), Newport (2 hrs.), and New London, Conn. (2 hrs.) seasonally, 860/442-7891, 860/442-9553; www.blockislandferry.com.
By Air: New England Airlines offers commuter flights from Westerly State Airport, 401/596-2460; 800/243-2460; www.blockisland.com/NEA.

First Steps
The best way to traverse this small island is by moped or bicycle, not by automobile. Moped rental is limited to 150 per day, but 2000 bicycles are available for hire from kiosks at the ferry docks in Old Harbor. Pick up a Block Island Trails and Information brochure at the ferry dock information

booth or at the Nature Conservancy office. The Nature Conservancy offers guided nature walks from mid June through Columbus Day.

Block Island Greenway Trails. Begin your exploration by renting a bicycle. Sounds incongruous, but 39 miles of state and town roads—often surprisingly steep—connect the nine access sites of the walking hermitages. Twenty-five miles of walking trails allow intimate access to Block Island's undeveloped moorlike landscape, which is punctuated by tiny ponds, remote beaches and dramatic cliffs.

Birders and environmentalists will be entranced with the walking trail treks into Block Island's outback. The ecologically significant habitat hosts more than 40 species of wildlife that are classified as rare or endangered. A major stop on the north-south route of the Atlantic flyway, the teardrop-shaped island hosts more than just tourists. Thousands of raptors, shorebirds, songbirds and waterfowl hang out here from time to time, too, seasonally calling Block Island "home."

Eleven miles of trails wind through Clay Head Preserve (1), 200 acres of magnificent scenery on the northeastern corner of Block Island. Accessed off Corn Neck Road, the trail runs toward the ocean, past Clay Head Swamp and Littlefield Farm. About 1/3-mile along the trail, a fork in the path allows you the option of walking down to the beach at Ball's Cove or climbing up the clay bluffs to "The Maze." Here, intertwining inland scrub trails lead through a 120-acre preserve, three-quarters of which are protected by conservation easements granted by the Lapham family. The preserve's fruit-bearing shrubs attract yellow warblers, red-winged blackbirds, song sparrows, bank swallows, American kestrels and barn owls.

Clay Head Trail terminates at Settler's Rock (2), a large fieldstone that marks the spot where first settlers landed on the island in 1661. From Settler's Rock you can follow a beach path along Sandy Point, a tangle of beach plums and dune grass that skirts Sachem Pond and the Block Island National Wildlife Refuge, a protected reserve sheltering American oystercatchers and piping plovers. A scramble over the dunes ends at North Light (3), a granite lighthouse built in 1867, abandoned by the Coast Guard in 1972 and now restored by the village of New Shoreham and opened as a maritime museum in 1993.

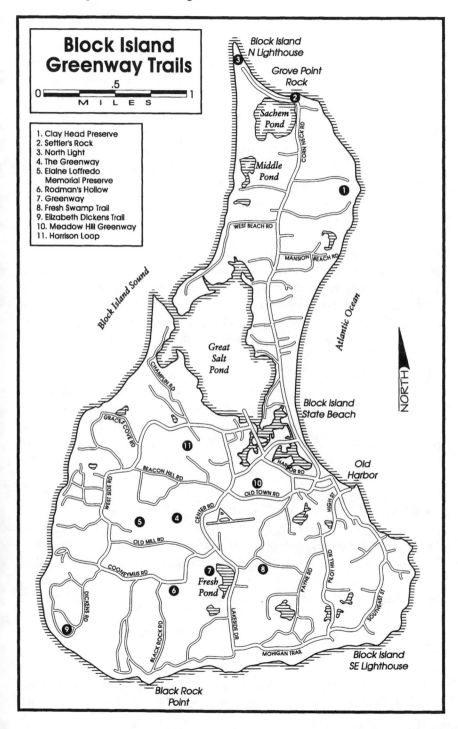

Block Island Greenway Trails

0 |———— .5 ————| 1
M I L E S

1. Clay Head Preserve
2. Settler's Rock
3. North Light
4. The Greenway
5. Elaine Loffredo
   Memorial Preserve
6. Rodman's Hollow
7. Greenway
8. Fresh Swamp Trail
9. Elizabeth Dickens Trail
10. Meadow Hill Greenway
11. Harrison Loop

Block Island
N Lighthouse

Grove Point
Rock

Sachem
Pond

Middle
Pond

CORN NECK RD

WEST BEACH RD

MANSION BEACH RD

Block Island Sound

Atlantic Ocean

NORTH

Great
Salt
Pond

CHAMPLIN RD

GRACE'S COVE RD

BEACON HILL RD

WEST SIDE RD

Block Island
State Beach

HARBOR RD

Old
Harbor

OLD TOWN RD

CENTER RD

OLD MILL RD

COONEYMUS RD

HIGH ST

PAYNE RD

PILOT HILL RD

SOUTHEAST ST

Fresh
Pond

LAKESIDE DR

DICKENS RD

BLACK ROCK RD

MOHIGAN TRAIL

Block Island
SE Lighthouse

Black Rock
Point

Landowners on the southern end of Block Island have allowed paths to be cut through their property, creating 12 miles of cleared trails called The Greenway (4). The habitat of Nathan Mott Park and Turnip Farm trails supports the endangered "bushy rockrose" and "northern blazing star." The Enchanted Forest trail leads through a recently planted forest of red pines, maples and spruce, a shady enclave that also sports a healthy smattering of poison ivy. The habitat of Elaine Loffredo Memorial Preserve (5) is a mix of scrub and meadows that attracts myriad nesting birds. Elaine Loffredo lost her life in the TWA flight 800 crash. Her husband, Robert, dedicated this highland preserve—which enjoys panoramic views of Block Island Sound, Eastern Long Island and Montauk—to her memory.

Perhaps the most dramatic trail in southern Block Island is Rodman's Hollow (6), a ravine described in geological circles as a "glacial outwash basin." The hollow is actually below sea level, but its porous sandy soil neither can hold rainwater to form a pond nor support the tilled crops of a farm. Covered with bayberry, shadbush and arrowwood, the scrubland ecosystem hosts the endangered northern harrier and the Block Island meadow vole. A trail climbs to the top of Rodman's Hollow knoll for a panoramic vista over the Atlantic. The more laborious route follows a sinuous path that leads to the bottom of the hollow and connects with Smilin' Thru Greenway (7), named for the 1920s show tune written by Block Islander Arthur Penn. This trail, whose terrain is often steep and rough, connects Rodman's Hollow Trail and Fresh Swamp Trail (8), which leads through the dense scrub and open field habitats of nesting birds.

Southwest of Rodman's Hollow, the Elizabeth Dickens Trail (9) winds along the edge of the bluffs and through the open fields of the 218-acre Lewis-Dickens Sanctuary, once a farm owned by Elizabeth Dickens. Called "the bird lady," Dickens taught bird study and natural history in Block Island schools from 1916 through 1963 and is credited with jump-starting the conservation movement on the island.

Meadow Hill Greenway (10), created by Captain John R. Lewis, founder of the Block Island Conservancy, loops along the edge of a cattail marsh. Beginning and ending on Old Town Road, it winds through huge expanses of shadbush, which bloom spectacularly in mid May. The newest walking trail in the Greenway system is the Harrison Loop (11), named for the benefactors who gifted the land to the Conservancy. The loop connects West Side Road, at Great Salt Pond and New Harbor, with Beacon Hill Road and Black Rock in the northern interior. The trail leads past Island Cemetery, the scenic resting-place of early islanders, whose gravestones date back to the late 1600s.

Village of Wickford

A quintessential sleepy, picturesque Rhode Island seaside village, Wickford sleeps in a time warp. Founded by Lodowick Updike in 1707 and called Updike's Newtowne by locals in spite of its official naming, Wickford played a colorful role in the Revolutionary War: Villagers kept the British ships away by firing week-old lobster bait at them from a cannon. The maritime economy thrived for a time and the town prospered, but by the end of the 19th century, the village relied on lobstering and shellfishing and a growing tourist trade.

Information
North Kingston Chamber of Commerce, 401/295-5566, www.wickford-village.com.

Getting There
From the north, take I-95 to Rte. 4, exit 9, then go south on Rte. 102, exit 5A. Take Rte 102 through intersection with Rte. 1, then turn left onto Brown Street to the village. From the south, take I-95 to Rte. 102, exit 5. Take Rte. 102 south for 10 miles. Turn left on Brown Street.

First Steps
Park in the harbor parking lot off Brown Street.

Village of Wickford. This compact little town lives its history. Its shops, cafes, offices and inns all occupy well-preserved 18th-century historic residences, and the shellfishing fleet still sets off from the docks in Wickford Cove. Stroll down Brown and Main Streets and poke into the shops along the harbor. Cut down Church Lane, which is lined with colonial residences, for a look at the Old Narragansett Church, c.1707. One of the four original colonial parishes in Rhode Island, Old Narragansett features box pews, a wineglass pulpit, a slave gallery and a 1680 pipe organ. One Sunday each August—deemed Queen Anne

Sunday—a colonial service is reenacted, complete with communion using the Queen Anne silver. You'll be able to explore this quaint village in about an hour, but don't leave without trying some Rhode Island clam cakes.

Ninigret Conservation Area, Quonochontaug

If "Life is a Beach," it doesn't get any better than this.

Information
South County Tourism Council, 4808 Tower Hill Rd., Wakefield, RI 02879; 401/789-4422; 800/548-4662; www.southcountyri.com.

Getting There
Take I-95 to exit 92, Rte. 2, to Rte. 78, to Rte. 1 north. Turn right on East Beach Road.

First Steps
Park at the Blue Shutters Beach.

Ninigret Conservation Area. Kick off your shoes, roll up your pant legs, don your shades and start beachcombing on Rhode Island's finest. Leave the crowded public beach behind and walk east, along the state-owned East Beach. You can walk for six uninterrupted miles with the crashing Atlantic on your right hand, Rosa rugosa and dune grass on your left. No dwellings and only a smattering of four-wheel-drive vehicles are allowed on the sand road behind the dunes here, so you'll be at one with Mother Nature. You can walk as far as Charlestown Breachway, the inlet to Ninigret Pond, if you are fit enough for this 12-mile roundtrip junket.

Napatree Point, Watch Hill

Separating Little Narragansett Bay from the Atlantic Ocean is an ecologically fragile spit of sand beach and rolling dunes known as Napatree Point.

Information
Greater Westerly-Pawcatuck Chamber of Commerce, Chamber Way, Westerly, RI 02891; 401/596-7761; 800/732-7636.

Getting There
Take I-95 north to exit 92, Rte. 2, to Rte. 78. Cross Rte.1 to Airport Rd. At rotary take Winnapaug Rd., then turn right on Watch Hill Rd.

First Steps
You can access the 1-mile walk from the beach parking lot in Watch Hill.

Napatree Point. At the end of the beach parking lot, walk around the end of the snow fence to the beach path. This is a conservation area so stay on the path, do not step on the dune grass and avoid any fenced off bird nesting sanctuary areas. Surrounded by water, you'll be treated to spectacular ocean vistas and a good view of the Watch Hill Lighthouse. At the end of the point lie the ruins of Fort Mansfield, built in 1898 to protect the coast during the Spanish-American War. Look for the gun turret.

When you return from your walk to the Point, stop at Watch Hill's Flying Horse Carousel on Bay Street. The horses are suspended from a center frame, not attached to the floor, and they swing out in a flying motion as the carousel turns. Brought to Watch Hill in 1883, the carousel's horses are hand-carved from a single piece of wood and sport real manes and tails, agate eyes and leather saddles. Sadly, only children are allowed to ride the Flying Horse Carousel today.

Rainy Day Options

Built in 1748 for wealthy sea merchant Jonathon Nichols, **Hunter House** is one of the Newport mansions under the protection of the Preservation Society of Newport County. A colonial era dwelling, Hunter House displays many pieces of Townsend and Goddard furniture, handmade by the two 18th-century Newport craftsmen. The interior of the house has been faithfully restored, including the pine paneling in the southeast parlor, whose grain is painted to resemble walnut. Docents point out the distinctive design features of the Newport-made furniture. *(Take America's*

Cup Ave., to Long Wharf, then turn right on Washington St. Contact: Hunter House, 54 Washington St., Newport, 401/847-1000.)

The 1880 Newport Casino—a social and sporting club, not a gambling hall, used by the glitterati of Newport Society—once housed a riding ring, lawn tennis courts, a ballroom and a horseshoe piazza. The club hosted the U.S. National Lawn Tennis Championships—presently the U.S. Open—from 1891 to 1914. Now the **International Tennis Hall of Fame**, the complex is open to the public from May to October. Professional tournaments are still played here each summer. The museum, housed in the original casino building, traces the history of tennis, including profiles of the sport's famous champions. *(Take America's Cup Ave. to Memorial Blvd., then turn right on Bellevue Ave. Contact: International Tennis Hall of Fame & Museum, 194 Bellevue Ave., Newport, 401/843-3990.)*

Lodging

The short distance between cities in Rhode Island allows you to choose one central base and explore attractions as day trips. For more lodging options, consult the New England-wide accommodations websites and reservation services listed in How to Use This Book or check out www.VisitRhodeIsland.com.

Hugging the Cliff Walk and a scintillating history, **Cliffside Inn** ($$$+, 2 Seaview Ave., Newport, 401/847-1881; 800/845-1811; www.distinctive inns.com), c.1876, creates a romantic, elegant ambiance "to the manor born." Cotton baron Andrew Turner bought the mansion as a summer-house in 1907, where he secluded his artist daughter, Beatrice, from Newport society. Until her death in 1948, Beatrice painted 3000 works here, 1000 of which were self-portraits, many nude. Cliffside Inn showcases 125 of the paintings.

Stay in the keeper's house of **Rose Island Lighthouse** ($+, Newport, 401/847-4242; www.RoseIslandLighthouse.org), a working lighthouse on Rose Island in Newport Harbor. Operated by the Rose Island Lighthouse Foundation, the keeper's house is a Victorian living history museum by day, a two-bedroom eco-lodge by night. You'll be on your own on Rose Island, so pack in your meals and pack out your trash. Nevertheless, this is high romance and adventure rolled into one.

The Admirals Inns ($-$$$, 401/848-8000; 800/343-2863; www.admiralsinns.com) encompass three historic homes near Newport's waterfront, all pristinely decorated in period antiques and reproductions. Choose among: Admiral Farragut (31 Clarke St.), c.1702, outfitted with Shaker-style four-poster beds and English antiques; Admiral Benbow (93 Pelham St.), built in 1855 and showcasing an antique barometer collection; and Admiral Fitzroy (8 Fair St.), c.1854, featuring hand-painted wall accents.

"The" place to stay on Block Island consistently remains **The 1661 Inn and Hotel Manisses** ($$$-$$$$, One Spring St., Block Island, 401/466-2421; 800/626-4773; www.blockisland.com/biresorts). The hotel, A Victorian landmark built in 1872, sits across Spring Street from 1661 Inn and Nicholas Ball Cottage, which perch high on the bluff overlooking the Atlantic. Dodge Cottage and Sheffield House are on High Street. The top-drawer amenities at all the facilities include candy, ice and a decanter of brandy in your room; a complimentary island tour; and wine and gourmet nibbles in the late afternoon.

Known as the Grande Dame of Providence, the **Providence Biltmore Hotel** ($-$$$, 11 Dorrance St., 401/421-0700, 800/294-7709; www.grandheritage.com), built in 1922, has been restored to its previous grandeur. From small economy rooms near the elevator to spacious suites overlooking Waterplace Park and the Providence skyline, the Biltmore offers accommodations for a variety of pocketbooks.

State House Inn ($, 43 Jewett St., Providence, 401/351-6111, www.providence-inn.com), circa 1889, offers 10 guestrooms featuring Shaker art and colonial furnishings, canopy beds and fireplaces. A short walk from downtown Providence, State House Inn offers comfort and value.

Built in 1863 as a rectory, **The Old Court** ($-$$, 144 Benefit St., Providence, 401/751-2002) sits in the shadow of the Rhode Island Courthouse. The Italianate-style bed-and-breakfast features 12-foot ceilings, ornate Italian mantelpieces and even antique Victorian beds, modified for 21st-century comfort.

Situated in the middle of historic Newport, **The Inns of Newport** (800/524-1386; www.InnsofNewport.com) re-create the pampering enjoyed in the Gilded Age: double whirlpool tubs, working fireplaces, featherbeds, tapestries and antiques. Choose among these three intimate historic inns: The 1705 Clarkeston ($$$, 28 Clarke St., 401/849-7397), Cleveland House ($$$, 27 Clarke St., 401/848-5300) or The Wynstone ($$$$, 232 Spring St., 401/849-7397).

A 1760 colonial mansion overlooking the waterfront, **The Francis Malbone House** ($$$, 392 Thames St., Newport, 401/846-0392; 800/846-0392; www.malbone.com) harbors a colorful past. It seems that Colonel Francis Malbone, the shipping merchant who originally owned the home, smuggled goods from his mooring dock to his cellars via a subterranean passageway. Today the 18 guestrooms offer elegant, gracious lodging.

Belonging to the Rose family for five generations, **The Rose Farm Inn** ($$, Roslyn Rd., Block Island, 401/466-2034) was built by James Rose in 1897 as a farm. Turned into an inn in 1980 by Robert Rose, Rose Farm exudes turn-of-the-19th-century casual country elegance. Sit a spell on the beach-stone porch and look out over the ocean.

Food and Drink

Seafood reigns in Rhode Island. For more dining options in Providence, visit the Italian neighborhood, Federal Hill, where it is almost impossible to find a bad meal. Consult www.VisitRhodeIsland.com for even more ideas.

One of the 19 restaurants in the great seafood chain, **Legal Sea Foods** ($$, 2099 Post Rd., Warwick, 401/732-3663) is located near T.F. Green Airport. Started as the Legal Seafood Market in Cambridge, Massachusetts, Legal Sea prides itself on the freshest seafood at a reasonable price.

Offering a trip down memory lane, **Brick Alley Pub and Restaurant** ($+, 140 Thames St., Newport, 401/849-6334; www.brickalley.com) showcases antique memorabilia from past decades, including a Texaco Flying Service truck cab and engine that flanks the salad bar. A toy train toots around the ceiling and '60s music pulsates from the jukebox. The eclectic menu is as sparkling as the dÈcor.

Situated in the 1880 Newport Casino, adjoining the International Tennis Hall of Fame, **La Forge Casino Restaurant** ($$-$$$. 186 Bellevue Ave., Newport, 401/847-0418) re-creates the sporty ambiance of the Gilded

Age. Dine in cozy Crowley's Casino Pub or in the glassed-in Victorian porch, awash in garden hues and hunter green, which abuts the grass tennis courts and viewing stands of the Horseshoe Piazza.

An institution in Newport sporting a history with the America's Cup races, **The Mooring Restaurant** ($$, Sayer's Wharf, Newport, 401/846-2260) overlooks the harbor and a marina full of visiting yachts. Known for its seafood, this is the perfect place for a long, leisurely, scenic lunch.

Choose between the elegant Victorian dining room at Hotel Manisses ($$$$, One Spring St., Block Island, 401/466-2421; 800/626-4773; www.blockisland.com/biresorts) or the more casual, less pricey, bistro-ish Gatsby Room. Either way, the menu showcases fresh local seafood, innovatively prepared. Herbs and veggies come from the hotel farm garden.

Directly across from the ferry landing at Old Harbor, **Harborside Inn** ($$, Water St., Block Island, 401/466-5074), c.1876, usually wins the annual chowder cook-off as well as rave reviews for stellar American cuisine. The patio dining is great for people watching.

To eat your fill of Maine lobster, fried clams and clear-broth Rhode Island clam chowder, go to **Ballard's** ($-$$, Old Harbor, 401/466-2231), a lobster house on the docks. Decor at this Block Island landmark is super-casual and the views over the Atlantic, unparalleled.

"Life is uncertain, order dessert first." So says the menu at XO ($$-$$$, 125 North Main St., Providence, 401/273-9090, www.xocafe.com), where dessert is listed first on the menu. The cuisine is as wonderfully eclectic as the decor—names are written with magic marker on the walls, which are hung with a panoply of art works from Rhode Island School of Design. XO exudes creativity. It's exquisite, funky and fun.

Garnering "Best of...." Awards, **New Rivers** ($$, 7 Steeple St., Providence, 401/751-0350) serves American cuisine with an international flair in a bistro atmosphere.

Deemed Newport's priciest and most historic restaurant, the **White Horse Tavern** ($$$$, 140 Thames St., Newport, 401/849-3600) combines a back-to-the-colonies atmosphere with topnotch upmarket American cuisine. A working eatery since 1687, the White Horse Tavern's plank floors, low-beam ceiling and massive hearths shimmer in the candlelight.

Massachusetts

Introduction

From the time the Pilgrims dropped Mayflower's anchor at the tip of Cape Cod, through the fight for independence, Massachusetts has played a leading role in our nation's history. After six weeks of Cape Cod's harsh winter climate, the Mayflower group of "saints" and "strangers" moved on to Plymouth and established the first New England colony. In 1628, England granted a group of Puritans, led by John Winthrop, the right to set up a fishing and fur-trading enterprise on the north shore of Massachusetts, which received a charter as the Massachusetts Bay Colony in 1630. The colony grew to 10,000 by 1634 and to 80,000 by 1700.

During the 18th century, Massachusetts established a booming sea trade economy, of which salted codfish was a mainstay. Along with colonies in Rhode Island and Connecticut, Massachusetts also shipped rum to Africa in exchange for slaves, which were traded in the West Indies for sugar and molasses to make the rum, as well as sizable amounts of money. Boston was the largest town in the British colonies by 1740 and had the busiest harbor in North America. Salem and Marblehead shipped codfish to the West Indies and the Mediterranean, and Gloucester carried fish to South America. Nantucket was the whaling center of the world.

Massachusetts was at ground zero during the growing resentment toward the English in the 1700s and remained the hot bed of the Revolutionary War, from the first shots at Lexington and Concord to the Battle of Bunker Hill and beyond. In the early months of the war, Cambridge became the headquarters of the colonial army.

Named by the Puritan settlers after Massasoit, the leader of the Wampanoag tribe, Massachusetts became the sixth state of the Union in 1788. The Bay State has it all—mountains, seashore, and a sparkling capital city, Boston, oft called with reverence the "hub of the Yankee universe," because it is also New England's cultural capital. The Berkshire Mountains, the lower extension of Vermont's Green Mountains, line the western part of the state. Cape Cod, a 60-mile-long spit of sand, juts out from the south coast like a beckoning arm, together with its two islands, Nantucket and Martha's Vineyard, a prime summer vacation spot. Still populated with an active fishing fleet as well as tourists, the tiny seacoast villages of Cape Ann poke into the sea on the northern coast.

All in all, Massachusetts must be considered the heart of New England—geographically, historically, and physically—for the pulse of our nation's birthplace still resonates from every corner of the state.

Greater Boston

Boston, the cradle of democracy, is widely regarded as America's walking city. Founded by the Puritans in 1630, thoughtfully laid out by our forebears around a massive public Common, and well-connected underground by subsequent city planners, Boston sizzles with a combination of well-preserved historic grandeur and 21st-century energy. Boston proudly showcases our "roots" with a number of well-documented walks through history. And its neighborhoods—from the Italian North End to Brahmin Back Bay to cobbled Beacon Hill—bring these tales to life.

Regional Information
Massachusetts Office of Travel and Tourism, 100 Cambridge St., 13th Floor, Boston, MA 02202; 617/727-3201; 800/447-MASS; www.mass-vacation.com.
Greater Boston Convention & Visitors Bureau, 2 Copley Place, Suite 105, Boston, MA 02116; 617/536-4100; 888/733-2678; www.bostonusa.com.

Getting There
By Air: All major carriers offer service to Boston's Logan International Airport.
By Rail: Amtrak offers service to Boston's South Station or commuter lines to North, South, or Back Bay Stations.
By Automobile: I-95 or Mass. Turnpike (I-90) to I-93. Driving into Boston is not advised until the construction congestion created by the Big Dig is finished (no completion date has been projected). But if you do choose to drive, use the Boston Common Underground Parking Garage on Charles St. or the garage at the Charlestown Navy Yard near the USS Constitution. Parking in Boston is very pricey, averaging as much as $20 per day.
By "T": The MBTA (617/222-3200; www.mbta.com) offers one, three, or seven consecutive-day passes for use of the underground "T."

Guided Walking Tours
Maritime Trail. Costumed guides take visitors along Long Wharf and lower State Street, narrating Boston's interesting maritime history. Contact

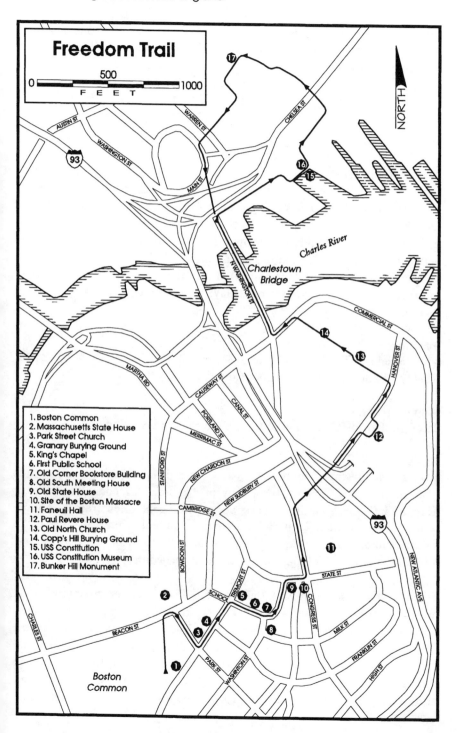

Freedom Trail

0   500   1000
FEET

NORTH

1. Boston Common
2. Massachusetts State House
3. Park Street Church
4. Granary Burying Ground
5. King's Chapel
6. First Public School
7. Old Corner Bookstore Building
8. Old South Meeting House
9. Old State House
10. Site of the Boston Massacre
11. Faneuil Hall
12. Paul Revere House
13. Old North Church
14. Copp's Hill Burying Ground
15. USS Constitution
16. USS Constitution Museum
17. Bunker Hill Monument

Charles River

Charlestown Bridge

Boston Common

the Boston History Collaborative, 617/574-5963; www.BostonbySea.org.
Boston By Foot. Guided walks tour the Freedom Trail, Back Bay, Waterfront, Beacon Hill or the North End, 617/367-2345.
Michele Topor's North End Market Tour. The sights, sounds and, most especially, the tastes of the Italian North End come alive during this 3-hour tour of the "neighborhood," 617/523-6032.

Freedom Trail

Perhaps the most famous walking trail in America, Boston's Freedom Trail tells the tale, step by step, of the birth of our country. A 2.5-mile red brick line leads you through downtown Boston, linking 16 historic sites between the Boston Common and Bunker Hill Monument. (There is a nominal charge at only three sites.) Along the way, costumed historical interpreters, the Freedom Trail Players, relate colorful stories from Boston's history.

Information
The Freedom Trail Foundation, 3 School St., Boston, MA 02108; 617/227-8800; www.thefreedomtrail.org.

Getting There
Take the Red or Green line of the "T" to the Park St. stop.

First Steps
Stop at the Boston Common Visitor Center on Tremont St., 100 yards from the Park St. "T" exit, for a copy of "Boston's Freedom Trail Visitor Map and Guide." National Park Service Rangers offer free 90-minute tours of the Freedom Trail daily, departing at regular intervals during the spring, summer, and autumn. Tours begin from the Park Service Center, 15 State St. Call 617/242-5642 for the daily schedule.

Freedom Trail. You can walk the Freedom Trail in either direction. These are the historic trail sites and other interesting places you will encounter, beginning at the Boston Common. Like most New England commons, the Boston Common (1), America's oldest public park, was a grazing pasture for colonial livestock. Later the militia trained here, and, for a short time during their occupation of Boston, the British used the Common as an army camp. Harboring a feisty history throughout the ensuing centuries, the Common has witnessed the words of Martin Luther King, Jr., Pope John Paul II and Vietnam War protesters, among others.

Situated on John Hancock's former cow pasture, the 1798 Massachusetts State House (2), the oldest building on Beacon Hill, looks majestically over Boston Common. Designed by Charles Bulfinch, the state capitol is topped with a 23-carat, gilded gold dome. (The dome was painted black during World War II to camouflage it from the enemy.) You can take a self-guided tour the State House or join one of the free guided tours that are offered daily at regular intervals. *(Contact: 617/727-3676; www.state.ma/sec/trs).*

For a time storing the gunpowder for the War of 1812 in a basement crypt, the beautiful Park Street Church (3), built in 1809, features a 217-foot Christopher Wren-style steeple. This church hosted abolitionist William Lloyd Garrison when he gave his first speech against slavery in 1829. Tours are given seasonally *(Contact: 617/523-3383; www.parkstreet.org.)*

Named for a granary that once stood across the street, the Granary Burying Ground (4) entombs such Patriot notables as Samuel Adams, Paul Revere, John Hancock, and Peter Faneuil. The two wives of Isaac Goose are buried here: Mary died in childbirth, and it is believed that Elizabeth—Mother Goose of nursery rhyme fame—took care of Mary's 10 children and had eight of her own. A marker relates that although she didn't live in a shoe, she might have lived on a shoestring.

The original King's Chapel (5) was a small, wooden structure built on the town burying ground in 1688 as America's first Anglican Church. In 1754, the granite Georgian-style Unitarian Church replaced the older chapel. Named after English King James II, the church is open for viewing *(Contact: 617/227-2155).* Next to the chapel on Tremont Street, the King's Chapel Burying Ground holds the remains of some of Boston's finest—former governor John Winthrop, Paul Revere sidekick William Dawes, Jr., and Mayflower passenger Mary Chilton.

The statue of Benjamin Franklin at the Site of the First Public School (6) is the first portrait statue erected in the United States. The first school, Boston Latin School, 1635, still operates today in the Fenway area of Boston.

Massachusetts literati such as Dickens, Emerson, Longfellow, and Thoreau hung out at the Old Corner Bookstore Building (7) when it was the Ticknor and Fields Publishing House in the mid 1800s. Built in 1718, the gambrel-roofed building now houses the Boston Globe Store, which is open daily *(Contact: 617/367-4004; www.historicboston.org)*. Across the street is the Boston Irish Memorial statue, which pays tribute to the immigrants who came to Boston to rebuild their lives after the Irish potato famine.

The Old South Meeting House (8)—built in 1729 as a meeting place for Puritan worshippers—evolved into a boiling pot of colonial discontent over British rule. Here on December 16, 1773, 5,000 angry citizens protested the British-imposed tea tax and gave birth to the revolutionary Boston Tea Party. Refurbished in 1997, Old South now offers an audio program that relives that historic day; a small admission fee is charged *(Contact: 617/482-6439)*.

Built in 1713 to house the government offices of the Massachusetts Bay Colony, the Old State House (9) witnessed the evolution of our country from an English colony to an independent nation. On July 18, 1776, the Declaration of Independence was shouted from the balcony of this building. Now a Boston history museum, the Old State House charges a nominal admission fee *(Contact: 617/720-3290; www.bostonhistory.org)*. Next to the Old State House is the site of the Boston Massacre (10), March 5, 1770. A ring of cobblestones marks the site of the historic event.

Faneuil Hall (11) is called the "Cradle of Liberty," for it was here that the Patriots gathered in the years leading up to the Revolution, discussing their dissatisfaction with British rule. Built by Peter Faneuil in 1742 and presented as a gift to Boston, the building housed a market on the first floor and a second-floor meeting hall, where National Park Rangers now present daily historical talks *(Contact: www.nps.gov/bost)*. Quincy Market, nearby, is now a riotous potpourri of eateries and shops.

As you walk the distance from Faneuil Hall to the North End, stop at the New England Holocaust Memorial. Six glass towers—etched with six million prisoner numbers in memory of the Jews who died in the Holocaust—are set over dark, smoldering chambers named for the Nazi concentration camps. Dramatic stories of victims and heroes are engraved along the black granite path.

Located in the North End—the Italian district packed with great restaurants and specialty food shops—the Paul Revere House (12) was home to the famed midnight rider from 1770 to 1800. A talented silversmith and engraver, Revere was a dedicated Son of Liberty at the time of the Revolution. Docents explain the history of the 1680 house, the era of Paul Revere and the significance of family furniture, silver and artifacts. A small admission fee is charged *(Contact: 617/523-2338; www.paulreverehouse.org)*.

Between Paul Revere House and Old North Church, the Freedom Trail passes St. Stephen's Church, where Rose Kennedy was baptized in 1890 and eulogized at her funeral in 1995. The trail then takes you through Paul Revere Mall, where a huge statue of Revere on horseback perches atop a large block of granite.

A rare confluence of art, history, and faith, the Old North Church (13), a Georgian-style structure inspired by the work of Christopher Wren, is singularly beautiful. From Old North's steeple in 1776, the church sexton, Robert Newman, displayed two lanterns to warn Paul Revere of the British activity on the eve of the Revolution. The church is still an active Episcopal Church, open for visitation and services *(Contact: 617/523-6676)*. The British placed cannons in nearby Copp's Hill Burying Ground (14), because the cemetery's hilltop location afforded them a good vantage point during the Battle of Bunker Hill.

Across the Charles River in Charlestown Navy Yard, the USS Constitution (15), launched in 1797, enjoys the distinction of being the world's oldest commissioned warship still afloat. Called "Old Ironsides" because she repelled cannonballs like pelted jellybeans and was undefeated in battle, the ship hosts guided tours daily. The nearby USS Constitution Museum features naval photographs, artifacts, memorabilia and exhibits *(Contact: 617/426-1812; www.ussconstitutionmuseum.org)*.

The Bunker Hill Monument (17), a 221-foot granite obelisk constructed 1843, commemorates the site of the first major battle of the American Revolution. Although the British captured the hill on June 17, 1775, half their forces were killed in the bloody battle. It is here that Colonel William Prescott supposedly gave colonists the legendary order, "Don't shoot until you see the white's of their eyes." You can climb the 294 steps to the top of the monument for a bird's eye view of Boston and the Freedom Trail *(Contact: 617/242-5641; www.nps.gov/bost)*.

Back Bay

No visit to Boston would be complete without a walk through Back Bay, formerly a swampy area along the Charles River that was filled in with dirt taken from Beacon Hill in the mid 1800s. By the 1870s, the area had been developed into a tony residential neighborhood filled with magnificent brownstone houses owned by wealthy Boston Brahmins.

Information
Greater Boston Convention & Visitors Bureau, 2 Copley Pl., Suite 105, Boston, MA 02116; 617/536-4100; 888/733-2678; www.bostonusa.com.

Getting There
Take the Red or Green line of the "T" to the Park St. stop.

First Steps
Stop at the Boston Common Visitor Center on Tremont St., 100 yards from the Park St. "T" stop, to pick up a "Walking Map" of Boston. This 1.5-mile walk combines the best of contemporary Boston with a few historical stops along the way.

Back Bay. Begin your exploration of Back Bay at the Public Garden (1), the small, well-manicured park across Charles Street from Boston Common. An odiferous tidal flat until the 19th-century landfill operation, the Public Garden is the first public botanical garden in the United States, featuring 350 varieties of trees. A lagoon dominates the center of the 24-acre park, where the famed Swan Boats have ferried visitors around The Lagoon, seasonally, since 1877. Don't miss the eight bronze ducklings that waddle behind a mother duck, statues commemorating Robert McCloskey's children's book, *Make Way for Ducklings*, which was set in the Public Garden.

Cross Arlington Street to the Commonwealth Avenue Mall (2), the grassy area between lanes of the wide boulevard. Stroll down the mall and check out the opulent late-19th-century brownstones. Turn left on Gloucester Street and left again on Newbury Street (3), whose brownstones now

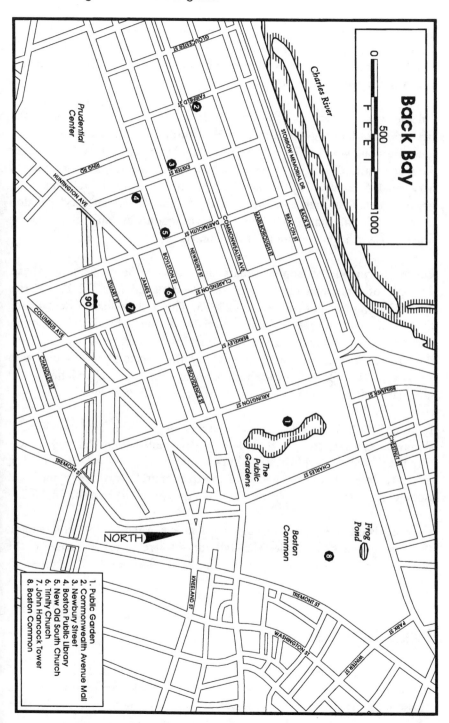

Back Bay

1. Public Garden
2. Commonwealth Avenue Mall
3. Newbury Street
4. Boston Public Library
5. New Old South Church
6. Trinity Church
7. John Hancock Tower
8. Boston Common

house upscale boutiques, posh restaurants, and interesting specialty shops. Follow Newbury for a bit of window-shopping, noshing, and people watching, then turn right on Dartmouth Street to explore Copley Square, which is flanked by historic buildings.

On the west, the imposing Boston Public Library (4), circa 1894, is the first public lending library in the United States. In addition to multitudinous volumes of rare books, the library showcases John Singer Sargent's vast "Triumph of Religion" mural on the third floor. Painted between 1890 and 1919, the mural depicts the evolution of religion, from pagan worship through medieval imagery to the "contemporary" religion of personal, internalized beliefs. Murals, sculptures, and paintings by other artists grace other floors of the library.

On the north side of Copley Square sits New Old South Church (5), an example of Ruskinian Gothic architecture designed in 1872 by Charles Amos Cummings and constructed in 1875. This architectural style calls for the use of multi-colored building materials, of which the church's roofing slates are a prime example. Over the years, fashion dictated painting over the structure's intricate stenciling, covering the stained-glass windows with Tiffany glass of deep purple, and removal of the gas chandeliers. The sanctuary was re-Ruskinized in 1984, restoring its former luster.

Built in 1877, Trinity Church (6), across the Square from the library, shimmers as a reflection in the 60-story glass-walled John Hancock Tower (7), the observatory of which offers a panoramic view of Boston. The intricate interior of the neo-Romanesque church features a piece of stonework from St. Botolph's, a 13th-century church in Boston, England.

Take Boylston Street back through the Public Garden to Boston Common (8), where you can wander through the 44-acre grassy expanse to the beginning of the Freedom Trail and the Black Heritage Trail, detailed in this section.

Black Heritage Trail

The first Africans in Boston were brought in as slaves in 1638. By 1705 the number of slaves grew to 400, but a free-Black community was also blossoming. By the end of the Revolutionary War, more free Blacks than slaves lived in Massachusetts, and by 1790, Massachusetts recorded no slaves at all. The Boston African American National Historic Site produces a fine, self-guided, 1.6-mile walking tour that explores the 19th-century pre-Civil War history of Boston's free African-American community.

Information
Boston African American NHS, 14 Beacon St., Suite 503, Boston, MA; 617/742-5415.

Getting There
From Park St. "T" Station, cross Boston Common toward the State House.

First Steps
Pick up the detail-packed walk brochure from the African Meeting House, 8 Court St., or from the Visitor Center kiosk in Boston Common. The National Park Service gives free 2-hour guided tours of the Black Heritage Trail (M-F—10am, noon, and 2pm during spring, summer, and autumn, and by reservation in the winter months). Tours depart from the Shaw Memorial across from the State House on Beacon St. and are limited to 30 people per tour.

Black Heritage Trail. The walk begins across from the gold-domed State House on Beacon Street at the August Saint-Gaudens bas-relief memorial sculpture of Robert Gould Shaw and the 54th Regiment, which was the first black regiment to be recruited in the North. It is not uncommon to see boutiques of fresh flowers tucked into Shaw's hands or the horse's bridle. The benefactor remains anonymous.

The walking loop encompasses 14 historic sites between Pinckney and Cambridge Streets and between Joy and Charles Streets, an area now known as the North Slope of Beacon Hill. Beacon Hill, the only remaining hill in Boston, retains its cobblestone streets and gas-style lanterns. The points of interest include structures that served as residences, schools, and Underground Railroad stops that for a time sheltered runaway slaves from the South. Today, most of the buildings are private residences. The last stop on the tour, the African Meeting House on Smith Court, is the oldest Black church building in the United States. Dedicated in 1806, it has been restored to the way it was in 1855. The ground floor houses the gallery for the Museum of Afro-American History.

Historic Cambridge and Harvard University

This 3.5-mile walk covers the original village of Newtowne, established by the founders of the Massachusetts Bay Colony in 1630, who thought it a more defendable position than Boston. In 1636, Harvard was established as an institution to educate the settlement's clergy and political leaders, and Newtowne was renamed Cambridge in honor of the English university that many of the residents once attended.

Information
Cambridge Office of Tourism, 15 Brattle St., Cambridge, MA 02138; 617/441-2884; 800/862-5678; www.cambridge.usa.org.
Cambridge Historical Commission, 831 Massachusetts Ave., Cambridge, MA 02138; 617/349-4683.
Cambridge Chamber of Commerce; 617/876-4100; www.cambridge-chamber.org.

Getting There
Take I-93 to Massachusetts Ave. or take the MBTA Red line.

First Steps
The Cambridge Office of Tourism and the Cambridge Historical Commission together have produced a wonderful, detailed, self-guided walking tour of historic Cambridge and Harvard University. Stop at the information booth at Harvard Square on Massachusetts Ave. to pick up a copy of "Walking Tour: Old Cambridge." Student led Harvard Yard tours explore America's oldest university (M-S, 10 and 11:15am; 2 and 3:15pm; Sun., 1:30 and 3 pm. Contact: Harvard Information Center, Holyoke Center, 1350 Massachusetts Ave., Cambridge; 617/495-1573.)

Historic Cambridge and Harvard University. Your walk along the city of Cambridge's brick sidewalks will take you to 27 locations, spanning four centuries of its rich and colorful history. The walk begins across from Harvard Yard, where the first residents laid out a settlement with a meeting house and marketplace in the middle, surrounded by houses, gardens and a common grazing area, then ringed with farmlands and pastures. The prescribed route takes you through Radcliffe Yard, where, beginning in 1879 and continuing until 1943, Harvard faculty instructed women students in separate classes.

Newtowne's livestock once grazed on Cambridge Common. Ensuing centuries saw religious, political and social gatherings take over the grassy green. Today, the tranquil Common showcases three British cannons captured in 1775 as well as a granite statue of Abraham Lincoln dedicated to Civil War veterans. Of particular note in the Common is a poignant cast-bronze statue, created in 1997 and dedicated to the Irish "great hunger." A mother holding an emaciated babe in her arms reaches out to a man who is holding another hungry child. The engraved quote says: "Never again should a people starve in a world of plenty.

On weekends, you can take a guided tour of the First Church Congregational, on the corner of Mason Street, near the Common. This imposing granite structure showcases beautiful stained-glass windows, a stark-white interior and a huge pipe organ. Your walk will lead you up and down Brattle Street, called "Old Tory Row," where you will see notable examples of well-preserved 17th- and 18th-century Loyalist mansions. (Historical markers in Cambridge are bright blue ovals with white printing.) The Longfellow National Historic Site closed until 2001 for renovations) was the 1759 home of Loyalist John Vassal, Jr., and then the quarters of George Washington during the Siege of Boston. Henry Wadsworth Longfellow bought the home after his marriage to Frances Appleton in 1843. His descendents granted it to the National Park Service in 1974.

At Winthrop Square—a marketplace in 1635—you'll see a tutorial sign citing the history of the Massachusetts Bay Colony and the founding of Boston and Newtowne. The tour routes you past 18th-century Hicks House on South Street and the 19th-century Governor Thomas Dudley House on Dunster Street as well as several of Harvard's 20th-century undergraduate houses before taking you back to Massachusetts Avenue, near where you began.

Here you will enter the near-sacred Harvard Yard, whose majestic red brick buildings take your breath away. (It is called the "yard," because the original college was surrounded by cowyards.) The self-guided tour leads you past some of Harvard's most significant buildings—such as Massachusetts Hall (1718), the oldest standing building, and Harvard Hall (1764), which housed the first classroom. But, at this point, your best bet is to join one of the free, daily, student-led tours of the university where you'll learn about Harvard's classic architecture, history, and lore. Top off your day by exploring Harvard's renowned museums: Carpenter Center for the Visual Arts, Fogg Art Museum, Busch-Reisinger Museum, Sackler Museum, Harvard Semitic Museum, and the Museums of Cultural and Natural History.

Lexington, Concord and Minute Man National Historic Park

Concord and Lexington share the bedrock of our country's democratic beginnings as the birthplace of the American Revolution. The Revolution's historic first battle on April 19, 1775, was played out along the famed Battle Road (now Lexington Road and a portion of Massachusetts Avenue) that links Lexington and Concord. Minute Man National Historical Park preserves and interprets the significant historic sites, structures, and landscapes associated with the Battles of Lexington and Concord, offering a fascinating walk through history.

Information
Minute Man National Historical Park, 174 Liberty St., Concord, MA 01742; 508/369-6993, ext. 22; www.nps.gov/mima.
Lexington Chamber of Commerce, 1875 Massachusetts Ave., Concord, MA 01742; 617/862-1450.
Concord Chamber of Commerce, 2 Lexington Rd., Concord, MA 01742; 508/369-3120.

Getting There
Take I-95/128 to exit 30B, Rtes. 2/2A.

First Steps
Stop at the Minute Man Visitor Center on Route 2A, Massachusetts Avenue where you can pick up an interpretive map and view the film "Road to Revolution." Allow more than one day to fully explore this history-packed area. Concord Guides offers a guided walking tour. Contact them at 978/287-0897; www.members.aol.com/concordweb.

Minute Man National Historical Park. Although the militiamen may have traversed the area on foot, busy roads and long distances between attractions dictate that you should drive between walking explorations. And, since Concord was the home and resting place of a number of

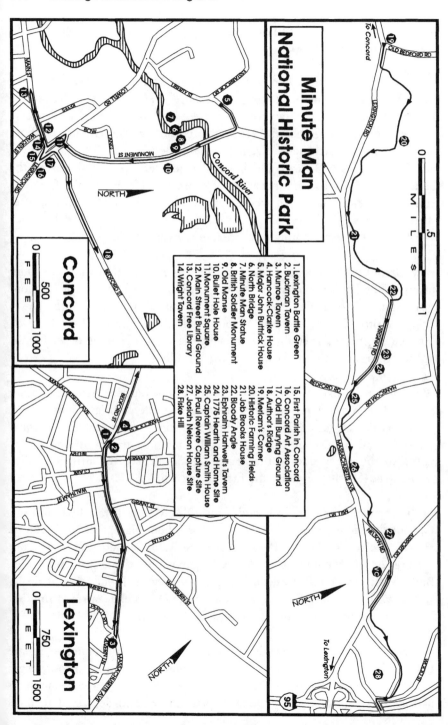

Minute Man National Historic Park

NORTH

0 .5 1
MILES

Concord

0 500 1000
FEET

Lexington

0 750 1500
FEET

1. Lexington Battle Green
2. Buckman Tavern
3. Munroe Tavern
4. Hancock-Clarke House
5. Major John Buttrick House
6. North Bridge
7. Minute Man Statue
8. British Soldier Monument
9. Old Manse
10. Bullet Hole House
11. Monument Square
12. Main Street Burial Ground
13. Concord Free Library
14. Wright Tavern
15. First Parish in Concord
16. Concord Art Association
17. Old Hill Burying Ground
18. Author's Ridge
19. Meriam's Corner
20. Historic Farming Fields
21. Job Brooks House
22. Bloody Angle
23. Ephraim Hartwell's Tavern
24. 1775 Hearth and Home Site
25. Captain William Smith House
26. Paul Revere Capture Site
27. Josiah Nelson House Site
28. Fiske Hill

distinguished American authors, this on-foot exploration enables you to discover their roots as well.

Begin where the battle began, at the Lexington Battle Green (1), where the first shots of the American Revolution were fired. Here you'll find the Buckman Tavern (2), now home of the Lexington Historical Society, where the militia gathered before the battle on the Green. A short distance up Massachusetts Avenue is Munroe Tavern (3), circa 1695, which served as a British field hospital when they retreated during the battle. If you follow Hancock Street from the Green, you'll find the Hancock-Clarke House (4), where Paul Revere and William Dawes, after their infamous ride from Boston, alerted Samuel Adams and John Hancock that the British were coming to confiscate the Patriots' arms.

Now drive toward Concord on Massachusetts Avenue following the route taken by the British soldiers on April 19, 1775. (At the center of Concord turn right on Monument Street and then left on Liberty Street to the North Bridge Visitor Center, and park.) Here you'll find the Major John Buttrick House (5). Buttrick is credited with being the first to give the order for the militia to fire into the ranks of the British soldiers.

Walk down the path to North Bridge (6), where Buttrick issued his order as the British were retreating from torching the militia's ammunition hidden at Barrett farm. Here you'll find the Minute Man Statue (7), which was sculpted by Daniel Chester French to honor the militia of 1775. Cross to the other side of the bridge and you'll see the British Soldier Monument (8), site of where the first enemy fell.

Walk through the meadow and tour Old Manse (9), which housed Concord's early ministers in the 1770s, then Nathaniel and Sophia Hawthorne from 1842 to 1845, and where Ralph Waldo Emerson wrote *Nature*. Across Monument Street is a large, yellow private residence called Bullet Hole House (10). Legend has it that a Redcoat fired a shot at Elisha Jones, who was standing in his doorway. The bullet missed him but lodged above the portal and is still visible to this day.

Return to your car and drive down Monument Street to Monument Square (11) in the center of Concord. (Park in a municipal spot.) On foot, begin your exploration of historic Concord by examining the three monuments in the Square (actually an oblong-shaped grassy area) dedicated to local soldiers who have died in America's wars from the American Revolution onward. Here, on the south side of the Square, the founders of Concord made a treaty with the Indians under the shelter of "Jethro's Tree," long gone but now marked with a plaque.

Turn right on Main Street. (City streets with historical significance are marked with oval plaques that give the street's history or the story of the person for whom the street is named.) Known as the Milldam, this was the site of an Indian fishing weir and was laid out along the dam soon after the settlement of the town in 1635. Walk to the Main Street Burial Ground (12), which contains many quaint, interesting stones marking the graves of the early settlers.

Proceed to the Sudbury Street fork to the Concord Free Library (13). An octagonal room in the library's center displays a statue of Emerson and busts of Thoreau, Louisa and Bronson Alcott, Hawthorne, and other honored Concordians. A table used by U.S. presidents from Madison to Grant graces the trustees' room.

Cross Sudbury and walk down the opposite side of Main Street to Wright Tavern (14). The shops along this stretch have old-English-style signs out front that illustrate what goods or services are offered within. Amos Wright was operating the historic Wright Tavern, c.1747, when, on April 19, 1775, the British commandeered it as their headquarters as they briefly held the town. (It is now an office building.)

Turn right on Lexington Road. The Meetinghouse of the First Parish in Concord (15), 1636, site of the first and second Provincial Congress of 1774, is now the imposing Unitarian Universalist Church, whose steeple is topped with a gold clock and cupola. Cross Lexington Road to #37, Concord Art Association (16), where you'll find changing exhibits of contemporary arts and crafts. Continue down Lexington past the Old Hill Burying Ground (17), where many of Concord's first settlers are buried.

Turn right on Bedford Street and walk to Sleepy Hollow Cemetery (entrance is just past Partridge Street) and head up to Author's Ridge (18) by taking the right fork up and around the hill. The Thoreaus, Hawthornes, and Alcotts, who all lived around the same time and all were friends, are buried in close proximity here. The Emersons rest apart, in a large, chained-in area surrounded with stone pillars. Ralph Waldo's grave is marked with a huge indigenous granite boulder.

Back in your car, drive down Lexington Road to Meriam's Corner (19), where the Minutemen ambushed retreating British soldiers. This is the beginning of the 5.5-mile Battle Road Trail, which traverses over much the same route taken by the American and British fighting forces on that fateful April day and connects many of the historic sites. (The actual battle road is one foot under the present surface.) You can either walk the entire trail (there is no public transportation back to your starting point, however) or drive to select sites and explore the surrounding trail areas on foot.

The Battle Trail leads through the Historic Farming Fields (20), which have been tilled since the 17th century, then past the Job Brooks House (21). The trail becomes a boardwalk, crossing over the protected Elm Brook Wetland. (In colonial times, a tannery utilized the water from Elm Brook here.) Some of the most intense fighting occurred at Bloody Angle (22). Travelers to and from Boston in 1756 stopped at Ephraim Hartwell's Tavern (23), which is now staffed with a costumed interpreter conducting a living history demonstration. (You can drive to this spot, park, and explore.) The foundation and central fireplace system of the 1775 Hearth and Home Site (24) of Sergeant Samuel Hartwell is .25 mile down the road.

As you follow the Battle Road Trail you'll pass the Captain William Smith House (25), c.1693, and a stone monument marking the approximate site where Paul Revere was captured (26). His companions on the "midnight ride" were luckier: William Dawes turned back, and Samuel Prescott escaped, successfully issuing the warning to the militia in Concord. (You can drive to this spot, park, and explore.)

The trail leads to the Minute Man Boulder and the Josiah Nelson House Site (27) as well as the site of Parker's Revenge, all of which are marked with plaques interpreting their historical significance. The historical park ends at Fiske Hill (28), just beyond the Minute Man Visitor Center, where British and Americans fought a bitter skirmish before the retreat and battle continued all the way to Bunker Hill in Boston.

Walden Pond State Reservation

Forever linked to Walden Pond, Henry David Thoreau spent two years here, in the middle Walden Woods—1845 to 1847—developing his theory of forest succession, then laid the foundation for our modern study of ecology. Thoreau kept a journal of his thoughts and observations during his time at Walden Pond, which he published in 1854 as the book, *Walden*.

Information
Walden Pond State Reservation, 915 Walden St. (Rte. 126), Concord, MA 01742; 978/369-3254.

Getting There
Take I-95 or I-495 to Rte. 2 to Rte. 126 south.

First Steps
Pick up a trail map at reservation headquarters before walking down to the pond.

Walden Pond. Considered the birthplace of American conservationism, Walden Pond is a 103-foot-deep glacial kettle hole of 62 acres, fed by underground springs, with no inlets or outlets. A 1.8-mile trail leads around the pond, passing, about every 200 yards, a narrow set of concrete steps that lead to the water. Here, the public is encouraged to commune with nature, to wade or swim in the pond or to simply sit, read, and drink in its tranquil beauty. (To experience Walden Pond as Thoreau did, come in the spring or fall; the summer months attract so many visitors that the area feels more like Coney Island.)

Begin at Red Cross Beach. Here, follow Pond Path counterclockwise around Walden Pond to Thoreau Cove, where Thoreau's original house was situated. (A replica of his home is near the parking area across Rte. 126.) At Ice Fort Cove, at the far end of the pond, ice was once harvested, stacked, and then loaded on railroad cars of the Fitchburg Railway, which passed nearby. Proceed to Long Cove, where it is not unusual to spot anglers fishing for brown or rainbow trout.

From Long Cove you have the option of continuing along the water on Pond Path or diverting to Esker Trail, which leads upland. From here you can take Emerson's Cliff Trail to Emerson's Cliff. Ralph Waldo Emerson, a close friend of Thoreau, owned much of the land surrounding Walden Pond. In 1922, Emerson and two other families who owned property in Walden Woods granted land to the Commonwealth of Massachusetts with the stipulation that it be pristinely preserved for public enjoyment. (Admittance is limited to 1,000 people per day.)

From Esker Trail you can take the boat-launch road back down to Pond Path to Main Beach or follow it in the opposite direction for a short distance to Rte. 126.

Rainy Day Options

This is a must-see for all Kennedy-philes. **The John F. Kennedy Library and Museum** showcases 25 dramatic exhibits of John F. Kennedy's Irish ancestry, his career, family and time in the Oval Office. Three theaters and period settings re-create Camelot. This memorial to our 35th President of the United States sits on a 10-acre waterfront park. *(Take the Red Line "T" to JFK./U.Mass Station, where a free shuttle will take you to the library and museum. Contact: John F. Kennedy Library, Harbor Point, Morrissey Blvd., Dorchester, MA 02125; 617/929-4523; www.cs.umb.edu/jfklibrary.)*

A group of literary geniuses lived and worked in Concord over the centuries. Three of their homes, filled with personal memorabilia and furnishings, are open for guided tours: **The Emerson House** *(Cambridge Turnpike, 978/369-2236)* was the home of Ralph Waldo from 1835 until his death in 1882. The 17th-century **Wayside** *(455 Lexington Rd., 978/369-6993)* was owned, successively, by the Hawthornes, Alcotts and then Margaret Sidney, who wrote Five Little Peppers. The Alcotts lived in **Orchard House** *(399 Lexington Rd., 978/369-4118)* from 1858 to 1877, where Louisa May wrote Little Women. These homes of literary Concord are within walking distance of each other.

Galleries and period rooms of the **Concord Museum** showcase exhibits and collections that provide a multi-faceted overview of Concord's colorful history. You'll see Emerson's study, as it was arranged when he died in 1882, and Thoreau's bed, desk, and chair from his time at Walden Pond. Six "Why Concord?" galleries trace Concord History from the first Native American settlement through the 20th century. *(Contact: Concord Museum, Cambridge Turnpike, Concord, 978/369-9609.)*

Lodging

Lodging in greater Boston is expensive, running the gamut from small inns to luxury hotels. For more comprehensive choices, consult the New England-wide accommodations websites and reservation services listed in the "How to Use This Book" or check out www.mass-vacation.com/lodging/greater_boston.phtml.

Smack-dab in the middle of the Big Dig, the **Harborside Inn** ($$, 185 State St., 617/723-7500, www.hagopianhotels.com) will enjoy its primo location near the waterfront and Faneuil Hall once the construction stops. Reinvigorating an 1858 mercantile warehouse in the heart of Boston's financial district, the inn's 54 guest rooms front an inner 3-story, brick-wall "courtyard," decorated with photographs and paintings that depict Boston's colorful past.

An historic grand hotel in the heart of Back Bay, the **Fairmont Copley Plaza** ($$$$, 138 James St., 617/267-5300, 800/527-4727, www.fairmont.com) oozes with the opulence of a bygone era. The palatial 379-guest-room hotel, opened in 1912, has hosted royalty, film stars, and other glitterati over the ensuing decades and leaves no hospitality detail to chance. Known as the "Grande Dame of Boston," the Fairmont Copley Plaza treats you as the other half lived.

A Colonial-Revival built in 1892, **A Cambridge House** ($-$$$, 2218 Massachusetts Ave., Cambridge, 617/491-6300, www.acambridge-house.com) exudes Victorian-era romance. Four-poster beds, a riot of Waverly prints, period furnishings, and gas fireplaces adorn the 15 guest rooms. Complimentary fruit and pastries grace the drawing room by day, replaced from 5 to 8pm with an assortment of yummy appetizers.

Eclectically decorated with the owners' original artwork, handmade quilts, antique furnishings and period memorabilia, **Hawthorne Inn** ($$, 462 Lexington Rd., Concord, 617/369-5610, www.concordmass.com) sits aside historic Battle Road on land that once belonged to the Emersons, Alcotts, and Hawthornes. Built in 1870, the seven guest rooms of the bed-and-breakfast offer serene lodging in the cradle of history.

An operating inn since 1716, Longfellow's **Wayside Inn** ($+, Wayside Inn Rd., Sudbury, 978/443-1776; 800/339-1776, www.wayside.org) was immortalized by patron Henry Wadsworth Longfellow in 1862 in *Tales of a Wayside Inn*. A self-guided walking tour of the 106-acre property reveals the Wayside Grist Mill, Martha-Mary Chapel, and the Redstone School of "Mary Had A Little Lamb" fame, as well as a museum of authentically preserved rooms throughout the inn itself. Be sure to inquire about the "Secret Drawer Society" and the Sudbury Ancient Fife and Drum Corps concerts.

An elegant brownstone in Back Bay with 32 guest rooms, **Newbury Guest House** ($+, 261 Newbury St., 617/437-7666, 800/437-7668, www.hagopianhotels.com) was built in 1862 as a private residence. The inn's central location is its trump card.

Constructed as the Massachusetts Eye and Ear Clinic in 1824, the historic building that now houses the **John Jeffries House** ($+, 14 David G. Mugar Way, 617/367-1866) was converted in 1986 into a handsome urban inn of 46 guest rooms. You'll find it charming, clean, convenient, affordable, and although it sits on the edge of a busy thoroughfare, remarkably tranquil.

Sublimely luxurious, the 95 suites of the **Eliot Suite Hotel** ($$$$, 370 Commonwealth Ave., 617/267-1607, 800/443-5468, www.eliothotel-.com) supplies a pampering of private pantries, Italian marble baths, and goose-down pillows and comforters. Reminiscent of a sophisticated European hotel, the Eliot was built in 1925 by the family of Harvard College president Charles Eliot and is adjacent to the Harvard Club in Back Bay.

The 113-guestroom **Inn at Harvard** ($$-$$$$, 1201 Massachusetts Ave., Cambridge, 617/491-2222, 800/458-5886, www.theinnatharvard.com) overlooks Harvard Yard. The perfect location for a walk through historic Cambridge, the inn offers elegantly furnished guest rooms and all the amenities of a private ivy-league club.

The **Colonial Inn** ($$, 48 Monument Square, Concord, 978/369-9200, 800/370-9200, www.concordscolonialinn.com) has witnessed Concord's historical evolution since the mid-1600s. Comprised of three colonial residences that flank the village green, the inn's guest rooms are individually appointed with colonial furnishings that reflect the period. If you are spiritually inclined, check out #24, the ghost room.

Food and Drink

Great food rules in Boston. It is difficult to find a bad meal here. And because Boston has soooo many wonderful places to dine, I can't stop at ten. For even more options, consult www.marestaurantassoc.org.

Sleekly modern with slate-gray walls, hardwood floors, and a Chinese-red bar, **Radius** ($$$$, 8 High St., 617/426-1234) epitomizes romantic cosmopolitan dining at its very best. The indirectly lit semi-circular dining room, awash with candlelight and orchids, adds to the ambiance, which is punctuated by the chef's singular interpretations of classic New England ingredients. Radius is pricey, but worth the indulgence.

A palatial steakhouse set amid dark oak and mirrors, beneath the shimmer of Waterford chandeliers, the **Oak Room** ($$$$, 138 St. James Ave., 617/267-5300, 800/527-4727, www.fairmont.com) at the Fairmont Copley Plaza is classy, pricey, and prime time.

A Boston institution that for years has stood for fresh seafood at reasonable prices, **Legal Sea Foods** ($$, 617/783-8088) has grown to 19 restaurants nationwide. While most of the establishments are in the Boston area, the restaurant at Copley Place (100 Huntington Ave., 617/266-7775) is probably most centrally located. Call the corporate number for the other listings.

One of the brightest new stars in the North End's endless lineup of fine restaurants is **Limoncello** ($$, 190 North St., Boston, 617/523-4480). The upmarket decor feels subtly Mediterranean, befitting the flawless Calabrese-style cuisine and welcoming ambiance. A glass of limoncello, from which the restaurant takes its name, makes the perfect meal topper. The owner, once a waiter at another North End restaurant, won the million dollar lottery and used his windfall to create Limoncello.

For simply great Italian cooking, portions that could feed a family of five, and a palatably small bill, **La Familia Georgio** ($+, 112 Salem St., Boston, 617/367-6711) shines. This popular North End eatery offers its dishes in two sizes—piccolo (manageable) and grande (doggy-bag time). Although sharing is allowed, each diner must order at least one entrée.

A Cambridge classic, **Upstairs at the Pudding** ($$$, 10 Holyoke St., 617/864-1933) graces the dining rooms of Harvard's Hasty Pudding Club, whose walls are peppered with centuries-old theater posters. Summertime finds diners enjoying the candlelit garden terrace.

French and Cambodian cuisine served in a sophisticated city bistro amid the soft strains of live blues is the signature of the twin **Elephant Walk** restaurants ($$+, 2067 Massachusetts Ave., 617/492-6900; 900 Beacon St., 617/247-1500). The fusion presentations are otherworldly.

You'll find American home-style cooking at **Longfellow's Wayside Inn** ($$, Wayside Inn Rd., Sudbury, 978/443-1776; 800/339-1776, www.wayside-.org), which has been serving warmth and hospitality to weary travelers since David Howe first opened his two-room home as Howe's Tavern in 1716. If you dine on summer Wednesdays, the Sudbury Ancient Fife and Drum Corps will treat you to a costumed performance.

Located in an old brick firehouse in Concord, the **Walden Grille** ($$+, 24 Walden St., 978/371-2233) offers classic New England ingredients in imaginative presentations of new-American cuisine.

Consistently garnering "Best of . . ." awards, **Mamma Maria** ($$$, 3 North Square, Prince and Garden Sts., 617/523-0077) serves upscale Italian cuisine in a 1900s North End brownstone. Among the intimate dining rooms is a grappa library.

Three restaurants—same owners: **Antico Forno** ($, 93 Salem St., 617/723-6733)—small, bustling and casual—and its upmarket Italian sister restaurant **Tarramia** ($$, 98 Salem St., 617/523-3112) rank among North End favorites of locals, visitor, and even other restaurant owners. The newest addition to this North End group, **Taranta** ($$$, 210 Hanover St, 617/720/0052) incorporates Arab influences in its innovative Italian cuisine.

Charley's Eating & Drinking Saloon ($$, 284 Newbury St., 617/266-3000) is a good place to stop for a burger and a drink. The decor of this popular family establishment mimics a 19th-century saloon and it sports the largest patio on Newbury Street.

With its sidewalk cafe and skylit dining room, **Stephanie's on Newbury** ($$$, 190 Newbury St., 617/236-0990) offers sophisticated American cuisine and a superb people-watching location.

It is all about seafood at the **Famous Atlantic Fish Company** ($$, 777 Boylston St., 617/267-4000). Check the chalkboard and have it your way.

Perched atop the 52-story Prudential Tower, the award-winning **Top of the Hub** ($$$$, 800 Boylston St., 617/536-1775) serves up an unparalleled view of Boston along with stellar cuisine and live jazz every night.

For more than just a burger and brew, stop at **Back Bay Brewing Company** ($$, 755 Boylston St., 617/424-8300). Choose from a menu of globally inspired cuisine in either of two distinctive dining rooms.

Anthony's Pier 4 ($$$, 140 Northern Ave., 617/482-6262) offers a breathtaking view of Boston's waterfront and an internationally inspired menu.

Overlooking the Public Garden, **Hampshire House Library Grille** ($$$, 84 Beacon St., 617/227-9600) serves classic American cuisine amid a Victorian ambiance. Don't miss the Sunday jazz brunch.

When a **Locke-Ober** ($$$$, 3-4 Winter Place, 617/542-1340; www.locke-ober.com) regular patron passes away, his plate is turned over and his chair propped up, in remembrance. So goes one long-standing tradition at this singular Boston establishment that has been cosseting its customers for more than 100 years. Locke-Ober's cuisine and its colorful history warrant a stop.

The Gospel Sunday Brunch draws a crowd of blues worshipers at the **House of Blues** ($, 96 Winthrop St., Cambridge, 617/491-2583). You and your taste buds will be transported to the Mississippi Delta.

The North Shore and Cape Ann

Percolating with maritime history, this bustling seaside area just north of Boston combines a scintillating past with some of the most quaintly picturesque vistas in New England. You'll find Marblehead, Salem, and Cape Ann—Massachusetts' "other cape"—strung along the north shore of Massachusetts Bay in the Atlantic like jewels on an antique necklace.

Regional Information
North of Boston Convention and Visitors Bureau, 17 Peabody Sq., Peabody, MA 01960; 800/742-5306; 978/977-7760; www.northof-boston.org.
Cape Ann Chamber of Commerce, 33 Commercial St., Dept. NB, Gloucester, MA 01930; 978/283-1601; www.cape-ann.com/cacc.

Getting There
By Air: All major carriers offer service to Boston's Logan International Airport.
By Rail: Amtrak offers service to Boston's South Station. The Newburyport/Rockport Commuter Rail Line offers service from Boston's North Station.
By Automobile: I-95/128 north to Rte. 128 north; or I-93 north from Boston to I-95/128 north, exit 37A, to Rte. 128 north; or I-495 to I-95/128 north, to Rte. 128 north.

Historic Marblehead

Marblehead sits serenely on a peninsula that juts into Massachusetts Bay just 18 miles north of Boston. Marble was never found nor quarried here, so it is believed that the original village was simply named for the rocky cliffs upon which it perches. Settled in 1629 by hardy English fishermen, Marblehead became the commercial fishing hub of New England by 1660. This desirable port began a thriving overseas trading industry as well, becoming the sixth largest town in the colonies by 1760. The American Revolution claimed the lives of so many fishermen that the industry was in decline for years, rebounding only to be decimated once again when a horrific storm destroyed the entire fishing fleet in 1846. By the end of the 19th century, a surging national interest in boating and Marblehead's fine harbor turned it into a thriving summer resort. Today Marblehead is a residential suburb of Boston and a lively recreational yachting community.

Information
Marblehead Chamber of Commerce, 62 Pleasant St., Marblehead, MA 01945; 781/631-2868; www.marbleheadchamber.org.
Marblehead Historical Society, P.O. Box 1048, Marblehead, MA 01945, 781/631-1069.

Getting There
From Rte. 128 north, take exit 25 to Rte. 114 (1A). Take Rte. 114 (1A) through Salem bearing left on Rte.114 when 1A forks to the right. Rte. 114 turns into Pleasant St. in Marblehead. Take Pleasant to Washington St. and turn right.

First Steps
Pick up a map and walking tour brochure from the Marblehead Chamber of Commerce Information Booth at 62 Pleasant St. The Marblehead Historical Society has compiled the self-guided walking tour of Marblehead and also offers guided walking tours of the historic neighborhoods at predetermined times throughout the summer. Contact the society for a current schedule.

Historic Marblehead. Quaint crooked streets and a panoply of Colonial and Victorian architecture abound on this picturesque 4-mile route, where 'round every corner you'll see an exquisite view of the Atlantic Ocean.

Park on Washington Street along the square at Abbott Hall (1), where the famed "Spirit of '76" painting by Archibald M. Willard hangs in the Selectman's Meeting Room. Also known as "Yankee Doodle," the painting is considered one of the most inspiringly patriotic paintings in America. The 1876 building's giant brass bell, aloft in the clock tower, still rings the hours.

Cross the street and proceed on Washington past #187, #185, and #181, which were built in the mid-1700s for the prominent merchant and shipbuilding families, Lee and Hooper. The Jeremiah Lee Mansion, #161 (2), home of the Marblehead Historical Society, was built in 1768 by Colonel Lee. This pre-Revolutionary Georgian structure features original hand-painted English wallpaper and intricate carved woodwork. Its wooden façade sand-painted to look like stone, the house is surrounded

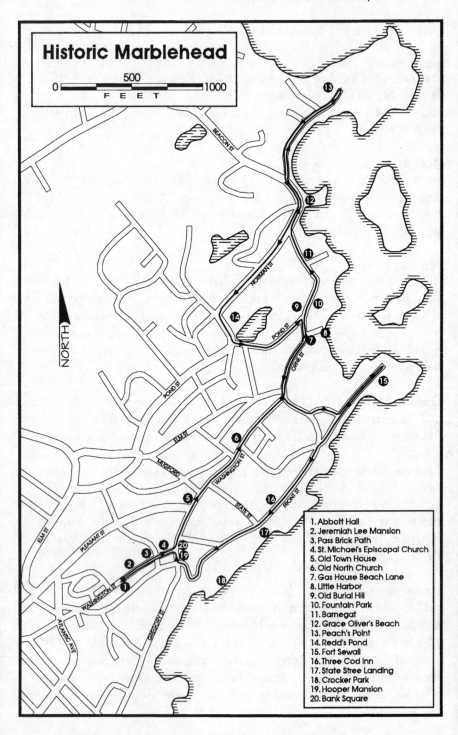

Historic Marblehead

500 FEET 1000
0 1000

NORTH

1. Abbott Hall
2. Jeremiah Lee Mansion
3. Pass Brick Path
4. St. Michael's Episcopal Church
5. Old Town House
6. Old North Church
7. Gas House Beach Lane
8. Little Harbor
9. Old Burial Hill
10. Fountain Park
11. Barnegat
12. Grace Oliver's Beach
13. Peach's Point
14. Redd's Pond
15. Fort Sewall
16. Three Cod Inn
17. State Stree Landing
18. Crocker Park
19. Hooper Mansion
20. Bank Square

by beautiful period gardens. House and gardens are open to the public for guided tours from mid-May through Oct. *(Contact: 781/631-1768).*

Head down Washington toward Summer Street. Pass Brick Path (3), the Tory headquarters in 1727, now the Brick Path Realty Trust. The vintage buildings along this stretch house antique stores and specialty shops. Go up hill on the left to St. Michael's Episcopal Church (4), built in 1714, which is readily distinguished by its tall white spire and gold weathervane and cupola. It is believed that after the signing of the Declaration of Independence, patriots rang the church bell so long and hard that it cracked. Paul Revere recast the bell, which is still in use today. The church was remodeled in 1832 in Gothic-Revival style with beautiful Victorian stained-glass windows.

Continue on Washington to the Old Town House (5) in Market Square, which was built by the citizens of Marblehead in 1727 as the center of town government. On the National Registry of Historic Landmarks, it is the oldest structure in continuous use as a public building since Colonial days. Remain on Washington to #41, the Old North Church (6). As Marblehead's first church, the congregational group began meeting in 1635. This structure was built in 1824 after the original church on Franklin Street burned. The codfish weathervane is constructed of gilded copper. Elbridge Gerry, one of the signers of the Declaration of Independence and James Madison's vice president during the War of 1812, once lived across the street at #44.

Continue straight as the street becomes Orne Street. (Use caution here as sidewalks end and the road proceeds around a blind corner.) Detour down Gas House Beach Lane (7) to the cove at Little Harbor (8). Goods were smuggled ashore in the mid-1700s, in an attempt to evade customs duties. A gas house stood here in the 1800s, whereby coal was converted to gas for lamp lighting and residential use. From here you can see Gerry's Island, which is now privately owned.

Return to Orne Street and turn right to Old Burial Hill (9). Established in 1838, Old Burial Hill is one of the oldest graveyards in New England. Marblehead's first meetinghouse was here. Go up the hill where six hundred Revolutionary War heroes are buried. The view of Cape Ann and the Atlantic from here is spectacular.

Across from Old Burial Hill, Fountain Park (10) also garners great views of the water. Continue along Orne as it turns into Beacon. (The road narrows; stay to the left and walk cautiously.) For centuries, this seafaring area called Barnegat (11) has housed marine-related businesses such as the Marblehead Lobster, Fish, and Seafood Company and the James E. Graves boatyard, which has been operating from here since the 1800s.

At Norman and Beacon, bear right on Beacon Street. To the right is Dolliber's Cove and Grace Oliver's Beach (12), site of an early settlement. Beyond you can see Peach's Point (13), a peninsula once supporting the farm and fish flakes of John Peach, now peppered with elaborate homes that were built as summer "cottages" in the 1800s. Retrace your steps and proceed down Norman to Pond Street and Redd's Pond (14), which was named after Wilmot Redd, a Marblehead woman hanged as a witch in 1692. (You also can see the bucolic pond from the top of Old Burial Hill).

Back at Old Burial Hill, go back down Orne Street, then turn left onto Franklin Street. Most of the houses on this street were built in the mid-1700s and are documented with historical markers. (The Hearth and Eagle House at #30 was immortalized in Anya Seton's historical novel of the same name.) Cross and turn left on Front Street, following the sidewalk along the harbor to Fort Sewall. At low tide the boats sit high and dry here.

Fort Sewall (15), built in the mid-1600s as a rough earthen barrier defense against French cruisers, was further fortified in 1742. The U.S.S. Constitution sought shelter under the fort's guns during a sea battle in 1814. Named after Samuel Sewall, chief justice of Massachusetts in 1814 and a Marblehead resident, the fort enjoys a spectacular vista encompassing historic Marblehead, Ocean Avenue, Devereux Beach, Marblehead Neck, and, directly across the harbor, Marblehead Light. Be sure to take the steps down the hillside to peep into the barred windows of the underground barracks, which once housed a Revolutionary War garrison.

Follow Front Street along the harbor toward the village center. A British frigate fired on the Three Cod Inn (16) (called "the old tavern" in 1680 and now a corner retail store, #82-84) from the harbor in 1775. One of the shots struck the front of the tavern and lodged there, but it was not discovered until the 20th century. A Marblehead Historical Society marker at the site tells the complete tale.

State Street Landing (17), Marblehead's public landing since the 1800s, is at State and Front Streets, where the wharves once bustled with fishing and trading vessels. Proceed past the historic houses on Front Street to a sign (opposite #40-42) noting Crocker Park (18). Turn left to the water where you'll enjoy a stunning view of the deep-water granite harbor.

Proceed along on Front Street, which is so narrow the houses literally sit on the street, and turn right at Union Street. When you get to Hooper Street turn right to #8. The Robert "King" Hooper Mansion (19) was built in 1728 and augmented in 1745 by Hooper, a respected and prosperous merchant who lived here until the Revolution, when as a loyalist he fled to Canada. The home features a wine cellar, slave quarters and a third-floor ballroom. The Marblehead Arts Association (*Contact: 617/631-2608*), which displays monthly exhibits of members' works, utilizes the building now. The house and a small but lovely rear garden are open to the public.

The intersection of Hooper and Washington Streets is called Bank Square (20) because the three major Marblehead banks were once located here. The National Grand Bank building, built in 1851, still stands next to Hooper Mansion. Retrace your steps up Washington Street to Abbott Hall.

Historic Salem

Infamous for the puritanical Salem Witch Trials of 1692, the city of Salem—16 miles north of Boston and minutes from Marblehead—more significantly harbors a glorious maritime and seafaring heritage. In 1626, Roger Conant led a group of adventurers from Gloucester, forming a settlement called Naumkeag as a commercial fishing station. The venture went bankrupt in a year and was acquired by the Massachusetts Bay Colony. The settlement was renamed Salem about 1629, reportedly short for Jerusalem. In 1630, Governor John Winthrop brought more than 100 colonists, many of which were Puritans, to settle in Salem.

By the mid-17th century, maritime trade with Europe was already prospering. Daily life in Salem, however, was riddled with tensions. Still under British rule, those accused of consorting with the devil were considered felons against the government, a crime punishable by hanging. More than 200 people were accused of witchcraft in 1692, but only 30-plus were hung. Unfortunately, more than 20 of those people were hung in Salem alone in a year's time, earning the city the reputation it would carry forever.

During the Revolutionary War, Salem merchant seamen turned their vessels into privateers, seizing or sinking a multitude of British vessels and keeping the spoils. By the end of the war, Salem boasted a population exceeding 5,000. Post Revolutionary trade with Africa, China, the West Indies, Russia, India, and Sumatra in the 18th and 19th centuries—called the "Great Age of Sail"—established Salem's sea captains as America's first millionaires. They built grand homes in what is now the McIntire Historic district, a neighborhood of well-preserved architecturally significant homes.

By the middle of the 19th century, most shipping commerce had moved to the ports of Boston and New York. Ships were being built so big that Salem's harbor was too shallow to accommodate them. Commerce in Salem turned to industry, prospering until the "Great Salem Fire of 1914," when many mills, factories, and tanneries, as well as parts of the residential center of the city, were destroyed. Today Salem—the third oldest city in America—is a relatively quiet residential town, bustling mainly with visitors exploring her bounteous historical treasures.

Information
Salem Office of Tourism and Cultural Affairs, Destination Salem, 10 Liberty St., Salem, MA 01970; 978-745-9595; 800/777-6848; www.salem.org.

Getting There
From Rte. 128 north, take exit 26 (Lowell St.) or exit 25A (Rte. 114 east). Follow tri-color signs to the Salem Historic District. Park at the Public Parking Garage on New Liberty St.

First Steps
Stop at the National Park Service Visitors Center on New Liberty St., where you'll find maps and brochures as well as a multimedia presentation on the colorful history of Salem. Be sure to pick up a

descriptive brochure of the McIntire Historic District for the second part of this walk.

Historic Salem. This 4-mile route links the Salem Heritage Trail and the McIntire District Walking Trail, thereby encompassing all Salem's colorful history. From the Visitors Center, walk to Essex Street and turn left at the trolley stop, following the red line on the sidewalk that denotes the Salem Heritage Trail. On your left is the Phillips Library (1), a part of the Peabody Essex Museum that houses rare books and manuscripts.

Turn left on Washington Square West. A statue sporting a swirling cape and a conical hat stands in the intersection with North Street, directly in front of the Salem Witch Museum. From a distance looking like a Puritanical witch, the statue is actually a likeness of Salem's founder, Roger Conant (2).

Cross Washington to Salem Common (3). Walk across the village green, now complete with a band-shell gazebo in its center. In the 17th and 18th centuries, this 9-acre site was used for grazing cattle and to train the militia. By the 19th century, the area was landscaped and called Washington Square, and grand homes of wealthy seamen were built around the perimeter.

Turn right on Washington Square East, then right on Essex Street and cross the street. At a small sign that denotes Salem Maritime National Historic Site entrance, walk down the wooden boardwalk and through a gate. (You will be leaving the red line route here temporarily.) The modest Narbonne House (4), built in 1672, was named for one of its last owners, Sarah Narbonne, a seamstress who operated a cent shop in the lean-to at the side of the house. Granite outlines of the foundations of a small dairy house and carriage house are on either side of the walk.

The wooden boardwalk becomes a brick sidewalk that cuts through the backyards of two historic houses. Derby House, Salem's oldest brick home, is on the left, Hawkes House straight ahead, Customs House to the right, all fronting Derby Street. The Georgian Derby House (5) was the home of Elias Haskett Derby—one of Salem's most successful ship owners—from 1762 until the 1780s, when he began building the much larger Hawkes House (6) next door. The Derbys never moved into "the new house," instead moving to a mansion in "uptown" Salem, away from the

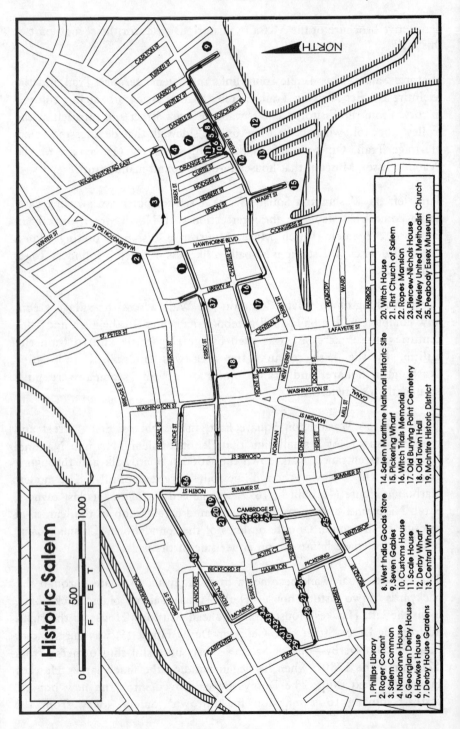

Historic Salem

FEET
0   500   1000

NORTH

1. Phillips Library
2. Roger Conant
3. Salem Common
4. Narbonne House
5. Georgian Derby House
6. Hawkes House
7. Derby House Gardens
8. West India Goods Store
9. Seven Gables
10. Customs House
11. Scale House
12. Derby Wharf
13. Central Wharf
14. Salem Maritime National Historic Site
15. Pickering Wharf
16. Witch Trials Memorial
17. Old Burying Point Cemetery
18. Old Town Hall
19. McIntire Historic District
20. Witch House
21. First Church of Salem
22. Ropes Mansion
23. Pierce-Nichols House
24. Wesley United Methodist Church
25. Peabody Essex Museum

waterfront. Derby used Hawkes House as a warehouse until his death in 1799. When the structure was sold in 1800, one-third of it was dismantled. The next year, Benjamin Hawkes remodeled the house to its present form.

The 18th-century Derby House Gardens (7) consist of six oval perennial beds—outlined and circularly inter-cut like a knot garden with borders of germander—and five triangular beds of antique and apothecary roses. Members of V.I.P, Volunteers in Parks, lovingly maintain the gardens. Some of the plants are harvested and used in the Stitch in Time program in the Salem Public Schools, where school children learn how to do colonial chores such as making herb sachets.

Follow the brick sidewalk to Derby Street, where you can see the front of these buildings. Cross the street and turn left down Derby Street to the West India Goods Store (8), where exotic imports from around the world and New England trade items were marketed in the early 1800s and are so offered today. Many of the vintage buildings on Derby Street house shops, cafes, and taverns named after witches, such as Witches Brew and Pig's Eye (see Food and Drink).

Cross Hardy Street to the House of the Seven Gables (9), 54 Turner Street, built by Captain John Turner in 1668. If you walk around the famous house, inspiration for Nathaniel Hawthorne's 19th century novel of the same name, you can count the seven gables. Tours of this complex of early houses and period gardens include Hawthorne's birthplace in 1804.

Backtrack to Derby Street, turn left, and proceed past Derby House and Hawkes House to the imposing Customs House (10), across from Derby Wharf. This stately 1819 red brick building—built in the Federal style with a cupola and gold eagle on top—stood at the center of port activity during Salem's foreign trade heyday. Here, sea captains presented their cargoes in order to pay import duties, about five percent of their value. Perhaps the most well known, though short tenured (1846 to 1849), customs surveyor was Nathaniel Hawthorne, who during this time conceived *The Scarlet Letter*. The Customs House is the centerpiece of the Salem Maritime National Historic Site, open at predetermined times for tours of historically furnished rooms. Behind the Customs House is the unassuming Scale House (11), which held the large scales that were used to weigh incoming shipments of goods.

Turn left onto Derby Wharf (12), once the longest and busiest in the nation. Positioned directly across from the Customs House, it was built by Elias Derby in 1762 and privately owned. (If the day is fine, you may want to walk to the lighthouse at the tip of the wharf in Salem Harbor, .5-mile each way.)

Beyond Derby Wharf, Central Wharf (13) was used in the 1870s for unloading raw materials such as lumber from Maine and coal from Pennsylvania. When Salem turned to manufacturing, the ships brought in cotton and hides to be later exported as textiles and shoes.

Proceed down Derby Street to the Orientation Center for the Salem Maritime National Historic Site (14). Here you can see an 18-minute movie on maritime Salem. By September 2001, the authentic reproduction of the ship *Friendship* will be moored here on Central Wharf, open to the public for tours. By her side will be *Captain's Gig*, which was built from scratch by a group of Salem volunteers. The Friendship was constructed at the Scarano Boat Building in Albany, New York, and completed and rigged out on site.

Stroll around Pickering Wharf (15), which features shops and cafes as well as the Museum of Myths and Monsters and the Salem Whale Watch office. Back out on Derby, cross the street, turn left and follow the Heritage Trail's red line once again. Derby Street takes you past the New England Pirate Museum. On the corner of Derby and Liberty Streets is the Salem Wax Museum of Witches and Seafarers.

Turn right on Liberty Street. On the left, enter the Witch Trials Memorial (16), a small courtyard ringed with a handcrafted u-shaped granite wall, to which are attached 20 cantilevered stone benches. Each bench is inscribed with the carved name and execution date of one of the victims hung in 1692 as a witch. (Fresh flowers often mysteriously appear on each stone bench, possibly placed by practitioners of Wicca, or modern-day witchcraft.) Inscribed on the memorial's threshold are victims' protests of innocence, interrupted in mid-sentence by the wall. This is designed to symbolize Salem's indifference to their oppression. Six black locust trees—last to flower and first to lose their leaves—grace the courtyard, planted to represent the stark injustice of the trials. Beyond the Witch Trials Memorial is the 17th century Old Burying Point Cemetery, where only the backs of tombstones are visible. This positioning serves as symbolic testimony that the people of Salem turned their backs in silent witness to the public persecutions.

Walk up Liberty Street and turn left at Charter Street, to the entrance of the Old Burying Point Cemetery (17), the oldest burying ground in the city. Among those buried in the cemetery, which dates back to 1637, are Captain Richard Moore, a Mayflower passenger, and Justice John Hathorne, member of the witchcraft court and ancestor of Nathaniel Hawthorne. (It is said that Hawthorne added the "w" to the family name to escape the curse of being related to one of the witch trial judges.)

Continue on Charter Street to Front Street. Cross Front at the Old Town Hall. Walk up the brick steps to Derby Square. The Old Town Hall (18) was built in 1816 on the site of Elias Haskett Derby's "uptown" mansion. It housed the city government until 1837, when a new City Hall was built on Washington Street. The Salem Chamber of Commerce maintains offices on the main floor.

At the top of Derby Square, turn left at the Essex Street Pedestrian Mall. Cross Washington Street and continue to the corner of Essex and North Streets, which begins the McIntire Historic District (19) of notable 18th and 19th century buildings. (Salem has over 600 buildings under historic protection.) Samuel McIntire was a self-taught architect who designed or influenced many of the structures in this area. Look for posts and sidewalk plaques marked with a sheaf of wheat along the McIntire Historic District route.

On this corner is the dark, brooding Witch House (20), c.1642, the restored home of Jonathan Corwin, who was one of the Salem witch trial judges. (The house is open to the public seasonally.) Leave the Heritage Trail and continue down Essex Street. On the right is the Gothic-Revival First Church of Salem (21), which was built of block granite in 1835. The congregation was founded in 1629 as the first Congregational Church in America.

Next door is the Ropes Mansion (22) and gardens, part of the Peabody Essex Museum. The house is named for loyalist Judge Nathaniel Ropes who was killed during a Patriot attack. The house itself is not open for public tours, but the magnificent English-style gardens should not be missed. Designed by John Robinson in 1912, the Colonial Revival-style geometric beds are filled with roses, annuals, perennials, and rare plants from around the world. In presenting the property to the Peabody Essex Museum, the two Ropes sisters' wills decreed that the garden should be forever maintained, a lecture series given regularly and garden gates kept open 24-hours a day.

Following the prescribed route of the McIntire Historic District Walking Trail, traverse Essex, Cambridge, Broad, Pickering, Chestnut, Essex, and Monroe Streets. (You'll find details of the historic structures here in the trail brochure.) When you get to Federal Street, turn right. Federal Street was laid out in 1766 on a ridge above the North River. The river was re-channeled in the middle of the 19th century, which must have dismayed homeowners of the Greek Revival-, Federal-, and Georgian-Colonial-style mansions whose back yards often reached back to the river's edge. Number 80, the Georgian-style Peirce-Nichols House (23), now is a part of the Peabody Essex Museum. Jerathmiel Peirce co-owned the merchant ship *Friendship*, which he docked on the river behind his house. This house is believed to be Samuel McIntyre's first architectural commission.

From Federal, cross North Street to Lynde Street and the stately Wesley United Methodist Church (24), built in 1888. Follow Lynde past the Witch Dungeon Museum, which has live reenactments of witch trials, and turn right on Washington Street. At the Essex Street Pedestrian Mall, turn left and follow Essex to the Peabody Essex Museum's (25) main building *(Contact: 978/745-9500; 800/745-04054)*.

When the Peabody Museum and the Essex Institute merged in 1992, they became the largest museum north of Boston. Thirty galleries house the international collections, and historic houses and gardens are sprinkled throughout surrounding streets. The museum offers daily tours of the 1684 John Ward House, the Georgian Crowninshield-Bentley House at 126 Essex Street, and the Federal-style Gardner-Pingree house. The museum will expand dramatically by 2003, when a new wing is scheduled for completion. The addition will include six new galleries, an auditorium, a fully reconstructed 18th-century Chinese house with furnishings, and a new public garden and memorial park. Return to the Visitors Center, which is across from the museum.

Sedgwick Gardens at Long Hill

Ellery Sedgwick, editor of the *Atlantic Monthly*, and his wife, Mabel Cabot, purchased the 114-acre Long Hill estate for a summer home in 1916.

Information
Sedwick Gardens at Long Hill, 572 Essex St., Beverly, MA 01915; 978/921-1944.

Getting There
Take Rte. 128 north to exit 18 in Beverly. Go left on Rte. 22 (Essex St.) for 1 mile, bearing right at the fork. At the brick gatepost and sign on left, proceed to parking area.

First Steps
Pick up an 18-point self-guided tour brochure from the Trustees office at Long Hill mansion and meander through the estate's charming maze of gardens, arbors and ponds, which are open from 8am to sunset daily.

Sedgwick Gardens. Mabel Sedgwick, an accomplished horticulturist, designed the extensive original gardens here. She utilized both native and exotic species to create a vast array of unique blooming beds that she connected with wandering grass paths and tranquil woodland pools. After her death from cancer in 1937, the second Mrs. Sedgwick—an Englishwoman named Marjorie Russell—carried on. Herself a distinguished gardener, Majorie added to the gardens, maintaining the style created by her predecessor.

The mansion itself features intricate woodwork, carvings, 19th century Chinese wallpaper and other interesting architectural details. The Sedgwick children donated the estate to the Trustees of Reservations in 1979. A 2-mile walking trail begins at the back of the formal gardens and winds through the estate's woodlands, ending in the apple and pear orchard near Essex Street. In most years, the peak blooming period is from the second week in April to mid-May.

Seaport of Gloucester

Settled in 1623, Gloucester has snagged the title of America's oldest seaport, and, during the 19th century, it was our country's largest as well. Its major industry still fishing, Gloucester was put back on the map in 1999 when Hollywood filmed "The Perfect Storm" here. The film is based on Sebastian Junger's true story of the daring Gloucester fishermen of the Grand Banks.

Information
Gloucester Tourism Commission, 22 Poplar St., Gloucester, MA 01930; 800/649-6839; 978/281-8865; www.1.shore.net/~nya/gloucester.html.

Getting There
Take Rte. 128 north to exit 14 (Rte. 133, Essex Ave.). Turn right on Rte. 127. Follow maroon signs with the picture of a mariner, which will lead to Gloucester Visitor's Welcoming Center at Stage Fort Park, Hough Ave.

First Steps
Pick up a mapped brochure at the Visitor's Center at Stage Fort Park.

Seaport of Gloucester. The Gloucester Tourism Commission has produced four mini self-guided walks, called the Gloucester Maritime Trail: Settlers Walk, Downtown Heritage Trail, Vessels View and Painters Path.

Most interesting and picturesque is Settlers Walk, which winds along Gloucester Harbor. Beginning at Tablet Rock (near the Visitor's Center), where Gloucester was founded by the Massachusetts Bay Colony in 1623, the trail visits a cliff peninsula that was a Revolutionary War fort used for defense against the British. The seaside promenade ends at the Fishermen's Memorial. Sculpted by Leonard Craske, this memorial to all Gloucester fishermen—also known as "The Man at the Wheel"—was made immortal in the MGM classic movie, "Captains Courageous."

Vessels View is less charming—a busy, noisy area along the docks that is teeming with truck and automobile traffic. The only real picturesque area here is the Gordon Thomas Park, a small park at the head of the harbor that provides unobstructed views of the fishing fleet. Of note on the Downtown Heritage Trail is the Fitz Hugh Lane House, a stately granite structure on a knoll overlooking the harbor. Be sure to look for a pair of bronze sandals perched on a rock near the house. The sculpture is so realistic and casually placed that you will be certain someone lost his shoes. Cape Ann Historical Museum at 27 Pleasant Street (*Contact: 978/283-0455*) showcases works by nautical painter Fitz Hugh Lane, as well as other artists who lived and worked on Cape Ann, including Winslow Homer and Milton Avery.

On the other side of Gloucester Harbor, Painters Path follows city streets through the Rocky Neck Art Colony, a working artist enclave since the 1890s, whose unique shops and galleries are open seasonally. (You can get a water shuttle from the Gus Foote Park on Rogers Avenue that will traverse the harbor and drop you at the Rocky Neck Art Colony.)

Village of Rockport

Located on the northern tip of Cape Ann, the once sleepy fishing village of Rockport is now a bustling summer tourist magnet.

Information
Rockport Chamber of Commerce, 3 Main St., Rockport, MA 01966; 978/546-6575; 888/726-3922.

Getting There
Take Rte. 128 north to Gloucester. At the rotary, go three-quarters of the way around and take Rte. 127 to Broadway. Turn left on Mount Pleasant to Dock Square.

First Steps
Pick up a mapped walking guide at the Chamber office. "Footprints" offers day or evening lantern tours of Rockport that regale the folklore of the former fishing village. Hands-on children's tours are also available upon request. Contact them at 3 North Road, Bearskin Neck, 978/546-7730.

Village of Rockport. The quaintly picturesque Bearskin Neck area sports campy shops and art boutiques as well as a smattering of seasonally operated seafood restaurants. From Dock Square, a walk down South Road to Bradley Wharf takes you past the oft-painted Motif #1. The familiar red fishing shack, built in 1884, is said to be the most painted and photographed building in America. Your stroll will end at Tuna Wharf.

Originally built for the processing of codfish in 1884, the wharf was renamed for the village "cash-cow" of the 1950s—tuna. At the end of Bearskin Neck you can spot the offshore Sandy Water Breakwater.

You can explore another dimension of Rockport by following a different pedestrian spoke from Dock Square—Main Street. Lined with shops for a short distance, Main Street also is home to the Old Sloop Congregational Church, built in 1803. Legend has it that during the War of 1812, a British frigate fired a shot from the harbor that landed in the tower support and remains lodged there to this day. Rockport is compact. You'll only need about 35 minutes to hit the high spots, but allow several hours to explore the fascinating shops and to sample the not-to-be-missed Portuguese clam stew.

Babson Farm Quarry Trail at Halibut Point State Park

Halibut Point State Park encompasses, within its 54 acres, a dramatic rocky coastline with sweeping vistas of Cape Ann and the Atlantic Ocean.

Information
Halibut Point State Park, P.O. Box 710, Gott Ave., Rockport, MA 01966; 978/546-2997.

Getting There
Take Rte. 128 north to Gloucester. At the rotary, go three-quarters of the way around and take Rte. 127 for 6 miles to Rockport. Turn left on Gott Ave.

First Steps
Pick up a brochure and bird list at park headquarters in the World War II tower building near the quarry.

Babson Farm Quarry Trail. An interesting 1-mile path winds through the now-abandoned Babson Farm Granite Quarry. Cape Ann granite was quarried here for almost 100 years and then loaded aboard stone boats and taken to East Coast cities for building projects. Known as "Haul-About" Point, the quarry was last owned by the Rockport Granite Company.

Big blocks of granite litter both sides of the wooded paths that wind through the park. Of particular interest is a mooring stone—one of the first objects to be made of Cape Ann granite—which was recovered from the bottom of Rockport Harbor. Fishermen used the 2-ton stone to anchor an oak post, to which they could tie their boats. (An informational plaque explains the fascinating process in detail.)

The path leads to the gin-clear waters of the Babson Farm Quarry, then forks left past a crude sculpture garden and winds up to a cliff. Here you'll enjoy sweeping vistas of the seaside heath moors, the grassy balds, Cape Ann, and the Atlantic Ocean. The trail will lead you back to the parking lot.

Rainy Day Options

A quirky mixture of Romanesque, Gothic, and 15th-century French facades, the **Hammond Castle Museum** showcases John Hays Hammond III's eclectic collection of European art, as well as his inventions. The 8,200-pipe Hammond organ resides in the castle's Great Hall. Considered America's second greatest inventor after Thomas Edison, Hammond held more than 800 U.S. patents. *(Contact: Hammond Castle Museum, Raymond St., Gloucester, MA 01930; 978/283-2080.)*

Most of the schooners, ships, and fishing vessels that sailed from Cape Ann ports in the 19th century were built in Essex, which was renowned as North America's leading producer of fishing schooners. **The Essex Shipbuilding Museum** housed in the 1834 Central School, showcases exhibits that highlight the village's 300-year shipbuilding history. Ship modeling demonstrations and a working shipyard add to the museum's authenticity. *(Contact: Essex Shipbuilding Museum, 66 Main St., Essex, MA 01929; 978/768-7541.)*

"Beauport" Sleeper-McCann House, the former "summer cottage" of Henry Davis Sleeper—a leading interior decorator, founder of the American Field Service and friend of John Hammond—is a 45-room mansion filled with Sleeper's collection of European antique and Early American art. Now open to the public as a museum, Beauport's innovative decorative treatments are a testament to Sleeper's creative use of light and color.

(Contact: Beauport, Eastern Point Blvd., Gloucester, MA 01930; 978/283-0800.)

Lodging

The North Shore offers accommodations ranging from inns in historic ship captains' homes to manor houses and 19th-century grand hotels on the ocean. For more lodging options, consult the New England-wide accommodations websites and reservations services listed in "How to Use This Book" or check out Bed & Breakfast Reservations, North Shore/Greater Boston/Cape Cod, 800/832-2632; 617/964-1606; www.bnbinc.com.

Listed on the National Register of Historic Places, the three buildings that comprise the **Salem Inn** ($$+, 7 Summer St., Salem, 978/741-0680; 800/446-2995; www.saleminnma.com) rub architectural shoulders with the other elegant houses in Salem's McIntire Historic District. Captain Nathaniel West built the 4-story Federal-style brick West House in 1834. Curwen House, c.1854, is a 3-story Italianate Revival. John P. Peabody constructed the Colonial-style Peabody House in 1874. The inn's 39 guestrooms have been painstakingly and authentically restored to their former grandeur.

Situated directly across from the Fishermen's Memorial Statue, **The Harborview Inn** ($, 71 Western Ave., Gloucester, 978/283-2277; 800/299-6696; www.harborviewinn.com) was built in 1839 as a private home that once sheltered descendants of the Gortons of Gloucester Seafood Company. The six guest rooms are individually decorated with a potpourri of matching floral wallpapers and fabrics.

An 18th-century Federal-style mansion located in the heart of the historic district, **Harbor Light Inn** ($$+, 58 Washington St., Marblehead, 781/631-2186; www.harborlightinn.com) combines the elegance of yesteryear—hand carvings, polished brass, fine antiques, and reproductions, period paintings, oriental carpets, glowing fireplaces—with warm and gracious hospitality. The romantic inn offers 10 distinctive guest rooms.

Brimblecomb Hill B&B ($, 33 Mechanic St., Marblehead, 617/631-3172) is a 1721 Federal-style house located in the heart of Marblehead's historic district, only a couple of blocks from the harbor. This reasonably priced lodging, which welcomes children, offers one guest room with a private bath and two that share a bath.

Built by a sea captain in 1879, the **CoachHouse Inn** ($, 284 Lafayette St., Salem, 978/744-4092, 800/688-8689, www.salemweb.com/biz/coach-house) oozes with Victorian charm. Located two blocks from the harbor, the inn actually serves a continental breakfast in each antique-filled guest room, so you can break the fast in bed.

The Stepping Stone Inn ($, 19 Washington Square North, Salem, 978/741-8900, 800/338-3022; www.go.boston.com/sites/steppingstone8) fronts the historic Salem Common. Built in 1846 for naval officer Benjamin True, the restored home now offers overnight hospitality in one of eight distinctive period-decorated guest rooms.

A stay at the **Hawthorne Hotel** ($$+, 18 Washington Square, Salem, 978/744-4080, 800/678-8946, www.hawthornehotel.com) seems almost like sleeping in a museum, so filled is this Salem landmark with vintage photographs, clippings, and memorabilia. Built as a grand hotel in the 1920s, Hawthorne Hotel is beautifully restored and continues to live up to its long-standing reputation.

Just footsteps from the harbor, **Julietta House** ($, 84 Prospect St., Gloucester, 978/281-2300; www.juliettahouse.com) was built in the Italianate style in the 1860s by sea captain Benjamin Low. Purchased in 1905 and embellished by the wealthy Proctor sisters, Julietta House features a treasure trove of architectural details and the gentile ambiance of yesteryear.

Emerson Inn By The Sea ($-$$$, Phillips Ave., Rockport, 978/546-6321; 800/964-5550; www.emersoninnbythesea.com), built in the mid-19th century, is a New England classic. Situated on 1.5 oceanfront acres, this Federal-style inn resembles a grand summer hotel of yesteryear—sweeping seaside lawns; gracious parlors; formal gardens; covered verandahs. The inn humbly began as Pigeon Cove House in the 1860s, whose most famous boarder was Ralph Waldo Emerson.

Seacrest Manor ($+, 99 Marmion Way, Rockport, 978/546-2211; www.seacrestmanor.com), a c.1911 Georgian mansion, perches on 2 acres, high above the sea. Eight spacious guest rooms, some with decks affording an ocean view, welcome guests. Walls of the inn are peppered with the works of notable Rockport artists.

Food and Drink

Seafood takes center stage on the North Shore, for fishing has long been a major industry here. For more dining options, log on to www.northofboston.org.

You'll find it difficult to decide which is most spectacular at **The Landing** ($$, 81 Front St., Marblehead, 781/639-1266), the seafood-studded cuisine or the view. The Landing showcases both. Situated on State Street Landing at water's edge overlooking the harbor, The Landing offers stellar dinner selections and a light but innovative luncheon menu.

The colorful cuisine offered at the upscale **Lyceum Bar & Grill** ($$, 43 Church St., Salem 978/745-7665) is a mere reflection of the rich history secreted by the building itself. Purpose-built in the early 1800s as a debate forum, the Salem Lyceum has provided an oratorical stage for Daniel Webster, John Quincy Adams, and Henry David Thoreau. In 1877, Alexander Graham Bell gave the first public telephone demonstration here. The food here is as interesting as its history.

At the cavernous **McT's** ($+, 25 Rogers St., Gloucester, 978/282-0950) on the wharf, the name-of-the-game is piscatory. From the ubiquitous New England clam chowder to a bivalve bonanza, seafood lovers won't be disappointed here.

As the name implies, **Passports** ($$, 110 Main St., Gloucester, 978/281-3680) offers internationally inspired cuisine from all corners of the globe. The menu reads like a United Nations roadmap, and the cozy bistro atmosphere adds to the feeling that you might well be seated in Paris or maybe Singapore.

Garnering rave reviews all the way to Boston, **Red Raven's Love Noodle** ($$, 75 Congress St., Salem, 978/745-8558) offers innovative cuisine with attitude. Sort of Thailand meets the California Bay area, this fusion is augmented by a panoply of "love liquids"—specialty martinis with provocative monikers.

Situated near Salem's House of the Seven Gables, the creatively named **Pig's Eye** ($+, 148 Derby St., Salem, 978-741-4436, www.inapigseye.-com) bills itself as the "home of the perfect pint." Mondays and Tuesdays are Mexican nights, when the traditional menu is augmented with humongous burritos and other Tex-Mex fare.

Burgers, brick oven pizzas, and award-winning beer distinguish the **Salem Beer Works** ($, 278 Derby St. Salem, 978/745-2337) a brewpub that offers tours by appointment. Situated along the Salem Heritage Trail across from Pickering Wharf, this happening place has an outdoor patio and often features live entertainment.

For a panoply of seafood like you've never seen—or tasted—before, visit **Woodman's of Essex** ($, Rte. 133, Essex, 978/768-6451, 800/649-1773, www.yankeetradition@woodmans.com). A true family affair restaurant, Woodman's boasts that Lawrence "Chubby" Woodman invented the first fried clam more than 80 years ago, and the awards have been rolling in ever since. This is a must-do when visiting the North Shore.

The moniker **My Place by the Sea** ($, Bearskin Neck, Rockport, 978/546-9667), heralds the picture-postcard setting of this outdoor eatery. Situated on the ocean at the end of Bearskin Neck, the restaurant serves up dishes from an inventively eclectic menu along with a breathtaking view.

Opened in 1995, the creative seafood offerings at **The Sea Garden** ($$$, 44 Marmion Way, Rockport, 978/546-3471) have been garnering rave reviews as far as Boston and beyond. The small but exquisite menu features unique treatments of classic entrees. Be sure to bring your own wine or spirits, because Rockport is a dry town.

Plymouth, Cape Cod and the Islands

America traces its beginnings to this 70-mile horseshoe of land encircling Cape Cod Bay, a glacial deposit bestowed by Mother Nature eons ago. Here the Pilgrims first landed at the tip of Cape Cod at Provincetown, when bad weather and high seas forced them to abandon their journey to the northern Virginia colony near Hudson Bay. Winter was closing in, so they set sail again for a more protected harbor, landing on December 21, 1620, in Plymouth. Today Plymouth shines as the keeper of our historical origins. And, for centuries harboring a colorful maritime history as sailors and whalers, Cape Cod, Nantucket, and Martha's Vineyard today shimmer as a summer playground of sand, salt and sea.

Regional Information

Plymouth County Convention & Visitors Bureau, P.O. Box 1620, Pembroke, MA 02359; 781/826-3136; 800/292-4145; www.plymouth-1620.com.

Cape Cod Chamber of Commerce (Visitors Center—U.S. Hwy. 6, east, exit 6), P.O. Box 790, Hyannis, MA 02601; 508/862-0700; 888/33capecod; www.capecodchamber.org.

Getting There

By Air: Boston Logan, Providence (RI) Green, or New York LaGuardia airports offer connecting service to Cape Cod's Barnstable Municipal Airport in Hyannis, Martha's Vineyard Airport, and Nantucket Memorial Airport.

By Automobile: I-93 or I-95 to Rte. 3, to U.S. Hwy.6; or Rte. I-195 or I-495 to Rte. 25 to U.S. Hwy. 6.

By Bus: Plymouth & Brockton Bus Lines motorcoach service to Plymouth and Cape Cod from Boston's South Station or Logan Airport (508/746-0378 508/771-6191; www.p-b.com).

By Ferry to the Islands: (Parking for all ferry crossings is limited. Plan to arrive at least one hour before departure time, as you may have to park a distance away and take a shuttle.)

• **Hy-Line Ferry and High Speed Catamaran to Nantucket and Oak Bluffs, Martha's Vineyard from Hyannis** (508/778-2600; 888/778-1132; www.hy-linecruises.com.): Cross Sagamore Bridge and take U.S. Hwy. 6 to exit 6, then south on Rte. 132 to the airport rotary. Take second right off the rotary to Barnstable Rd. Go through Main St. lights (road becomes Ocean St.) and continue straight at the South St. light. Continue on Ocean

St. for .25 mile and look to the left for Hy-Line Cruises.
• **Steamship Authority Ferry to Nantucket** from Hyannis (508/477-8600): Cross Sagamore Bridge and take U.S. Hwy. 6 to exit 7, Willow St. Turn left off exit, cross Rte. 28 at the lights and proceed to E. Main St. At stop sign, take a right on Main St. and the first left onto Pleasant St. The ferry leaves from South Street Dock at the corner of Pleasant and South.
• The **Steamship Authority Ferry to Vineyard Haven,** Martha's Vineyard from Woods Hole (508/477-8600; www.islandferry.com): At the Bourne Bridge rotary, take Rte. 28 south. Follow ferry signs to Falmouth/Woods Hole on Rte. 28.
• **The Island Queen to Oak Bluffs, Martha's Vineyard** from Falmouth Harbor (508/548-4800; www.islandqueen.com): At the Bourne Bridge rotary take Rte. 28 south. Turn left at first traffic light to Falmouth. Proceed for 1 mile. At the second light, turn right on Davis Straits and then proceed .25 mile to dock.

Historic Plymouth

All American schoolchildren study the Pilgrim story, look to the Mayflower as a national icon, and regard Plymouth Rock as legendary. So it is no surprise that the historic village of Plymouth—where the English separatists finally concluded their long journey and set up the first Pilgrim colony—attracts visitors the world over. All the major players are represented here, from the settlement's Governor William Bradford to Massasoit of the Wampanoag tribe.

Plymouth Rock, itself, has endured a turbulent history. The settlers never mentioned the rock in writings of 1621. In fact, it wasn't until 1741 that the rock became an issue. A debate arose when it was suggested that a new town wharf be built over a rock that Mayflower descendent Thomas Faunce claimed had been used by his forefathers as a disembarkation stone. The rock was spared but, in 1774, Colonel Theophilus Cotton used 30 yoke of oxen in an attempt to move the stone to a more public place and broke it in two pieces. The bottom remained embedded at the wharf and the top half was moved to Town Square, where it remained until 1834. After a short tenure within an iron fence at Pilgrim Hall, the two sections of Plymouth Rock were joined in 1880 and placed under a Victorian canopy at the harbor. Here it lay until 1920, when it was removed and repositioned under an elaborate portico in the redesigned

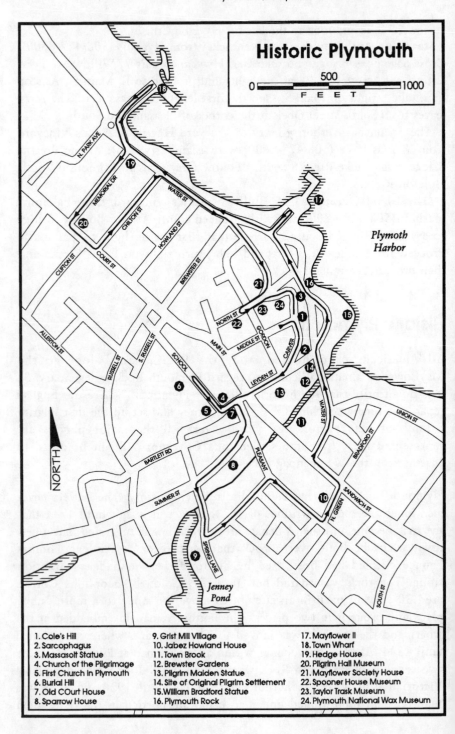

Historic Plymouth

0 — 500 — 1000
FEET

Plymoth Harbor

NORTH

Jenney Pond

1. Cole's Hill
2. Sarcophagus
3. Massasoit Statue
4. Church of the Pilgrimage
5. First Church in Plymouth
6. Burial Hill
7. Old COurt House
8. Sparrow House
9. Grist Mill Village
10. Jabez Howland House
11. Town Brook
12. Brewster Gardens
13. Pilgrim Maiden Statue
14. Site of Original Pilgrim Settlement
15. William Bradford Statue
16. Plymouth Rock
17. Mayflower II
18. Town Wharf
19. Hedge House
20. Pilgrim Hall Museum
21. Mayflower Society House
22. Spooner House Museum
23. Taylor Trask Museum
24. Plymouth National Wax Museum

waterfront in 1921. The tide now washes around Plymouth Rock, much as it must have in 1620, but preservation has tampered with ambiance, because the stone is encased in a clear protective shield.

Information
Plymouth County Convention & Visitors Bureau, P.O. Box 1620, Pembroke, MA 02359; 781/826-3136; 800/292-4145; www.plymouth-1620.com.

Getting There
I-95 or I-93 south to Rte. 3 south, exit 6, to U.S. Hwy. 44 (Samoset St.). Turn right on Court St., which turns into Main St. Take Main to Middle St. and park in lot or on the street.

First Steps
Most of the historic houses and museums along this 3-mile walk are open seasonally, usually from late Apr. or early May to mid-Oct. An information booth on Water St. along the route provides maps and brochures of other Plymouth attractions. Colonial Lantern Tours offers guided tours nightly from Apr. through Nov. (98 Water St., 508/747-4161; 800/698-5636).

Historic Plymouth. Begin your tour of historic Plymouth from the top of Cole's Hill (1), which enjoys a commanding view of the harbor, the Mayflower, and the village. During their first brutal winter, the colonists stealthily buried their dead here during the night, then planted corn atop the graves to hide their plight from the Native Americans. A sarcophagus (2) on the hill contains some of the skeletal remains. Also on the hill, a statue honors Massasoit (3), the Wampanoags' sachem, an ally and protector of the Pilgrims in 1621.

From Carver Street, turn right on Leyden, then Cross Main Street and head up the hill to Church of the Pilgrimage (4). This Congregational Church pays tribute to the original separatists. Continue on Leyden to the First Church in Plymouth, Unitarian Universalist (5), at the base of Burial Hill. This was the site of the Pilgrims' first meetinghouse in 1620, where a continuous ministry has been maintained ever since.

Follow the stone steps up Burial Hill (6), a steep hill whose summit was the site of the Pilgrims' watchtower and fort. Many Mayflower passengers are buried here, including William Bradford and William and Mary Brewster. Retrace your steps to the front of the church. Bear right to the Old Court House (7), the oldest wooden courthouse in America. It was the governmental colony site until 1749, then the county courthouse until 1820. (John Adams tried and won several cases here.) The restored and preserved structure now houses the Court House Museum.

Turn right on Market Street, then right again on Summer Street to #42, the Richard Sparrow House (8), c.1640. This is Plymouth's oldest house, now a gallery, open to the public. From Summer turn on Spring Lane to John Jenney Grist Mill Village (9), where a working replica of a water-powered mill and a museum of exhibits tells the story of the original 1636 mill used by the Pilgrims to grind corn, wheat, and rye. Exit the gristmill, taking the path to Pleasant Street, and walk down North Green. Turn left on Main Street to the Jabez Howland House (10), c.1667, the only remaining home of a Mayflower passenger. It is now a museum filled with 17th-century furnishings.

Cross Main to Water Street and walk to Town Brook (11), whose spring waters first attracted the Pilgrims to settle here. The brook runs through Brewster Gardens (12). The Pilgrim Maiden Statue (13) stands in this tiny park, dedicated to the spunky spirit of the Mayflower women. The original Pilgrim settlement was situated at the corner of Water and Leyden Streets (14), on the slope of land leading to Town Brook.

Walking below Coles Hill, cross Water Street to walk along the harbor. The William Bradford Statue (15) stands on the right, a life-size likeness of the former governor of the Plymouth Colony. A little further down, beneath a white-pillared canopy, under glass, lies the famed Plymouth Rock (16). Two-thirds of the stone is underground.

The highlight of historic Plymouth is undoubtedly a visit to the Mayflower II (17), a full-scale, in-water reproduction of the original ship. Costumed interpreters portray actual passengers and crew in a re-enactment of the fateful voyage of 1620 (see Plimoth Plantation in this section), which brought 102 passengers to the New World.

Continue down Water Street to the Town Wharf (18) to view the fishing fleet. Backtrack to126 Water Street and take the path to the Hedge House (19), a c.1809 Federal-style home that is now a museum showcasing porcelains and other items illustrating the 19th-century China trade that helped Plymouth to prosper. Exit left onto Memorial Drive to Court Street.

The Pilgrim Hall Museum (20), 75 Court Street, is thought to be America's oldest public museum. A Greek-Revival structure dating to 1824, the building is chock-a-block with authentic Pilgrim memorabilia, furniture, and artwork. Turn left on Chilton Street, then right on Water and angle onto Winslow Street. The Mayflower Society House (21), headquarters since 1941 of the Society of Mayflower Descendents, is a museum showcasing formal gardens, a "flying" staircase, and nine antique-furnished rooms. Edward Winslow constructed the building in 1754. Cross and take North Street to #27, the Spooner House Museum (22), c.1749. Now a museum displaying authentic furnishings from colonial times to the 20th century, this was the home of the Spooner family for almost 200 years.

Follow North Street toward Coles Hill, stopping at #35, Taylor Trask Museum of Early American History (23), c.1829. The museum highlights the lives of former residents of North Street, Plymouth's second oldest street. Peek into the Plymouth National Wax Museum (24), if you like, where 150 wax characters tell the Pilgrim story. A few steps further puts you back where you began at Coles Hill.

Plimoth Plantation

Plimoth Plantation is a living history museum that re-creates the Pilgrim colony of Plymouth. Costumed interpreters go about the daily tasks of the colonists, bringing the settlement to life. They remain in character at all times, invoking a 17th-century English dialect as they chat with visitors.

Information
Plimoth Plantation, P.O. Box 1620, Plymouth, MA 02360; 508/746-1622; www.plimoth.org. Plimoth Plantation is open 9 AM to 5 PM, daily, from Apr. through Nov.

Getting There
Take Rte. 3 to Plimoth Plantation Hwy., exit 4, then follow the signs.

Plimoth Plantation. Begin your tour of this multifaceted living-history museum, Plimoth Plantation, by viewing the 15-minute orientation film in the Visitors Center. Then head up the hill to the Carriage House Crafts Center, where a changing rota of artisans demonstrate such 17th-century pursuits as basket weaving, lace making, shoe making, and furniture carving. The authentically produced goods are sold in the adjoining gift shop.

Follow the path from the Crafts Center to the 1627 Pilgrim Village, the centerpiece of Plimoth Plantation. As you pass through the gates of the stockade, you will take a leap back in time. Wander through the dirt paths of the colony and you'll glean a voyeuristic peek into the tiny shelters of such notables as William Bradford, William Brewster, John Alden, and Myles Standish. Watch them wash clothes, cook, tend to the animals, weed the garden, even build new structures. Outgoing and gregarious, the colonists talk about their difficult lives in the New World.

Leave the protection of the stockade and venture down the Eel River Nature Walk to Hobbamock's Homesite. The boardwalk affords great views of Cape Cod Bay and Eel River estuary. Staff and native interpreters dress in Native American attire but use modern-day English in their re-enactment of life in a Wampanoag settlement, explaining Hobbamock's culture and his role as guide and adviser to the colonists.

On the waterfront in the village of Plymouth, adjacent to Plymouth Rock, is another part of Plimoth Plantation's living history museum, the Mayflower II. This re-creation of the famed Pilgrim ship combines exhibits, costumed interpreters, artisans who work on ship repair, and occasional demonstrations and on-board lectures to explain 17th-century navigation and the Pilgrim's voyage to America. Admission is included in your ticket to Plimoth Plantation.

Heritage Plantation—Cape Cod

Secreted away on 76 gloriously blooming acres in Sandwich, Heritage Plantation showcases three distinctive museums sprinkled amid the massive horticultural wonderland of the former Charles O. Dexter estate. Founded by the family of Josiah Kirby Lilly, Jr., Heritage Plantation shares the Lillys' vast personal collections—and those of other contributors—with a fascinated public.

Information

Heritage Plantation, Grove and Pine Streets, Sandwich, MA 02563; (508) 888-3300; www.heritageplantation.org. Heritage Plantatation is open daily from Mother's Day to mid-Oct.

Getting There

Go over the Sagamore Bridge on U.S. Hwy. 6, then take exit 2, Rte. 130 north to Sandwich village. Take a sharp left onto Grove St. (across from the Sandwich Glass Museum) and continue on Grove St. to the main gates.

Heritage Plantation. This is more than just a cultural "walk in the park." Heritage Plantation is situated on a rolling landscape abutting Upper Shawmee Lake that Charles Dexter transformed from an underutilized farm into a rhododendron showplace between 1921 and 1943, during his retirement years. He hybridized myriad varieties of rhododendrons, which now bear his name, and annually planted thousands of seedlings throughout the woods and fields of his property.

The resulting "forests" of 30-foot-high rhododendrons usually burst into full flowering regalia from Memorial Day through the first two weeks in June. Two miles of cedar-chip paths meander through the towering masses of blooms and a series of formal gardens. The herb, hosta, daylily, heather, and holly gardens take turns as headliners throughout the season.

J.K. Lilly III bought the Dexter estate to create a museum in which to house and display his antique automobile collection, undoubtedly the centerpiece of Heritage Plantation, which opened in 1969. He built a replica of the Hancock Village (Mass.) Shaker Round Barn as a circular forum to showcase his 37 pristine automobile classics.

A paved road winds throughout Heritage Plantation, a walker's paradise, linking the museums and the miles of rhododendron-lined paths. Lilly III built the Military Museum to house his father's antique firearms collection. The armament illustrates the range of firepower available from colonial times through the Spanish American War. He then bought back Lilly Jr.'s amazing assemblage of military miniatures from the Smithsonian

Institution, ultimately displaying them in the museum's lower level. About 2,000 lead soldiers are amassed as representative regiments, dating from 1620 to the beginning of the 20th century.

The three galleries of the Art Museum fan out from an authentic 1912 carousel. Built by Charles I.D. Looff, who also built the first Coney Island carousel in 1876, the antique attraction offers guests rides round yesteryear, on demand. The fascinating Folk Art Gallery features collections of carved shop signs and shipboard figures, primitive hand-sculpted weathervanes, Nantucket lightship baskets, and carved scrimshaw. The Lower Gallery showcases an extensive collection of Currier and Ives lithographs, a rookery of carved birds and decoys, Lilly III's antique toy collection, and a gravestone art exhibit. The Changing Exhibitions Gallery features a special exhibit every year.

Cape Cod National Seashore

President John F. Kennedy established the Cape Cod National Seashore in 1961, forever preserving 20,000 acres of coastline between the villages of Chatham and Provincetown.

Information
Cape Cod National Seashore, 99 Marconi Site Rd., Wellfleet, MA 02667; 508/349-3785.

Getting There
Take U.S. Hwy. 6 to the outer Cape towns of Eastham, Wellfleet, Truro, and Provincetown.

First Steps
Pick up a "Self-Guiding Nature Trails" brochure from the Salt Pond Visitor Center, U.S. Hwy. 6 in Eastham, between 9am and 4:30pm, which lists directions to each of the 11 trailheads. (Contact: 508/362-3225.) At most trailheads you will find an interpretive map of the specific walking route.

Cape Cod National Seashore. Eleven self-guided trails traverse this preserve, offering walkers a birds-eye view of the fragile spits of shoreline that make up the outer Cape. Flushed daily by the tides, the salt ponds and marshes of the National Seashore act as a nursery for quahogs, oysters, mussels, and fish as well as hosting shorebirds and wading birds. Wear good walking shoes; apply insect repellent; bring plenty of water; and wear a hat.

Cranberries

The cranberry is as indigenous to North America as are the Cape Cod Nauset Indians who first discovered the little red berry, which they called ibimi, or bitter berry. Native Americans used the berry to make pemmican, a high-protein combination of crushed cranberries, dried venison, and melted fat. They also treated arrow wounds with the berry and used the berry juice as a dye for rugs and blankets. Pilgrims named the fruit cranberry, or "crane berry," thinking the white blossom looked like the head of a crane.

The berries, which grow on low-lying vines in beds know as bogs, have been cultivated in Massachusetts since 1810, when Captain Henry Hall, of Dennis, noticed that wild cranberries in his bogs grew better when the wind covered them with sand. He transplanted his cranberry plants, put a fence around them, covered them with sand, and reaped a bountiful harvest. Commercial harvesting began on Cape Cod in 1816; Massachusetts now is the leading producer of cranberries. Harvest time is from mid-September through early November, when the bogs become a scarlet sea of berries. Bogs are visible from the roadway in many areas of Cape Cod, Nantucket, and the south shore of Massachusetts, and cranberry harvest festivals abound in the autumn. For more information, contact the Cape Cod Cranberry Growers Association: 508/295-4895

Eastham: The Fort Hill Trail (1.5 miles) connects with the Red Maple Swamp Trail (.5-mile boardwalk through the swamp), offering great views of Nauset Marsh and Nauset Spit and the Atlantic Ocean. (When charted by explorer Champlain in 1605, Nauset Marsh was a navigable bay.) The Buttonbush Trail (.25 mile) begins next to the Salt Pond Visitor Center, winding through the forest and across Buttonbush Pond via boardwalk bridge. The Nauset Marsh Trail (1 mile) traverses the edge of Nauset Marsh and Salt Pond, originally a freshwater kettle pond and now a tidal pond. From here you can opt to detour on the 1.5-mile Cedar Banks hiking trail, which will take you to Coast Guard Beach. Doane Loop Trail is a .5-mile paved trail, wheelchair accessible, that winds through pine and oak forests and offers a view of Nauset Marsh.

Wellfleet: The Atlantic White Cedar Swamp Trail (1.25 miles) meanders through stunted pines and oaks and emerges at a boardwalk that takes you through the picturesque swamp. The trail returns via an uphill sand road. The National Seashore's most difficult trail is also its most spectacular: The Great Island Trail (6 miles) follows a soft-sand stretch between Great Island and Great Beach Hill, then through an aged pitch pine forest. The views from Jeremy Point Overlook are magnificent, and part of the trail leads past a colonial-era tavern site. You'll have to check the tides for this one.

Truro: The Cranberry Bog Trail (.5 mile) explores an abandoned commercial cranberry operation. The Small Swamp Trail (.75 mile) leads through a forest once cleared as farmland by Pilgrim farmers. The Pilgrim Spring Trail (.75 mile), a short loop through pine and oak forest, highlights a freshwater spring representative of the type from which the Pilgrims would have drunk upon their arrival.

Provincetown: The Beech Forest Trail (1 mile) hugs the dunes, goes around Beech Forest Pond and ultimately leads into a beech forest.

Shining Sea Bikepath—Cape Cod

Shining Sea Bikepath is built over the roadbed of the former Old Colony Railroad, which brought provisions to Woods Hole and for Martha's Vineyard via steamship transport between 1872 and 1959. Shining Sea is named in honor of Katherine Lee Bates, a Cape Codder born in Falmouth in 1859. Her poem, "America the Beautiful" was the foundation of America's patriotic song by the same name.

Information
Falmouth Chamber of Commerce, 20 Academy Lane, Falmouth, MA 02531; 508/548-8550; 800/526-8532; www.falmouth-capecod.com.

Getting There
Take Rte. 3 to the Sagamore Bridge Rotary. Follow signs to Buzzards Bay/Falmouth, then cross the Bourne Bridge. Take Rte. 28 south to Falmouth. Fork right onto Locust St. Entry to the bikeway's parking is 1 mile on the right, just beyond the Pin Oak Way sign on the left.

Shining Sea Bikepath. Connecting the Cape Cod villages of Falmouth and Woods Hole, the Shining Sea Bikepath (3.3 miles each way) is a great route for walkers too. The paved bikeway follows the footpath of the seafaring Wampanoag tribe through 21.7 acres of locust, cedar, maple, and oak forests and through coastal acreage bordering salt marsh, salt ponds, and Vineyard Sound.

You'll see marsh vegetation such as purple loose strife and green willow, and clumps of bishop and rose hips, dune grass, and evening primroses. Swans and otters punctuate Salt Pond and Oyster Pond, and, because Cape Cod is on an aviary flyway, you'll be able to spot wide-ranging species of birds, such as mallards and buffleheads; herons, egrets, and osprey; and maybe even a yellow-breasted chat.

The Island of Nantucket

An Algonquin word meaning "far away island," Nantucket beckons walkers with its cobblestone streets and compact village. Purchased by Tristram Coffin in 1659 for the sum of 30 pounds and 2 beaver hats, the island—30 miles off the coast of Cape Cod—was named Nantucket and became a part of Massachusetts in 1795. By the 1820s and 1830s Nantucket was enjoying the "golden age of whaling," the capital of a thriving industry that captured sperm whales and marketed by-products around the world. Population of the island burgeoned to 7,000 people, and more than 60 whalers and 75 trading vessels regularly set off from its bustling port. Wealthy ship owners built grand Federal and Greek-Revival mansions on Upper Main Street, while the ships' captains lived in bungalows on Orange Street. The deathblow to whaling came in the 1850s when petroleum oil was first commercially produced, and Nantucket became a ghost town. Today Nantucket again is thriving as an upmarket resort community, whose resident population soars with the temperature.

Information
Nantucket Island Chamber of Commerce, 48 Main St., Nantucket, MA 02554; 508/228-1700; www.nantucketchamber.org.

Getting There
The Hy-Line Ferry docks at Straight Wharf and the Steamship Authority docks at Steamboat Wharf offer ferry service to Nantucket.

First Steps
Stop at the Whaling Museum on Broad St. to purchase a visitor pass for admission to the museums and historical properties encountered along our walk.

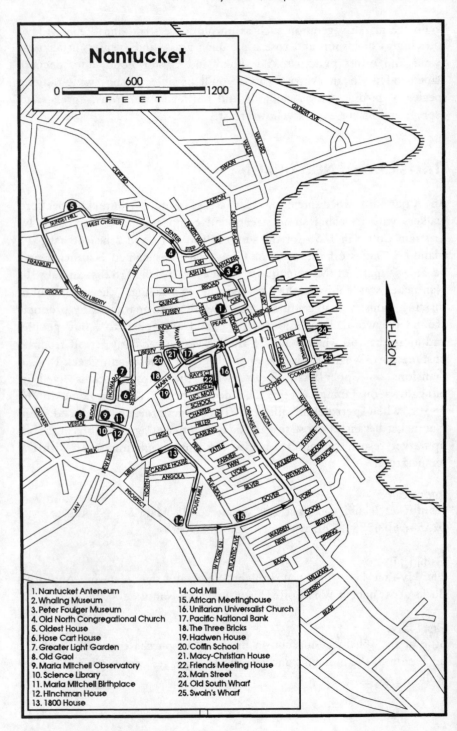

Nantucket

0 600 1200
F E E T

NORTH

1. Nantucket Anteneum
2. Whaling Museum
3. Peter Foulger Museum
4. Old North Congregational Church
5. Oldest House
6. Hose Cart House
7. Greater Light Garden
8. Old Gaol
9. Maria Mitchell Observatory
10. Science Library
11. Maria Mitchell Birthplace
12. Hinchman House
13. 1800 House
14. Old Mill
15. African Meetinghouse
16. Unitarian Universalist Church
17. Pacific National Bank
18. The Three Bricks
19. Hadwen House
20. Coffin School
21. Macy-Christian House
22. Friends Meeting House
23. Main Street
24. Old South Wharf
25. Swain's Wharf

Historic Nantucket. Walk up Straight Wharf—which is lined with a potpourri of inviting boutiques, shops, and restaurants—and turn right on South Water Street. Turn left on India Street to the Nantucket Atheneum (1), c.1847. One of the oldest libraries in the United States, the Atheneum's 40,000 volumes feature a treasure trove of Nantucket maritime history and interesting artifacts. Retrace your steps to South Water and turn right on Broad Street to the Whaling Museum (2). The Whaling Museum, built in 1847 as a spermaceti candle factory, displays historical memorabilia of the whaling industry, along with the skeleton of a 40-foot finback whale and artifacts from the ship *Essex*. The *Essex*, rammed by an angry sperm whale, was the inspiration for Herman Melville's *Moby Dick*.

Stop next at the Peter Foulger Museum (3). Here, the Nantucket Historical Association showcases its collections of artifacts, maps, charts, ship's logs, and photographs related to Nantucket's maritime history. Turn right on North Water Street, where former ship captains' bungalows, dating to the mid 1700s, flank the cobblestone street and brick sidewalks. Turn left on Step Lane, then right on Centre Street to #62, Old North Congregational Church (4), 1834. Climb the tower for a panoramic view of the sea and the entire island.

Angle left onto West Chester Street, then right on Sunset to the Oldest House (5). Built in 1686 by Peter Coffin and John Gardner as a wedding present to their marrying children, Jethro and Mary, this 17th-century saltbox, known as the Jethro Coffin House, is furnished with period artifacts.

Turn left on North Liberty, then jog right onto Gardner Street. Stop at Hose Cart House (6), erected in 1886, where you'll see "Cataract #6," a hand-pumper fire cart, as well as some vintage photographs of fire-fighting operations of old Nantucket. Detour down Howard Street to the charming Greater Light Garden (7), which fronts a former 18th-century livestock barn. Go back to Gardner and turn right onto brick-paved Upper Main Street.

Cut down Bloom Street—whose rose covered residences sit directly on the former horse path—to Vestal Street. Turn right to the Old Gaol (8), built in 1805 from heavy wooden timbers and iron straps. Murderers, drunks, and embezzlers were incarcerated here until 1933. Turn left down Vestal to the Maria Mitchell Observatory (9), c.1908, where you can get a guided tour, examine an outdoor solar system model, and view sunspots with a telescope. The Science Library (10), next door, houses a vast array of Mitchell's scientific journals and documents. Across the street is the Maria Mitchell Birthplace (11). Nantucket native Maria Mitchell was America's first woman astronomer (1818-1889), who sighted a comet from a telescope placed atop the Pacific National Bank on Main Street. The Quaker-design building and its contents typify Nantucket in the mid-19th century. The house features the only public rooftop "widow's walk" on Nantucket. (You'll need to purchase an admission ticket for these attractions, which also includes access to Hinchman House and the Maria Mitchell Aquarium on Washington Street).

At the corner of Vestal and Milk Streets, stop off at the Hinchman House (12), a natural history museum that displays native Nantucket flora and fauna. Walk down New Dollar Lane, which is lined with nicely restored clapboard houses that bear understated brass historical plaques. Jog left on Mill Street to the 1800 House (13), the house of Nantucket's 19th-century sheriff, Jeremiah Lawrence. Turn right on Pleasant, then right on South Mill Street to the Old Mill (14), which was built in 1746 and features handcrafted wooden gears. The mill still grinds corn daily in season.

Turn left onto West York and continue to Pleasant Street. On the corner is the post-and-beam African Meetinghouse (15), c.1827, the second-oldest structure in America built by free African Americans for their own use. (Slavery was abolished on Nantucket in 1773.) Walk down York Street and turn left onto Orange, continuing to the white-spired Unitarian Universalist Church, circa 1809 (16). Nantucket tradition dictates that a bride and groom climb the Old South Bell Tower and together ring the bell after the ceremony.

Turn left on Main Street at the early Federal-style Pacific National Bank building (17), c.1818. This portion of Main Street is lined with 19th-century mansions owned by Nantucket's whaling-ship owners and wealthy merchants. The "Three Bricks" (18)—#93, #95, #97—were built by Joseph Starbuck for his three sons. Stop at #96, Hadwen House (19), a large pillared Greek Revival built in 1845 by William Hadwen, who owned the village's candle factory. The house and gardens have been restored to their former splendor.

Walk back down Main to Winter Street. Turn left to Coffin School (20), founded in 1827 to educate descendents of Tristram Coffin, one of Nantucket's first settlers. (Legend has it that about 8,000 students qualified for admission.) The former school now is the home of Egan Institute of Maritime Studies, which houses maritime memorabilia. Proceed to Liberty Street and turn right to the Macy-Christian House (21), built in 1745 as the home of prosperous merchant Nathaniel Macy. The home features period-decorated rooms and a collection of 19th-century decorative arts. Turn down Walnut Street to Main, then right on Fair Street to the Fair Street Museum and Friends Meeting House (22), a former 1838 Quaker school that was converted to a meeting house in 1864. It now houses exhibits and collections of the Nantucket Historical Association.

Retrace your steps to Main Street (23) and head back toward the wharf, exploring the wonderful boutiques and specialty shops that line both sides of the cobbled thoroughfare. Don't miss the two pharmacies located side by side, each offering an old-fashioned soda fountain. Stop for an egg cream before you head back to the ferry. Be sure to detour to Old South Wharf (24) and Swain's Wharf (25), whose sea shanties and loading docks have been reinvigorated as shops and gardens.

The Island of Martha's Vineyard

Martha's Vineyard lies five miles south of Cape Cod between Vineyard and Nantucket Sounds and the Atlantic Ocean. Captain Bartholomew Gosnold discovered and named the vine-covered island in 1602 (the identity of "Martha" is still disputed). Farmed for a time, Martha's Vineyard—96 square miles—derived its early prosperity, like Nantucket, from the sea. A thriving resort community since the end of the 18th century, Martha's Vineyard has been made infamous in the last decades by the summer antics of the Kennedys and Clintons. The three major population centers down-island—Vineyard Haven, Oak Bluffs, and Edgartown—grew up surrounding fine harbors. The up-island Vineyard—Tisbury, Chilmark, and Aquinnah—is more rural. The spectacular terrain of the Vineyard's cliffs, streams, ponds, and beaches sets a dramatic stage for the sprinkling of quaint little villages.

Information

Martha's Vineyard Chamber of Commerce, P.O. Box 1698, Vineyard Haven, MA 02568-1698; 508/693-0085; 508/693-4486; www.mvy.com.

Getting There

From the ferry docks in Oak Bluffs or Vineyard Haven, take the Yellow Line Public Bus, which offers daily service between the six towns of Martha's Vineyard, or rent a car from one of the national companies that maintain offices adjacent to the ferry docks. Martha's Vineyard is so large that, unlike Nantucket, on-island transportation is necessary between the villages.

Historic Edgartown

Edgartown is a tiny, elegant village of meticulously maintained, mostly white Colonial, Federal, and Greek-Revival ship captains' homes that still exudes the aura of the bygone era when it was the principal whaling port of Martha's Vineyard. Hitting its pinnacle of prosperity between 1830 and 1845, this compact community's high notes can be easily explored on foot in a couple of unguided hours.

Information

Martha's Vineyard Preservation Trust, 99 Main St., Edgartown; 508/627-8017.
Martha's Vineyard Historical Society, School and Cooke Streets, Edgartown; 508/627-4441.

Getting There

From the ferry dock in Vineyard Haven take Edgartown Rd; from Oak Bluffs take Beach Rd. to Edgartown Rd.

First Steps

Stop first at the Dr. Daniel Fisher House, headquarters of the Martha's Vineyard Preservation Trust, at the corner of Pease Point Way and Main St., to pick up a map of Edgartown.

Historic Edgartown. Martha's Vineyard Preservation Trust conducts seasonal tours of the Fisher House, a restored Federal-style residence, as well as of the Vincent House Museum, next door, and the Old Whaling Church. Built in 1672 and occupied by generations of the same family for 250 years, the Vincent House still contains original brickwork, hardware and woodwork. The Greek-Revival-style Old Whaling Church, constructed in 1843 and showcasing six imposing columns, is now Martha's Vineyard's performing arts center, offering concerts, plays, and film classics.

A walk down Main Street passes the picturesque courthouse, St. Elizabeth Church, and the Edgartown Town Hall before quickly turning into a tourist haven of shops and boutiques. At the end of Main, turn left on North Water Street and walk along the harbor to Edgartown Lighthouse, where a short hike through the beach grass nets a panoramic view of the sea. North Water Street, and its sister on the other side of Main, South Water, are flanked by a sentry of elegant historic residences. Backtrack to South Water and look for Edgartown's famous Chinese pagoda tree, planted as a seedling by Captain Thomas Milton.

From South Water Street, Cooke Street leads to the Historical Society's Vineyard Museum complex (corner of Cook and School Streets). The Thomas Cooke House, c.1765, showcases 12 rooms chockablock with antiques, scrimshaw, ship models, and whaling gear. Dedicated to Martha's Vineyard's marriage to the sea, the Captain Francis Pease House features three galleries of exhibits highlighting the island's colorful history. The Carrriage Shed houses an 1854 fire engine, a Norman's Land whaleboat, and an old peddler's wagon, among other Vineyard memorabilia. The 1856 two-story fresnal lens and clockwork that was removed from Gay Head Lighthouse in 1952 is also on display at the museum. You can examine its inner workings and actually watch the light turn on as the sun goes down.

Oak Bluffs Camp Meeting Grounds/Tabernacle

Reminiscent of a stage set for Alice in Wonderland, the Camp Meeting Grounds and Tabernacle of Oak Bluffs combine a fascinating history with a riot of Easter-egg hued, gingerbread-bedecked Victorian cottages.

Information
Martha's Vineyard Camp-Meeting Association, Oak Bluffs; 508/693-0525

Getting There
From the ferry dock, take Lake Ave. to Dukes County Ave.

Oak Bluffs Camp Meeting Grounds/Tabernacle. Beginning in 1835, an Oak Bluffs grove and pasture became the annual meeting spot for groups of Methodists on a summer prayer retreat. Referred to as the Wesleyan Grove, the Oak Bluffs Camp Ground meetings became such a phenomenon that, by the 1850s, more than 12,000 people were staying and praying in communal tents.

Over the years, the growing number of faithful pitched family tents, then began building wooden cottages in a spiderweb-like spoke from the central hub of an all-steel tabernacle structure built in 1879. The tiny doll-like cottages—which incongruously combine stained glass, turrets, and all manner of Gothic detail—were elaborately decorated with wooden curls, scrolls, and cut-outs called "gingerbread" and painted the riotous colors of a circus clown.

By the end of the 19th century, more than 30,000 "campers" attended Illumination Night, the annual closing ceremony of the summer season, marked by the simultaneous lighting of a fairyland of Japanese lanterns strung throughout the Tabernacle, from tree to tree and from cottage to cottage. Today, Oak Bluffs creates an annual Illumination Night on a predetermined night in mid August. As in the days of the Methodist camp meetings, the program begins with a community sing, and the Vineyard Haven Band plays. Some of the lanterns date back more than 100 years, many others are now electrified, but the illumination is still dramatically choreographed.

Walk through the maze of narrow lanes that encompass the tabernacle green, and you'll marvel at the individuality of the closely packed cottages, which often stand only three feet apart. Today, their colorful history pristinely preserved, the gingerbread houses are private residences bearing such colorful names as: "Clamity Cottage," "Lavender and Old Lace," "Oops," "Lullaby" and, yes, "Alice's Wonderland." A unique enclave that spawned the development of Oak Bluffs as a summer vacation mecca, this is history in Technicolor.

Rainy Day Options

Cranberry World, sponsored by Ocean Spray Cranberries Inc., traces the history of the cranberry, from colonial times to the present, by means of a fascinating interactive program, an outdoor demonstration bog, and exhibits of the growing, harvesting, and marketing of Cape Cod's favorite berry. *(Contact: Cranberry World Visitors Center, Water St., Plymouth, 508/747-2350).*

The granite tower at the **Provincetown Museum**, the tallest all-granite structure in the United States, commemorates the Pilgrim's historic landing on Cape Cod in 1620. An exhilarating climb to the very top of the tower will net you a fantastic view of Provincetown and Cape Cod Bay. The museum details the history of the Cape as well as its cranberry industry. *(Contact: Provincetown Museum, High Pole Hill, Provincetown, 508/487-1310.)*

The voice of Walter Cronkite on a documentary video at the **JFK Museum** evokes memories of a man . . . and his son . . . that we can never forget. This tiny compilation of family photos and memorabilia allows a voyeuristic peek into the sun and fun enjoyed by the entire Kennedy clan at their Hyannis Port, Cape Cod compound. *(Contact: JFK Museum, 397 Main St., Hyannis, 508/790-3077.)*

Lodging

The magnificent homes of former ship owners and whaling captains have been converted into great lodging venues all over Cape Cod. For more lodging options, consult the New England-wide accommodations websites and reservation services listed in the "How to Use This Book" chapter or check out www.mass-vacation.com/lodging/cape_cod.phtml.

Foxglove Cottage ($, 101 Sandwich Rd., Plymouth, 508/747-6576, 800/479-4746, www.foxglove-cottage.com) is a charming three-guestroom bed-and-breakfast minutes from Plimoth Plantation. The main part of this "full cape" dates to 1820, showcasing a hand-turned staircase and wide-plank flooring. Surrounded by 45 acres of woods and meadows, Foxglove offers fine accommodation at good value.

The Belfry Inne ($+, 8 Jarves St. in Sandwich, 508/888-8550, www.belfryinn.com), a desanctified Roman Catholic Church and Rectory, garners the most-unusual-former-life-of-an-inn award for sure. While the nine guestrooms of the Drew House rectory are classic Cape Cod, the recently reinvented Abbey is otherworldly. **The Abbey's** six guest rooms—named for the days of Creation, Monday through Saturday—feature a bath in the bell tower, flying buttresses, headboards that were once pews, and stained-glass images of Gabrielle and Archangel Michael.

Wequasset Inn ($$-$$$$, Pleasant Bay, Chatham, 508/432-5400, 800/225-7125, www.wequasett.com) offers a Cape Cod resort experience that encompasses pool, tennis, golf, beach, croquet, and sailing the blue Atlantic. Situated on 22 acres on a secluded cove, Wequassett—which means "crescent on the water"—features 104 guest rooms divided among 20 "cottages," all decorated in casual early Americana.

Light, bright, and filled with Laura Ashley prints, springtime flowers, 4-poster beds, antique quilts, and a stuffed bear in every room, the **Whalewalk Inn** ($$+, 220 Bridge Rd., Eastham, 508/255-0617), c.1830, is located minutes from Cape Cod National Seashore. The Whalewalk Inn is homey, comfortable, and unpretentious, yet leaves no amenity to chance.

Built in 1883 by Captain William Swain and situated among other grand ship's captains' homes, **76 Main** ($$, 76 Main St., Nantucket, 508/228-2533) offers cozy rooms, a central location, and good value. Imaginative muffins and scones, homemade each morning, top the continental breakfast of this charming B&B.

Exquisitely elegant in every detail, including the fresh flowers in every room, the **Victorian Inn** ($$-$$$$, 24 Water St., Edgartown 508/627-4784; www.thevic.com), on Martha's Vineyard, is the former home of Captain Laffayette Rowley. Furnished with four-posters and family antiques and flanked by an English garden courtyard, the inn combines the restoration of the home's romantic past with the creature comforts of the 21st century.

Located in the very center of historic Martha's Vineyard village, **The Colonial Inn** ($$+, North Water St., Edgartown, 508/627-4711; 800/627-4701; www.colonialinnmvy.com) offers a good family base from which to explore the village. Built as a harbor-front hotel in 1911, the inn's clientele has included Somerset Maugham and Howard Hughes. A third-floor covered porch offers a gull's eye view of the sea.

Class-to-the-max, **The Charlotte Inn** ($$$$, 27 South Summer St., Edgartown, 508/627-4751; www.relaischateaux.fr/charlotte) recreates the opulence exuded during the golden years of whaling in the 19th century. An elite Relais & Chateaux property, Charlotte Inn's rooms and suites embrace two ship captains' homes, a 1705 garden house, a carriage house, and an old-fashioned garage—all exquisitely restored and nestled amid wisteria vines, rose gardens, and flower arbors. This is the place to stay when your ship comes in.

The Captain House Inn ($$$, 369-377 Old Harbor Rd., Chatham, 508/945-0127, www.captainshouseinn.com) occupies a compound of buildings surrounding the 1839 Greek-Revival home of Captain Hiram Harding. The finely appointed guestrooms in the main house, former stables, carriage house, and cottage—which are named after Hardings's family and ships—feature period reproductions and antiques, pumpkin pine floors, and fireplaces.

The stately Federal-style brick mansion of wealthy ship owner Jared Coffin welcomes guests with the aura of the prosperous whaling era. **Jared Coffin House** ($-$$$$, 29 Broad Street, Nantucket, 508/228-2400, 800/248-2495, www.jaredcoffinhouse.com), actually 60 guest rooms in six buildings, is awash with period reproductions, antiques, and artwork, its softly lit chandeliers casting the shadows of the history it harbors within.

Food and Drink

Don't forget to try the classic Cape Codder—cranberry juice and vodka. For more dining options, consult www.marestaurantassoc.org.

Founded in 1971 when "Happy Days" was a hot television comedy, **Arnold's** ($, Rte., 6, Eastham, 508/255-2575)—a rustic, minimalist seafood "shack"—makes the best fried clams on the Cape. The eatery serves a meal every 30 seconds during the summer season, and it is not uncommon for lines to be out the door. You might have to wait a bit, but your taste buds will thank you.

As you would expect from an Irish pub, the good cheer, conviviality and toe-tapping music are as good as the grub. That said, you won't be disappointed at the **Olde Inn** ($$, 348 Main St., West Dennis, 508/760-

2627). Be sure to catch the lively tunes and Irish sing-alongs on the weekends.

Innovative cuisine and a sophisticated bistro ambiance belie the name **Brewster Fish House** ($$, Rte. 6A, Brewster, 508/896-7867). But one thing's for certain, the seafood here is outstanding.

Abbicci ($$+, Rte. 6A, Yarmouth Port, 508/362-3501) showcases its upmarket Italian cuisine with the continental flair of a cosmopolitan trattoria. You will be hard-pressed to choose between the pasta and secondi piatti offerings, so plan to order both.

Stellar American cuisine with a fresh-from-the-sea accent marks the menu at **21 Federal** ($$-$$$, 21 Federal St., Nantucket, 508/228-2121). Popular with locals and visitors alike, you'd better make reservations if you want to dine here on a summer weekend.

Something of an institution on Martha's Vineyard, **The Black Dog Tavern** ($, Beach St., Extention, Vineyard Haven, 508/693-1991) has been packin' 'em in since Hector was a pup. Equally as famous for their logo-emblazoned t-shirts and roadside bakery of temptations, The Black Dog leaves a distinguished gustatory mark as well.

Sandwiches, burgers, wings, ribs, and chowder are hot off the press at **The News from America** ($, 23 Kelly St., Edgartown, 508/627-4397). Be sure to order a rack of beers—a mix and match sampling of five brews—at this cozy, dark Martha's Vineyard pub. And, don't forget fries, which come in a paper bag.

Nothing fancy at **Lobster Hut** ($, Town Wharf, Plymouth, 508/746-2270), just a stand-up window and tons of fresh, fresh seafood. The Hut offers most everything fried, but you can find lobster rolls and a smattering of broiled fish.

The divine cuisine at **Genesis** in the Belfry Inne ($$, 8 Jarves St., Sandwich, 508/888-8550) is no play on words. Situated in the Abbey, a newly renovated desanctified Roman Catholic Church, the restaurant has recycled the confessional as a wine cooler and church pews for bar paneling. A prism of light radiates through the stained glass windows, all in all creating a heavenly experience.

Be it seafood by candlelight in the dining room or prime rib in the tap room pub, Jared's ($$, Jared Coffin House, 29 Broad St., Nantucket, 508/228-2400; 800/248-2495; www.jaredcoffinhouse.com) is renowned for serving superior cuisine with style. You'll find lunch in the adjoining garden courtyard the perfect antidote for an historic walk through the village.

Central Massachusetts

Wedged between metropolitan Boston and the Berkshires, the treasures of Central Massachusetts often go unheralded and undiscovered. You'll find a wealth of diversity to explore on foot in the center of the state, from an 1830 New England village re-created as living history to picturesque botanical gardens and a smorgasbord of geologic wonders.

Regional Information
Worcester County Convention & Visitors Bureau, 33 Waldo St., Worcester, MA 01608; 508/755-7400; www.worcester.org.

Getting There
By Air: All major carriers offer service to Boston's Logan International Airport.
By Rail: Amtrak offers service to Boston's South Station.
By Automobile: I-95 or I-495 to Mass. Turnpike (I-90) or Rte. 2 west.

Old Sturbridge Village

You will step back in time the moment you walk through the portals of Old Sturbridge Village, an outdoor living-history museum that authentically re-creates a rural 1830s New England village. More than 40 historical buildings—most original 19th-century structures moved from other places in New England—shelter costumed history interpreters, who routinely go about the daily activities of the era, answering questions and demonstrating skills long ago forgotten by modern society. An ever-changing rota of special events—such as the annual 1830s Agricultural Fair that features a ploughing match, cattle show, and exhibition of the heirloom vegetable harvest—further illustrates life in New England between 1790 and 1840.

Information
Old Sturbridge Village, 1 Old Sturbridge Village Road, Sturbridge, MA 01566; 508/347-3362; 800-733-1830; www.osv.org.

Getting There
Take the Mass. Turnpike (I-90) to exit 9, or I-84 to exit 2. Then take U.S. Hwy. 20 into Sturbridge and watch for signs.

First Steps
Old Sturbridge Village is open daily from mid-Feb. through Dec. and on weekends from Jan. 1 through mid-Feb. Call for hours, which change by season. You'll receive a self-guided map with your admission fee.

Old Sturbridge Village. Begin your exploration of Old Sturbridge Village in the Visitor Center (1), at the J. Cheney Wells Clock Gallery of period timepieces. Special historical exhibits change every year or so. Exit the Visitor Center and enter the virtual 1830 village. Follow the dirt road to Friends Meetinghouse [c.1796, Bolton, MA] (2), where the Society of Friends, or Quakers, worshiped.

Proceed to the Center Meetinghouse [c.1832, Sturbridge, MA] (3), a quintessentially New England white clapboard church with a tall steeple that would have been a common spot for town meetings. The Shoe Shop [c.1800-1850, Sturbridge, MA] (4) portrays the cottage industry manufacture of peg-soled men's shoes. Across from the road, the Town Pound (5) temporarily held stray livestock until claimed by their owners.

As you walk "into the countryside," you'll see the non-graded District School [c.1800-1810, Candia, NH] (6), where, typically, village children would take their lessons between December and March, when they were not needed on the farm. The Pottery [c.1819, Goshen, CT] (7) features a skilled redware potter, who demonstrates the process of making earthenware from local clay. Pots are fired in the reproduction Kiln (8) across the road. Local militia stored gunpowder in the Powder House [c.1806, Oxford, MA] (9).

Walk to the Freeman Farm (10), whose buildings include the farmhouse [c.1810-1815, Sturbridge, MA]; barn [c.1830-1850, Charlton, MA]; corn barn [c.1830-1860, Thompson, CT]; and the smokehouse [c.1800, Goshen, CT]. OSV staff sows and harvests the fields, milks the cows, and works in the buttery. Heirloom vegetables are stored in the farm's root cellar. The interpreters use the produce, cream, and butter in household cooking demonstrations at Old Sturbridge Village.

Visit the neighboring Cooper Shop [c.1840, Waldoboro, ME] (11), where village coopers explain and demonstrate the craft of making buckets, barrels, and pails typically used by villagers. A panoply of barrels—for cider, meat, apples, grain, and flour—crowd the shop. At the nearby

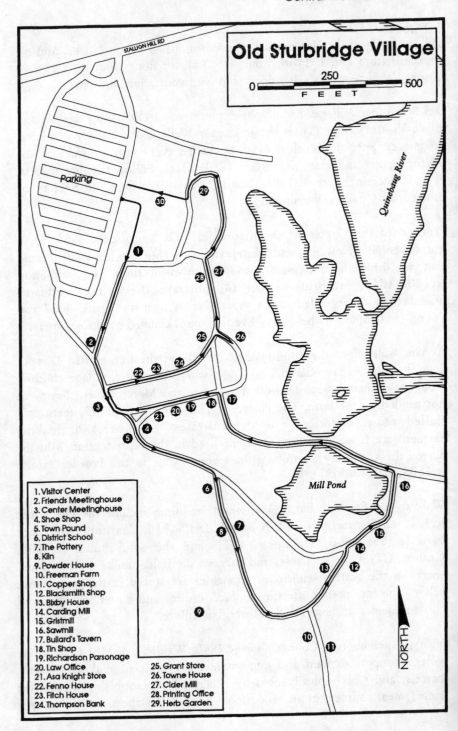

Old Sturbridge Village

0 — 250 — 500
FEET

STALLION HILL RD

Parking

Quinebaug River

Mill Pond

NORTH

1. Visitor Center
2. Friends Meetinghouse
3. Center Meetinghouse
4. Shoe Shop
5. Town Pound
6. District School
7. The Pottery
8. Kiln
9. Powder House
10. Freeman Farm
11. Copper Shop
12. Blacksmith Shop
13. Bixby House
14. Carding Mill
15. Gristmill
16. Sawmill
17. Bullard's Tavern
18. Tin Shop
19. Richardson Parsonage
20. Law Office
21. Asa Knight Store
22. Fenno House
23. Fitch House
24. Thompson Bank
25. Grant Store
26. Towne House
27. Cider Mill
28. Printing Office
29. Herb Garden

Blacksmith Shop [c.1802-1810, Bolton, MA] (12), a skilled craftsman explains and demonstrates, over a charcoal fire, the creation of such ironwork as farm tools and household utensils. The country blacksmith's family would have lived across the street at the Bixby House [c.1800-1810, Barre, MA] (13), where they might have supplemented the household income by braiding straw or selling cheese and butter.

Walk around Mill Pond and explore the mills. The Carding Mill [c.1840, South Waterford, ME] (14) prepared wool for spinning by means of water-powered mechanization. The carding machines brush the picked wool into rolls or batting. The water-powered Gristmill (15) is a reproduction made from both new and old wood timbers. Its machinery came from a mill in Hebron, Conn.; the millstones and original wheel are from South Egremont, Mass. This mill, which would have ground rye and corn, sits on the actual site of an early 1800s gristmill. The reproduction Sawmill (16) illustrates the patented "up and down" saw process common before 1840. It is built on the very spot that David Wight had his mill in the 1790s.

Walk through the covered bridge, which came from Dummerston, Vermont. Stop at Bullard's Tavern (17) at the village green for a bite to eat if you like. At the top of the village green, visit the Tin Shop [c.1800-1850, Sturbridge, MA] (18), where "tinners" demonstrate their craft, creating skimmers and sconces, dippers, and funnels. Tinware was a growing industry in the years after the Revolution, directly competing with the sale of redware pottery.

The Richardson Parsonage [c.1748, East Brookfield, MA] (19) is a 19th-century lean-to structure that often housed the village minister and his family. Carrots, beets, peas, beans, squash, and other heirloom vegetables and herbs common in the 1830s grow in the raised beds of the progressive kitchen garden. A fenced dooryard garden features such vintage flowers as ragged robin, belladonna roses, and sun drops.

The Law Office [c.1796, Woodstock, CT] (20) illustrates the working environment of a country lawyer in the 1830s, while at Asa Knight Store [c.1810, Dummerston, VT] (21), most residents of the village would barter produce, cheese and butter, farm animals, and crafts in exchange for manufactured or imported goods. Only a fraction paid for merchandise with cash.

Continue around the green, past the Center Meetinghouse and visit Fenno House [c.1704, Canton, MA] (22). The oldest structure in Old Sturbridge Village, this house is interpreted as the residence of an elderly widow and her spinster daughter. The neighboring Fitch House [c.1737, Willimantic, CT] (23) is designed as the home of an upwardly mobile printer and his family. Their adjoining garden reflects an interest in planting "new" varieties of plants. The Fitch Children's Garden is based on a plan described in the 1833 children's book, *The Young Florist*. Here, concentric circles of plantings around a birch arbor showcase such antique flowers as love-in-a-puff and catch-fly.

Walk on to Thompson Bank [c.1835, Thompson, CT] (24), a pillared Greek-Revival structure chartered in 1833. The original interior includes the cashier's desk, a massive safe vault, astral lamps and a regulator clock. Grant Store (25), next door, houses an Old Sturbridge Village gift shop. Also fronting the green is Towne House [c.1796, Charlton, MA] (26), home of the prosperous Salem Towne, Jr. and his large family. The home is furnished as if the Townes still lived there—wall-coverings, curtains, and carpets attesting to their wealthy status within the village. Of particular note here is Mr. Towne's formal cutting garden, geometrically patterned beds edged with hyssop and featuring a riot of brilliant orange-red corn poppies and delicate five-petal singular rubrifolia roses.

At the Cider Mill [c.1835, Brookfield, NH] (27), a horse-powered crusher and hand-operated screw-press turned autumn's apple harvest into the village's favorite beverage. (The Cider Mill operates weekends in October.) Across the path, interpreters demonstrate 19th-century printing methods at the Printing Office [c.1780, Worcester, MA] (28). You will pass a number of vintage structures along the road housing museum collections that illustrate life in the early 1830s: Glass; Firearms, Fibers and Fashion; Early Lighting; and Rural Industries.

An extensive, terraced Herb Garden (29) contains 400 varieties of herbs, grouped and labeled by usage. The lower garden contains early 19th-century medicinal herbs such as lamb's ear, used to stop bleeding; rhubarb, whose roots were used as a powerful laxative; and foxglove, for regulating the heart. The middle tier grows culinary herbs still recognizable today. The top terrace features household herb plants that were used to make dye, potpourri, brooms, or straw hats. Interspersed in the Herb Garden are a wild woodland bed of native plants and a classic knot garden.

End your walking tour of Old Sturbridge Village in the gift shop and bookstore just beyond the Herb Garden. The shop features an amazing selection of books on the history through which you've just walked, as well as volumes on heirloom vegetables, fruits, flowers, and historic gardens. You can purchase heirloom seeds here and even the exquisitely scented antique rose plants you've seen grace so many of Old Sturbridge Village's cottage gardens.

Purgatory Chasm State Reservation

This 900-acre park, designated a state reservation in 1919, surrounds one of Massachusetts' natural wonders, the dramatic Purgatory Chasm. Believed to have been formed 14,000 years ago when large volumes of dammed-up glacial meltwater suddenly released from Ramshorn Pond, Singletary Pond, and Casey Brook in the western part of Sutton and flowed through Purgatory Brook valley, the chasm runs for .25 mile between 70-foot-high granite walls. Large blocks of granite, which were broken away with the torrent of rushing water, now litter the bottom of the chasm.

Information
Massachusetts Forest and Park Service, Purgatory Rd., Sutton, MA 01590; 508/234-3733.

Getting There
Take Rte. 146 south to Purgatory Road in Sutton. Follow signs to Purgatory Chasm.

First Steps
Pick up a trail map at the Purgatory Chasm State Reservation Visitors Center. Park is open daily, sunrise to sunset.

Purgatory Chasm State Reservation. The state park service has mapped five trails that can be looped together to fully explore the bold and unique landscape of Purgatory Chasm: Chasm Loop Trail (.5 mile), Charley's Loop (1 mile), Old Purgatory Trail (.75 mile), Forest Road Trail (.5 mile) and Spring Path (.25 mile).

Chasm Loop Trail, which has blue blazes painted on the rocks, is the most dramatic and popular. You must be in good physical condition for this one, and wear hiking boots or sturdy sneakers, because you will be climbing through the chasm—up, down, around, and between the granite boulders—which can sometimes be slippery or deceiving. You'll see evidence of eskers, which are long ridges of glacially deposited course gravel, and gneiss, bands of gray metamorphic rock in which minerals are deposited in layers. Labeled rock formations carry fancifully descriptive names: The Corncrib, Fat Man's Misery, The Coffin, The Pulpit, Lovers' Leap, and His Majesty's Cave.

In 1793 historian Peter Whitney wrote: "Many visitors come to the chasm to experiment with dropping pebbles, to marvel at the icicles visible in May or June and to climb the boulders and explore the small caverns. After all, no description given of this place by another will enable persons to form just and adequate conceptions of it." He was so right.

Tower Hill Botanic Gardens

An easy day trip from Boston and a must-see when exploring Central Massachusetts, Tower Hill Botanic Gardens—whose master plan was unveiled in 1988—offers gardening enthusiasts, flower lovers, and trail trippers the opportunity to bask in blooming New England. Home of the Worcester Horticultural Society, Tower Hill sits high on a knoll with spectacular views of Wachusett Reservoir and Mount Wachusett. A confluence of formal gardens, meadows, and woodland trails on 132 acres creates a "living museum of plants."

Information
Tower Hill Botanic Gardens, 11 French Dr., Boylston, MA 01505; 508/869-6111; www.towerhillbg.org.

Getting There
Take I-495 to I-290 west, to exit 24 (Church St.. Proceed on Church St. for 3 miles, toward Boylston. Tower Hill will be on your right.

First Steps
Tower Hill is open year round, Tues. through Sun. and on Mon.

holidays. Admission is charged. Pick up a garden map in the Stoddard Education and Visitors Center.

Tower Hill Botanic Gardens. The Society's self-guided garden map allows you to explore this floral wonderland at your own pace. The Lawn Garden, resplendent with more than 350 varieties of flowering trees, shrubs, and perennials, features a double pergola that overlooks a Secret Garden of floral pastels. Cottage and Vegetable Gardens surround a 1740 farmhouse on the property (now housing administrative offices). From here, a short path leads to the Wildlife Garden, actually a naturalized area surrounding a vernal pond that is sprinkled with bird and bat houses and feeders. Stone benches secreted in the undergrowth afford a voyeuristic peek at the wildlife.

An unblazed, interconnected trail system winds around the eastern and northern perimeters of the property. Some trails are short and steep. The Belvedere and Tower Hill Summit offer the best views. Perhaps most popular is the 1-mile Loop Trail, which winds past the Harrington Orchard. The Davenport Collection of 119 heirloom apple varieties ripen here in September and October. Rare varieties such as Smokehouse, Winter Banana, Pawpaw, Twenty Ounce, and Black Oxford are on display for sale during the Columbus Day weekend "Apple Daze Celebration."

Something is blooming at Tower Hill Botanic Gardens in every season. Seas of flowering bulbs take center stage in mid-April and May. From May through early June is the best time to see the spring-blooming trees, shrubs and the extensive collection of peonies. The apple orchard blossoms in mid May and the wildflower meadow in June. The perennial gardens hold court from May through October while the annuals shine from July through September. But only in the 18th-century Orangerie—a "coolhouse" that features winter-blooming exotics from temperate and tropical regions—can plants survive a New England winter.

Rock House Reservation

During winter hunting forages, Native Americans once sought shelter beneath the massive cavelike rock lean-to that is now the focal point of a relatively unknown haven called Rock House Reservation. Created by the retreat of the last glacier more than 12,000 years ago, the Rock House sits on farmland that was owned by the William Adams family during the later part of the 19th century. Decades later, Arthur Carter used the property as a tree farm, planting red and Norway spruce and red pine and creating a pond by damming up a small stream. He built a cabin on the shores of the pond.

Information
The Trustees of Reservations, 572 Essex St., Beverly, MA 01950-1530; 508/921-1944. Rock House Reservation, 508/840-4446.

Getting There
Take the Mass. Turnpike (I-90) west to exit 8, Palmer. Go north on Rte. 32. At the intersection of Rte. 32 and Rte. 9 in Ware, bear right on Rte. 9 east for 1.1 miles.

First Steps
Rock House Reservation is open daily from 8am to sunset. You'll find an interpretive trail guide at the kiosk near the parking lot.

Rock House Reservation. The Trustees of Reservations owns the 75-acre Rock House Reservation. A marked system of easy-to-moderate trails winds throughout the boulder-strewn former farm: Inner Loop (.6 mile), Outer Loop (.4 mile), Summit Trail (.6 mile) and Fire Road (.6 mile). At every intersection of trails there is a trail map, and you can easily combine all the short trails into one meandering loop (2.5 miles).

From the parking lot follow the flat, well-maintained, cedar bark path to Carter Pond. The pond is loaded with frogs, turtles, and water snakes and is frequented by great blue herons and belted kingfishers. Big outcroppings of granite rock pepper the landscape. Fork to the right around the pond and follow either the short Inner Loop or the longer Outer Loop through the tree farm to the Butterfly Meadow. A work in progress, Butterfly Meadow is a grassy area constantly cleared for power lines that traverse it. Species of plants that attract butterflies are being added to the meadow. For example, violets and butterfly weed are favored food for the caterpillars, and summer-sweet butterfly bush and globe thistle provide nectar for adult butterflies.

Follow the Summit Trail to the Vista and then backtrack, or proceed directly to Balance Rock, which precariously perches atop a granite ledge.

Just beyond you'll find Carter's cabin, now used as a small nature center. Bear left at the fork after the cabin and look for the imposing Rock House, which is made up of gneiss, or reheated and metamorphosed granite, 20- to 30-feet high. The shelter captures the early morning sun with its southeasterly exposure and will capture your imagination as well.

Chesterfield Gorge and Westfield River

Only the chirping of resident birds and the humming of the river's lazy swirls and churning rapids interrupt the tranquility of this walk.

Information
The Trustees of Reservations, 572 Essex St., Beverly, MA 01950-1530; 508/921-1944. Chesterfield Gorge: 413/684-0148. An honor-system admission donation is requested at the gorge.

Getting There
Take the Mass. Turnpike (I-90) west to I-91 north, to Rte. 9 west, to Rte. 143 west. At intersection of Rte. 143 and Ireland St. in Chesterfield, take Ireland St. west 0.8 mile to River Rd. Entrance and parking area are on the left.

Chesterfield Gorge and Westfield River. Peer over the handrail into Chesterfield Gorge for a dramatic view of rushing water through a granite canyon that was carved through the ages by the East Branch of the Westfield River. Then walk through the parking lot and take the gently sloping gravel road to the left, past the Chesterfield Four Seasons Club, to the river. The road (now open to foot and bicycle traffic only) follows the river for 10 miles, bordering a forest of hemlocks, ash and oaks that tower over ferns, wildflowers, and lichen-covered rocks. Streams and small waterfalls cascade through the forest to the river, sometimes flowing under the road, often times trickling across the path. And though the road is about 6-feet wide, level and compact, this could be a muddy trek in the spring or after a heavy rain.

You will marvel at the incredible masses of fissured granite erratics that punctuate the woods. You can picnic at the gorge, though not along the river. But bring your fishing rod, because catch-and-release angling for Atlantic salmon—using lures only—is allowed here.

Old Deerfield

Settled in 1669 by former Massachusetts Bay colonists who endured constant Indian attacks, Deerfield was totally destroyed in the Deerfield Massacre of February 29, 1704. Attracted by the fertile land and undaunted by savage threats, a new wave of settlers rebuilt Deerfield in 1707, which has remained populated ever since. The 1-mile street first settled in 1669 sits within the confines of the Old Deerfield National Historic Landmark. Meticulously preserved much as it was in the 18th and 19th centuries, this main thoroughfare, called The Street, is itself a museum of antiquity.

Information
Historic Deerfield, P.O. Box 321, Deerfield; 413/774-5581; www.historic-deerfield.org.

Getting There
Take the Mass. Turnpike (I-90) to I-91 north. Take exit 24 (from north) or exit 25 (from south) and go 6 miles on Rte. 5/U.S. Hwy. 10. Turn left into the village. Park along "The Street."

First Steps
Begin your tour of Old Deerfield by stopping at the Hall Tavern Information Center, across from the Deerfield Inn, to purchase a "Walking Tour of Deerfield" guide—featuring a detailed narrative of 88 places on "The Street"ñ and an Historic Deerfield ticket. Historic Deerfield's museum houses are open daily from 9:30am to 4:30pm.

Old Deerfield. The preservation of Deerfield began in 1936, when the Henry Flynts of Greenwich, Conn., discovered the sleepy village while dropping off their son at the Deerfield Academy (founded in 1797). One by one, as the vintage houses came up for sale, the Flynts purchased and restored them to period authenticity. Fourteen houses later and incorporated as Historic Deerfield since 1952, this street museum—which mingles with the private period-structures on The Street—displays more than 25,000 Americana artifacts used between 1650 and 1850.

The best way to explore the village is to do both the self-guided walk of Old Deerfield and the guided tours of Historic Deerfield. (The interiors of the museum houses are only open during the group tours.) On the hour,

Historic Deerfield guides conduct narrated tours of Hinsdale and Anna Williams House, Wright, Ashley, Stebbins, Frary, Wells-Thorn, and Dwight Houses and the Barnard Tavern. Tours of the silver and metalware collection, the textile museum and Allen House leave from the Information Center twice daily. Unlike the museum houses, Historic Deerfield's Memorial Hall Museum, Sheldon-Hawks House, and the Flynt Center of Early New England Life may be toured on your own. Allow two days in Old Deerfield if you plan to see all the museums and collections.

Doane's Falls/Tully Lake Hiking Trail

By 1753, the waters of Lawrence Brook at Doane's Falls provided the power for dozens of prosperous local mills. Doane's Falls was named after Amos Doane, who built the last working mill here in the early 1800s. Portions of foundations and old millstones still litter the terrain.

Information
The Trustees of Reservations, 572 Essex St., Beverly, MA 01950-1530; 508/921-1944. Doane's Falls, 508/840-4446.

Getting There
Take Rte. 2 west to exit 18, Rte. 2A. At the intersection of Rte. 2A and Rte. 32 in Athol, follow Rte. 32, crossing the Millers River bridge. Bear right on Chestnut Hill Rd. and follow it for 4 miles. Trailhead is on the left at the intersection with Doane Hill Rd., just after the stone bridge over Lawrence Brook in Royalston. Parking is limited.

First Steps
Pick up a trail map at the kiosk at the top of the falls. Be sure to pack a lunch, wear sturdy hiking boots, copiously apply insect repellent, and take two bottles of water per person for this excursion.

Doane's Falls/Tully Lake Hiking Trail. This beautiful 4-mile hike over sometimes moderately difficult terrain will take you along a sheer-granite-walled gorge dominated by the 200-foot cascade of Doane's Falls, then through pine and deciduous forests, across massive Tully Dam, and around tranquil Tully Lake. From the parking area, take the path along the gorge until you see the beginning of the yellow-blaze system and follow the blazes to the right along Lawrence Brook. The trail will take you out of the woods to Doane Hill Road for a short distance, where it crosses Tully River, then it cuts back in at the Old Tully Campground. Pick up the trail again on the right side of the campground, directly opposite the brown entrance booth.

Follow the trail around the lake, through thickets of mountain laurel and stands of birch, maple, oak, and hemlock. Halfway around the lake you'll find picnic tables and public bathrooms and then you must climb a grassy knoll to cross Tully Dam via the Athol-Richmond Road. After you pass the gatehouse, scramble back down the hill on the other side of the dam. As you look at the lake, you'll see a metal stake with a yellow blaze, near the woods toward the right. Follow the blazed trail back into the forest and continue around the lake. The hike back up the bedrock to the top of the falls is by far the most strenuous, but worth the effort because the abutting waterfalls and dark, swirling eddies are phenomenal.

Rainy Day Options

Fruitlands—The Museum of the New England Landscape sits atop Prospect Hill on 200 glorious acres of land with a 50-mile view of the Nashua River Valley spread at its feet. Conceived by Bronson Alcott in 1843 as a 19th-century utopia that would live off the "fruits of the land," Fruitlands now is a compound of four museums that tells the story of the daily life, art, and beliefs of the Shakers, Trancendentalists, Native Americans, and Hudson River painters. These four diverse groups shared a belief in the importance of harmony with nature, and they respected the land above all else. Knowledgeable interpreters host guided tours in each of the museums.

Fruitlands Farmhouse was Alcott's home, from which he started his short-lived commune. The house is now a museum dedicated to memorabilia of the Transcendentalist movement. The Shaker Museum is an 18th-century building, moved from Hancock Shaker Village in Pittsfield, which displays typical artifacts of the Shaker community. The Picture Gallery houses collections of paintings by artists of the 19th-century Hudson River School, who celebrated the beauty of the landscape in their works. The Indian Museum displays two spectacular Indian bronze statues and "One Thousand Generations," the story of 10,000 years of our native peoples. Four nature trails wind through the surrounding meadows and woodlands. Some areas are steep. Flies, mosquitoes and poison ivy dominate much of the area in the summer months, so if you're up for a hike, come prepared with insect repellent and a fly-switch. *(Contact: Fruitlands, 102 Prospect Hill Rd., Harvard, 978/456-3924.)*

Lodging

The mid-state location of Central Massachusetts also allows you the option of staying in the greater Boston area or in Western Massachusetts and exploring attractions as day trips. For more lodging options, consult the New England-wide accommodations websites and reservation services listed in "How to Use This Book" or check out Folkstone Bed & Breakfast Reservation Service, 508/480-0380; 800/762-2751.

Like the adjacent Old Sturbridge Village, **Old Sturbridge Village Lodges and Oliver Wight House** ($, Rte. 20, Sturbridge, 508/347-3018, www.osv.org) offer a choice between antique and reproduction buildings. The Oliver Wight House, built in 1789, once was a wayside tavern. Completely restored to period authenticity in 1985, the 10 guest rooms feature Federal-style antiques and reproductions. The 47 Village units, in newer buildings that mimic traditional 19th-century architectural styles, surround a swimming pool and playground.

The Publick House ($, Rte. 131, Sturbridge, 508/347-3313, 800/782-5425, www.publickhouse.com), on Sturbridge Common, has sheltered weary travelers since Colonel Ebenezer Crafts first hosted guests before the Revolutionary War. You can choose to stay in the historic inn itself or opt for one of the 100 rooms of the Country Lodge or a suite in the Colonel Crafts Inn. The rooms offer modern amenities, but are furnished with period reproductions and exude an antique New England aura.

When the **Deerfield Inn** ($$, 81 Old Main St., Deerfield, 413/774-5587, 800/926-3865, www.deerfieldinn.com) first opened it doors in July 1884, guests arrived on horseback or in carriages and bedded their steeds in the stables out back. Today, the inn's 23 guest rooms—which are named after notable Deerfield residents of centuries past—graciously shelter visitors exploring Old Deerfield's historic mile—The Street. The spirited should ask to stay in one of the two ghost rooms.

Clark Tavern Inn ($, 98 Bay Rd., Hadley, 413/586-1900, www.clarktaverninn.com), a three-guestroom bed-and-breakfast, is a 1742 Georgian Colonial sporting the wide-plank floors and 12-over-12 windows so indicative of the era. Furnished with antiques, the inn features welcoming touches such as a guest refrigerator stocked with complimentary water, soft drinks, wine and snacks.

Just minutes from Rock House Reservation, The Wildwood Inn ($, 121 Church St., Ware 413/967-7798, 800/860-8098) is a seven-guest-room Queen Anne Victorian that was built in 1880. Furnished with antiques and heirloom quilts, the bed-and-breakfast features a wrap-around porch overlooking two wooded acres.

Only 10 miles from Old Deerfield, the Allen House Victorian Inn ($, 599 Main St., Amherst , 413/253-5000, www.allenhouse.com) is a Queen Anne stick-style structure built in 1886 and restored to its former splendor. The seven-guestroom bed-and-breakfast, which is filled to the brim with antiques, still retains its original woodwork and hand-carved cherry mantels. Guests enjoy 21st century amenities as well as a hearty country breakfast.

The Lord Jeffery Inn ($$, 30 Boltwood Ave., Amherst, 413/253-2576, www.pinnacle-inns.com/lordjefferyinn), circa 1926, offers 48 individually appointed colonial-style guest rooms. Enjoying a central location, this warm and unassuming historic small hotel overlooks a charming colonial garden as well as the village green.

The 99-guestrooms and common areas of The Hotel Northampton ($-$$$, 36 King St., Northampton, 413/584-3100, 800/547-3529, www.hotelnorthampton.com) exude the aura of an architectural museum. Loaded with Chippendale, Federal, and Duncan Phyfe antiques, the 1927 vintage hotel retains the luster of an opulent bygone era.

Yankee Magazine heralds Bear Haven Bed and Breakfast $, 22 Mechanic St., Shelburne Falls, 413/625-9281, www.bearhaven.com) as "a rest home for teddy bears." Indeed, this small cozy 1850 Victorian is chock-a-block with the cuddly creatures, the owners' stuffed bear collection. Be sure to visit the nearby Shelburne Falls Bridge of Flowers.

You'll find working fireplaces in every room of The Seven Hearths Bed &

Breakfast ($, 412 Main Rd., Rte. 143, Chesterfield, 413/296-4312, www.hamphillsbandb.com/sevenhearths). The 1891 Dutch Gambrel picturesquely sits on 2 rural acres in the vicinity of Chesterfield Gorge.

Food and Drink

For more options, consult www.marestaurantassoc.org.

Good basic Yankee cooking keeps 'em coming back to the **Publick House** ($$, Rte. 131, Sturbridge, 508/347-3313, 800/782-5425, www.publick-house.com), on Sturbridge Common. Renowned for their bread-basket—which brims with warm sticky buns, corn sticks, and pumpkin bread—the Publick House also serves up a walloping Farmer's breakfast. You'll really have to plow the back 40 after you tuck into this one: hot mulled cider, hot cereal, eggs, potatoes, red flannel hash, and warm, deep-dish apple pie topped with a huge slab of cheddar cheese.

A culinary jewel tucked in the Massachusetts countryside, the **Salem Cross Inn** ($$, Rte. 9, West Brookfield, 508/867-2345) secrets both a fascinating history and gastronomic delights. Built in 1705, the building's front door latch bears the Salem Cross hex mark (a symbol believed to ward off witchcraft). And with perhaps supernatural coincidence, a family named Salem has, since 1955, owned and operated Salem Cross Inn. The inn features a chestnut-beamed ceiling, an enormous fieldstone fireplace, and a working beehive oven. The Salem Cross Inn is renowned for their authentic 1700s drover's roasts, fireplace feasts and summer herbal dinners.

Like the museum homes that line The Street of Old Deerfield, the dining room of the **Deerfield Inn** ($$$, 81 Old Main Street, 413/774-5587, www.deerfieldinn.com) re-creates a 19th-century ambiance of prosperous comfort and sates the appetite with sparkling New American cuisine. The Deerfield Inn offers the casual option of a tavern supper menu in its cozy spirits room, as well as light bites during the day in the Terrace Cafe.

Situated in a historic Greek Revival building, the **Whistling Swan** ($$$, 502 Main St., Sturbridge, 508/347-2321) offers intimate dining with an international flair. More casual fare is offered upstairs in the Ugly Duckling Loft.

Overlooking the colonial garden of the Lord Jeffery Inn, **Elijah Boltwood's Tavern** ($-$$, 30 Boltwood Ave., Amherst, 413/253-2576, 800/742-0358, www.pinnacle-inns.com/lordjefferyinn) offers a potpourri of light fare as well as stellar country American cuisine. Serving breakfast, lunch and dinner daily, the Tavern's sunset menu, served between 4 and 6pm, is a particularly good value.

The Windowed Hearth ($$$, 30 Boltwood Ave., Amherst, 413/253-2576, 800/742-0358, www.pinnacle-inns.com/lordjefferyinn), the fine dining restaurant of Amherst's Lord Jeffery Inn, derives its name from the warmth and hospitality its flickering fire offered travelers in colonial times. Innovative presentations of classic New England ingredients—such as duck, rabbit, pheasant, and halibut—set this eatery apart.

The Fresh Pasta Company ($, 249 Main St., Northampton, 413/586-5875), a small neighborhood bistro, offers large portions of good pasta at great prices. Need I say more?

An eclectic eatery for soups, sandwiches, salads, pizza, Tex-Mex, and burgers, **Fitzwilly's** ($, 23 Main St., Northampton, 413/584-8666) is a family affair that has sated hungry locals and visitors for 25 years.

Moved from its original 1786 location in Hopkinton, New Hampshire, **The Wiggins Tavern** ($$, 36 King St., Northampton, 413/584-3100, 800/547-3529, www.hotelnorthampton.com) was painstakingly reconstructed as part of Hotel Northampton some 141 years later. The interior's carved paneling, hand-hewn beams and brick hearths set a warm and cozy colonial backdrop for its fine offering of American cuisine.

Light upmarket fare is offered in The Northampton Hotel's **Coolidge Park Cafe** ($, 36 King St., Northampton, 413/584-3100, 800/547-3529, www.hotelnorthampton.com). Named for Grace and Calvin Coolidge, who had an estate in Northampton, the cafe is filled with greenery and artists' floral renditions.

Western Massachusetts and the Berkshires

The beneficiary of Mother's Nature's bountiful goodness, Western Massachusetts basks in the glory of the Berkshire Mountains. Attracting wealthy industrialists from Boston and New York in the 1800s, who built summer mansion cottages, the region burgeoned as a magnet for the arts. Today, summer in the Berkshires means a smorgasbord of live music, theater, and dance amid a treasure trove of historical villages and a still-pristine wilderness.

Regional Information
Berkshire Hills Visitors Bureau, Berkshire Commons, Plaza Level, Pittsfield, MA 01201; 413/443-9186; 800/237-5747.

Getting There
By Air: All major carriers offer service to Boston's Logan International Airport.
By Rail: Amtrak offers service to Boston's South Station.
By Automobile: I-95 or I-495 to the Mass. Turnpike (I-90) or Rte. 2 west.

Norman Rockwell's Stockbridge

The village of Stockbridge softly sleeps in a valley at the base of Monument Mountain in the southern Berkshire Hills, full of quaint charm and history. Originally a mission to the Mahicans, Stockbridge incorporated in 1739. Known as Indian Town, the two factions lived peacefully together until 1785, when the Mahicans moved to New York and then on to Wisconsin. By the 1800s Stockbridge was reincarnated as the "inland Newport" by wealthy industrialists who built "cottage" mansions on Main Street and infused the community with capital and culture.

Information
Stockbridge Chamber of Commerce, 6 Elm St., P.O. Box 224, Stockbridge, MA 01262; 413/298-5200; www.stockbridgechamber.org.

Getting There
Mass. Turnpike (I-90) to exit 2, Lee, then Rte. 102 south to U.S. Hwy. 7 south. Park on the street.

Pick up maps and brochures at the Stockbridge Bluebird Visitors' Center information booth on Main Street (Rte. 102), across from the Red Lion Inn.

Norman Rockwell's Stockbridge. If the village of Stockbridge looks like something out of a Norman Rockwell painting, it is because the artist, who described Stockbridge as "the best of America, the best of New England," immortalized the village in many of his illustrations. Originally from Vermont, Rockwell moved to Stockbridge in 1953, where he lived—for 25 years—died and is buried. Rockwell painted "Main Street at Christmas" for McCall's magazine in 1967. Every year the scene is re-created on the first Sunday of December by the townsfolk of Stockbridge. Anyone owning a vintage automobile, circa 1960s, parks the car on Main Street for the day. And mimicking the painting, a Christmas tree is set atop a 1967 classic and placed in front of the Red Lion Inn. Rockwell also classically depicted Stockbridge in "78th Spring," which shows Rockwell, his wife and two friends bicycling down Main Street on a spring day, passing in front of the Children's Chime Tower, the Congregational Church and the Town Hall.

This captivating 1.5-mile walk through Main Street U.S.A. will transport you into the peaceful, bucolic scene of Rockwell's illustrations. From the information kiosk, cross Main Street to the Red Lion Inn (1). Built on the site of a onetime stagecoach stop and colonial meeting spot in 1773 as the Inn at the Sign of the Red Lion, the Red Lion Inn still percolates as the hub of Stockbridge. Like an illusion from a Rockwell drawing, rocking chairs line the expansive front veranda, usually occupied with folks just sittin' a spell. Norman Rockwell's house and carriage barn once sat across the street from the Inn.

Head North on Main Street, passing the brick bank building, to 1884 House (2). Originally the Stockbridge town offices and now the Yankee Candle Company, the high-ceilinged 1884 House sports interior walls of old brick that are peppered with vintage photographs of the old town hall. You'll see this building in Rockwell's "The Marriage License." His first studio was above the nearby general store.

Down the cul-de-sac just past 1884 House, the Mews embosoms a potpourri of shops. At an alleyway a little further down Main Street, a

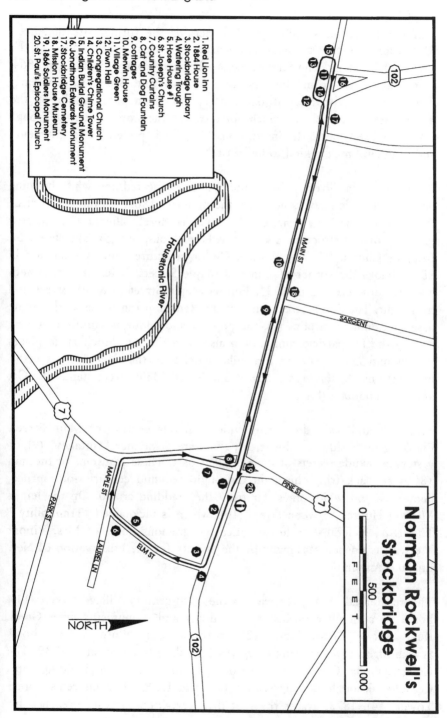

Norman Rockwell's
Stockbridge

1. Red Lion Inn
2. 1884 House
3. Stockbridge Library
4. Watering Trough
5. Hose House #1
6. St. Joseph's Church
7. Country Curtains
8. Cat and Dog Fountain
9. cottages
10. Merwin House
11. Village Green
12. Town Hall
13. Congregational Church
14. Children's Chime Tower
15. Indian Burial Ground Monument
16. Jonathan Edwards Monument
17. Stockbridge Cemetery
18. Mission House Museum
19. 1866 Soldiers Monument
20. St. Paul's Episcopal Church

NORTH

sign for Theresa's Stockbridge Cafe heralds the former site of Alice's Restaurant, which was made famous in the Arlo Guthrie song. At the corner of Main and Elm Streets, the Stockbridge Library (3), built in 1864, stores artifacts—from the Mahican Indians and Stockbridge's early days—in the Historical Room. Still perched in the middle of the intersection that once saw much horse traffic, the stone Watering Trough (4), circa 1881, bears the inscriptions: "Utility is preferable to grandeur" and "Merciful man is kind to his beast."

Turn down Elm Street. You should recognize the red and white building on the right side emblazoned with the numbers 1862. An integral part of Rockwell's "The New American LaFrance is Here!" illustration, the now privately owned structure is known as Hose House #1 (5). The stately St. Joseph's Church (6), a gray stone Gothic structure built as a mission in 1862, flanks the corner of Elm and Maple Streets. It features a stained-glass window created in 1531. Follow Maple Street to South Street and turn right. The South Street wing of the Red Lion Inn serves as the home base of Country Curtains (7), the popular and enduring curtain company run by the Fitzpatrick family, who also own the inn. Stockbridge places statues and monuments in triangular patches in the middle of its many intersections. At the crossroads of South and Main Street stands the Cat and Dog Fountain (8).

Turn left and walk down this wide, gracious portion of Main Street. Flanking both sides of the street, the stately summer "cottages" (9) of yesteryear exude secrets of their opulent past. These mansions of the mid 1800s sit back from the main thoroughfare amid centuries-old spruce, hemlocks, and white pines, far from the madding crowd. On the left is Merwin House, 14 Main Street (10), which is nicknamed "Tranquility." The 1825 Federal-style house, once the gracious home of Mrs. Vipont Merwin, is opened seasonally by the Society for the Preservation of New England Antiquities.

The residential area gives way to the 19th-century Village Green (11), home to a number of historic buildings and monuments. The Greek Revival-style Town Hall (12), with striking white pillars, hosts Stockbridge's town meeting every year, a village tradition since 1739. The Congregational Church (13) also occupies the Green. The building dates to 1824, although its congregation began in 1739. The Children's Chime Tower (14), 1878, graces the spot that Rev. John Sargeant preached his first message to the Mahicans. At the request of David Dudley Field, the tower's benefactor, the bells chime every day at 5:30pm. from "apple blossom time until frost" as a memorial to his grandchildren. A stone obelisk on the Green, called the Indian Burial Ground Monument (15), honors the settlement's Native Americans.

Proceed across Main Street. In the middle of the intersection triangle of Main and Church Streets stands the marble Jonathan Edwards Monument (16), erected in 1872 by the descendents of the fiery 18th-century preacher. On the corner, gravestones of the Stockbridge Cemetery (17) date back to the 18th and 19th centuries. Those of the early settlers are on the left. Giant evergreen trees planted at the head of the graves of these long-deceased citizens of Stockbridge shadow the rows of graves. Norman Rockwell, who died at age 84, is buried here.

Continue north on Main Street. Rev. John Sergeant, a missionary to the Mahicans, built a home in 1739 to use as a Christian school for the Indians. The structure was moved here from its original location and restored in 1920. Now open seasonally as the Mission House Museum (18), Sargeant's former abode is surrounded with Colonial-Revival gardens, and authentic furnishings evoke the early pre-Revolutionary era. The period gardens are planted with only varieties commonly found in a colonial plot.

At the intersection triangle at Main and Pine Streets, the 1866 Soldiers Monument (19) honors the Stockbridge soldiers of Gettysburg for bravery and patriotism. On the northwest corner, the Gothic/Romanesque-style St. Paul's Episcopal Church (20), which was constructed in 1884 of stone, showcases a Tiffany window in the nave and a LaFarge window in the chancel. You are now a few steps from the information kiosk at which you began.

Williams College, Williamstown

Nicknamed "the Village Beautiful," Williamstown sparkles as the quintessential New England college town. Settled as the tiny outpost of West Hoosuck in 1750 during the French and Indian Wars, the community didn't really grow much until peace was established in 1760 and farmers came from Connecticut to work the fertile lands. The

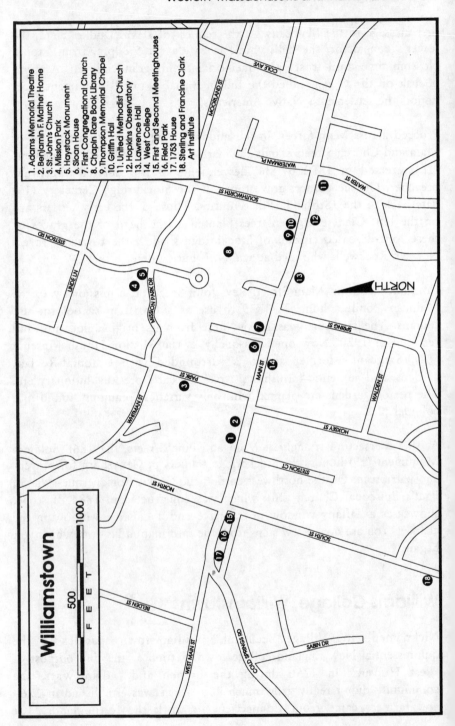

Williamstown

FEET
0   500   1000

NORTH

1. Adams Memorial Theatre
2. Benjamin F. Mather Home
3. St. John's Church
4. Mission Park
5. Haystack Monument
6. Sloan House
7. First Congregational Church
8. Chapin Rare Book Library
9. Thompson Memorial Chapel
10. Griffin Hall
11. United Methodist Church
12. Hopkins Observatory
13. Lawrence Hall
14. West College
15. First and Second Meetinghouses
16. Field Park
17. 1753 House
18. Sterling and Francine Clark Art Institute

agricultural community incorporated in 1865, but not as West Hoosuck. Feeding his considerable ego, Ephraim Williams, a colonel who had led the war's northern defense, left money in his will to establish a free school in the village on one condition: West Hoosuck must change its name to Williamstown, in his honor. The English Free School and Academy was established in 1791 and ultimately became Williams College in 1793. After the Civil War, the areas surrounding Williamstown turned to manufacturing and with the subsequent downturn of that industry became economically depressed. But Williams College infused the village with cultural lifeblood, beating as the very heart of Williamstown to this day.

Information
Williamstown Chamber of Commerce, Town Hall, 31 North St., Williamstown, MA 01267; 413/458-9077; 800/214-3799; www.williamstownchamber.com.
Williamstown House of Local History; Town Library, Field Park at Rte. 2 & U.S. Hwy. 7; 413/458-2160.

Getting There
From Boston take I-95 or I-495 to Rte. 2 west. From Stockbridge or Pittsfield, take U.S. Hwy. 7 north. Park at the Adams Memorial Theatre lot, accessed from Adams Memorial Drive on Rte. 2.

First Steps
Pick up a map and the Williamstown Points of Historical Interest brochure at the information booth, corner of Rte. 2 and U.S. Hwy. 7.

Williams College, Williamstown. This 2.5-mile walk leads you through the hallowed and historic grounds of Williams College. Begin your exploration of Williams College by visiting Adams Memorial Theatre (1), an intimate playhouse that is home to the Williamstown Theatre Festival. The WTF produces classic and original plays, featuring both students and internationally known actors. As you head down Main Street you'll pass the home of Benjamin F. Mather (2), now the admissions office, #988. Mather, a 9th-generation descendent of renowned New England puritan Cotton Mather, built the house in 1800. With his son Charles, Benjamin ran a general store during the 1800s on the site of the Adams Theatre.

Detour left on Park Street to St. John's Church (3), a stately 1895 structure made completely of fieldstone. Exquisite stained-glass windows and a vaulted ceiling grace the lovely sanctuary. Cross Park Street to Mission Park (4), a 10-acre park punctuated by the Haystack Monument (5). This 12-foot-tall marble column, which was quarried and crafted in the Berkshires, supports a globe that is 3 feet in diameter. It marks the spot where students in a college prayer meeting sought shelter in the lee of a haystack during an 1806 thunderstorm. Their epiphany reportedly inspired them to form "The Brethren" in 1808, as a foreign mission.

Walk between Williams and Chapin Halls, past Sage and Baxter Halls to the Sloan House, 936 Main Street (6). This gracious building, built in 1802 by wealthy farmer Sam Sloan, has sheltered the presidents of Williams College since 1858 and is commonly referred to as President's House. A design of the late Federal period, the house features side porches with intricate balustrade railings on three stories.

> **Culture in the Berkshires**
>
> Summer finds the mountains of the Berkshires turned into a virtual cultural mecca, encompassing the arts of music, theater, and dance. The offerings in the Berks prove that all New England culture does not lie just in Boston. The Tanglewood Music Festival, in Lenox, summer home of the Boston Pops since 1936, offers an outdoor music series that also includes chamber music, jazz, and pop performances. Jacob's Pillow Dance Festival, in Becket, oldest dance festival in America, presents innovative contemporary dance programs throughout the summer. Seasonal live theatre abounds in the Berkshires as well: Shakespeare & Company and Berkshire Opera Company in Lenox; Williamstown Theatre Festival in Williamstown; and the Berkshire Theatre Festival in Stockbridge. Contact the Berkshire Visitor's Bureau for more information: 800/237-5747; www.Berkshires.org

Proceed down Main Street once again, crossing Chapin Hall Drive to the First Congregational Church (7), whose steeple is topped with a brass weathervane. The church itself is part of Williams College, but the village of Williamstown has owned the steeple clock since the early days when it was the town's only timepiece. This was the site of the meeting house of the First Congregational Church of the United Church of Christ, organized in 1765. The present building was erected in 1869, a brick structure of the Romanesque-Revival style. In 1914 the church was "modernized" in the Neoclassical style, its brick covered over with white clapboard.

Just past the turret tower of Hopkins Hall, turn down the drive to Chapin Library/Stetson Hall. A marble staircase leads to the Chapin Rare Book Library (8), which was established in 1915. On permanent display under glass you'll find—The Declaration of Independence, 1776; Articles of Confederation and Perpetual Union, 1777; Committee of Style draft of The Constitution of the United States, 1787; House of Representatives version of The Bill of Rights, 1789; and George Washington's copy of The Federalist Papers. The library houses more than 25,000 rare books.

Retrace your steps back to Main Street to the imposing stone fortress, Thompson Memorial Chapel (9). Built in honor of a former alumna, the chapel features a bell tower meditation room that is open during the academic year. Of significance here is a John LaFarge stained-glass window, which was dedicated to President James A. Garfield, an 1856 graduate of Williams College. A minuteman statue stands on the grassy knoll in front of Griffin Hall (10), which was constructed in 1828 as a chapel and now houses classrooms.

Cross Main Street to the red brick United Methodist Church (11) on the corner, built in 1877, and proceed back up Main Street to the Hopkins Observatory (12). Constructed in 1836-38 of East Mountain stone, Hopkins is the oldest working observatory in the United States, offering planetarium shows and the opportunity to look through the college telescopes. Don't miss the Mehlin Museum of Astronomy's interesting astronomy exhibits.

Just beyond East College—which was rebuilt in 1841 after a devastating fire—lies the Williams College Museum of Art in Lawrence Hall (13), another must see. Built in 1846 as the college library, the hall now showcases 11,000 works of art in 14 galleries.

Walk past the imposing Morgan Hall and head up the hill, a great vantage point from which to photograph the picturesque First Congregational Church across the street. The building on the hilltop, now called West College (14), is the original academy that was built with the proceeds of Ephraim Williams's will in 1791.

The walk up Main Street leads past Spencer, Brooks, Perry, and Wood, all grand mansions that are now college buildings. Cross South Street to Field Park and the site of the First (1768-1797) and Second (1798-1866) Meetinghouses (15), now noted with a historical marker. The small, crudely built first meetinghouse was moved to make way for the second, which burned in 1866. These grassy areas of Field Park (16) are all that remain of the town green, which in those days was used for grazing cattle.

The 1753 House (17), in the park, is a replica of a "regulation" house, constructed for Williamstown's bicentennial. To qualify for a lot title, early settlers had to build a house on a 5-acre parcel of land that measured "at least 15 feet by 18 feet with a 7-foot stud." These were the "regulations." A quick peep inside yields a fascinating look at 18th-century construction methods.

Detour here for a brisk walk to 225 South Street (18), the Sterling and Francine Clark Art Institute. *(Contact: 413/458-9545)*. Francine and Robert Sterling Clark, who was heir to the Singer sewing machine fortune, purpose-built this museum to showcase their extensive private collection of French Impressionist and 19th-century American art. Monet, Degas, Homer, Sargeant, Remington and more than 30 Renoirs are on view here, as well as collections of sculpture, porcelain and silver. Special exhibitions spotlight collections from other major museums.

Mt. Greylock State Reservation

Long an inspiration for writers and poets, Mount Greylock, at 3,491 feet, presides as the grand majesty of the Berkshires, its summit offering sweeping vistas of New York, Vermont, New Hampshire, Massachusetts, and Connecticut. A road leads to the top of the 440 million-year-old mountain, where Bascom Lodge, a rustic stone and timber building built in the 1930s by the Civilian Conservation Corps as a hospitality center for hikers, is now run by the Appalachian Mountain Club. About 20 minutes from the summit, Mt. Greylock Visitor's Center showcases a large diorama, depicting the 50 miles of varied trails that wind throughout the 11,000-acre reservation.

Information
Mt. Greylock State Reservation, Rockwell Road, Lanesborough, MA 01237; 413/499-4262.

Getting There
Mass. Turnpike (I-90) to exit 2, Lee. Take Rte. 20 north to U.S. Hwy. 7 north. Continue north to Lanesboro. Watch for Mt. Greylock Reservation

and Visitor Center signs on the right, 2 miles north of Lanesboro. Turn right on Main St. and follow signs.

First Steps
Stop at the Mt. Greylock Visitor Center on North St., just before the reservation, to pick up a trail map.

Mt. Greylock State Reservation. A Mt. Greylock naturalist suggests six walks in the reservation with varying levels of difficulty. All feature interesting geologic structures or fantastic views.

Round's Rock (1) is an easy 1-mile loop through low-bush blueberry barrens, which peak during August. A good family hike, the trail goes by the ruins of a 1945 airplane crash and affords great views of Mt. Everett, the Taconic Mountains, and Housatonic Valley. The trailhead is a small gravel turnoff on the right side of Rockwell Road, 3.1 miles from the Visitor's Center. Access Deer Hill Trail (2) from the Sperry Road campground parking lot via the Roaring Brook Trail. This moderately difficult, 2-mile loop trail winds through old growth forest of 250- to 300-year-old red spruce and hemlocks—unique in this area—into the heart of Greylock. The trails cross Roaring Brook and pass by Roaring Brook Falls amid some of the prettiest woodland flowers in the region. The hike out from Deer Hill is steep.

Robinson's Point (3) is a quick 1/3-mile, 15-minute descent—accessed off a Notch Road pullover—perfect for sunset viewing. The climb out will take 30 minutes. Bring a flashlight. With great views of the summit, Stony Ledge Trail (4) is the naturalist's personal favorite, with wonderful views of Mt. Greylock and Hopper Ravine to March Cataract Falls. Remnants of old homesteads litter the edges of the lower trail and remains of charcoal pits of the 1800s pepper the southwest slopes.

The Overlook Trail (5), which is accessed from the summit, is a 2.4-mile moderate loop that winds through mixed conifer and hardwood forest, peppered with wildflowers in the spring. Steep at both the beginning and the end, Overlook Trail crosses two tributaries of Bacon Brook, offering the possible sighting of a black-throated blue warbler. Following the Appalachian Trail for a distance, Overlook Trail affords a view of the Hopper and passes Old Pump Pond, Massachusetts's highest manmade pond. March Cataract Trail (6) leads from Sperry Road campground for .8

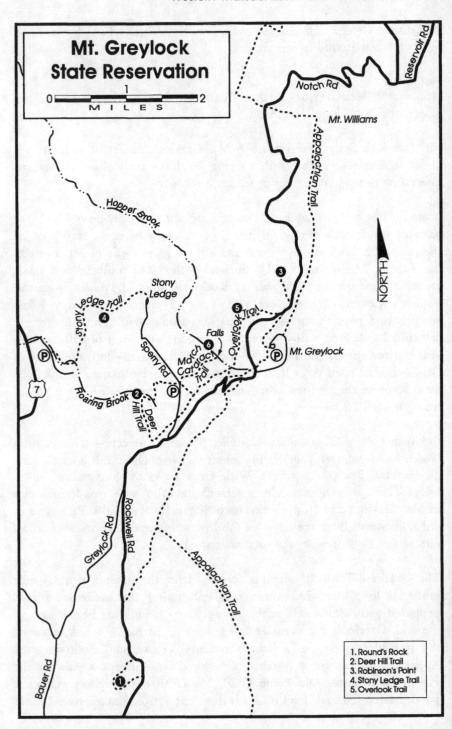

Mt. Greylock State Reservation

0 — 1 — 2
MILES

NORTH

Notch Rd

Reservoir Rd

Mt. Williams

Appalachian Trail

Hopper Brook

Stony Ledge

Stony Ledge Trail

❹

❸

❺

Overlook Trail

Falls

❻

Match Cataract Trail

Sperry Rd

❻ Mt. Greylock

Ⓟ

Ⓟ

Roaring Brook

❷

Deer Hill Trail

Ⓟ

Ⓟ

❼

Greylock Rd

Rockwell Rd

Appalachian Trail

Bauer Rd

❶

1. Round's Rock
2. Deer Hill Trail
3. Robinson's Point
4. Stony Ledge Trail
5. Overlook Trail

miles, ending at March Cataract Falls on Bacon Brook. This short moderate trail, which is occasionally steep, lies in a transitional zone known as the Hopper.

Hancock Shaker Village

Turn back the clock for a visit to the Shaker community at Hancock, home to the "United Society of Believers in Christ's Second Appearing" from 1790 to 1960. Hancock Shaker Village, comprised of the restored buildings that remained in 1960 when the Shaker community dissolved, now functions as a living history museum that interprets three centuries of Shaker life.

Information
Hancock Shaker Village, P.O. Box 927, Pittsfield, MA; 413/443-0188; 800/817-1137; www.hancockshakervillage.org.

Getting There
From Boston take the Mass. Turnpike (I-90) to exit 2, Lee, then U.S. Hwy. 20 north to U.S. Hwy. 7 north to Pittsfield. Hancock Shaker Village is at the junction of U.S. Hwy. 20 and Rte. 4.

First Steps
Pick up an easy-to-follow walking tour brochure at the Visitor's Center and wander the paths of yesteryear. Hancock Shaker Village is open daily from Apr. through Nov. An admission fee is charged.

Hancock Shaker Village. Living a simple existence devoted to God, members of the commune practiced celibacy, equality and separation of the sexes and combined practicality and ingenuity in the invention of many items we have long taken for granted. Known as Shakers because of the trembling and shaking gyrations they endured when the "spirit moved them," the group sought perfection in all things. Three hundred Shakers lived in the Hancock community at its peak in the 1830s.

Costumed "sisters" and "brothers" interpret everyday life, demonstrating chores such as spinning, working a loom, harvesting the garden or tending to the cattle. The restored function-driven buildings date to the 18th and 19th centuries. Of particular interest is the round dairy barn, built of stone in 1826. Hancock Shaker Village offers workshops in a variety of Shaker crafts such as forging iron roses, chair seat weaving, and oval box construction.

Natural Bridge State Park

This .5-mile exploration is more a discovery on foot than a walking tour, but Natural Bridge is a singular geological wonder that should not be missed. Meltwaters from mile-thick glaciers cut deeply through the marble bedrock here 500 million years ago, sculpting the Hudson Brook chasm and forming a "natural bridge." This phenomenon is repeated nowhere else on this continent.

Information
Natural Bridge State Park, P.O. Box 1757, North Adams, MA 01247; 413/6636392 (May-Oct.); 413/663-6312 (Nov.-Apr.).

Getting There
From Boston take I-95 or I-495 to Rte. 2 west. From Stockbridge or Pittsfield, take U.S. Hwy. 7 north to Rte. 2 east. From North Adams, take Rte. 8 north for .5 mile.

First Steps
The park is open daily from Memorial Day through Columbus Day. A vehicle fee is charged.

Natural Bridge State Park. Located on the site of the former Hoosac Marble Company quarry, a series of steps and boardwalks winds up-and-down, in-and-out, around-and-through the intricately eroded stone. Water cascades over the lichen-covered white marble dam, manmade in 1800, and percolates through a series of potholes as if falling from teacup to teacup. The potholes in the chasm are formed when stones caught by depressions in the streambed are tumbled by the rushing water, drilling deep, circular holes into the bedrock.

Nathaniel Hawthorne was a frequent visitor to Natural Bridge. In 1838 he wrote in *American Notebook*: "The cave makes a fresh impression upon me every time I visit it—so deep, so irregular, so gloomy, so stern . . ." The area continues to stimulate the arts. Massachusetts Museum of

Contemporary Art (Mass MoCA) installed speakers in the neighboring mined-out marble quarry. For 15 minutes each day at sunset, a series of computer-generated tones—designed by Walter Fahndrich—plays softly and subtly, creating an eerie counterpoint to the sounds of rushing water. (Gates to the upper parking lot close at 4pm so you must walk up to the quarry from the lower lot.)

Rainy Day Options

Situated on 36 scenic acres of the former Linwood estate, the **Norman Rockwell Museum** houses the world's largest collection of original Rockwell art as well as changing exhibits by other renowned illustrators. Rockwell spent his final 25 years in Stockbridge, immortalizing the village in a number of his works. Frequent gallery talks illuminate Rockwell's life and work. The artist's last studio, the one he liked best, was moved from downtown Stockbridge to the museum grounds in 1986. Open for viewing, the cozy lofted studio looks like Rockwell simply stepped out for a cup of tea, for it is chockablock with easels, palettes, brushes and personal momentos. *(Contact: Norman Rockwell Museum, Rte. 183, Stockbridge, 413/298-4100.)*

Nestled into the side of Prospect Hill with sweeping vistas over the Housatonic River valley, **Naumkeag** justifies its Native American name, "haven of peace." Joseph Hodges Choate—an affluent lawyer and successful diplomat—built the Shingle-style summer house in 1885. A riot of gables and towers, alcoves and porches, the 26-room mansion is surrounded with terraced lawns punctuated with a confluence of paths and gardens. Both the interior furnishings and the extensive grounds reflect the Choates's extensive travels to Europe and the Far East. The rooms are filled with Chinese porcelain, antique furniture, tapestries, and original artwork. The landscaping, which was designed by Fletcher Steele, features a Japanese pagoda amid Japanese maples, a walled Chinese garden, and an English rose garden. The home is open seasonally for guided tours. *(Contact: Naumkeag, Prospect Hill Rd., Stockbridge, 413/298-3239.)*

Opened in May 1999 in a 19th-century former factory complex, Mass MoCA, the **Massachusetts Museum of Contemporary Art** is the largest center for contemporary visual and performing arts in the country. The cavernous multi-story galleries on the 13-acre one-time industrial site showcase contemporary works of gargantuan proportion, many of which have never before been exhibited because of their grand scale. Artists whose works are displayed at Mass MoCA tend to be on the cutting edge of expression. Of particular note is "The 1/4 Mile or 2 Furlong Piece" by Robert Rauschenberg, a 20-year mixed media endeavor—still a work-in-progress—that spans the football field-size second-floor gallery of Building 5. A 10,000 square-foot theater provides the vehicle for innovative live theater and dance performances as well as avant-garde film productions. *(Call for directions, which are complicated. Contact: MassMoCA, 87 Marshall St., North Adams, 413/664-4481, www.massmoca.org.)*

Lodging

For more lodging options, consult the New England accommodations websites and reservations services listed in "How to Use This Book" or check out www.mass-vacation.com or the Berkshire Bed & Breakfast Homes reservation service, 413/268-7244.

Immortalized by Norman Rockwell's "Main Street at Christmas," the three-story **Red Lion Inn** ($+, 30 Main St., Stockbridge, 413/298-5545, www.redlioninn.com) dominates the village in both stature and hospitality. The main inn of the Red Lion, built as a hostelry in 1897 on the site of a 1773 tavern/stagecoach stop, features 110 guest rooms. Seven vintage houses nearby—including the old firehouse—have been converted for guests as well.

"To the manor born" may have been coined to describe **Devonfield** ($$, 85 Stockbridge Rd., Lee, 413/243-3298, 800/664-0880, www.devonfield.com). The Federal-style manor house overlooks a sweeping birch-dappled meadow in the shadow of the Berkshire Hills. Wide hallways with planked flooring and oriental rugs lead to six guest rooms and three suites, which are decorated in period furnishings and wall coverings in understated elegance. Hospitable touches, such as a stocked guest pantry, set Devonfield apart.

The Orchards ($$+, 222 Adams Rd., Williamstown, 413/458-9611, 800/225-1517, www.orchardshotel.com), within walking distance of Williams College, reflects the elegant ambiance of an English manor house with lazerlike attention to details. With a pencil-post bed, so high it comes with its own set of stairs, to goose-feather pillows, down comforters and a wood-burning fireplace, each of the 49 guest rooms exudes the Old World charm enjoyed by America's aristocratic ancestors.

The Inn at Stockbridge ($$, Rte. 7 North, Stockbridge, 413/298-3337, 888/466-7865, www.stockbridgeinn.com), a turn-of-the-last-century Georgian-Colonial on 12 acres, exudes the ambiance of an English country house. Complimentary wine and cheese, candlelit breakfasts, and a houseful of antiques, all make this place special. The inn is secluded but not far from the action.

The former Tom Ball Farm, built in 1776 by Revolutionary War soldier Christopher French, found new life in 1952 when it became **The Williamsville Inn** ($$, Rte. 41, West Stockbridge, 413/274-6118, www.williamsvilleinn.com). The inn offers a unique package of New England charm—cozy guestrooms, a barn full of sheep and goats, 10 acres of gardens and a candlelit gourmet restaurant. Each summer the inn's meadow is transformed into a regional sculpture garden.

Four-poster canopy beds and claw-foot tubs pamper weary walkers at **Windflower** ($+, 684 S. Egremont Road, Great Barrington, 413/528-2720, www.windflowerinn.com), a former Berkshire estate built in the 1850s. The 13 guestrooms—several with working fireplaces—are cozy and inviting. Afternoon "tea," complete with homemade pastries, is served each day in the casual living room or on the screened porch, where guests look out at sweeping lawns, manicured gardens, and the swimming pool.

The 12 country guest rooms at **The Weathervane Inn** ($+, Rte. 23, South Egremont, 413/528-9580, 800/528-9580, www.weathervaninn.com), a 1785 farmhouse with an 1835 Greek-Revival addition, welcome visitors to the Berkshires. Friendly and relaxing, this is a good place to get away from it all.

A 32-room Colonial inn built in 1771, **The Village Inn** ($-$$$, 16 Church Street, Lenox, 413/637-0020, www.villageinn-lenox.com) sits in the middle of Berkshire culture. All rooms are furnished with country antiques and reproductions. Accommodations are available across three price categories, depending upon size of room and amenities such as wood-burning fireplaces and whirlpool tubs. The inn features a candlelit dining room and a cellar pub tavern with a light-fare menu.

An elegant Tudor on 85 acres in the Berkshire Hills, **Blantyre ($$$$**, Blantyre Rd., Lenox, 413/637-3556, www.blantyre.com) enjoys Relais & Chateaux status. Reminiscent of an aristocratic castle, Blantyre is conveniently situated near Tanglewood, the Berkshire cultural oasis. Andrew Harper's Hideaway Report calls Blantyre, "America's consumate estate sanctuary."

In 1878 Luther Noyes bought land abutting the town green, now Field Park. He built a house and sold it to spinster sisters Cordelia and Lydia Paige in 1884. Today, reincarnated as the **Williamstown Bed and Breakfast** ($, 30 Cold Spring Rd., Williamstown, 413/458-9202, www.williamstownbandb.com), the Victorian home, furnished with period antiques, offers guests gracious yet affordable accommodations in the heart of historic Williamstown.

Food and Drink

The restaurant scene in the Berkshires mirrors the creativity of its other cultural offerings. Dining choices abound. For more dining options, log on to www.berkshires.com.

Dark, cozy and casual with rough-hewn wide-plank floors and red-checkered tablecloths, the **Widow Bingham's Tavern ($$$**, 30 Main St., Stockbridge, 413/298-5130), at the Red Lion Inn, oozes with colonial charm. Offering the same gourmet cuisine as The Red Lion's cavernous formal dining room (jackets required there for men), Widow Bingham's provides an intimate colonial setting. **The Lion's Den ($)** in the inn's cellar offers pub fare and live entertainment.

A railroad passenger depot serving the New York, New Haven, and Hartford Railroad from 1893 to 1971, **Sullivan Station ($$**, Railroad St., Lee, 413/243-2082) now serves great down-home cookin' with atmosphere. Sullivan Station offers a sure-fire meal ticket at a palatable price.

A vision of hunter-green upholstered walls, soft lighting and pink pastel linen, **The Orchards ($$$$**, 222 Adams Rd., Williamstown, 413/458-9611) creates its cuisine like Michelangelo might have sculpted David—with vision and acute attention to detail. Elegance is the order of the day here, and the prices reflect it, but every single bite is worth the indulgence.

Situated on the site of the former Alice's Restaurant of Arlo Guthrie fame, **Theresa's Stockbridge Cafe** ($, Main St., Stockbridge, 413/298-5498) offers steaming soups, thick sandwiches, salads, and quiches. The unpretentious eatery serves its fare atop small marble-top tables.

The Williamsville Inn ($$, Rte. 41, West Stockbridge, 413/274-6118, www.williamsvilleinn.com) serves elegant country cuisine nightly in July and August, and on Thursday through Sunday the rest of the year. The intimate **Tom Ball Tavern** ($) offers lighter fare. From November through April, Sunday at the Williamsville Inn means a prix fixe menu and the popular storytelling night, where noted authors, poets, and performers share the romance of language with readings and interpretations of their work.

Once the last and best known Alice's Restaurant, operated by Arlo Guthrie and Alice Brock until 1979, the **Apple Tree Inn** ($$, 10 Richmond Mountain Rd., Lenox, 413/637-1477) serves dinner Thursday through Sunday evenings and every night during Tanglewood season. Located in a 120-year-old inn across from Tanglewood, the summer home of the Boston Symphony Orchestra, the restaurant creates gastronomic music of its own.

Candlelight and linen, fine crystal and china, the gentle notes of a harp, even the good silver—this is dinner at **Blantyre** ($$$$, Blantyre Rd., Lenox, 413/637-3556, www.blantyre.com). If you shut your eyes as you sample the fine cuisine, you may be able to imagine yourself as lord of the manor.

Pittsfield's newest upscale gathering place, **Dewey's** ($, 1 West St., Pittsfield, 413/499-2000), in the Crowne Plaza Hotel at Berkshire Common, is a library-themed cocktail lounge. Patrons enjoy libations from a full bar, as well as a pub menu that includes sandwiches, salads, clam chowder, and buffalo wings.

Specializing in New England regional cuisine, **The 1896 House** ($$, Rte. 7, Williamstown, 413/458-1896) offers four "period" dining rooms in an historic barn. The Common Room's candlelit tables flank a fieldstone fireplace, and the Publick Room is a small, intimate parlor. **The Tap Room** ($) features a round bar and "Yankee comfort fare." A special function room is dubbed the Great Room in honor of Christopher and Dana Reeve, who met here.

Moonlight Diner & Grill ($, 408 Main St., Rte. 2, 413/458-3305, www.moonlightdiner.com)—it's '50s; it's good; it's cheap; it's All-American; it's got attitude! Need I say more?

Vermont

Introduction

Vermont has less level ground than almost any other state in the United States. French settlers named the area "verdmont," or green mountains, because of the preponderance of green deciduous trees on the mountains. The English later dropped the "d." The Green Mountains were formed 425 million years ago by subterranean pressures on either side of a fault line, which effectively thrust half of New Hampshire atop Vermont. The resulting towering mountains eroded to Pre-Cambrian rock, making the Green Mountains one of the oldest ranges in North America.

The Green Mountains are lower (tallest peak is 4,000 feet) and more fertile than the White Mountains of New Hampshire. Early settlers farmed the area, grazing their cattle in mountain pastures. Vermont still is very rural in character, left relatively unchanged by the Industrial Revolution. Its population is among the smallest in the United States, and the federal government ranks it as most rural of all the states. The Green Mountain State has more cattle, fewer cities and less manufacturing than other states in New England. Dairy products remain a chief industry, along with the quarrying of granite and marble, the underlying rock of the Green Mountains.

Both New York and New Hampshire claimed Vermont until 1777, when it declared independence, forming a separate republic with its own coinage, postal system, and foreign minister. Ethan Allen's Green Mountain Boys fought the "Yorkers" until the Revolution, when all the colonies united against the British. New York blocked Vermont's admittance to the Union until 1790, when Vermont paid New York $30,000 for the privilege of statehood, which it achieved in 1791. The Green Mountain National Forest attracts nature enthusiasts in all seasons, especially during the spectacular autumn months when hordes of leaf-peepers invade the state. By mid October the mountains are ablaze with prismatic foliage, punctuated by the scarlet leaves of the sugar maple, Vermont's state tree.

Some say, tongue-in-cheek, that Vermont has six seasons, adding mud season and black fly season to the traditional four. Mud season is generally during the months of April and May, when spring runoff saturates the soil. Hikers are urged to stay off higher elevation trails during these months because the trails in these areas are particularly vulnerable to erosion and vegetation damage. Black fly season follows the spring runoff and lasts until the end of June. Black flies buzz hikers incessantly, attacking with vicious bites. Strong insect repellent and veiled hats help repel the pests, but most native Vermonters wisely wait until black fly season ends before taking to the woods.

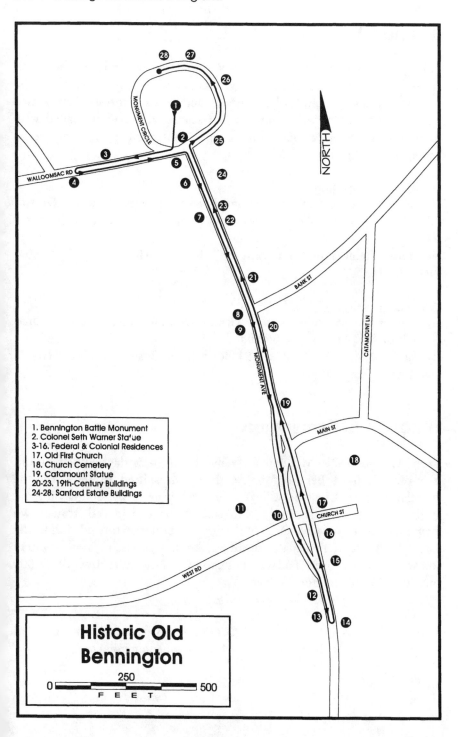

1. Bennington Battle Monument
2. Colonel Seth Warner Statue
3-16. Federal & Colonial Residences
17. Old First Church
18. Church Cemetery
19. Catamount Statue
20-23. 19th-Century Buildings
24-28. Sanford Estate Buildings

NORTH

MONUMENT CIRCLE

WALLOOMSAC RD

BANK ST

CATAMOUNT LN

MONUMENT AVE

MAIN ST

CHURCH ST

WEST RD

Historic Old Bennington

0 ——— 250 ——— 500
F E E T

Southern Vermont

Pastoral and picturesque, Southern Vermont nestles amid the southern range of the Green Mountains—a virtual canvas of white church spires, barn-red farms, peaceful village greens and verdant forests. Pretty as a postcard, especially during autumn leaf season, this area is loaded with natural wonders, great outlet shopping, quaint country inns and stellar dining establishments.

Regional Information

Vermont Department of Tourism and Marketing, 6 Baldwin St., Drawer 33, Montpelier, VT 05633-1301; 800/Vermont; www.1-800-Vermont-.com.
Vermont Chamber of Commerce, P.O. Box 37, Montpelier, VT 05601; 802/223-3443.

Getting There

By Air: Major carriers offer service to Boston's Logan International Airport or U.S. Airways to Rutland.
By Automobile: MA Rte. 2 to I-91 north (from Boston) or U.S. Hwy. 7 south (from Rutland).

Historic Old Bennington

From 1761 to 1820, Monument Avenue hummed as the main street and economic hub of Bennington. As the town shifted to industry, the population moved to the "valley" nearer the waterpower sources for the mills and the newly built railroad. Now considered downtown Bennington, this area of mills, foundries and potteries thrived during the late 19th century, producing furniture, knitted goods, toys and pottery known the world over. Today Bennington is a residential town of 17,000 and home of Bennington College.

Information

Bennington Area Chamber of Commerce, Veterans Memorial Dr., Bennington, VT 05201; 802/447-3311; www.bennington.com.

Getting There

Take I-91 to Rte. 9 west. Follow Rte. 9 (West Main St.) through

Bennington center. At Old First Church, take a sharp right onto Monument Ave. Park in the Bennington Monument parking area.

First Steps

Pick up a copy of "Two Walking Tours of Bennington, Vermont" from the Chamber of Commerce, Veterans Memorial Dr. (Rte. 7), which details two historic walking tours. The best walk is Monument Ave. (1.5 mile), whose high points are featured below. The Downtown Bennington (2.75 mile) tour actually is better explored by automobile. The architectural points of interest along this route—mainly late 19th century commercial and public buildings—are scattered over a large area with many unremarkable structures in between.

Historic Old Bennington. Begin and end this walk at the Bennington Battle Monument (1), a 306-foot phoenix rising from the top of Monument Hill. The monument marks the spot where Brigadier General John Stark's American forces and the Green Mountain Boys defeated the army of British General John Burgoyne in the summer of 1777. Commemorating the battle, believed to be the turning point of the Revolution, the Bennington Monument, erected in 1891, sits on the site of the arsenal depot the two sides were fighting over. You can take an elevator to an observatory at the top of the monument, where you'll enjoy a 360-degree panorama that encompasses vistas of the Green Mountains, New York State and even Mount Greylock in Massachusetts.

At the corner of Monument Circle stands a granite statue honoring Colonel Seth Warner (2), commander of the Green Mountain Boys, whose in-the-nick-of-time arrival during the Battle of Bennington turned the tide, allowing the Americans to be victorious. Follow the prescribed route down the right side of the wide boulevard, Monument Avenue, where you'll pass by late 18th- and early 19th-century Federal- and Colonial-style private residences (3-16) whose histories are noted in the walking tour brochure. Cross the street at the Dewey House (14), c. 1800, homestead of Bennington's first minister. In Colonial days, the village preacher was granted the "minister's right" of 420 acres of land in the town center in return for his services.

Of particular note on this historic walk is the Old First Church (17), c.1805. A scalloped picket fence surrounds its fascinating cemetery (18), which predates the church. Among those buried here are Revolutionary

War soldiers, five Vermont governors and poet Robert Frost (signs lead to his grave and family plot). The intricately carved 18th-century headstones in this cemetery are amazing.

Beyond the church, on Monument Avenue, a bronze statue (19) of a catamount (wild cat) commemorates the site of the former Catamount Tavern, which was destroyed by fire in 1871. Ethan Allen and the Green Mountain Boys met here to form the Republic of Vermont. Several of the early 19th-century structures (20-23) you'll encounter between the statue and Bennington Monument, now private homes, were constructed of brick or stone, unlike the predominantly wooden structures across the street. The Federal-style brick structure (20) was built as an academy in 1821 and housed the district school. Old Bennington's sole remaining stone structure (23), c.1781, served as a blacksmith shop.

Back at Monument Circle you'll see the four buildings of the former Sanford estate (24-28), shingle-style structures built between 1896 and 1900. They still enjoy a commanding view of the countryside from atop the hill. The grassy circle is a great place to spread a picnic after your walk.

Equinox Preservation Trust, Manchester Village

At 3,835 feet, Mount Equinox is the highest peak in Vermont not traversed by the Long Trail. The Equinox Preservation Trust is a not-for-profit organization created in 1993 by Equinox Resort Associates. Together with the Vermont Land Trust, the Vermont Institute of Natural Science and The Nature Conservancy, the Trust dedicates itself to the preservation, protection and wise environmental management of the wilds of Mount Equinox. A series of multi-use blazed trails are open to the public. The trails are rated "easy," "more difficult" and "most difficult."

Information
Equinox Preservation Trust, Rte. 7A, Manchester Village, VT 05254; 802/362-4700.

Getting There
Take Rte. 2 west to I-91 north. Then take exit 2 in Brattleboro, to Rte. 9 west to U.S. Hwy. 7 north to Rte. 7A in Manchester. Turn left for one

mile to The Equinox Resort.

First Steps
Pick up an Equinox Preservation Trust Trail Guide in the Equinox Resort.

Equinox Preservation Trust. From the parking lot of the Equinox Resort, follow the gravel path to Union Street and turn right at the fork (water tower will be on left). Proceed to Red Gate where you'll begin this walk. Follow the merged Red Gate and Blue Trails to the Snicket Trail. Turn left on this yellow blazed trail, which is a narrow, winding path through a stand of white paper birch and other mature hardwoods. (You'll encounter a glacial erratic the size of a VW Beetle.) Bear left on the lower loop of the Red Gate Trail, past the Main Gate and follow Pond Loop Trail halfway around Equinox Pond, where you'll see anglers trying their luck at fly-fishing. (Pond Loop Trail is flat and "easy;" Red Gate and Snicket Trails are rated "more difficult," which means you'll encounter intermittent, short ascents and descents.)

A gin-clear brook babbles from the pond, passing under a small wooden footbridge. At the fork, bear left on the Mountain Bluff Trail, which is rated "most difficult." (If you want to continue on the flat, easy Pond Loop Trail, bear right.) Mountain Bluff Trail is the most challenging in the Equinox Preservation Trust. You'll traverse steep ascents and descents and climb to an elevation of 1,580 feet.

This trail through third-growth forest is blazed red. You can hear the rushing water of Upper Spring and Middle Spring to your far left. The trail jogs sharply to the right—on the left is an abandoned slate-roofed shed built directly over a cascading stream—and proceeds up an extremely steep incline. Don't despair, this killer ascent is as bad as it gets. The trail reaches a plateau and traverses it for a distance. Bear left at the fork, down a steep hill, turn right and follow the mountain stream that cascades along the descending trail.

If you have the stamina left, detour .5-mile up Robin's Lookout, where you'll enjoy a sweeping view of Equinox Pond, the Batten Kill Valley and the Green Mountains. Trillium Trail joins Mountain Bluff Trail from the left for a short distance, then forks to the right. At the fork, follow Trillium Trail to Pond Loop Trail. Turn left on the blessedly flat path to the Main Gate and exit the Equinox Preservation Trust.

Go out the black iron gates and walk down Pond Road. Mountains ring the residential street. Turn left on Prospect Street, then right on Taconic Road. Well-manicured, grand Federal-style homes with outbuildings line this street, some with horses and ponies grazing in the back yard.

Cross Route 7A to the Dellwood Cemetery, a bucolic resting place filled with tall pines, silver birches, brooks and waterfalls. Enter the main gates and look for Orvis Circle, the burial compound of generations of the Orvises, the family who began their famous fly-fishing business here in Manchester. A tall stone crypt with 12 graves marks the center, 16 more headstones line the grassy perimeter. Notice that near the gates is a solitary Orvis grave. This appears to be the black sheep of the family, banished from the family circle even in death.

Cross back over Route 7A and follow the marble sidewalks back to the Equinox Resort. (Manchester Village has more than 17 miles of marble sidewalks.) The street is lined with large white houses, all with hunter-green, colonial-blue or black trim and shutters. Of no one architectural style, the massive buildings appear to have had wing upon wing added over the centuries. Dominating the tiny village green is the grand Equinox Resort, almost as long as a city block, (see Lodging) and the picturesque First Congregational Church, whose carillon tower chimes in song each evening at 6 PM. A monument to the men of Manchester who served in the Revolutionary War, the War of 1812, the Mexican War and the Civil War stands in the middle of the green. End your 5.5-mile trek with a glass of lemonade taken atop the wide, gracious verandah of the Equinox.

Grafton Ponds Trails, Grafton Village

Grafton Village is unique among New England villages, not a re-creation but the actual restoration and preservation of a living, breathing 18th-century community. Settled in 1780, Grafton always had more sheep than people—10,000 by 1850—and probably still does. (The human population is now a whopping 600.) Life in the village revolved around the general store and the inn ñThe Old Tavern (see Lodging)—which are still the centerpieces of the town. In 1963 the Windham Foundation began restoring many of Grafton's beautiful historic buildings. (The Foundation now owns about half the buildings in the village.) Scattered around the tiny village you'll find these Foundation enterprises, operating much as they did in the 19th century: Grafton Village Cheese Company, the Grafton Blacksmith Shop, Grafton Village Store, Idyll Acres Farm and The Old Tavern. Explore them, then head to the Grafton Ponds Trails for the walk detailed below.

Information
Windham Foundation, Inc., Grafton, VT 05146; 802/843-2211; www.windham-foundation.org.
Grafton Ponds Nordic Ski & Mountain Bike Center, Townsend Rd., Grafton VT 05146; 802/843-2400.

Getting There
Take I-91 north to exit 5 (Bellows Falls). Bear right off the exit to the "T" at the end of the road. Turn left on Rte. 5 north for 2 miles to the first set of traffic lights. Turn left to Rte. 121 west for 12 miles to Grafton.

First Steps
Stop at the Information Center on Townsend Rd. (802/843-2255) for a trail map, then proceed to the parking lot of the Graftons Ponds Nordic Ski and Mountain Bike Center. You'll find trails labeled "easier" and "more difficult." All are clearly marked with capital letters.

Grafton Ponds Trails. A series of well-groomed cross-country ski and snowmobile trails are maintained as walking and mountain-biking trails in the other seasons. For this 3-mile walk—rated "easier"—which combines portions of a number of trails, take Main Trail past I to K, where you'll find the Village Overlook. Look across the alpine meadow, where you'll see two white church spires, The Old Tavern and the white buildings of the village. Follow the gradual incline of the trail past M, along the top of Lee Wilson Loop to Q. Make a sharp right to P, then a switchback left onto Big Bear Trail. Cut to the right up a steep incline to T, then at the fork, turn right again continuing on Big Bear Trail.

Covered Bridges

Undoubtedly, you will encounter the quintessentially New England covered bridges in your on-foot explorations. New Englanders built covered bridges for many reasons. The roof of the covered bridge kept the roadway dry, preventing water and snow from seeping into the joints of the road, where it might freeze during the winter or cause rotting during the summer. The walls and roof of the covered bridge strengthened the structure, the added weight making the bridge more solid. And the covered bridge looked much like a barn, a calming influence on the animals, which really did not like crossing a rushing river.

Big Bear Trail runs up the ridge through a deciduous forest. At the top of Big Bear Trail you'll find a warming shed with a picnic table, where you can rest and sit a spell. (This is a great spot for lunch.) You'll be rewarded for your climb with a panoramic view, through the birches, of the valley and the mountains beyond.

Now, you can begin your trek down the mountain. Follow Big Bear past the entrance to Little Bear Trail at U and continue to the fork at E. Turn left on Chivers Trail. At the base of Chivers the trail leads you through a meadow. (A big bull's eye is painted on the mountain across the meadow.) The trail leads along the top of Windham Pond and markers C and D.

Leave the path at the sign noting Grafton Ponds Tube Hill and walk through the meadow to the top of Grafton Pond, whose center features a manmade fountain. Turn right and follow the wooden boardwalk around the pond, which fronts the winter warming house buildings, back to where you began. You'll find solitude and good bird watching on the Grafton Ponds Trails.

White Rocks-Ice Beds Trail

The White Rocks National Recreation Area is located in the northern section of the Manchester District of the Green Mountains National Forest. Logged until the 1930s, the 36,000 acres are covered with third and fourth growth forest. The White Rocks National Recreation Area was created in 1984 with passage by the U.S. Congress of the Vermont Wilderness Act. The recreation area has blazed trails for every ability level. White Rocks-Ice Beds is one of its most fascinating.

Information
Green Mountain National Forest, Manchester Ranger District, Rtes. 11 and 30; RR 1, Box 1940; Manchester Center, VT 05255; 802/362-2307; www.fs.fed.us/r9/gmfl/hiking/white_rocks.
Green Mountain Club, 4711 Waterbury-Stowe Rd., Waterbury Center, VT 05677; 802/244-7037; www.greenmountainclub.org.

Getting There
Take U.S. Hwy. 7 north to Rte. 140 east. After 2.1 miles, bear right on Sugar Hill Rd., (gravel road), then bear right again and follow signs to

White Rocks National Recreation Area.

First Steps
From the White Rocks picnic area, look for the White Rocks-Ice Beds Trail sign at the southwest side of the parking lot. No trail maps are provided, but the trail is clearly marked with blue blazes.

White Rocks-Ice Beds Trail. This moderate 2.5-mile round-trip hike may test your endurance at times but is well worth the effort. Cross a small stream and climb a series of switchbacks up the rocky ridge to the Parapet, a granite-laden cliff that affords you a dramatic view of the northwestern side of White Rocks Cliff. The trail continues its steep incline to the top of a knoll, where you'll be rewarded with another fantastic vista at the White Rocks Overlook. You can see Otter Creek valley and the Taconic Mountains.

From the knoll, follow the blue blazes and descend until you reach a jeep trail. Bear left on this trail, crossing a small stream. The trail then follows the brook upstream to the Ice Beds. In the thousands of years since the last ice age, freezing and thawing of water in the White Rocks Cliff has caused large pieces of quartzite rock to break off the face in big chunks and cascade to its base. Today, during the winter, ice forms in the recesses of the mountainous rock pile, where rain and snow become virtually trapped.

Because this gigantic mass of rocks lies in a shaded, protected ravine, the ice does not melt readily and remains hidden within the rocks of the Ice Beds well through the summer. The ice melts gradually, and the water flows from the base of the rocks in a chortling, icy stream. The simmering Ice Beds and 40-degree meltwaters cause a cool draft in the ravine, where the temperature is about 10 degrees cooler than the rest of the trail.

A scramble up the rock slide nets an impressive view of the surrounding mountains and forests. If your day is warm and sunny, bring a snack and lounge on one of the granite "tables" of the Ice Beds.

Rainy Day Options

Abraham Lincoln's eldest son, Robert, first came to Manchester when he was in college in 1863, accompanied by his mother, Mary Todd Lincoln, and his brother Tad. They stayed at the Equinox House (now the Equinox Resort). Forty years later Robert Lincoln purchased a large parcel of land on which he built a 24-room Georgian Revival summer home he named **Hildene**. The Robert Lincoln family and later their descendents summered here until 1975. Guided tours of this fascinating estate are offered seasonally, from mid-May through October. The magnificently restored mansion showcases furnishings and personal memorabilia from five Lincoln family homes, including a 1908 Aeolian pipe organ. The gardens also have been restored to their former grandeur. Three nature trails traverse the extensive grounds. (*Contact: Hildene, Rte. 7A south, Manchester, 802/362-1788, www.hildene.org*).

You'll find the largest public collection of paintings by Grandma Moses at the **Bennington Museum**. Anna Mary Robertson Moses, a.k.a. Grandma, began painting at age 75 and became an internationally regarded artist by her death at the age of 101. The schoolhouse she attended in nearby Eagle Bridge, New York, was moved to the museum and houses the collection, which includes several of her paintings of Bennington. The Bennington Museum also showcases the Bennington Battle Flag and other military and historical artifacts as well as collections of Vermont-created glassware, furniture, sculptures and paintings. The museum is open daily 9am to 5pm. Fee for admission. (*From U.S. Hwy. 7, turn right on Rte. 9, West Main St., in the center of Bennington. Contact: Bennington Museum, West Main St., Bennington, 802/447-1571.*)

Lodging

The charming inns of Vermont redefine the term "country breakfast." For more options, consult the New England-wide accommodations websites and reservation services listed in "How to Use This Book" or check out www.lodgingvermont.com or www.visitvt.com/vlra/lodging.

Exuding elegance and opulence in the relaxed, casual, unpretentious style of old money, **The Equinox** ($$-$$$$, Rte. 7A, Manchester Village, 802/362-4700, www.equinoxresort.com) dominates the village in both structure and stature. Begun as Marsh Tavern in 1769 and evolved into a premier resort by 1864, the 183-room Equinox Resort includes two restaurants, a fitness spa, Gleneagles Golf Course, British School of Falconry, Land Rover Driving School and Equinox Preservation Trust. You'll never be at a loss for things to do here, and, rest assured, Equinox sates your creature comforts too.

Details, details, details. Every amenity has been carefully considered at **The Inn at Ormsby Hill** ($$$$, 1842 Main St., Rte. 7A, Manchester Center, 802/362-1163, www.ormsbyhill.com). All ten romantically decorated "bed chambers" of this 18th-century Federal mansion have fireplaces and luxurious bathrooms, complete with two-person whirlpool tubs, perfumed bath salts, candles and a family of rubber duckies. A plate of freshly baked cookies welcomes you, and breakfast is outrageously memorable.

Since 1801, the historic guest roster of **The Old Tavern** ($$, Rtes. 35 & 121, Grafton, 802/843-1801, www.old-tavern.com) has read like "Who's Who": Grant, Hawthorne, Emerson, Kipling, Thoreau, Webster. Restored by the Windham Foundation in 1965 with detailed authenticity, the inn's wide plank floors, hand-hewn beams, pewter and polished brass evoke a bygone era. The 35 amenity-filled rooms and six historic guesthouses eschew phones and TV sets. Be sure to visit the exquisite Phelps Barn for a drink.

Built in 1910 atop the foundation of the original burned out c.1783 structure, **The Four Chimneys Inn** ($+, 21 West Rd., Rte. 9, Old Bennington, 802/447-3500, www.fourchimneys.com) was the estate of Peter Jennings, a prominent Bennington businessman until 1949. The eleven guestrooms, including the renovated icehouse and carriage house, have been recently refurbished, offering modern amenities amid old-world charm.

The Inn on Covered Bridge Green ($$, 3587 River Rd., Arlington, 802/375-9489; www.coveredbridgegreen.com) was Norman Rockwell's last home in Vermont. Located on 5.5 acres on the Batten Kill River, next to the c.1852 West Arlington covered bridge, the pristine guestrooms of this charming bed-and-breakfast are furnished with country reproductions and antiques. An 18th-century barn has been morphed into a honeymoon cottage, and Rockwell's former studio has been converted for groups of four or more.

Surrounded by 150 acres of woodland and perched on the mountainside overlooking the Batten Kill Valley, **West Mountain Inn** ($$+, River Rd., Arlington, 802/375-6516, www.westmountaininn.com), c.1849, evolved over the decades from farmhouse, to gristmill, to lumber mill, to hostelry. A welcoming basket of fresh fruit and a trail map inviting a hike into the "back 40" grace each of the 18 homey rooms and suites in the main inn, the Cottage in the Pines and the Historic Millhouse. Rates include country breakfast, pre-dinner hors d'oeuvres and "good cheer," and candlight dinner for two.

The Village Country Inn ($$-$$$$, 3835 Main St., Rte. 7A, Manchester, 802/362-1792, 800/370-0300, www.villagecountryinn.com) is a self-described haven for romance. The exquisite B&B offers lavishly decorated guestrooms and suites for most budgets. The common areas are warm and inviting, and lush gardens sprinkled with marble fountains surround the outdoor pool. Inn guests are offered a five-course candlelight gourmet dinner in the Rose Room at a special price.

Painted a dramatic purple, **The Reluctant Panther** ($$$+, 17-39 West Road, Manchester Village, 802/362-2568; 800/822-2331; www.reluctantpanther.com) distinguishes itself from other inns by more than its exterior color. Built in 1850 by a wealthy blacksmith, the inn features 21 elegantly decorated guestrooms and suites, some with fireplaces and whirlpool tubs. Rates include breakfast and dinner for two in The Reluctant Panther Restaurant.

The Inn at Manchester ($+, Rte. 7A, Manchester Village, 802/362-1793, 800/273-1793; www.innatmanchester.com) offers a self-avowed "peace, pancakes, and pampering." Who can resist? Open year round, this 19th-century Victorian and renovated carriage house sits on more than 4 acres, with incredible mountain views, a secluded pool in a meadow, 14 guest rooms, and four suites with fireplaces.

A restored 1880 Colonial, **Cornucopia of Dorset** ($$, Rte. 30, Dorset, 802/867-5751, 800/566-5751, www.cornucopiaofdorset.com) offers four guest chambers and a cottage suite, which feature four-poster beds adrift with down pillows and comforters, designer toiletries and period reproductions or antiques. You'll be greeted upon arrival at this charming bed and breakfast with a champagne welcome, and you'll find a pre-breakfast wake-up tray at your door each morning, complete with coffee, tea and fresh flowers.

Food and Drink

As the hub of gourmet dining in Southern Vermont, the Manchester area attracts diners from near and far like a magnet. For more dining options, consult www.visitvt.com/dining or www.manchesterandmtns.com/dining.

The original structure of the **Equinox Resort, Marsh Tavern ($$+,** Rte. 7A, Manchester Village, 802/362-4700, www.equinoxresort.com) first opened in 1769 and was a favorite meeting place for American Revolutionaries, including the Green Mountain Boys. Today subdued, masculine and casually chic with muted lighting and hunter-green walls, Marsh Tavern offers traditional tavern fare updated as New American cuisine.

The cuisine is far more imaginative than the minimalist décor at **Bistro Henry ($$,** Rtes. 11 & 30, Manchester Center, 802/362-4982), which is situated adjacent to the Chalet Motel. The upmarket bisto fare utilizes fresh local ingredients, and while the menu isn't extensive, the flavors are refined and refreshingly innovative.

Flickering candlelight, understated elegance and great cuisine distinguish the dining room at **The Old Tavern ($$,** Rtes. 35 & 121, Grafton, 802/843-1801, www.old-tavern.com). Feeding hungry horse traders, cattle dealers, clothing merchants and weary travelers since Enos Lovell converted his home into an inn in 1801, The Old Tavern carries its reputation as a first-rate eatery and watering hole into the 21st century.

Campily located in an authentic 100 year old train depot, **Bennington Station ($,** 150 Depot St., Bennington, 802/447-1080) features an extensive menu of classic American fare.

A *Yankee Magazine* Editor's Pick in 2000 and a favorite eatery in Bennington since the 1940s, the **Blue Benn Diner ($,** Rte. 7, Bennington, 802/442-5140) has refined traditional diner fare to cater to the more sophisticated taste buds of this 21st-century college town.

The ever-changing prix fixe menu at the **West Mountain Inn** ($$$$, River Rd, Arlington, 802/375-6516, www.westmountaininn.com) includes four courses plus a spot of Ben & Jerry's sorbet to cleanse the palate. So, although this may appear to be a pricey dinner, you'll get good value for your dough. Sup by candlelight in the inn's wood-paneled dining room by the flickering fire.

Even the name is unique—**The Perfect Wife's** ($$, 2594 Depot St., Rtes. 11&30, Manchester, 802/362-2817, www.perfectwife.com) approach to cuisine is like an artist's brush to canvas. Eat in the greenhouse garden room or the cobblestone piano room. The eclectic menu of upscale New American dishes offers satiation of your gourmet cravings.

Chef/Proprietor Robert Bachofen of the **Reluctant Panther** ($$$, 17-39 West Road, Manchester Village, 802/362-2568; 800/822-2331; www.reluctantpanther.com) serves up his uniue blend of European- and Swiss-influenced American cuisine with aplomb. The menu changes nightly and is presented in the Greenhouse room or aside the giant fieldstone fireplace in the main dining room.

Bringing a wealth of experience from Ondine's in Sausalito, Le Cirque in NYC and The Homestead in Greenwich, Conn., chef/owner Richard Whisenhunt's culinary talents explode at **The Black Swan** ($$, Rte. 7A, Manchester, 802/362-3807). Situated in the c.1834 Munson Farmhouse, The Black Swan offers tastes of the big city with country-village charm. The cuisine is upmarket, elegant and innovative.

A favorite with locals in Southern Vermont who love the chateaubriand and Caesar salad, the chef-owned **Chantecleer Restaurant** ($$, Rte. 7A, East Dorset, 802/362-1616) is a culinary oasis offering fine Continental cuisine that tempts gourmands from all over.

Central Vermont

A bastion of rural America, Central Vermont mixes a potent natural cocktail—rolling hills, challenging mountains, surging rivers, quiet villages. While the light of this area's riches isn't exactly kept under a barrel, its breathtaking scenery is often encountered off the beaten path, down winding country roads.

Regional Information
Central Vermont Chamber of Commerce, P.O. Box 336, Stewart Rd., Barre, VT 05641; 802/229-5711; www.central-vt.com.

Getting There
By Air: Major carriers offer service to Boston Logan International Airport or Burlington International Airport.
By Rail: Amtrak service from Eastern Seaboard cities, including Washington, D.C., New York City, and Boston to Montpelier, Waterbury, and Randolph (800/USA-RAIL; www.amtrak.com).
By Automobile: I-91 north to I-89 north.

Silver Lake Trail, Leicester

Silver Lake—1 mile long and 0.25 mile wide—is a glacial basin that nestles 1,260 feet above sea level surrounded by mountains. Artifacts discovered along its shores indicate that Native Americans fished and hunted here long ago. Frank Chandler created a religious camp on the shores of Silver Lake in 1879. The camp morphed into a hotel that subsequently was abandoned in 1911 after a dam constructed by Central Vermont Public Service Corporation (who owned water rights) caused the water level to rise 10 feet. The camp complex was completely destroyed by fire in the late 1930s, and Chandler's heirs deeded the pristine property to the Green Mountain National Forest in 1947.

Information
Green Mountain National Forest, U.S.D.A. Forest Service, Middlebury Ranger District, RD 4, Box 1260, Middlebury, VT 05753; 802/388-4362.

Getting There
Take I-89 north, to U.S. Hwy. 4 west, to Rutland. Then follow U.S. Hwy.

7 north, to Rte. 73 east, to Rte. 32 north (Goshen-Ripton Rd.). Turn on Forest Road 27 (Silver Lake Rd.). Follow brown signs to parking lot.

First Steps
Pick up an interpretive "Silver Lake" brochure at the trailhead. This round-trip loop is 3.7 miles.

Silver Lake Trail. From the parking lot, follow the Goshen Trail for .6 mile through thick deciduous forest down to Silver Lake. The Silver Lake Trail goes around the perimeter of the lake, and the brochure's "Rocky Point Interpretive Trail" points out the cultural and natural history of the area keyed to 31 interpretive markers.

You'll enter the 2.5-mile Silver Lake Trail loop between markers #23 and #24, which indicate growths of wild lily of the valleys and partridge berries. You can proceed around the lake in either direction, but for purposes of this descriptive narrative, turn right on the level dirt road. At intervals, unofficial paths cut into the woods and lead to the lake, following the shoreline for a distance.

You'll encounter the ruins of the Silver Lake Hotel, such as Old Fence Row, a large stand of Northern red oaks planted in the late 1800s at the time when visitors here "got religion." Only a few of the hotel's foundation stones remain, and a sprinkling of apple trees still can be found in the forest that has reclaimed the hotel's sizable orchard. Look for blackberries in the old fields if you're walking this trail in late August.

The trail leads past Silver Lake Dam on the north shore. Interpretive markers on the western shore point out the varied vegetation you are encountering, such as field horsetail, American hornbeam, sphagnum moss and liverwort lichen. Chandler Ridge looms over the trail here. The ridge's extremely hard core is known as Cheshire quartzite. (Quartzite comprises most of the western edge of the Green Mountains.) Divert down the short side trail to Rocky Point, where scuba divers discovered two Abenaki-era dugout canoes sunken in the lake.

At the south end of the lake, look for the "wood duck nest boxes" that the U.S. Forest Service has placed high in dead trees in an attempt to foster nesting among the declining wood duck population. Continue along to the eastern shoreline, which is called a kame terrace. The melting glacier deposited sand and gravel here, creating a porous landscape that early settlers found easier to cultivate than the western shore.

When you've finished the loop, return the .6 mile up the steep Goshen Trail to the parking area. Silver Lake remains a hidden gem in Vermont's environmental crown.

Robert Frost Interpretive Trail, Ripton

This easy, interesting walk commemorates the poetry of Robert Frost, who lived and worked less than a mile from here. For 23 summers Robert Frost lived in a small cabin north of Rte. 125 in Ripton, Vermont. A number of his poems are displayed in appropriate settings along the trail, carved into wooden boards that have been allowed to weather naturally. The poems displayed reflect the feelings of the poet, feelings ignited by walking through this natural environment.

Information
Green Mountain National Forest, U.S.D.A. Forest Service, Middlebury Ranger District, RD 4, Box 1260, Middlebury, VT 05753; 802/388-4362.

Getting There
Take I-89 north, to U.S. Hwy. 4 west, to Rutland. Then follow U.S. Hwy. 7, to Rte. 125 east for 2.1 miles, to Ripton.

First Steps
Begin this 1-mile loop at the trailhead just beyond the parking area. Interpretive markers are placed along the groomed path in lieu of a trail map. The first .3 mile is suitable for wheelchairs.

Robert Frost Interpretive Trail. The juxtaposition of poetry and nature is inspiring. Follow the poetry trail. A grassy pond area: "The Secret Sits." A canopied forest: "Stopping by Wood on a Snowy Evening." A log bridge over a chortling brook: "Come In." On the other side of the bridge is posted "The Road Not Taken," with an arrow pointing to the right. Aptly placed at this fork in the road, Frost's poem reads: "Two forks diverged in the yellow wood; Sorry I could not travel both; And be one traveler long I stood; And looked down one as far as I could; To where it bends in the undergrowth."

Benches are placed just off the path in scenic areas for meditation . . . and inspiration. A stand of towering hardwoods: "In Hardwood Groves." A dell of yellow birch trees: "Yellow Birch." A look through a clearing nets a sweeping vista of Firetower Hill, Bread Loaf Mountain, Battell Mountain, Kirby Peak and Burnt Hill, prompting: "Heaven gives its glimpses only to those not in position to look too close," from Frost's "A Passing Glimpse." A bench aside the south branch of Middlebury River invites reflection: "Going for Water."

The U.S. Forest Service uses prescribed fires (controlled conditions in spring and early summer) to perpetuate a meadow of low-bush blueberries. (Low-bush blueberries must be regenerated by fire once every three to four years for maximum production.) The old farm fields here are maintained by prescribed fires in early summer, just after the leaves emerge, creating what are called upland wildlife openings The burned woody vegetation is replaced by native grasses and native ground flora within two to three weeks. The Frost poem accompanying this instructional information is "The Last Mowing."

The trail leaves the meadow and follows the brook once again, canopied by the forest. Cross back over bridge and you'll returned to where you began, "Where the Secret Sits."

Texas Falls Nature Trail, Hancock

Unlike most woodland walks highlighted in this book, the most dramatic moment—the sighting of Texas Falls—happens before you ever reach the trail.

Information
Green Mountain National Forest, U.S.D.A. Forest Service, Middlebury Ranger District, RD 4, Box 1260, Middlebury, VT 05753; 802/388-4362.

Getting There
Take I-89 north, to U.S. Hwy. 4 west, to Rutland. Then follow U.S. Hwy. 7 to Rte. 125 east.

First Steps
Pick up a "Day Hikes" brochure at the Texas Falls Recreation Area above

the falls. This U.S. Forest Service publication lists 26 other trails in the Middlebury & Rochester Ranger Districts, most rated "moderate" or "difficult," should you want to try a challenging hike. Six trails in the Breadloaf Wilderness are unrated "in the wilderness ethic of self discovery."

Texas Falls Nature Trail. This 1.2-mile loop resembles the forest primeval . . . or maybe Eden. As you cross the rustic footbridge that leads to the trail, you will see the tumbling falls on either side. Texas Falls is comprised of a series of dramatic but small cascades that flow through a narrow gorge that was carved aeons ago by glacial meltwater.

Bear left after you cross the bridge and follow Texas Brook. You'll see that the torrents of swirling meltwater have drilled potholes in the bedrock of the stream. The shady canopy of the forest and the rushing roar of the falls and rapids provide a tranquil respite in every season. But be advised, this is an extremely popular spot for summer day-trippers (picnic facilities are provided), so if you plan a summer walk here, go in the early morning or late in the day for maximum peace and solitude.

Montpelier Architectural Tour

Montpelier—named after Montpellier, France—became a town in 1791, the same year Vermont was made a state. In 1805, when the state was seeking a permanent capital, the citizens of Montpelier trumped the legislature's decision by suggesting an offer they couldn't refuse—land and cash to build a wooden capitol building. A more substantial government building, stone with granite columns, was constructed in 1837, but a winter fire destroyed it in 1857. The present State House was built in 1859. Montpelier, which has the smallest population of any state capital in the U.S. (8,800), is committed to preserving the 19th-century character of its downtown.

Information
Vermont Historical Society, Pavilion Building, 109 State St., Montpelier, VT 05609; 802/828-2291; www.state.vt.us/vhs.

Getting There
By Rail: Amtrak service is offered from Eastern Seaboard cities, including

Washington, D.C., New York City, and Boston, (800/USA-RAIL; www.amtrak.com).
By Automobile: I-89 north.

First Steps
Stop at the Vermont Historical Society office on State Street and pick up a copy of "Three Walking Tours of Montpelier." Capitol Walking Tour offers a 1.5-hour guided architectural and historical heritage tour of Montpelier. Contact them at 134 State St., 802/229-4842.

Montpelier Architectural Tour. The Montpelier Heritage Group, Inc. has compiled three walking tours: State Street, Main Street and College Street, which detail the architectural features of the predominantly brick buildings, constructed in the late 1800s. Small and compact, the intersecting streets can be easily explored in under an hour. This little city appears caught in a time warp, a 19th-century movie set shadowed by a halo of mountains.

Dominating State Street is the Vermont State Capitol, constructed in 1859 in the Renaissance-Revival style. The gold-leafed dome, which is topped with a statue of Ceres, goddess of agriculture, is strikingly beautiful against the backdrop of the Green Mountains. The capitol's interior has been restored in recent years and features permanent and changing exhibits. (Free guided tours are available by calling 802/828-2228.)

A replica of the exterior facade of the c. 1876 Pavilion Hotel was built at the corner of State Street and Governor Davis Avenue in 1971, and the reconstructed period building now houses the Vermont Historical Society. Built in an architectural style known as Steamboat Gothic, the structure features massive verandahs on two stories and a mansard roof and is constructed of bricks that were made from 19th-century molds. Another striking structure on State Street is the Washington County Courthouse, a barn-red brick building sporting four dramatic white pillars. A brick jailhouse stands behind this Greek-Revival building.

Lower Main Street is lined with the commercial "block" buildings, such as Blanchard Block and French Block, so common in 19th-century American cities. Today, the towering brick structures house much of Montpelier's retail trade. Montpelier City Hall, c.1901, is built in the Italian Renaissance style of yellow brick and granite. Photographs of historic

Montpelier are displayed inside. Another interesting Main Street structure is the Main Street Depot, c.1880, a three-story station for Montpelier's turn-of-the-last-century rail service (now shops and offices).

Two buildings are of particular interest on Upper Main Street: The Methodist Church, c.1874, features beautiful stained glass windows and ten chimes in its carillon. The imposing Kellogg-Hubbard Library, c.1894, is constructed of rough granite blocks and features pink North Conway granite columns. Its interior showcases marble staircases and fireplaces and oak wainscoting.

The seven architecturally significant buildings that comprise the College Street tour—all on one city block—can be more easily inspected with a drive-by, since they are a distance from the intersecting Main and State Streets with several blocks of unremarkable structures in between.

If you are a 19th-century architecture bluff, you'll enjoy the 1.5-mile stroll along Main and State Streets. But even if you're not, this exploration reveals a pulsating city hidden within Montpelier's historic confines.

Quechee Gorge Trail, Quechee

Called Vermont's "Little Grand Canyon," Quechee Gorge was formed by the constant scouring of glacial meltwaters through a bedrock ridge more than 13,000 years ago. In 1875 Woodstock Railroad Company built a bridge spanning the gorge. Trains went from White River Junction to Woodstock, carrying passengers and supplies. With the growing popularity of the automobile, railway service ceased in 1933 and the beds were converted into a highway (Rte. 4). Waters of the Ottauquechee River rush under the bridge through Quechee Gorge.

Information
Quechee State Park, 190 Dewey Mills Rd. (Rte. 4), White River Junction, 802/295-2990.

Getting There
Take I-91, to I-89 west, to U.S. Hwy. 4 west.

First Steps
Pick up a Quechee Gorge brochure from the kiosk at the entrance to Quechee State Park. Park in lot at Quechee Gorge Gifts on U.S. Hwy. 4.

Quechee Gorge Trail. In 1962, the Army Corps of Engineers built a causeway between Dewey Mill Pond and the Ottauquechee River, which is now a walkway and wildlife sanctuary. Begin your 2-mile exploration of Quechee Gorge by walking out onto the bridge that spans the river (Rte. 4). The Ottauquechee River rushes dramatically 162 feet below, and the views both up-gorge and down-gorge are spectacular.

From the bridge, walk down to the hard-packed, wide path and follow it to the right, along the cliff, downhill, as it shadows the gorge on your right. At the bottom of the path you'll be at water level. Walk out onto the exposed flat boulders that carpet the riverbed. (You can fish for rainbow or brown trout if you have a Vermont fishing license.) Retrace your steps up the gentle but constant incline to the bridge. The mixed forest of hemlocks, beech, maples, pines and birch to your right is alive with songbirds and wildflowers.

The path leads under the automobile bridge, where it becomes a cedar chip trail. (The gorge will be on your left.) Follow the trail to a picnic area, which overlooks a dam and waterfalls. The dam was once the location of the Dewey Woolen Mill. The trail continues all the way to the dam itself. At the trail's terminus, you'll note a jarring contrast between the roaring waters that cascade over the dam and the calm, tranquil Dewey Mill Pond on the other side, which is set before the picturesque backdrop of the Green Mountains. Retrace your steps to where you began.

Woodstock Village Architectural Walk

Called "the prettiest small town in America" by *Ladies Home Journal*, Woodstock takes historical preservation seriously—half the village was listed on the National Register of Historic Places by 1973. Nestled between the Qttauquechee River and foothills of the Green Mountains, Woodstock was settled in 1765. By 1785 it was the Shire Town, or governmental seat, of Windsor County. Business and professional people, mainly from Connecticut and Massachusetts, were attracted to the picturesque village, bringing a modicum of culture with them to rural

Vermont. Shops and cottage industries burgeoned around the Village Green in the late 1800s, and agriculture, milling and animal husbandry flourished in the outlying areas. With the advent of the railroad, commerce declined; the population of Woodstock peaked in mid 19th century. The Old Woodstock Inn opened in 1892, and the village has been a year round resort town ever since.

Information

Woodstock Historical Society, 26 Elm St., Woodstock, VT 05091; 802/457-1822.

Woodstock Area Chamber of Commerce, 18 Central St., P.O. Box 486, Woodstock, VT 05091; 802/457-3555; 888/WOODSTOCK; www.woodstockvt.com.

Getting There

Take I-91 north, to I-89 north, to Rte. 4 west (exit 1) for 11 miles.

First Steps

Stop at the Chamber of Commerce Information Booth on the Village Green and pick up a copy of "Woodstock—A Walking Guide." Escorted walking tours start from the Chamber of Commerce Information Booth on the Village Green twice daily during the summer months.

Woodstock Architectural Walk. The Woodstock Historical Society has detailed a walking guide to Woodstock, which they call a "sampler" (55 locations) of the more than 200 historical structures in the village. This is an especially good, thorough walking guide. Each of the featured buildings is pictured in the brochure, alongside its architectural history, and a foldout map traces your prescribed route.

Begin your walk at the elliptical Village Green, which since 1793 has been the heart of the village. Walk along the top of the Green, past the stately Federal-style homes—many of which are made of brick. Note Middle Bridge, which crosses the Ottauquechee River on Mountain Avenue. It is the first authentic covered bridge built in New England this century, c.1967. Continue past the historic residences that line the Green and enter Church Street, where you'll see the Town Hall, built as a music hall in 1899, and the Unitarian-Universalist Church, a pretty, white Greek-Revival structure, c.1835.

Continue on along Prospect Street and South Street to the Woodstock Inn & Resort, c.1969, the most dominant building fronting the Green. A bustling hostelry has operated on this site since the Eagle Hotel opened in 1792. Of particular note on the south side of the Green are the Italianate-Revival Windsor County Court House and the Norman-Romanesque Norman Williams Public Library. Be sure to step into the library to view its interesting interior.

Continue down Central Street, which was designed as Woodstock's business district in 1800 and is lined with brick commercial "blocks"—French, Cabot, Whitcomb, Phoenix—mainly Italianate in style. A linseed oil mill constructed in the 1800s perches on a tributary of the Ottauquechee River further down this street. From here follow Bond Street to Pleasant Street and turn right on Elm Street. These streets are lined with wonderfully preserved Federal-style brick residences.

Cross the Elm Street Iron Bridge and walk .3 mile to the Marsh-Billings National Historical Park, which includes Billings Farm & Museum, a working dairy farm and museum of rural Vermont life. The park is a gift from Laurence S. and Mary French Rockefeller. Mrs. Rockefeller was the granddaughter

Maple Sugaring

The first sign of spring in New England is the annual ritual of sugaring—gathering the sap from the sugar maple trees to make maple syrup. From late February through early April, farmers in nearly every New England village invade the woods armed with buckets, tubing, and drills to gather the sap. Early settlers learned sugaring from Native Americans, who collected the sap in hollowed-out logs and dropped in hot stones to evaporate the water and reduce the sap to syrup.

Sugar found in the sap is made by the leaves of the sugar maple during the previous summer. (Trees with large, full crowns of leaves produce the best sap.) Trees need to be at least 8 inches in diameter to be tapped, which is done by drilling a small hole, 3- to 4-inches deep, several inches above the ground. A hollow metal drip peg is inserted in the hole. The peg has a wooden hook on which the sap bucket is hung.

Best weather for maple sugaring requires nights with temperatures below freezing and daytime temperatures between 45 and 50 degrees. Once the sap has begun to flow, buckets are emptied at least once a day into a gathering tank in the sugarhouse. The sap in boiled down in an evaporator until the syrup reaches the proper density. It takes 40 gallons of sap to make one gallon of syrup. Syrup is reviewed for density, color, and taste, then graded to federal government standards before being sold.

For information on sugarhouses open to the public, contact: Massachusetts Maple Producers Association, www.massmaple.org; Maple Syrup Producers Association of Connecticut, Inc., 860/974-1235; Vermont Maple Promotion Board, www.vermont-maple.org; www.visitnh.gov; or, visit the New England Maple Museum, Rte. 7, Pittsford, Vermont, 802/483-9414.

of Frederick Billings, who established his dairy farm in 1871 and began reforestation of the area based on the principles of George Perkins Marsh, one of America's first conservationists and an earlier owner of the property. You can explore the dairy farm and museum as well as the farmhouse, which has been restored to its 19th-century splendor (May through October; fee charged). Guided tours are offered of the Marsh-Billings-Rockefeller mansion as well as its grounds and gardens (June through mid-October; separate fee charged). Guided tours also are offered of the network of carriage roads that wind through Mount Tom Forest.

Retrace your steps for a .3-mile trek back to Elm Street and follow the thoroughfare to the Village Green. Take particular note of the Congregational Church, c.1807, which is known as the "Old White Meetinghouse." The original Revere bell, c.1818, cracked in 1976 and is now displayed on the south porch. The church features beautiful Tiffany windows. This entire street is lined with fabulous Federal-style residences. Back at the Village Green, you are sure to agree Woodstock earns it moniker as "the" quintessential New England village.

Vermont Raptor Center Nature Walk

The Vermont Raptor Center operates as an educational center, clinic and living museum devoted to birds of prey under the auspices of Vermont Institute of Natural Science. Located at the Bragdon Nature Preserve, the Vermont Raptor Center's birds have all been permanently injured and cannot survive alone in the wild.

Information
Vermont Institute of Natural Science, Vermont Raptor Center, 27023 Church Hill Rd., Woodstock, VT 05091; 802/457-2779.

Getting There
Take I-89, to U.S. Hwy. 4 west to Woodstock, then angle left on Church Hill Rd.

First Steps
When you stop at the remodeled dairy barn that is the Center's office to pay your entrance fee, you'll be given a map of the Raptor Center and a trail guide. Here you can borrow "Interrelationships," a booklet

highlighting the nature stations you'll encounter on the Gordon Welchman Nature Trail.

Vermont Raptor Center. A walk through the outdoor museum aviary of the Vermont Raptor Center is fascinating. The raptors are sheltered in their natural habitats, enclosed by gigantic cages. You'll encounter nine species of owls, ranging from the great horned owl to the snowy owl. And, you'll never get closer to a bald eagle than this. Both the male and female are within spitting distance, much larger "in the feather" than you'd expect from a fleeting glimpse in the wild. Other center residents include American kestrels, a merlin and a peregrine falcon, turkey vultures, golden eagles, seven species of hawks and common ravens. Their beady-eyed demeanors suggest that perhaps you are the one being inspected.

Surrounding the Vermont Raptor Center is the Bragdon Nature Preserve, which has three trails you can explore. The 0.25-mile Pond Loop Trail can be combined with the 9/10-mile Communities Nature Trail, which traverses fields and forests of pine and hardwoods. The most interesting option is the Gordon Welchman Nature Trail. A series of marked nature stations are placed along the 1.5-mile trail. They correspond to the guidebook you can borrow from the Raptor Center office. The book points out the flora you'll see on the trail and explains the complex interrelationships the plant life maintains with insects, birds, other wildlife and the earth itself. All nature lovers will love the Vermont Raptor Center.

Rainy Day Option

Born on the fourth of July, Calvin Coolidge, 30th president of the United States, is immortalized at the **President Calvin Coolidge State Historic Site.** Tiny Plymouth Notch, Coolidge's birthplace, rests in a time warp, a preserved example of an early 20th-century Vermont hill town. Very little has changed here since the turn of the last century.

A number of historic sites are open to the public. Wilder Barn exhibits 19th-century farm implements. Wilder House, the childhood home of President Coolidge's mother is now the coffee shop. The rooms of Coolidge Homestead, the president's boyhood home, are furnished exactly like they were in 1923. (It was here that as vice president,

Coolidge learned of the death of Warren Harding and was administered the oath of office). Plymouth Cheese factory was built by Colonel John Coolidge in 1890. You still can buy original-recipe "granular curd" cheese here. Generations of Coolidges worshipped at the Union Christian Church, c.1849, which features hard-pine woodwork made at a local mill. The actual Calvin Coolidge birthplace is a room attached to the General Store, where the president's father was storekeeper. You also can visit the Plymouth Cemetery across Route 100A, where six generations of Coolidges are buried. *(Contact: Calvin Coolidge State Historic Site, Rte. 100-A, Plymouth Notch, 802/672-3773.)*

Lodging

Some of Central Vermont's country inns offer networks of cross-country ski trails on their property, which they maintain in the other seasons for their hiking guests. For more lodging choices consult the New England-wide accommodations websites and reservation services listed in "How to Use This Book" or check out www.lodgingvermont.com or www.visitvt.com/vlra/lodging.

Off the beaten track but well worth the trip, **Blueberry Hill** ($, RR3, Goshen, 802/247-6735, 800/448-0707, www.blueberryhillinn.com)—a restored 1813 farmhouse nestled at the foot of Romance Mountain aside a spring-fed pond—entertains you like an old family friend. The cookie jar is always full, breakfast is sumptuous and each evening you are treated to an hors d'oeurves hour followed by a four-course dinner. (The inn does not have a liquor license so bring your own.) An extensive network of trekking trails through the Moosalamoo section of the Green Mountains begins at the inn's back door.

Hike 35 km of trails on the 17-acre estate encompassing the **Green Trails Inn** ($, Brookfield, 802/276-3412, 800/243-3412, www.quest-net.com/gti). Situated across the street from the floating bridge in Sunset Lake, at a crossroads known as Pond Village, the two 19th-century buildings that comprise the bed-and-breakfast tick and chime with the owners' antique clock collection. The 13 spacious, period-decorated guestrooms are simple, comfortable and win the author's pillow award (four rooms have shared baths).

An 1880 restored Victorian townhouse, **The Canterbury House** ($, 43 Pleasant St., Woodstock, 802/457-3077, www.thecanterburyhouse.com) shimmers with the gracious hospitality of a bygone era. The inviting common room of the bed-and-breakfast glows with oriental rugs over hardwood floors; an oak hearth fronts a flickering fireplace; and a fine wood banister leads the way to eight guestrooms, which are adorned with stenciling, quilts and lace. Best of all though, are the warmth and good humor of your hosts.

Betsy's Bed and Breakfast ($, 74 East State St., Montpelier, 802/229-0466, www.central-vt.com/business/betsybb), offers charm and value in one sweet package. The 12 homey rooms and suites occupy two turreted Victorians and a carriage house and are furnished with prints, chintz and antiques.

A brick Georgian, built in 1832, the **Shire Inn** ($$, Main St., Chelsea, 802/441-6908, 800/441-6908; www.shireinn.com) offers six guest rooms, each with 10-foot ceilings, wide-plank flooring, and tall windows. Named after Vermont's original shires, the rooms feature canopy beds and wood-burning fireplaces.

Mountain Top Inn and Resort ($$+, Mountain Top Rd., Chittenden, 802/483-2311, 800/445-2100; www.mountaintopinn.com) offers a cornucopia of outdoor sporting adventures—winter or summer—amid a spectacular setting in the Green Mountains. The inn, once a barn for a turnip farm in the late 1800s, has evolved into a gentrified country lodging, even frequented by presidents (Eisenhower, 1955).

Tucked away in the tiny village of Chittendam, **Tulip Tree Inn** ($$+, 40 Dam Rd., Chittendam, 802/483-6213, 800/707-0017; www.Tulip-TreeInn.com) offers an oasis of comfortable lodging and fine dining (see Food and Drink). Rates here include dinner and breakfast, which is a virtual feast. Fluffy towels and rubber duckies grace the bathrooms and the nine graciously appointed rooms span a range of budgets.

The rambling 144-room **Woodstock Inn & Resort** ($$$, Fourteen the Green, Woodstock, 802/457-1100, 800/448-7900, www.woodstockinn.com), a bastion of modern comfort with old-world ambiance, offers all the amenities you could hope for in a resort: golf, tennis, skiing, fitness center, great dining. The centerpiece of Woodstock's

Village Green, the Woodstock Inn & Resort began as Eagle Hotel in 1792, was replaced and renamed Woodstock Inn in 1892, and rebuilt again by Laurence S. Rockefeller in 1969.

An 1890 Victorian mansion, **The Jackson House Inn** ($$- $$$, 1143 Senior Lane, Woodstock, 802-457-2065, www.jacksonhouse.com) is surrounded by five acres of gardens and meadows, complete with a trout-filled pond. The 15 guestrooms are eclectically decorated in country New England, turn-of-the-last-century or French-Empire styles. Complimentary wine, champagne and hors d'oeuvres are offered at sunset.

Irish for "The Great House," the **Ardmore Inn** (23 Pleasant St., Woodstock, 802/457-3887, www.ardmoreinn.com) lives up to the Gaelic boast. The five guestrooms of the restored 1850 Greek-Revival Victorian are furnished with antiques and oriental rugs and offer a home away from home in both amenities and gracious hospitality.

Food and Drink

Since Central Vermont is so rural in nature, many of the country inns offer lavish dinners included in their room rates. Consult www.visitvt.com/dining for more options.

Occupying a converted 19th-century residence at the crossroads known as Pond Village, **Ariel's Restaurant** ($+, At the Floating Bridge, Brookfield, 802/276-3939) is a little-known culinary jewel. Weekdays you can sup in the cozy bistro-like pub room, where the chalkboard choices are upmarket, eclectic and reasonably priced. Weekends you can opt for the elegant formal dining room, where the cuisine is more intricate and pricier, but equally as tasty. Ariel's offers a wide selection of great wines by the glass.

Bentleys Restaurant & Cafe ($, 3 Elm St., Woodstock, 802/457-3232), dark and shiny as a Victorian parlor, offers fine eclectic cuisine, a good selection of microbrews and lively weekend entertainment. Situated in a landmark building in the center of Woodstock's historic district, Bentleys is a favorite of visitors and locals alike.

Recommended even by their competition, you know that the classic Vermont cuisine at **The Village Inn of Woodstock** ($+, 41 Pleasant St., Woodstock, 802/457-1255) has to be great! Dine amidst the stained-glass windows, carved oak mantles and tin ceilings of the turn-of-the-last-century drawing room or enjoy a leisurely meal outside on the verandah.

Eat while they learn. The restaurants of the **New England Culinary Institute** (www.neculinary.com) offer good food and value: The Main Street Grill & Bar ($, 118 Main St., Montpelier, 802/233-3188); Chef's Table ($$, 118 Main St., Montpelier, 802/229-9202); La Brioche Bakery & Café ($, 89 Main St., Montpelier, 802/229-0443).

The wood-fired flatbreads at **Firestones** ($, Rte. 4, Waterman Place, Quechee, 802/295-1600) are legendary, but their inventive pasta dishes vie for center stage too. You'll also find super burgers, salads, sandwiches and ales, which you can enjoy outdoors on the rooftop deck if you like.

Situated in a restored 1803 mill overlooking the Ottauquechee River, falls and covered bridge, the **Simon Pearce Restaurant** ($$, off Rte. 4 at the covered bridge, Quechee Village, 802/295-1470, HYPERLINK http://www.simonpearce.com www.simonpearce.com) serves its stellar cuisine on hand-thrown pottery and hand-blown glass made in the Simon Pearce manufacturing facilities in Windsor. The food is as magnificent as the view.

At the **Woodstock Inn & Resort** ($-$$$$, Fourteen the Green, Woodstock, 802/457-1100, 800/448-7900, www.woodstockinn.com), four restaurants stand ready to meet your dining needs. The formal dining room offers imaginative preparations of New American cuisine amid candlelight and soft music. The Eagle Café is more casual and less pricey. Richardson's Tavern features classic pub fare and live entertainment on weekends. And Woodstock Country Club serves its offerings *al fresco*, on a deck overlooking the links.

Offering a palate-tingling extravaganza rarely tasted this side of Manhattan, The Jackson House Inn Restaurant ($$$$, 1143 Senior Lane, Woodstock, 802-457-2065, www.jacksonhouse.com) opened in 1997 and garners raves for its cuisine, style and service. Choose between three prix fixe dining options: two courses plus dessert; a vegetable tasting of six courses; or a chef's-choice six-course tasting menu with wine pairings. Prepare to arrive hungry!

Bon Appetit says of **The Prince & The Pauper** (24 Elm St., Woodstock, 802/457-1818): "While the ambiance is laid back, the cooking is not." The dinner menu changes daily, reflecting the chef's culinary inspirations. And those with small appetites have the option of choosing from the Bistro menu, which served in the tavern.

Winner of the *Wine Spectator* Award every year since 1991, **Tulip Tree Inn** ($$$, 40 Dam Rd., Chittendam, 802/483-6213, 800/707-0017; www.TulipTreeInn.com) is renowned for their fine cuisine. The wine cellar includes 250 wines from all over the world.

Northern Vermont

From the shores of Lake Champlain to the Green Mountains and beyond to the lakes, streams and peaks of the Northeast Kingdom, Northern Vermont proffers a rich bounty of environmental goodness to explore on foot. Its villages small and quaint, it cities few and far between, its hillsides redundantly beautiful, this area of Vermont takes living in the woods to new heights.

Regional Information
Vermont Department of Tourism and Marketing, 6 Baldwin St., Drawer 33, Montpelier, VT 05633; 800/Vermont; www.1-800-Vermont.com. Vermont Chamber of Commerce, P.O. Box 37, Montpelier, VT 05601; 802/223-3443.

Getting There
By Air: Commuter service offered from Burlington International Airport.
By Rail: Amtrak service from Eastern Seaboard cities to Burlington/Essex Junction and Waterbury/Stowe stations (800/USA-RAIL; www.amtrak-.com).
By Automobile: I-91 north to I-89 north.

Little River State Park History Hike, Waterbury

A community of subsistence farmers inhabited this part of the 4,000-acre Ricker Block of Mount Mansfield State Forest in the early 1800s, eventually abandoning it for greener, more fertile pastures. The forest has reclaimed much of the settlement, but a ghost town of artifacts still remains. Little River State Park was created in 1962.

Information
Little River State Park, 3444 Little River Rd., Waterbury, VT 05676; 802/244-7103 (summer only); 800/658-6934 (Jan.-May).
Agency of Natural Resources Vermont Department of Forests, Parks & Recreation, www.vtstateparks.com.

Getting There
Take I-89 to Rte. 100 south (exit 10) for 0.25 mile. Then take Rte. 2 west for 10.25 mile. Turn right on Little River Rd. for 3.5 miles to the end.

First Steps
Stop at contact station kiosk for the History Hike trail guide (parking fee charged). Follow the signs for History Hike parking. Trailhead is in a mowed area on the left of the road.

Little River State Park History Hike. The history of subsistence farming springs to life on this 5-mile loop through the abandoned community that once toiled on the rocky slopes of Ricker Mountain. Joseph Ricker first settled here in the early 1800s and by mid century was joined by others—Hill, Goodell, Herbert, Montgomery, Carney, Clossey, Randall, Fuller, Ayer. By century's end more than 50 families lived in the Little River community.

Theirs was a hardscrabble existence, farming the crops, cattle and chickens they needed to survive. The community made tools from the preponderance of timber on the mountain, and marketed by-products such as maple syrup, tannic acid, soap and building materials via the railroad, which came through Waterbury by the middle of the 19th century. The thin soil of Ricker Mountain proved unsuitable for long-term farming, however, so by the late 1800s most of the families began abandoning their homesteads for more fertile, free-for-the-asking land in the valley.

This terrific walk takes you past the ruins and remains of the virtual ghost town at Ricker Basin. The comprehensive trail guide leads you to 18 locations, where it recounts the tales of the pioneers who lived and worked here. You'll encounter a dozen cellar holes—one even has rusting maple sap buckets still inside—two cemeteries, old roads and bridges, even the boiler, band saws and concrete foundations of the Waterbury Last Block Company Sawmill. Only the abandoned farmhouse of Almeron Goodell remains standing. All the others were either moved or destroyed.

For the most part, the trail follows the Dalley Loop Trail, diverting at intervals down other labeled trails to seek out the spirits of Little River. Your trek through Little River State Park is truly a journey through time.

Trapp Family Lodge Chapel Trail, Stowe

The hills are alive here at the Trapp Family Lodge, no doubt about it. Immortalized in "The Sound of Music," the Baron and Baroness von

Trapp and their nine children discovered Stowe in 1942 and fell in love with Vermont. They converted a hillside farm on 2,200 acres into a 27-room guesthouse in 1950, and the rest is history (see Lodging). The lodge's cross-country skiing trails double as hiking trails from late spring through fall, and the public is welcome to hike here at no cost. More than 90 species of birds, such as the broad-winged hawk, and rare, close-to-extinct species of wildflowers, such as purple trillium, can be found in this forest, which overlooks Nebraska Valley.

Information
Trapp Family Lodge, 42 Trapp Hill Rd., Stowe, VT 05672; 802/253-8511; 800/826-7000; www.trappfamily.com.

Getting There
Take I-91 north, to I-89 north, to Rte. 100 north (exit 10). Proceed for 8 miles, then turn left at Moscow Rd. for 1 mile. Turn right on Barrows Rd. to stop sign. Turn left, up the hill, for 1 mile and follow signs to Trapp Family Lodge.

First Steps
Stop at the Ski Touring Center for a "Nature Trails" map. The 2-mile Chapel Trail loop, a moderate hike, is detailed below. If you'd like another interesting challenge, try Sugarhouse Chute.

Trapp Family Lodge Chapel Trail. The trail segments here are blazed with red boxes, and intersections are signed like streets. From the Ski Touring Center, take Sugar Road to Maria Plaza and turn right toward Fox Track. At the fork take another right up the incline toward the chapel. As you pass through a forest of sugar maples, notice the maze of purplish flexible tubing strung from tree to tree. These trees have been tapped to collect sap for making maple syrup. In late March, the tubes drain the sap to sap buckets. When full, the sap buckets are emptied into 200-gallon gathering tanks that are taken for processing to the Sugarhouse by a sleigh drawn by a team of Belgian draft horses, just as the von Trapps did decades ago.

Hike up the short, steep ascent to Our Lady of Peace Chapel. Known as Maria's Chapel, the tiny stone structure is topped with a metal bell, and a now-rusty iron cross hangs over the marble keystone. Inside, a wooden icon of the Virgin Mary hangs over a small altar, which is laid with a Bible, candles and a heart-shaped box full of handwritten prayers. Pens and paper are supplied so that you can add your own prayer to the collection.

Continue on the path beyond the chapel, a slow but steady switchback ascent. At the summit, Johannes Rest, a ridge 1,100 feet above sea level, you'll find a thoughtfully positioned park bench, upon which you can catch your breath. Then fork to the right at the sign pointing back toward the lodge. The trail leads you out of the forest into a sudden clearing, where you'll be assaulted with a spectacular panoramic view of the verdant valley below and tiers of terraced mountains beyond that look almost surreal. You may be inspired to break into song.

Follow the Luce Trail along the ridge behind the Trapp Family Lodge. The vistas remain unparalleled. As you descend through the meadow, which is the setting for free music concerts in the summer months, you can almost imagine actress Julie Andrews twirling her peasant skirt and warbling, "The hills are alive with the sound of music."

Stowe Recreation Path, Stowe

After more than 10 years of intense community effort, the Stowe Recreation Path was completed in 1989, a total of 5.3 miles of path created at a cost of $680,000. Funding came from a wide variety of sources, including the creative venture of selling pieces of the path at $2 per inch, $15 per foot, $45 per yard and on through chains, rods and lengths.

Information
Stowe Recreation Path Greenway Information: 800/24-STOWE; 800/247-8693; 802/253-7321.
Stowe Area Association, Main St., Stowe, VT 05672; 802/253-7321; 800/247-8693; www.stoweinfo.com/saa.

Getting There
Take I-91 north, to I-89 north, to Rte. 100 north (exit 10), to Stowe Village.

First Steps
Stop at the Visitor Center on Main Street to pick up a Stowe Recreation Path map.

Stowe Recreation Path. The Stowe Recreation Path roughly follows the serpentine route of the West Branch River, through fields and woods and near some commercial and residential areas. At 10.6 miles roundtrip, this is quite a hike to do in its entirety, unless you are able to leave an automobile at both ends. You can choose among any of the seven entrances to design a shorter walk if you like. The primary access (1) in the center of Stowe is behind Stowe Community Church, a picturesque white structure with a tall steeple on Main Street (Rte. 100). A small park—Lintilhac Park—fronts the beginning of the path, named in honor of Claire Lintilhac, who conceived of the path as a way to get walkers off busy Mountain Road and spearheaded the effort to create the Recreation Path in the early 1970s.

Many of the other access points—all off Rte. 108, Mountain Road—are rather camouflaged, and the small, oblong white signs

> **Long Trail**
> The Long Trail is the largest and most varied trail system in Vermont, extending for more than 265 miles from the Massachusetts border to Canada, through the Green Mountains. More than 85 side trails crisscross the Long Trail, creating a 445-mile honeycombed network. Trails are marked with white blazes and secondary trails with blue blazes, handiwork of the Green Mountain Club, which maintains and protects the trails and publishes a wide variety of helpful hiking guides. Overnight sites are situated in 70 locations on the Long Trail, each about a full-day hike apart. For more information on the Long Trail System, contact the Green Mountain Club, 802/244-7037; www.greenmountain-club.org.

with black lettering that indicate the Stowe Recreation Path parking, rather obscure. Other access points are: (2) behind the Stowe Cinema next to the Baggy Knees Shopping Center; (3) near McDonald's where the path crosses the Rusty Nail Restaurant parking lot; (4) Cape Cod Road—no parking here, though; (5) Chase Park on Luce Hill Road, where the path follows an underpass beneath the road; (6) Thompson Park which is not well marked but is between Sugarhouse and Cottage Club Roads, on the opposite side of the Mountain Road. The terminus (or beginning if you so choose) is off Brook Road, just before a charming covered bridge. Here the path closely parallels the river for a while.

Now that you know how and where to access the Stowe Recreation Path, what will you see? The paved path attracts more bicyclists and rollerbladers than walkers, but your trek will be scenic, nonetheless. The path winds through meadows, past Bouchard Farm, shadows West Branch river and tributary streams, crosses 10 iron bridges and rambles under a forested canopy. The citizens of Stowe are justifiably proud of their special path.

Weissner Woods, Stowe

In memory of her husband Fritz—a conservationist with an adventurous spirit—Moo-Moo Wiesnner and her children entrusted 80 acres of woods to the Stowe Land Trust so that the public may always be able to enjoy this pristine forest. Trails are marked with the icon of the great horned owl, because Mrs. Wiesnner once nursed two such owlets back to health.

Information
Stowe Land Trust, P.O. Box 284, Stowe, VT 05672; 802/253-7221. Stowe Area Association, Main St., Stowe, VT 05672; 802/253-7321; 800/247-8693; www.stoweinfo.com/saa.

Getting There
From Stowe Village, take Rte. 108 (Mountain Rd.) for 3.5 miles to Edson Hill Rd. Turn right (pass entrance to Stowehof Inn) and take next drive on the right. Park on the left in Wiessner Woods parking lot and follow signs to trailhead.

First Steps
Stop at the Stowe Area Association Visitor Center on Main Street to pick up a trail map.

Wiessner Woods. For this quintessential walk in the woods, follow the trail through a meadow to the edge of the woods. The Catamount Trail leading into the forest is blazed blue, yellow and green, but the three diverge in different directions at Four Corners. Bear right on Hardwood Ridge Trail, blazed at this point both blue and green. The pine needle path winds through ferny undergrowth beneath a cathedral of mature pines, whose dead lower branches create a spooky, forest-fire-was-here feeling. Actually this old-growth forest is reaching for the sun; only the tops are green.

Bear right on Sugar House Loop, blazed green, where the Howard Carrol Memorial Bridge crosses a wide chortling stream. Dappled by sunlight, ferns and pine needles carpet the forest floor. Walk through an opening in a stone fence, some of which contains pieces of marble. Turn left on Sugar Shack Lane, following the green blazes, then turn right on Hardwood Ridge Trail, blazed blue.

At the end of Hardwood, continue straight onto Meadow Trail, blazed yellow, which is a gentle incline that leads to a scenic overlook. Rest a bit on the park bench and gaze over the meadow to the Green Mountains beyond. Take Meadow Trail back to Four Corners and follow the triple blaze back to the trailhead. This remote, tranquil 2-mile loop guarantees an all-but-private commune with nature. Walk quietly and you may meet pileated woodpeckers, songbirds, squirrels and deer.

Shelburne Museum, Shelburne

Possibly the most extensive, fascinating amalgamation of collections on the planet, Shelburne Museum rates a two-thumbs up . . . with all ten fingers! Thirty-seven exhibit buildings and historic structures house huge collections, so diverse you'd expect them to be in the Smithsonian Institution. Electra Havemeyer Webb founded Shelburne Museum in 1947 to showcase her extensive eclectic collections. Electra bought buildings she discovered on her travels in New England, had them dismantled and moved them to Shelburne, where they were reassembled. Hence, Shelburne Museum is now an outdoor art and history museum, displaying 80,000 amazing objects.

Information
Shelburne Museum, 5555 Shelburne Rd. (Rte. 7), Shelburne, VT 05482; 802/985-3346; www.shelburnemuseum.org.

Getting There
Take I-89 to U.S. Hwy. 7 south (exit 13), 7 miles south of Burlington.

First Steps
The museum is open daily from late May to late October. Only selected buildings are open by guided walking tour in the other months. Pay your

admission fee at the Museum Store, then enter the village of collections through the rear exit (you will receive a map).

Shelburne Museum. Begin your exploration of Shelburne Museum at the Electra Havemeyer Webb Memorial Building, whose interior was designed to re-create six rooms of the founder's New York City apartment. Upon her death, her children moved entire rooms to the museum, providing a window into the life of Electra and her husband, James Watson Webb, grandson of William Henry Vanderbilt. Showcased here is the Webb's private art collection, which includes works by Degas, Monet, Manet and Cassatt.

Next, visit the Lighthouse, c.1871, which was moved from Colchester Reef in Lake Champlain in 1952. Exhibits illustrate life in a lighthouse and Lake Champlain history. Nearby, Bostwick Garden, a walled planting of annuals and perennials surrounds a bronze sculpture by Edith Parsons called "Turtle Baby." The garden commemorates Electra Webb Bostwick, the founder's daughter.

From Bostwick Garden, cut over to the Webb Gallery, which houses a collection of 19th-century portraits and landscapes by such artists as Winslow Homer, Grandma Moses and Andrew Wyeth. Walk to the Sawmill, a re-creation of the Trescott-Shepard sawmill in South Royalton, Vermont, which showcases the mill's equipment, dating back to 1787. The original waterwheel was replaced with a historically accurate replica in 1990.

Sawyer's Cabin, the one-room house next door, was moved from East Charlotte. Constructed of hand-hewn and dovetailed timbers, the c.1800 log cabin was probably built by a French-Canadian logger. Move on to Dorset House, c.1832, a Greek-Revival house transported from East Dorset, which displays the largest collection of decoys for public viewing in the world.

The c.1845 covered bridge, the last double-lane bridge with a footpath in Vermont, was moved from Cambridge, where it spanned the Lamoille River. It now spans a manmade pond. Continue on to the Stagecoach Inn (c.1783, Charlotte), a Georgian building that features 10 fireplaces and two ham-smoking chambers. Displayed within are a folk art collection, tobacconists' figures, trade signs and ship figureheads.

Walk to the Schoolhouse (c.1840, Vergennes), a brick structure topped with a bell tower. The brickwork was removed, piece by piece, and reassembled on site in 1947. It is furnished as a 19th-century one-room school. The Variety Building next door (c.1835)—the only structure originally on the site of Shelburne Museum—is a rambling brick farmhouse that exhibits collections of decorative arts such as English ceramics, Chinese porcelain, American pewter and scrimshaw. The second floor gallery displays Mrs. Webb's 1200 antique dolls and her collection of dollhouse miniatures.

Adjoining the Variety Building, the Toy Shop displays miniature transportation toys such as steamboats, trains and fire wagons, as well as early cast-iron toys, banks and music boxes. The Hat and Fragrance Textile Gallery next door (c.1800, Shelburne) was originally a distillery, then the Shelburne town barn. Now it houses Electra Webb's extensive collection of quilts, rugs, hatboxes and costumes.

Proceed to Jail. The former Castleton jail, c.1890, is built entirely of slate and is reinforced with railroad irons. The nearby Shaker Shed (c.1840, Canterbury, NH), made of timber strengthened by five stone pillars, exhibits a collection of woodworking tools, cobbler and harness-maker tools and fire-fighting equipment.

Continue on to the Weaving Shop and the Ben Lane Printing Shop, both reproductions built on site in 1955. The Weaving Shop offers demonstrations of spinning and weaving, using an 1890s Jacquard loom. On display is a collection of vintage blankets, tablecloths and yard goods. The Printing Shop re-creates an early 20th-century village print shop, which demonstrates the workings of a variety of early presses.

Now explore the fascinating Horseshoe Barn and Annex. Here you'll find the carriage collection of Electra Havemeyer Webb's father-in-law, Dr. William Seward Webb. The barn is an on-site reproduction constructed in 1947 from hand-hewn beams collected from 12 other Vermont barns and stone from two gristmills. Here you'll see 225 horse-drawn vehicles, such as sleighs, coaches and fire equipment.

Proceed to the Meeting House, c.1840, a Greek-Revival-style church with trompe l'oeil walls, built by a Methodist congregation in Charlotte. Across the lane is Vermont House, c.1790, which Electra Webb had refurbished and designed to represent the home of a wealthy sea captain. Here she displayed her collections of Queen Anne and Chippendale furniture and European decorative accessories. Stop at the Blacksmith Shop, c.1800, where you'll see blacksmithing demonstrated as it was done in the early 20th century.

Next, visit the General Store (c.1840, Shelburne Center) and Apothecary Shop, which look like Hollywood movie sets. The fully stocked shelves display the type of goods found in a general store in the late 1800s. The attached Apothecary Shop was built on site in 1959 and re-creates a druggist shop during the same era. Most of this exhibit was salvaged from actual pharmacies that closed in the early years of the 20th century.

Visit the Stencil House (c.1804, Columbus, N.Y.) across the lane, a small gabled house whose interior walls and furnishings were hand-stenciled between 1810 and 1830. The neighboring Prentis House (c.1773, Hadley, Mass.) displays William and Mary furnishings, English delftware ceramics and oriental carpets. Next stop in at the Pleissner Gallery, which displays the work of artist Ogden Minton Pleissner, a close friend of the Webb family. His Manchester, Vermont, studio is reproduced here.

Continue on to the most incongruous, and perhaps most interesting, acquisition of the Shelburne Museum. Sitting high and dry in the middle of a grassy green is the steamboat Ticonderoga, which ferried passengers on Lake Champlain from the early 1800s to the middle of 20th century. An exploration of Ti's meticulously restored interior is fascinating, a time capsule to another era.

And just when you think this place can't get any better, you'll discover the Railroad complex. The Locomotive 220, built in 1915, was the last coal-burning, steam-driven 10-wheeler used on the Central Vermont Railway. It was retired from service in 1956 and given to Shelburne Museum for preservation. The Rail Car Grand Isle (c.1890), which belonged to Vermont Governor Edward C. Smith, reflects the grand manner of travel enjoyed by the rich at the turn of the last century. The Railroad Station, built for Rutland Railroad President William Seward Webb in 1890, served as the Shelburne railroad depot. Flanking the station, the Railroad Freight Shed, a replica of a station outbuilding, erected in 1963, houses a collection of railroad lanterns.

Stop at Beach Lodge and Beach Gallery, constructed on site in 1960 to look like an Adirondack camp. Named after the Beaches, hunting buddies of the Webb's, the log buildings—built of timbers from the founders' northern New York property—display hunting trophies, canoes, Native American artifacts and a collection of paintings depicting the American wilderness.

Finally, don't miss the Circus Building, a unique, horseshoe-shaped building that exhibits a magnificent 3000-piece, 500-foot-long miniature circus parade as well as 40 authentic, full-size carousel figures. The miniatures are carved on a scale of 1-inch to 1-foot. As you exit this unusual museum, stop at the McClure Visitor Center and Round Barn (c.1901, East Passumpsic), whose lower two floors display annually changing exhibits. Plan to spend the day at Shelburne Museum.

Burlington Waterfront Bike Path— Lakeshore Segment

Burlington, Vermont's largest city, hugs the eastern shores of Lake Champlain, a 136-mile freshwater lake, ranked as sixth largest in the U.S. The lake is named for Samuel de Champlain, a French explorer who discovered the coveted body of water in 1609. In the 1990s Burlington began restoring its waterfront. Part of that renaissance is the bike path, which runs for 6.5 miles along Lake Champlain, built upon a former railroad bed.

Information
Lake Champlain Regional Chamber of Commerce, 60 Main St., Burlington, VT 05401; 802/863-3489; www.vermont.org.

Getting There
By Air: Commuter service to Burlington International Airport
By Rail: Amtrak service to Burlington/Essex Junction.
By Auto: I-89 to Rte.2 (exit 14), Main St. to the waterfront.

First Steps
You won't need a map to traverse this easy-to-find path. But the winds blowing off Lake Champlain can be chilly, even in the warmest weather. Bring a sweater or jacket with you.

Burlington Waterfront Bike Path—Lakeshore Segment. This picturesque segment of the bike path, which follows the waterfront of Lake Champlain for 2.5 miles, nets fabulous views of the brilliant-blue Lake Champlain, the Adirondack Mountains of New York State across the lake and the Green Mountains on the Vermont side. Begin at Union Station at the base of Main Street. The railway depot operated from 1916 to 1953, serving passengers on the Rutland and Central Vermont railroads.

The initial leg of the path extends from Oakledge Park to the mouth of the Winooski River. Here you'll pass the Burlington Community Boathouse, built in 1991 and the Lake Champlain Basin Science Center, where you can experience hands-on ecological and cultural exhibits. The path continues on past the U.S. Coast Guard Station and the Lake Champlain Community Sailing Center.

Battery Park overlooks the waterfront. American troops camped here during the War of 1812, when British troops were within firing range. From the park, walk a long, uninterrupted stretch of lakeshore, passing the Urban Reserve, an active haven for waterfowl, ducks and sandpipers. Continue on to North Beach Park, a fine sandy beach and on to Leddy Park, the end of this segment of the bike path. Retrace your steps, completing the 5-mile loop.

Vermont Wildflower Farm, Charlotte

The Vermont Wildflower Farm is a commercial venture that opens its gardens to the public from May through October for a small fee. You'll see a short video, "Wildflowers through the Seasons," before venturing through the botanical trails, which identify 357 different plant species.

Information
Vermont Wildflower Farm, Rte. 7, Charlotte, VT 05445; 802/425-3500.

Getting There
Take I-89 to Shelburne exit just south of Burlington, then U.S. Hwy. 7 south.

First Steps
The self-guided path through the 6-acre wildflower farm leaves from the

back door of the retail office. You must pay an admission fee before you can access the trail.

Vermont Wildflower Farm. Garden enthusiasts will not want to miss this walk. Follow the gravel path through the main flower field, then through the woodland habitat. The plants are labeled with red, blue or white discs. Each numbered disc explains the plant's common and botanical name; whether the plant is biennial, perennial or annual; the season of bloom; maximum height of the plant; and flower color. Red discs identify species that have been introduced by seeding, such as Baby Blue Eyes, Iceland Poppy and Desert Bluebell. Blue discs mark plants that originally were growing on the property or were introduced with mature plants, such as False Solomon's Seal, Purple-Flowering Raspberry and Monkeyflower. White discs label species that are not usually considered wildflowers—ferns, sedges and grasses, such as Interrupted Fern and Floppy-top Sedge (an endangered species in Vermont), and trees, shrubs and other woody plants, such as Trembling Aspen, Wild Currant and Tartarian Honeysuckle.

Frequent explanatory signs share legends, historical uses and other interesting information about the plants that you are encountering. Blooms, of course, vary by season, so no two outings here will be exactly the same. You can buy wildflower seeds by the packet or by the pound—specially mixed for the growing conditions of the Northeast, Southwest, Wild West, Pacific Northwest, Southeast or Midwest—to create your own wildflower meadow.

Mt. Pisgah South Trail at Willoughby State Forest, Westmore

Lake Willoughby is a long, narrow glacially carved lake surrounded by dramatic rock cliffs. Known as Vermont's Lake Lucerne, the lake nestles beneath the shoulders of the surrounding mountains—Hor, Moose, Wheeler, Hedgehog, Pisgah and Bartlett. The Westmore Association maintains the trails at Willoughby State Forest. This state forest has no developed facilities.

Information
Vermont Dept. of Forest, Parks and Recreation, Waterbury, VT 05671; 802/241-3655.

Getting There
Take I-91 north, to Rte. 16 east at Barton, to Rte. 5A south at Westmore. Follow the shores of Lake Willoughby to the trailhead, on your left, which is marked with a small, square Mt. Pisgah sign, .4 mile after the campground. Parking is on the right side of the road, at the CCC gravel access road.

First Steps
This trail is unmapped and the powder-blue blazes are not too plentiful, but the path is well trodden.

Mt. Pisgah South Trail. This 3.5-mile roundtrip trek is for the hale and hearty. The narrow trail parallels the steep rock face of Mt. Pisgah and rewards those who persevere with spectacular views of Lake Willoughby and the surrounding mountain ranges. With an elevation gain of 1,450 feet, for the most part you will be walking steadily uphill or downhill.

Fall Foliage

Fall foliage season is a much-anticipated event in New England. Whereas all six states have colorful autumn leaves, the most popular viewing destinations are New England's mountains and foothills—White Mountains (New Hampshire and Maine), Green Mountains (Vermont), Berkshires (Massachusetts), and Litchfield Hills (Connecticut). Foliage season begins in late September and usually peaks around Columbus Day Weekend.

Why does Mother Nature treat New England to such a prismatic kaleidoscope? Native Americans thought the yellow leaves represented their campfires and that the red leaves symbolized the "killing of the Great Bear of the Heavens." Scientists have another theory: Food-making in the leaves produces chlorophyll, which gives the leaves their green color in spring and summer. But as the shorter days and cooler temperatures of autumn signal the approach of winter, the leaves stop making food, chlorophyll breaks down, and the green disappears, revealing the previously masked chemical pigments ñyellows, oranges, reds, and browns. Whatever the scientific explanation, New Englanders know that leaf season is magic.

Hints to the wise: Make hotel reservations as much as a year in advance. Go leaf peeping midweek if you can. Don't miss the back roads. Don't worry about hitting peak season because the colors are fantastic all during the autumn. And take a walk in the woods. There is no substitute for up-close-and-personal. For more information on New England's leaf season contact: www.mass-vacation.com/foliage; Maine Office of Tourism, 888/624-6345; New Hampshire Foliage Report, 800/258-3608; www.ctbound.org; www.1-800-vermont.com.

The trail initially descends an embankment and crosses a mud flat and Swampy's Pond via footbridges. Follow the trail to the left along a hogback and then turn right and head uphill. About 1 mile up the steep incline you'll encounter a dramatic rock outcropping called Pulpit Rock, where peregrine falcons often nest. If you're not an acrophobe, carefully walk out on the granite perch. Here you can enjoy a great view of Lake Willoughby, about 550 feet below, and also Mount Hor, Moose Mountain and Wheeler Mountain across the lake. (If you are experiencing any physical difficulties from the hike, turn around at this point. The trek to Pulpit Rock is terrific in and of itself.)

Continue up the steep incline another .75-mile to the grassy area that tops Mt. Pisgah, where you'll be able to see as far as the White Mountains of New Hampshire. Retrace your steps down the steep descent, still challenging though an easier cardio-vascular exercise. Or, if you are still raring to go, descend on North Trail, which you can follow down the other side of the mountain to Rte. 5A. However, this option means you will have to hike 3 more miles, along the highway, back to your car!

Darling State Park Summit Trail, East Burke

Burke Mountain, elevation 3,267 feet, is a popular ski area in Vermont's Northeast Kingdom. A paved road built by the Civilian Conservation Corps snakes its way to the parking lot at the top. From here, a footpath leads to the summit, affording panoramic views over the valley below.

Information
Vermont Dept. of Forest, Parks and Recreation, Waterbury, VT 05671; 802/241-3655.

Getting There
Take I-91 north, to Rte. 114 (exit 23) to East Burke. Turn right on Burke Mountain Rd. and follow it to the top of the mountain.

First Steps
The trail is unmapped and unblazed but well trodden. You'll find the trailhead to the left of the parking area at the top of Burke Mountain.

Darling State Park Summit Trail. Shortly into this 1.5 -mile roundtrip walk you'll encounter two forks to the right. These turnouts go the cliff's edge, affording sweeping views of the surrounding countryside. Continue on the main trail and at the next fork take the Summit Trail (to your left) to the top of Mount Burke. Climb the steps to the clearing. The view is spectacular—the summit is literally ringed with mountains. You can see Quebec, New Hampshire, and the Green Mountains. A fire tower is built on top of a big granite boulder here, and, if you are not bothered by extreme heights, climb the 124 steps to the viewing platform, where the phenomenal 360-degree vista will blow your socks off.

Retrace your steps from the summit to the fork and this time take the Under Profile Trail, an easy, flat path that hugs the side of the mountain. The trail leads between giant boulders, and huge rock formations hang over the trail. The trail becomes steep, narrow and rocky, with moss and lichens carpeting both sides, and then ends at an enormous rock outcropping that is covered with pines. At the risk of sounding redundant, the view here is magnificent. Retrace your steps back to parking lot.

Rainy Day Options

Create your own teddy bear in the "Make a Friend for Life" production room of the **Vermont Teddy Bear Factory**. A "beary" nice worker stuffs the bear body shell by machine to your specs. From the big dial, pick the whimsical ingredients that will be added to the your bear's stuffing. For instance, stuff the legs with love, the head with dreams and the tummy with giggles. A heart is placed in the bear and its final seam is sewn up. Choose an outfit for your bear to wear, pick a name and then the staff will issue your bear a birth certificate. A short tour of the actual factory is laden with "beary" corny jokes. *(Contact: Vermont Teddy Bear Factory, Rte. 7, Shelburne, 800/829-BEAR; www.vtbear.com.)*

"Moooooove on in" to the Cow Over the Moon Theatre at **Ben & Jerry's Ice Cream Factory** and see a short flick about how Ben and Jerry got their start in the ice cream business. Learn how the different flavors got their crazy names. After you enjoy the "moooovie," head to the tank room for a tour of the factory itself. You'll find out the secret ingredient in Ben & Jerry's ice cream—"dairy-air." No kidding, the ice cream is made with 17 to 25 percent Vermont air! And at the end of the tour, free samples are offered to all. *(Contact: Ben & Jerry's Ice Cream Factory, Rte. 100, Waterbury, 802/882-1240; www.benjerry.com.)*

Lodging

Wonderful inns and resorts nestle in the northern Green Mountains. For more lodging choices consult the New England-wide accommodations websites and reservation services listed in "How to Use This Book" or check out www.lodgingvermont.com or www.visitvt.com/vlra/lodging.

Experience a touch of Austria at the **Trapp Family Lodge** ($$, 42 Trapp Hill Rd., Stowe, 802/253-5764; www.trappfamily.com). This sprawling resort—begun by *the* Trapp family that Maria immortalized in song—offers 93 rooms in two lodges, all sporting refined Alpine-style décor and majestic vistas of the Green Mountains and valleys. Offering all the amenities of a first-class resort, you'll find plenty to do here. And you will hear music . . . nightly in the Lounge and at summer concerts in the meadow.

Every detail of the **Green Mountain Inn** ($+, 1 Main St., Stowe, 802/253-7301, 800/253-7302, www.greenmountain.com) has been restored or authentically reproduced. Originally built as a private residence and neighboring train depot in the early 1800s, the inn's 64 guestrooms feature stenciled walls, wainscot paneling, canopy beds, country quilts, antique furnishings and American folk art, and many offer fireplaces and whirlpool tubs. A health club, outdoor pool and two restaurants complete the picture.

Classic country in appearance but built in 1989, **The Inn at Essex** (70 Essex Way, Essex Jct., 802/878-1100, 800/727-4295, www.innatessex-.com) appoints its 97 rooms with period reproductions, decorator fabrics, comfortable sitting areas and in many cases, working fireplaces. Combining the amenities of a big-city hotel with the friendliness of a village inn and the upmarket cuisine of the New England Culinary Institute, the Inn at Essex seems to have found the recipe for success.

Situated at the north end of Lake Willoughby in the Northeast Kingdom, **Willough Vale Inn** ($+, Rte. 5A, Westmore, 802/525-4123, 800/594-9102, www.willoughvale.com) offers casual country comfort in its eight guestrooms and four lakeside cottages. Mt. Hor and Mt. Pisgah seem to rise from the lake like twin giants, an inspirational scene more reminiscent of the Swiss Alps than Vermont. Robert Frost wrote "A Servant to Servants" after he stayed here in 1909. Enjoy complimentary use of canoes, kayaks and bikes.

Internationally acclaimed, **Topnotch Resort and Spa** ($$$$, 4000 Mountain Rd., Stowe, 802/253-8585, 800/451-8686; www.topnotch-resort.com) combines European high-end amenities with Vermont country charm. Choose between 90 guestrooms and suites or 15 townhouses. Either way, you'll enjoy all the resort has to offer—14 tennis courts, 2 pools, fitness center, equestrian center, spa, sauna and whirlpool.

Situated on the Stowe Recreational Path, **The Siebeness Inn** ($+, 3681 Mountain Rd., Stowe, 802/253-8942, 800/426-9001, www.siebeness-.com) is surrounded by 70 scenic acres of meadow in the foothills of Mount Mansfield. The 12-guestroom bed-and-breakfast welcomes adults only. For maximum romance, take a moonlight dip in the outdoor pool or a soak in the hot tub.

An inn since the 1930s, **The Gables Inn** ($$+, 1457 Mountain Rd., Stowe, 802/253-7730, 800/422-5371, www.gablesinn.com), a c.1850 farmhouse, sits in the shadow of Mount Mansfield, the highest peak of the Green Mountains. Choose your lodging from among the 13 guestrooms in the inn, the four carriage-house rooms or two river-view suites. This warm and welcoming hostelry offers canopy beds, whirlpool tubs, fireplaces,country décor peppered with antiques and a relaxing greenhouse solarium.

Originally built for Vermont State Senator Charles Woodhouse in the 1880s, the **Willard Street Inn** ($+, 349 South Willard St., Burlington, 802/651-8710, 800/577-8712, www.willardstreetinn.com) was restored and transformed into a 15-guestroom inn in 1996. Loaded with interesting architectural details—check out the outside marble staircase, which leads to elaborate gardens—the inn is situated in the 19th-century mansion-lined Hill Section of Burlington. Three guestrooms do not have private baths.

The Inn at Shelburne Farms ($-$$$$, 102 Harbor Rd., Shelburne, 802/985-8686; www.shelburnefarms.org/comevisitus/inn) was the 19th-century country home of Dr. William Seward and Lila Vanderbilt Webb. Twenty-four bedrooms and cottages, in an entire spectrum of price ranges, reflect the gentile lifestyle of its owners, who designed Shelburne Farms as a model agricultural estate in 1886. This national historic site is a 1,400-acre working farm as well.

A family resort like no other in Vermont, **Smugglers' Notch** ($$+, 4323 Vermont Rd., Rte. 108 south, Smugglers' Notch, 802/644-8851; www.smuggs.com) was voted the #1 Family Resort in the Northeast by Disney's *FamilyFun* Magazine in 2000. Kid camps take care of the little ones, so parents can partake of the many adult activities, including walking the miles of groomed trails, even at night with a headlamp and a guide!

Food and Drink

Northern Vermont's lake and mountain country offers the option of dining in a romantic inn or amid the bustle of Stowe and Burlington bistros and trattorias. For more options, consult www.vermont-.com/dining or www.visitvt.com/dining.

Drink in the phenomenal views and savor the Continental-style cuisine at **Trapp Family Lodge** ($$, 42 Trapp Hill Rd., Stowe, 802/253-5764; www.trappfamily.com). European-trained chefs prepare seasonal Vermont specialties designed as three- or five-course prix fixe meals. The dining room is casually elegant and a harpist will serenade you.

Dine in the cozy, dark grillroom of the **Whip Bar and Grill** ($+, Green Mountain Inn, 1 Main St., Stowe, 802/253-7301, 800/253-7302, www.greenmountain.com) or opt to eat outside on its sunlit poolside patio. Either way, the food is great. Named for the collection of antique buggy whips that hang on its walls, the Whip offers full meals of innovative New American cuisine or light-bite salads, sandwiches, burgers and pub fare. The Whip Bar and Grill received the first liquor license ever granted in Stowe.

Your taste buds are in for a treat at **Butler's Restaurant** ($$, The Inn at Essex, 70 Essex Way, Essex Jct., 802/878-1100, 800/727-4295, www.innatessex.com) because this cozy, elegant restaurant is operated by the New England Culinary Institute. You'll be treated to cutting-edge cuisine and solicitous service here—this school turns out some of the brightest culinary stars in America. The four-course prix fixe menu is a great value. Enjoy casual pub fare in **The Tavern** ($).

You can't beat the view from the dining room at the **Willough Vale Inn** ($-$$, Rte. 5A, Westmore, 802/525-4123, 800/594-9102, www.willoughvale.com), which sits on the shores of the fjordlike Lake Willoughby. All windows look over the wide verandah and gazebo, creating a relaxed and casual atmosphere to enjoy first-rate Vermont-inspired country cuisine.

Don't give up the search for **Gracie's** ($+, Main St., Carlson Bldg., Stowe, 802/253-8741), though it is a bit tricky to find—tucked behind Carlson Real Estate. Boasting the biggest burgers in the state as well as great steaks and seafood, most of Gracie's menu offerings carry the name of a dog breed. Don't miss the signature dessert, the Doggie Bag—"a white-chocolate bag filled with peppermint schnapps-flavored chocolate mousse on a bed of hot fudge." That will take a bite out of your diet!

For exotic pizzas, inventive pastas, eclectic starters and internationally inspired bistro plates, stop at **Olives Bistro** ($+, Stowe Center Shops, 802/253-2033). Rumor has it the martinis are over-sized here.

Enjoy upmarket innovative gourmet cuisine and spa fare at **Maxwell's** ($$$, Topnotch Resort and Spa, 4000 Mountain Rd., Stowe, 802/253-8585, 800/451-8686; www.topnotch-resort.com). Whether you choose to take the high road or low road calorie-wise, neither the riot of taste sensations nor the sensational view of the Green Mountains will disappoint you.

The enticing aroma emanating from the wood-fired oven will lure you into **Sweet Tomatoes** ($, 83 Church St. Burlington, 802/660-9533), and their extensive offerings of innovative pizzas and Italian specialties will keep you there. You'll find two more of these popular family-style trattorias in Rutland and Lebanon, N.H.

Stop for a tantalizing bite at **NECI Commons** ($, 25 Church St., Burlington, 802/862-6324), owned and operated by the New England Culinary Institute. Tomorrow's famous chefs practice their craft today. Your taste buds will thank you.

Italian tapas? An inspired idea! **Villa Tragara** ($+, Rte. 100, Waterbury, 802/244-5288) serves lots of small-size portions, allowing you to mix, match, taste, sample and share. You can also enjoy full dinners of upmarket Neapolitan cuisine in the theatre barn (dinner theatre on Mondays, live nightclub entertainment on Fridays) or within the glassed porch of the restored 1820 farmhouse.

New Hampshire

Introduction

Named after the English county of Hampshire and nicknamed the "Granite State" because of its extensive granite quarries, New Hampshire became our nation's ninth state in 1788. Known for its fierce independence and state pride—New Hampshire levies no income tax or sales tax—the state proudly boasts the motto "Live free or die." Copious natural resources grace New Hampshire, which is only 180 miles long and 50 to 93 miles wide. More than 6,000 miles of hiking trails honeycomb the state.

Glaciers covered New Hampshire four times during the Ice Age, carving out rivers and lakes and sculpting the notches of the White Mountains, the centerpiece of the state. These mountains run north and south in the northern tier of the state and are marked by four distinctive notches—Pinkham, Crawford, Franconia, and Dixville. Called "New England's Switzerland," the peaks of the White Mountains form the Presidential Range, which is topped by Mount Washington. The famous face of "Old Man of the Mountains"—state symbol of New Hampshire—juts in profile 1,500 feet above Franconia Notch. Lake Winnipesaukee (71.5 square miles), Lake Sunapee and a galaxy of smaller lakes and ponds shimmer across the central portion of the state. New Hampshire has only 18 miles of coastline on the ocean.

First inhabited by the Algonquin Indians, the region saw European exploration as early as 1603. The first permanent white settlement was a fishing village at Odiorne Point in 1623, now the coastal town of Rye. Then, in 1638, Strawbery Banke (Portsmouth) was settled, followed by Dover, Exeter, and Hampton. In 1679 the King of England gave New Hampshire a charter making it a separate royal province.

Early colonists traded in fish, fur, and lumber, supplying giant white pines for ship masts to England from 1634 to 1773. Although New Hampshire sent troops to fight in the Revolutionary War, no battles touched New Hampshire soil. New Hampshire was the first colony to write its own constitution (1775-76). It became a state in 1788.

The advent of the railroad in the mid 1850s increased lumber trade and brought tourism to the White Mountains, still the primary businesses in the state today. Relentless logging all but destroyed the forests by 1900.

The Society for Protection of New Hampshire Forests was formed in 1901, and the federal "Weeks Act of 1911" deemed most of the White Mountains (800,000 acres), nearly one-third of the state, a national forest preserve. Logging is still allowed, but regulated.

Famous New Hampshirites include Dr. Seuss, Nelson Rockefeller, and Robert Frost.

Southern New Hampshire

The southern tier of New Hampshire includes the seacoast region that borders the Atlantic Ocean, the central, more heavily populated and industrialized areas of Nashua, Concord, and Manchester, and the tranquil southwestern corner, which sits in the shadow of giant Mount Monadnock.

Regional Information
Southern New Hampshire Convention & Visitor Bureau, Manchester, NH 03103; 603/645-9889.
New Hampshire Office of Travel and Tourism Development, Box 1856, Concord, NH 03302-1856, 603/271-2343; www.visitnh.gov.

Getting There
By Air: Major carriers offer service to Boston's Logan International Airport or Manchester Airport.
By Automobile: Access the southeastern region via I-95. For the southwestern region, take I-93 and then state roads west.

Southeastern Region

Although New Hampshire can boast of only 18 miles of seacoast, this historically and environmentally rich area offers a wealth of discoveries. From the working harbor of Portsmouth, to inland bays and estuaries, to cultural and archaeological enclaves, New Hampshire's southeastern region yields fascinating adventures on foot.

Portsmouth Harbor Trail

Portsmouth, which sits on the banks of the Piscataqua River, 4 miles inland from the Atlantic Ocean, was originally settled by English colonists as Strawbery Banke in 1632 and incorporated as the village of Portsmouth in 1653. Serving as colonial New Hampshire's capital until 1679, Portsmouth developed into a prosperous shipbuilding and maritime trade center in the 17th and 18th centuries, spurred by the founding of the Naval Shipyard by the U.S. Congress in 1800. Like other New England coastal towns, the arrival of the railroad in the 1840s created an industrial expansion that lasted well into the 20th century. Portsmouth, which is still an active New England seaport, took steps to preserve and revitalize its historic buildings in the 1960s.

Information
The Greater Portsmouth Chamber of Commerce, 500 Market St., Portsmouth, NH 03801; 602/436-1118; www.portcity.org.

Getting There
Take I-95 to exit 7 and bear right on Market St. to Market Square.

First Steps
Pick up a copy of the Portsmouth Harbour Trail Map & Guide (fee charged) at the information kiosk in Market Square (Memorial Day through Labor Day) or at the Chamber of Commerce office on Market St. Guided tours are available from early July through Columbus Day.

Portsmouth Harbour Trail. This walking tour—well-documented by words and color photos by the Portsmouth Chamber of Commerce—is divided into three sections: "Downtown and the Waterfront," the "South End," and "State Street to Haymarket Square and Congress Street." Each section takes about one hour to explore. The complete walking tour highlights 71 historic locations in Portsmouth.

The "Downtown and the Waterfront" trail begins at Market Square, which has been the commercial pulse of Portsmouth since the 1700s. Although many of the original structures here were destroyed in an 1802 fire, they were impressively rebuilt of brick. Among the highlights of this walking tour are the Athenaeum, c.1823; Moffatt-Ladd House, c.1763; USS *Albacore* and Albacore Park (site of the world-famous experimental submarine); and Warner House, c.1716, all of which are open for public tours. The brick buildings of Market Street, Merchants Row, and Bow Street—once merchants' offices, storerooms, and warehouses—retain much of their early 18th-century character. Just as they have since the 1930s, picturesque tugboats still line the Ceres Street docks on the Piscataqua River.

The "South End" tour explores the commercial buildings along Pleasant Street and State Street and then winds through the residential area of the South End, as well as exploring Strawbery Banke Museum (see Rainy Day

Option Box in this section). Historic homes open for tours here include Governor John Langdon House and Garden, c.1783; Wentworth-Gardner House, c.1760; and Tobias Lear House, c.1740. The Point of Graves Burial Ground is Portsmouth's earliest cemetery, with stones dating to 1682. This walk nets sightings of Peirce Island, Four Tree Island, and the Portsmouth Naval Shipyard, which all harbor colorful early histories but have evolved over the centuries into bustling 21st-century waterfront facilities. Also colorfully adorning this walk are Prescott Park—a decaying blighted area purchased in the 1930s by the Prescott sisters and converted into a flowering waterfront public green space—and Liberty Gardens, which features experimental blooms planted each spring by the University of New Hampshire.

The third walking tour begins at the intersection of Pleasant and State Streets. Most of this area was developed in the 19th century, although some older structures still remain. Rundlet-May House, c.1807; John Paul Jones House, c.1761; and Richard Jackson House, c. 1664, all are open for tours. Tony mansions were built in the 1800s along Haymarket Square, which was a hay and farm products market in the 1700s. Other interesting buildings on this walk include Kearsage House, c.1866, Portsmouth's only bow-front brick structure, and South Church, c. 1826, Portsmouth's only granite church.

Seacoast Science Center and Odiorne Point State Park, Rye

Scottish fishermen landed at Odiorne Point in 1623, founding the first European settlement in New Hampshire. Later, the British camped here before heading to Cape Ann and Cape Cod. John Odiorne joined the community in 1660, acquiring several coastal acres, which he farmed and fished. Odiornes worked this land for generations. Much of Odiorne Point was filled with summer homes and a grand hotel by the early 1900s. In 1942, the federal government purchased all the land between Little Harbor and the Sunken Forest. Here they built an Army base, Fort Dearborn, to protect Portsmouth Harbor from possible attack. Odiorne Point State Park, which was sold to the State of New Hampshire in 1961, now features 300 coastal acres, including walking paths labeled with interpretive panels that reveal Odiorne Point's layered history. The area is alive with gulls, cormorants, eiders, scoters, and other sea ducks.

Information
Seacoast Science Center, 570 Ocean Blvd., Rye, NH 03870; 603/436-8043.

Getting There
Take I-95 to exit 5, Portsmouth. At the traffic circle, follow U.S.1-Bypass toward "Beaches and Hampton." Continue on U.S. 1 and turn left at Elwyn Rd. At Foyes Corner intersection, turn right on Rte. 1A, heading south. After 1.1 miles, look for Odiorne Point State Park's north parking area and boat launch on the left. Continue on for .7 mile to the main entrance of Seacoast Science Center.

First Steps
Stop at the Seacoast Science Center and pick up a walking map put out by the New Hampshire Division of Parks and Recreation. (A nominal admission is charged.) For a truly comprehensive guide for this walk, purchase *Footsteps in Time*, compiled by Howard S. Crosby, Wendy W. Lull, and Richard T. MacIntye, which is available at the Seacoast Science Center for $15. The book contains a wealth of historical, maritime, and ecological information about Odiorne Point, as well as more than 75 photographs.

Seacoast Science Center, Odiorne Point State Park. Begin your 2.3-mile exploration of Odiorne Point by visiting the Seacoast Science Center, where exhibits of tidepools, marshes, woodlands, and the undersea world explain the habitats you will encounter. Head first to the Sunken Forest at the southern rim of the park. Go to the right of the Science Center's main building and follow the grass path to the water, bearing left at the fork, keeping the water on your left. From here you can see the Isles of Shoals. At low tide you can see the trunks and roots of an ancient forest that extended east to the Isles of Shoals and beyond. Scientists have carbon-dated the trees at 3,500 years old. Glacial melting drowned the forest. You can walk across exposed rock outcroppings and actually touch the petrified wood. An old cannon mount remains here as well.

Retrace your steps back to the main building and follow the path along the Gulf of Maine, which will be on your right, to Frost Point. Frost Point was named for the Frost family, who acquired it in the mid-1700s. Along the way you will pass freshwater ponds and marshes and a number of World War II batteries, now overgrown with foliage and a profusion of rugosa roses. Bear right at Battery Seaman and walk to the end of the stone breakwater, completed in 1903 by the U.S. Army Corps of Engineers, where you will be rewarded with a panoramic view of the sailboat-filled Little Harbor. From here you can see the town of New Castle, Fort Stark, and the imposing old Wentworth Hotel across the harbor, as well as Whaleback Light and Kittery Point to the right. (This is a great place to enjoy a picnic lunch.)

Return to Battery Seaman and pass it on the gravel road to the right. World War II buffs will enjoy exploring the remains of this battery, where you'll be able to note both the northerly and southerly gun mounts. You can detour to the top of the casemate, where you'll be treated to a spectacular vista. Spread before you are the salt marshes that feed into Little Harbor, the Maine coast, the Isles of Shoals, and the freshwater marshes dotting Odiorne Point, which in spring and fall are filled with migrating birds.

From here you can divert along a trail that shadows Rte. 1A and take a detour around a freshwater pond, or return the way you came. Either way, be sure to stop at the Dolphin Fountain, a masonry structure flanked by stone benches, built before World War II on the former Marvin/Straw estate. A scallop shell and dolphin are cast in relief, and a metal pipe extends from the dolphin's mouth. In the 1920s and 1930s, a windmill pumped well water to the fountain.

On your return to the Seacoast Science Center, you'll see the remains of many of the homesteads that once graced this property. Interpretive markers tell the residents' historic stories. Stop at Battery 204 before returning to the main building.

America's Stonehenge, North Salem

America's Stonehenge has long fascinated historians, archaeologists, and astronomers, and it is an intriguing discovery for the general public as well. Thought to be prehistoric and one of the largest and oldest stone-constructed sites in all of North America, America's Stonehenge has been deemed by researchers to be "an accurate, astronomically aligned calendar." Owner Robert E. Stone of Derry, N.H., opened the site to the public in 1958 for research and preservation.

Information
America's Stonehenge, P.O. Box 84, N. Salem, NH 03073; 603/893-8300; www.stonehengeusa.com.

Getting There
Take I-93 to exit 3, then Rte. 111 east to the intersection of Island Pond and Haverhill Rds. Follow Haverhill Rd. south for 1 mile to the entrance.

First Steps
Pick up a detailed Tour Guide Map at the Visitor Center when you pay your admission fee. Site is open daily from Apr. through Nov. Call for hours in Mar. and Dec.

America's Stonehenge. This exploration on foot yields fascinating discoveries for adults and children alike. From the Visitor Center, follow the prescribed trail to the 32 viewing stations. The comprehensive guide describes the phenomena you'll discover at this 4,000-year-old archaeological site. Excavations have netted artifacts that scientists have radiocarbon dated. The 30-acre site, which contains precisely placed 4- to 10-ton capstones, much like England's Stonehenge, is enclosed by a series of stone walls. Researchers believe either a European culture or a Native American culture constructed the site, long before Columbus ever visited our shores.

The 3/4-mile path, blazed with orange arrows on white signs, will take you past the remains of a number of post-colonial stone structures, including the Pattee Area, whose foundations are still remarkably intact. Here you can walk through a maze of caves, cellar holes, and stone chambers, and you can examine stone walls, a fireplace, steps, and an 8-ton roof slab.

One of the most significant areas of the site is the 2,000 BC Excavation. While not showy on the surface, the area has been excavated, recovering the charcoal that set the timetable for the site. Also fascinating is the "Oracle Chamber, two passages in the shape of a T." Here you'll find a "Secret Bed," which is a stone cubby just large enough for one person to be completely hidden. A small opening near the floor allows the person to spy on others outside. A "Speaking Tube" runs from the chamber to the "Sacrificial Table." Words spoken into the tube give the impression that the table itself is talking. The 4.5-ton sacrificial stone table has a channel carved on its surface.

An astronomical viewing platform has been constructed at the point where you can see all the major astronomical alignment stones, and the trees have been cleared here for an unobstructed view. A separate Astronomical Trail takes you to the stones, which are marked by round, white pieces of wood, painted with black letters A-N. Among the stones you'll see here are the equinox alignment, true north stone, summer and winter solstice sunrise and sunset stones, and the May Day stone.

The path takes you back toward the main museum building. Here you'll find several wonderful outdoor exhibits for children. "Animal tracks" features a sand table and rubber presses of the footprints of the animals and birds that a child may encounter in the area. A kid's archaeological dig tells about the science of archaeology and allows children to dig in the sand to discover stones, shells, and other artifacts. The short Pope Road Nature Trail features interesting wooden sculptures, such as an owl on a stake and a squirrel attached to a stump. Trees and plants are labeled, and the Three Sisters Garden showcases the vegetables the Iroquois thought were gifts from the Great Spirit. A Native American dugout canoe, drying rack, wigwam, bed, and fire pit are all descriptively labeled so children can understand their functions. Finish your walk at the museum/visitor center, where you can view many of the artifacts discovered during the excavations at America's Stonehenge.

Canterbury Shaker Village, Canterbury

Shakers founded their village in Canterbury in 1792, one of 19 "Shaking Quakers" colonies established in the eastern United States, from Maine to Kentucky. Members of the United Society of Believers in Christ's First and Second Appearing, Shakers took a vow of celibacy, and in this work-oriented commune, men and women of all races were considered equal. Their motto was: "Put hands to work and hearts to God." The Canterbury Shaker Village, now 24 buildings on 694 acres, endured for 200 years. The last sister died in 1992. The village is now a private, non-profit historic site museum.

Information
Canterbury Shaker Village, Canterbury, NH 03224; 603/783-9511; 800/982-9511; www.shakers.org.

Getting There
Take I-93 to exit 18 and follow signs to Canterbury Shaker Village.

First Steps
Stop at the visitor center to pay admission and pick up a site map. Two guided tours, A and B, alternate every 30 minutes. Allow 2.5 hours to tour the entire property. Since many of the buildings are open by guided tour only, plan to take the tours, which are part of the admission fee. Canterbury Shaker Village is open daily, May through Oct. and on Sat. and Sun. in Apr., Nov., and Dec.

Canterbury Shaker Village. You can leisurely stroll through Canterbury Shaker Village, following the briefly described self-guided map, but for a comprehensive look into the 200-year-old Shaker culture of the village, first take the guided tours. At the village's peak in the 1850s, 300 people resided here. They farmed the land, sold seeds and herbs, and manufactured herbal medicines and crafts.

You'll see the Meeting House, the house of worship where the brothers entered on the left and the sisters on the right. The ministry lived separately from the masses, a decision thought to help them maintain their objectivity. You'll visit their lodging and the residences of the Elders and Eldresses, the infirmary, and the Sisters Shop, where the women produced many of the goods sold to the outside world. The former carriage house is now a gift shop that sells authentic Shaker crafts and offers periodic broom-making demonstrations.

The tour encompasses the creamery, carpenters shop, firehouse, powerhouse, and North Shop, currently housing the print shop, which also gives demonstrations. Medicinal syrups were produced in the Syrup Shop. The laundry was powered by steam; Ivy League college-sweaters were produced on the second floor. In the early days of the one-room schoolhouse, the boys attended in the winter and the girls in the summer; later both Shaker children and other children from Canterbury attended all year long. A bee house, cart-shed, and woodshed round out the buildings of the village.

After you have explored the village, walk to the gardens and find the start of the nature trail around the ponds, near the orchards. At the fork between the two ponds, bear right, counterclockwise around the pond. Lily pads and cattails dot the bucolic ponds, which are graced by a pair of resident nesting swans and several great blue herons. The path, which is shadowed by sugar maples, is flat, level, and well marked.

Evelyn Browne Trail at Adam's Point, Durham

Freshwater rivers meet the salt water of the coast at the Great Bay Estuary, which is a drowned river valley estuary. The surrounding 4,471 acres of tidal waters and mud flats, 48 miles of shoreline, 800 acres of upland habitat, salt marsh, and open fields are home to myriad species of fish, birds, and migratory waterfowl. Adams Point is a great, easily accessed bird-watching location.

Information
Great Bay National Estuarine Research Reserve, N.H. Fish and Game Dept. Marine Fisheries Div., 225 Main St., Durham, NH 03824; 603/868-1095.

Getting There
Take I-95 to Rte. 101 west, to Rte. 108 north, to Durham Point Rd. After about 3.8 miles, turn at U.N.H. Jackson Estuarine Laboratory sign and follow to Adams Point.

First Steps
Park in the small parking lot, then walk up the road to Jackson Estuarine Laboratory, where you'll find a trail guide in a kiosk at the trailhead.

Evelyn Browne Trail at Adam's Point. This easy 45-minute walk traverses the historic peninsula that separates Little Bay from Great Bay. The trail is dedicated to the memory of Evelyn Browne, an instructor at University of New Hampshire, who lived on Crommet Creek on the back side of Adams Point and cherished her surrounding environment. When Aristotle Onassis proposed building the world's largest oil refinery in her backyard in the 1970s, Evelyn organized the Great Bay Estuarine System Conservation Trust, which successfully fought off the initiative. The area was designated the Great Bay National Estuarine Research Reserve in 1989. Evelyn Browne died in 1994.

The first residents of Adams Point were the Native Americans, who used the area as a camp, harvesting oysters and clams and leaving mounds of shell middens uncovered here. In the early 1800s, "Reformation" John Adams (the same dynasty as the two American presidents) preached here at revival meetings. Four generations of Adams held the land until they sold it to the state of New Hampshire. The Adams House, which was a popular resort from the mid-1800s until the early 20th century, stood at the site of the present-day Jackson Estuarine Laboratory's parking lot until the 1960s.

The trail takes you through a field, where a tall obelisk, erected in 1854 of Durham granite and Carrara marble, marks the tomb of the Adams family. Twenty-four members of the family are buried here. Along the eastern shoreline, atop a steep cliff, you'll walk along "Lovers' Walk." As you follow the well-marked trail through the forest, you'll encounter artifacts of a bygone era: crumbling stone walls, a rusting hay rake, tree stumps, and shell casings. The fields have long since overgrown into a mixed forest of pines, hardwoods, and birches.

If you tread softly, you may encounter small animals, such as fox, rabbit, or even a bobcat, as well as white-tailed deer. Songbirds are prolific in the marsh and field areas. The nutrient-rich estuary is a favored stopping-off point on the migratory route of waterfowl and shorebirds along the Atlantic flyway. They feed and breed in the protected coves.

Once you reach the salt marsh, look for cordgrass and salt marsh hay, which can tolerate having their roots constantly in salt water. As you get to the shallows of Great Bay, eelgrass becomes one of the dominant habitats, sheltering juvenile fish and shellfish. Larger fish and horseshoe crabs live in the deeper channels. The Adams family used the blue clay that lines the bottom of the bay to make bricks. Material from their brickyard was used to build the fashionable townhouses in Boston's Beacon Hill.

Boats called gundalows—shallow-draft, barge-like vessels with sails—transported bricks, lumber, salt hay, and fish from Great Bay at Adams Point to market from the 1650s until 1900. (A 69-foot full-size replica is moored at Stawbery Banke in Portsmouth during the summer. See Rainy Day Options Box in this section.)

Cross the road to the Little Bay side of Adams Point. This manmade causeway floods in heavy rains, making Adams Point once again an island. Little Bay is deeper and narrower than Great Bay. Lobsters seek out the deep holes here and the throaty chugging of lobster boat motors are commonly heard in the bay. Here you'll see a shingle beach, so called because the tidal action of the bay has caused the bedrock of the shore of Adams Point to fracture. The water-worn "shingles" of rock are visible at low tide.

Your last landmark will be Pulpit Rock, a huge, square granite slab that legend holds was the site of Sunday worship services for boarders at Adams House. If you look intently over Furber Strait, you may spot an American bald eagle or an osprey, both of which have started to frequent the area once again.

Monadnock Region

Mount Monadnock, one of the most climbed mountains of the world, dominates the southwest region of New Hampshire, bordered by Massachusetts on the south and Vermont on the west. Visible from many parts of the area, Monadnock provides a dramatic backdrop for the unfolding scenic New Hampshire countryside.

Pack Monadnock, Miller State Park, Peterborough

Algonquin for "mountain that stands alone," Mount Monadnock is a climb for serious, seasoned hikers. Pack Monadnock, or little Monadnock, on the other hand, is a strenuous but achievable challenge for the average walker. The reward for perseverance to the summit of Pack Monadnock, 2,090 feet, is a panoramic view of the tri-state area.

Information
New Hampshire Division of Parks and Recreation, P.O. Box 856, Concord, NH 03302-0856, 603/924-3572.

Getting There
Take Rte. 101 east from Peterborough for 3 miles. Miller State Park is on the left.

First Steps
Stop for a trail map at the parking lot kiosk at Miller State Park. The park is open from Memorial Day through Labor Day. An admission fee is charged. The total loop for this hike of Pack Monadnock is 2.8 miles, with an optional summit trail of .4 mile once you reach the top. The Marion Davis Trail is more gradual than the Wapack Trail, which is a rocky scramble all the way. Unless you hike regularly, I suggest you take the Marion Davis Trail to the summit and the Wapack Trail back down. In any case, wear sturdy footgear and bring plenty of water.

Pack Monadnock. Miller State Park was founded in 1891 and dedicated to General James Miller, Peterborough's favorite son, hero of the Battle of Lundy's Lane in the War of 1812. In the late 1800s, families would travel by horse and buggy up a windy road to Pack Monadnock's summit to picnic on Sundays. (You'll find picnic tables at the summit too.) Cattle were driven to the summit to graze, and a hotel called the Pioneer House operated here also for a time.

Expect a steady uphill climb on the 1.4-mile Marion Davis Trail (blazed blue), sometimes over boulders and glacial erratics. The trail is heavily wooded with deciduous trees and ferny undergrowth. You'll see prolific wildflowers in the spring and a profusion of blueberries and chokeberries in the summer. A 27-foot steel tower, built in 1939 as a forest fire watchtower, tops the summit. If vertigo is not a problem for you, climb it. On a clear day you can see all the way to Boston. Take the optional .4-mile Summit Loop Trail around the perimeter of the mountaintop if you like, before heading down the Wapack Trail.

The 1.4-mile Wapack Trail (blazed yellow), which runs from the summit of Pack Monadnock to the Miller State Park parking lot, is actually a part of the a much larger footpath. The complete Wapack Trail extends for 21 miles, from Mt. Watatic in Ashburnham, Mass., to North Pack Monadnock in Greenfield, N. H. Unlike the trek uphill on the Marion Davis Trail, the Wapack Trail is surrounded with old-growth pine forest, which is blanketed in pine needles. The path is narrow and you may be descending as much on your derriere as on the soles of your feet, because the trail is often a maze of giant granite slabs, upended at all angles. As you scramble along the edge of the mountain amid precarious footing, it is easy to concentrate so much on your journey that you forget to look at the scenery. The vistas are magnificent. Be sure to sit down and drink in the view.

Rhododendron State Park, Fitzwilliam

More than 16 acres of wild rhododendrons have earned Rhododendron State Park National Natural Landmark status—deservedly. This profusion of *Rhododendron maximum*—one of the largest natural groves north of the Allegheny Mountains—peaks in mid-June, but even without blooms, this 1-mile stroll will take your breath away.

Information
Mondadnock State Park, P.O. Box 181, Jaffrey, NH 03452, 603/532-8862.

Getting There
Take Rte. 12 to Rte. 119 west, to Fitzwilliam. Continue on Rte. 119 for 0.5 mile. Turn right on Rhododendrum Rd. and continue for 2 miles. Rhododendron State Park is on the right; parking lot is on the left.

First Steps
Pick up an informational brochure at the trailhead kiosk. The short intertwining paths are clearly marked.

Rhododendron State Park. Growing at the northern limits of their range, this 16-acre stand of *Rhododendron maximum* is the largest of 19 similar clusters in central and northern New England. Thought to have descended from the magnolia, the rhodies are actually members of the heath family, which includes mountain laurels, heathers, blueberries, and cranberries.

A series of footpaths link together in one plant-filled, wildlife loop. Begin on the Rhododendrum Trail (0.6 mile), a crushed stone path beneath a feathery pine canopy. At the fork, bear right and stay on the Rhododendron Trail. (About 0.2 mile into the walk, if you'd like a challenging climb, you have the option to detour up the Little Monadnock Mountain Summit Trail, 1.1 mile, to the 1,883-foot mountaintop.)

Rhodies grow wild on both sides of the narrow Rhododendron Trail. Butterflies are flying everywhere here, and it feels like walking through a jungle of greenery. In some areas the rhododendrons create an absolute canopy over the trail. A glimpse through the pines reveals more blossoming stands. Cross the wooden Mary Lee Ware Bridge over a wetlands area, where you may spot some migrating waterfowl, and take the Wildflower Loop. The wildflowers here, best seen in the spring, are labeled for easy identification. Benches pepper the sun-dappled trail as it winds through the dense pine forest, which is carpeted with pine needles and sprinkled with ferns.

As you round the loop, you'll see a sign for the Laurel Trail, a horseshoe shaped footpath that lies between the Wildflower Loop and the Rhododendron Trail. The forest here is blanketed with running pine, a tiny pine groundcover, and quite a few mushrooms. Large stands of mountain laurel profusely dominate the landscape. Picturesque and tranquil, this short tiptoe through the rhodies will take you only about a half hour.

Chesterfield Gorge, Chesterfield

A local Chesterfield farmer, George White, bought the land surrounding the gorge in 1936 to keep it from being clear-cut by loggers, and then he sold 15 acres to the Society for the Preservation of New Hampshire Forests, who donated it to the State of New Hampshire.

Information
Pisgah State Park, P.O. Box 242, Winchester, NH 03470, 603/239-8153.

Getting There
Take Rte. 9 west from Keene for 6 miles. Look for the the Chesterfield Gorge sign on the right.

First Steps
This short, 0.7-mile walk is barely a stroll, but the geologic wonder that it borders is a must-see. A visitor center staffed by volunteers is open

three-bedroom cottages, all freshly renovated and blooming with flowered chintz, delicate lace, and period antiques. A centuries-old barn graces the 105-acre property, surrounded by organic flower and vegetable gardens. This charming inn earned a coveted "Editor's Pick" by *Yankee Magazine* in 2001.

Food and Drink

For more dining options, consult www.virtualnh.com or www.seacoastnh.com.

You'll enjoy cutting-edge comfort food at **ffrost Sawyer Tavern** (Three Chimneys Inn, 17 Newmarket Rd, Durham, 603/868-7800; 888/399-9777; www.threechimneysinn.com). Dine in the "Maples," ($$$$) the original living/kitchen area of the 1649 homestead, which now showcases Georgian furnishings amid its four fireplaces. The "Tavern" ($$) is darkly cozy with granite walls, beamed ceilings, and an open-hearth summer kitchen fireplace. In fine weather, eat in the "Conservatory," ($$) outside aside the grape arbor.

Whether you choose the formal Terrace Restaurant ($$) or casual, leather-accented lounge ($), you'll enjoy the New American cuisine of **The Inn of Exeter** (90 Front St., Exeter, 603/772-5901, www.someplaces-different.com). Sunday brunch here has garnered awards.

A tiny gourmet deli offering big, big tastes, **Lindy's** (One Range Rd., Rtes. 28 and 111, Salem, 603/890-1133) is wallpapered with movie posters and promotes the stars with its stellar panini sandwich offerings. The choice is difficult. Sharon Stone or Michael Douglas? Pacino Pastrami or Schwartzenegger Reuben? Demi Moore or Meg Ryan? Julia Roberts Vegetarian or the Jane Fonda Garden Burger? Whatever the marquee, however, you won't leave this place hungry.

An elegant picture: mauve and cream linens, stenciled walls, oriental carpets over wide-planked floors, soft classical music, and panoramic windows looking out to a lighted garden. The dining room of the **Colby Hill Inn** ($$$$, 3 The Oaks, Henniker, 603/428-3281, 800/531-0330, www.colbyhillinn.com) sets the stage for the stellar New American cuisine that marches out of the kitchen. From the chef's complement to the brimming dessert menu, be prepared to dine in style.

Situated in a restored vintage building on the historic Main Street in Jaffrey, **The Inn at Jaffrey Center** ($$, 379 Main St., Jaffrey, 603/532-7800) serves up classic American country fare as well as a couple of outstanding pasta dishes. Popular with the locals (who usually know where to find the best meal in town) The Inn tops off its reliable menu with a handful of decadent dessert offerings too tempting to resist.

Akin to attending a fine dinner party, dining at the **Chesterfield Inn** ($$+, Rte. 9, Chesterfield, 603/256-3211, 800/365-5515, www.chester-fieldinn.com) is something special. The chef designs a menu of new creations everyday, winning raves from visitors, locals, and even well-known chefs and food writers, who recognize that classic country cuisine has been elevated to new heights. This is altogether a gourmet's nirvana.

Eat in or takeout, **Twelve Pine** ($, 11 School St., Peterborough, 603/924-6140) offers gourmet soups, sandwiches and entrée dishes, plus a fabulous array of breads and desserts. Wash down your vittles with something from the fresh juice or coffee bars.

Housed in Portsmouth's former Custom House of the early 1800s, **Anthony Alberto's Ristorante Italiano** ($$+, 59 Penhallow St., Portsmouth, 603/436-4000, www.anthonyalbertos.com) pairs remarkable antipastos, pastas, and entrees with a candlelit ambiance. The original brick and stone cubbyholes and arched alcoves, exposed beams, and mahogany walls enhance the romantically charged atmosphere.

Named "one of the top 25 restaurants in America" by the American Association of Restaurant Scientists, **The Hancock Inn** ($$$$, 33 Main St., Hancock, 603/525-3318, 800/525-1789, www.hancockinn.com) offers authentic American fare, such as cranberry pot roast, whose recipe was lauded by *Bon Appetit* magazine. Servers are garbed in period attire.

Del Rossi's ($+, Rte. 137, Dublin, 603/563-7195, www.delrossi.com), open only Wed. through Sun., offers tasty homemade pasta and Old World Italian dishes. Sometimes on autumn weekends you can catch the live bluegrass and folk music sessions.

Central New Hampshire

Central New Hampshire is blessed with two distinctive areas of beauty—the Darmouth/Sunapee Region in the west and the Lakes Region in the east. The Connecticut River, Mount Sunapee, and Lake Sunapee punctuate the farmland of the west, while massive Lake Winnipesaukee and surrounding satellite lakes and mountains dominate the east. Both areas abound in rich natural attractions, which beg to be explored on foot.

Dartmouth/Lake Sunapee Region

It's easy to see why the bountifully beautiful Sunapee Region of New Hampshire attracted the likes of John Hay and Augustus Saint-Gaudens, summer visitors who ultimately succumbed to the area's considerable charms and stayed forever.

This region borders the Connecticut River along the state's western border. It is named for Dartmouth College, the Ivy League college chartered in 1789 in Hanover, and the sublime recreation areas of Lake Sunapee and Mount Sunapee.

Regional Information

Hanover Chamber of Commerce, Hanover, NH 03755, 603/643-3115, www.valleynet/-han_area_chamber.
Lake Sunapee Business Association, Sunapee, MH 03782, 603/763-2495, 800/258-3530, www.sunapee.vacations.com.

Getting There

Take I-91 or I-89 to state and county roads.

Saint Gaudens National Historic Site, Cornish

Cornish, a small village on the Connecticut River—which forms the natural border with Vermont—was originally called Mast Camp, because it was the point where pine masts were shipped down the river, eventually heading for England. The longest covered bridge in the United States connects Cornish with its Vermont sister across the river, Windsor. Calling Cornish home for much of his lifetime, Augustus Saint-Gaudens lived and worked here from 1885 to his death at age 59 in 1907. Now preserved as the Saint-Gaudens National Historic Site, the home, **gardens, studios, galleries, gardens,** and woodlands of the Irish-born sculptor illuminate the artist's amazing talents.

Information
Saint-Gaudens National Historic Site, RR3, Box 73, Cornish, NH 03745; 603/675-2175, www.nps.gov/saga.

Getting There
From I-89, exit 20, take Rte. 12A south for 12 miles. From I-91, exit 8, take Rte. 131 east to Rte. 12A north. Saint Gaudens is 2.5 miles from the Cornish/Windsor covered bridge.

First Steps
The grounds are open year round until dusk. Buildings and exhibits are open May through the end of Oct., 9am to 4:30pm. With your admission fee you will receive a self-guided tour brochure to the 15 noteworthy sites of the Saint Gaudens estate. You can tour the spots in any order you like. Guided tours of the grounds are offered at 2pm daily. Or, for a small additional fee you can rent a self-paced audio tour, which yields a wealth of information.

Saint Gaudens National Historic Site. Born to a French father and Irish mother in Dublin, Ireland, Augustus Saint-Gaudens immigrated to the United States at age 6 months. By age 13 he apprenticed as a cameo cutter, also taking art classes at Cooper Union and the National Academy of Design. At 19 he studied in Paris, then went to Rome as a student of classical art and architecture. There he met and married American Augusta Homer in 1877.

The Saint-Gaudens estate encompasses 150 acres of gardens, meadows, and woodlands. The c.1800 house, named "Aspet" after the artist's father's birthplace in France, is a gracious Federal-style brick mansion, originally built as an inn. (A separate ticket is needed for the house tour, which is scheduled several times during the day. Sign up at the entrance kiosk.) A 110-foot thornless honey locust planted in 1886 dominates the front yard.

The gardens and three exhibition galleries showcase original works and recasts of Saint-Gaudens famous sculptures. Saint-Gaudens received his first commission in 1876, a monument to Civil War Admiral David Glasglow Farragut, which was unveiled in New York's Madison Square in 1881. His talent and fame grew exponentially. One of his best-known works, the Robert Gould Shaw Memorial, depicts Shaw and the 54th regiment, the famed black Civil War unit immortalized in the movie, "Glory." Described as a "symphony in bronze," the sculpture took 14 years to complete and was unveiled across from the Massachusetts State House on Boston Common in 1881. Other Saint-Gaudens sculptures are permanently exhibited in Chicago (seated Lincoln, Grant Park), Boston (Phillips-Brooks monument at Trinity Church), and New York (Sherman monument at GAR Plaza).

Saint-Gaudens designed the Little Studio Pergola after a trip to Italy in 1889. Adorned with Doric columns, red stucco walls, and casts from the Parthenon frieze, the studio exudes a decidedly Mediterranean air, incongruous in the bucolic New Hampshire estate setting. Here, Saint-Gaudens developed the concepts and original models for his works, then directed students and apprentices, who finished the sculptures. Drawings, models, and recasts are displayed here.

A picture gallery features seasonally changing exhibits, and a Roman-style atrium gallery with reflecting pool, called the New Gallery after the former building was destroyed by fire, features Saint Gaudens' designs of gold coinage and medals, carved cameos, and bas relief portraits, which are considered the most complicated and difficult type of sculpture. Saint Gaudens completed more than 100 commissioned relief portraits in his lifetime, using bronze, wood, marble, or plaster.

The gardens are equally striking. Terraced perennial gardens, a 6,000-square-foot cutting garden, a birch grove with Pan fountains, and the 350-foot allée (tree-lined walk) are unique, but the outdoor galleries framed by 100-year-old, 12- to 14-foot-high white pine and hemlock hedges provide the high drama. Here, framed by greenery, are recasts of the haunting Adams Memorial (a funerary sculpture of Clover, the wife of historian Henry Adams) and the aforementioned Farragut Monument. The final version of the Shaw Memorial, which is slightly different from the original that Saint Gaudens placed in Boston, is also showcased here. One of the evergreen rooms is preserved as a bowling green for lawn bowls.

Two trails wind through the woodlands of the Saint-Gaudens National Historic Site. The Ravine Trail, a steep, rugged quarter-mile trail leads from the Ravine Studio (summer home to an artist in residence, who demonstrates the intricate process of bronze sculpting), following an old cart path along Blow-Me-Down Brook. The longer Blow-Me-Down Trail begins just beyond the Temple, which was designed in 1905 as a play set for a local dramatic production honoring Saint-Gaudens on the 20th anniversary of his permanent move to Cornish. The Temple was later rebuilt as a marble crypt, now the final resting place of the Saint-Gaudens family. The 2.5-mile trail descends to a millpond and through an 80-acre natural area. You'll find a guide to the natural area at the trailhead.

Dartmouth College, Hanover

Named for William Legge, the Second Earl of Dartmouth, Dartmouth College was founded by Eleazar Wheelock, a Congregational minister from Connecticut in 1769. Now an Ivy League educational institution, Dartmouth—America's ninth oldest college—beats as the pulse of Hanover, New Hampshire. Famous graduates include: Daniel Webster (1801) and Theodor Geisel, a.k.a. Dr. Seuss (1925).

Information
Hanover Chamber of Commerce, 216 Nugget Building, Hanover, 603/643-3115,
Dartmouth College, Dartmouth, 603/646-1110, www.dartmouth.edu.

Getting There
Take I-93 north to I-89 north at Concord. Get off I-89 at exit 18 in Lebanon onto Rte. 120 north. (A sign says that it is the exit for Dartmouth College.) After 4.1 miles, fork right at a traffic light. Follow Rte. 120 for 0.5 mile on South Park St., to the second traffic light. Turn left at the light, onto East Wheelock St. Follow East Wheelock for 2/10 mile, to the Hopkins Center (left) and the Dartmouth Green (right).

First Steps
Guided campus tours are offered daily. Times vary seasonally. Call 603/646-2875 for information. Pick up the "Self-guided Walking Tour of Darmouth College" booklet from the information kiosk on the Green.

Dartmouth College. Like at Harvard and Yale, a walking tour of Darmouth is most interesting when guided. You do, however, have the option of exploring the college by yourself. The self-guided booklet guides you around Darmouth's historic inner core around the Green. You'll begin in the southeast corner at Reed Hall and proceed counterclockwise along "Dartmouth Row" to Thornton Hall and Dartmouth Hall, which was the college's first permanent structure. Begun in 1784, the building took seven years to complete. The last building of "Dartmouth Row" is Wentworth Hall.

To the left of "Dartmouth Row" is Rollins Chapel, a neo-Romanesque building constructed in the 1880s. On the north side of the Green, Webster Hall—named after Daniel Webster, class of 1801—is an imposing Greek Revival structure that now houses the Rauner Special Collections Library. Behind Webster Hall, a 207-foot tower tops Baker Library. The "Baker Bells" ring out to call students to denote the start and finish of classes as well as appropriate holiday chimes. The interior is amazing. Be sure to explore each floor; the walls are a virtual art gallery of historic murals and portraits.

Cross North Main Street to Rockefeller Center and Silsby Hall. Go into Rockefeller Center, which is named after Nelson A. Rockefeller, to the Class of 1930 Room, where a plaque lists Rockefeller and more than 200 other Dartmouth graduates who have been state governors or held national elective office. You can divert further up North Main Street, if you like, to visit Webster Cottage, built in 1780. Webster lived here part of his student days. It is now a small museum open Wed., Sat., and Sun. afternoons.

Retrace your steps to the Green, passing the Blunt Alumni Center/Crosby Hall, once the home of Dr. Dixi Crosby. In his laboratory Crosby tested a black, sticky substance that was irritatingly showing up in the fields of Pennsylvania farmers. The analysis turned out to be the surprising discovery of oil. Continue along the west side of the Green past the massive stone halls ñParkhurst, McNutt, Robinson—and Collis Center.

The Hanover Inn (see Lodging in this section) and the Hopkins Center/Hood Museum of Art dominate the south side of the Green. The "Hop" is the creative and performing arts center of Dartmouth. The Hood

Museum of Art showcases more than 60,000 works of art as well as special exhibitions that change annually.

Conclude either your guided or self-guided tour with a stroll down South Main Street, which houses the commercial establishments at the heart of Dartmouth—its campus bookstore, shops, pubs, and eateries (see Food and Drink in this section).

The Fells Historic Site and John Hay National Wildlife Refuge, Newbury

The Fells is the former summer retreat of John Hay, who in his lifetime was private secretary to President Abraham Lincoln, assistant secretary of state to President Hayes, and secretary of state to Presidents Theodore Roosevelt and McKinley. Hay also authored a 10-volume biography of Lincoln. Built in 1891 on the shores of Lake Sunapee among 900 acres of wilderness, the Fells—a Celtic term from northern England meaning hillside pastures—is a turn-of-the-last-century Colonial that has been extensively remodeled by the three generations of summering Hays. Clarence Hay—third generation—donated 675 acres of the site to the Society for Protection of New Hampshire Forests in 1960, sold off the dairy farm on the property, then gave the 163.5 acres to the U.S. Department of Fish and Wildlife for preservation as a refuge.

Information
The Fells Historic Site and John Hay National Wildlife Refuge, Rte. 103A, Newbury, 603/763-4789, www.thefells.org.

Getting There
Take I-89 north to exit 9 and go west on Rte 103 to Newbury. Then take 103A north for 2.2 miles. The Fells is on the left.

First Steps
Gardens and grounds are open dawn to dusk, year round. House tours are offered Sat. and Sun., Memorial Day to Columbus Day (fee charged). Park at the Gatehouse Visitor Center and walk down the driveway to the main house.

The Fells Historic Site and John Hay National Wildlife Refuge. About sixty acres of the pristine property surrounding the Fells is now managed by the Friends of John Hay National Wildlife Refuge. The rooms of the home are unfurnished but well maintained and provide a glimpse into the opulence enjoyed by this historic family over the century. The home is surrounded with fabulous gardens, which were the enduring passions of Clarence and Alice Appleton Hay. (Alice donated the Fells to the refuge upon her death.)

Begin your exploration of this national treasure at the 100-foot-long perennial border—1930s style in pink, blue, and white. It sets the scene for Alice Hay's pride and joy, the rose terrace, which she planted in 1924. A brook trickles from the rose terrace to a Japanese water lily pool in the Alpine garden, where Clarence Hay planted more than 500 rare plants between 1929 and 1935. (Only the hardy remain today.) High stone walls surround a series of three garden rooms, which are planted with shrubs, vines, and flowers and are furnished with benches, fountains, pots, and statues.

The centerpiece of the John Hay National Wildlife Refuge is the John Hay II Forest Ecology Trail. From the house and gardens, follow the path to the trailhead, where you'll find an interpretive guide that illuminates the wonders of forest succession, of which this woodland is a prime example. This 1-mile walk, over easy, flat terrain, leads to the shores of Lake Sunapee. Once fields and pastures abandoned more than 100 years ago, the area is now populated with stands of white and yellow birch, red and white pine, sugar maple, and red spruce.

Two virgin hemlocks, each 300 to 400 years old, dominate the shoreline of Lake Sunapee. Ferns, mosses, and wildflowers blanket the forest floor. Mount Sunapee looms across the lake. Two enormous glacial erratics, deposited 10,000 to 12,000 years ago, wear cloaks of brilliant green lichens. The crystalline waters lap against the rock-lined banks. You may be tempted to abandon your shoes—or your clothes—for a dip before you follow Beech Brook back to Grassy Road and the Fells.

Mount Sunapee State Park
Lake Solitude Trail, Newbury

Mount Sunapee's summit looms 2,743 feet above the Sunapee region. At its base lies a massive lake, also called Sunapee, an Indian name loosely translated as Goose Lake (the lake used to be seasonally filled with wild geese). Together, the mountain and the lake have attracted visitors for generations. Lake Solitude lies 400 feet below the summit, an exquisite jewel secreted in the depths of the forest.

Information
Mount Sunapee State Park, Rte. 103, Newbury, 603/763-2356, www.mt-sunapee.com.

Getting There
From I-89, take exit 9 to Rte. 103 west for about 16 miles through Newbury. Entrance is on the left. From I-91, take exit 8 (in Vermont) to Rte. 103 east through Claremont and Newport. Entrance is on the right.

First Steps
Take the aerial sky ride (fee charged) to the top of Mount Sunapee. The views of the mountains and myriad lakes from the chairlift are breathtaking. The chairlift operates from 10:30am to 5pm daily, from mid June to Labor Day, then weekends until Columbus Day (weather permitting; sky ride may not operate in case of heavy fog or thunder storms). From the summit, follow arrows to Lake Solitude Trail.

Mount Sunapee Lake Solitude Trail. Follow the steep gravel road to the left of the chairlift down a steep incline to the trailhead, where you will take the sinuous 1-mile path to solitude—Lake Solitude, that is. The trail goes over sharply undulating terrain through the forest—up and down, up and down—ultimately terminating at White Ledges, an area composed of enormous slabs of pink granite perched on a precipice 400 feet lower than the top of the mountain but high above Lake Solitude, which lies directly below. The vista of Lake Solitude from the edge of the granite carpet is dizzyingly spectacular.

This is a great place to enjoy a picnic lunch, but if you really are looking for solitude, make your trek early in the day and take breakfast instead. A relatively easy hike, this is the most popular summer attraction atop

Mount Sunapee, also a bustling New Hampshire skiing destination in the snowy months. Retrace your steps for the 1-mile trek back to the chairlift.

If you are an experienced, hearty hiker, you can opt for several more challenging hikes at Mount Sunapee State Park. If you can position automobiles at both the base of the chairlift and on Mountain Road, you can descend from White Ledges to Lake Solitude itself and continue for 1.8 mile on the Andrew Brook Trail. Alternately, you can hike from the base of the mountain to the summit on the Summit Trail and then do the Lake Solitude and the Andrew Brook Trail. Or simply take the chairlift to the top, hike the 2-mile loop to White Ledges overlooking Lake Solitude and then return to the parking lot via the 1.8-mile Summit Trail.

Lakes Region

Dominated by the largest lake in New England, Lake Winnipesaukee—an Indian word meaning "smile of the great spirit"—the Lakes Region is awash with a galaxy of 273 ponds and lakes, all nestled in the foothills of the White Mountains.

Regional Information
Lakes Region Association, P.O. Box 430, New Hampton, NH 03256; 603/744-8664, 800/605-2537; www.lakesregion.org.
Meredith Chamber of Commerce, 272 Daniel Webster Hwy., P.O. Box 732, Meredith, NH   03253-0732; 603/279-6121, 877/279-6121, www.meredithcc.org.

Getting There
Take I-93 north, then specified state and county roads east.

Science Center of New Hampshire, Holderness

A cross-generational audience thrills to discoveries of this 200-acre sanctuary. The mission of the Science Center is "to advance understanding of ecology by exploring New Hampshire's natural world." It was founded in 1966 to teach visitors first-hand about the ecosystems and habitats of local wildlife.

Information
Science Center of New Hampshire, P.O. Box 173, Holderness, NH 03245; 603/968-7194, www.sciencectrofnh.org.

Getting There
Take I-93 to exit 24, then U.S. Rte. 3 for 4 miles to the junction of Rte. 113. The Science Center is on the left.

First Steps
Pick up a trail map when you pay your admission fee. The trails are open to the public from May through Oct.

Science Center of New Hampshire. Four trails traverse the Science Center at the south end of Squam Lake. Perhaps the most unusual and fascinating for all ages and ability levels is the 0.75-mile Gephart Exhibit Trail. More than 30 animals, which have been injured or orphaned, are housed in open pens or cages that replicate their natural environment. (Brought to the Center by the New Hampshire Fish and Game Department and the Humane Society, only animals that adapt well to captivity are accepted.) Like an outdoor classroom, this trail introduces you to bears, white-tailed deer, foxes, otters, owls, bald eagles, hawks, and more. All the wildflowers and trees along the trail are labeled.

From the visitor center follow the trail over a wooden boardwalk that spans a wetlands area and proceed through the forest. Suddenly you begin encountering the wildlife exhibits, actually the camouflaged abodes of the resident animals and birds. Interpretive signs share their personal habits and lifestyles. After you visit the raptor exhibit, divert onto the Ecotone Trail, a short 0.5-mile loop along the edge of the forest, where you'll see native trees, shrubs, and flowers. Allow 1.5 hour to explore the environmentally rich Exhibit and Ecotone Trails.

Two other trails offer other options. The Mount Fayal Trail is a 1-mile loop to the summit of 1,067-foot Mount Fayal, where you'll be treated to stunning views of Squam Lake. Wear sturdy footgear for this one, and plan to allow at least one hour for the trek. The Forest Trail is a 2/3-mile hike through some of the Science Center's 30 wooded acres. The loop goes part way up Mount Fayal, but cuts back down to the Ecotone Trail.

The Science Center also gives live-animal presentations hourly during July, which provide insights into the wonders of nature.

Paradise Point Nature Center, Hebron

This property on Newfound Lake offers trails through an old-growth forest, rare in New Hampshire because most of the state was completely logged in the 18th and 19th centuries. Trails vary in difficulty and the habitats through which they transverse.

Information
Paradise Point Nature Center & Wildlife Sanctuary, North Shore Rd., East Hebron, NH 03222, 603/744-3516 (July to Sept.), 603/224-9909 (Sept. to July).
The Audubon Society of New Hampshire, 3 Silk Farm Rd., Concord, NH 03301, 603/224-9909, www.nhaudubon.org.

Getting There
Take I-93 north to exit 26 west, Rte. 25, to Rte. 3A south. At a sign saying: "Sculptured Rocks, Paradise Point, Wellington State Beach," turn right (North Shore Rd., but no sign) for 1 mile, then turn left on Paradise Point access road and park in the lot.

First Steps
Pick up a map at the nature center building, which is open daily during the summer months. The trails are always open.

Paradise Point Nature Center. Begin on the 5/8-mile Ridge Trail (yellow blazes). At the split, bear to the right over a boggy area, where you'll see lots of mushrooms growing. A short, steep incline will take you to the top of a ridge in the 100-year-old hemlock forest, whose floor is covered with pine needles and littered with pinecones and massive glacial erratics.

When the Ridge Trail dead ends at Paradise Point, proceed on the 0.5-mile Lakeside Trail (blue blazes) along the shores of Newfound Lake. (Wooden benches front the lake, a great place to have lunch.) The 180-foot-deep lake was formed by glacial erosion. Native Americans called the lake "pasquaney," which refers to the area's prevalent birch trees, the bark of which they used to build canoes. Notice the lichen growing on the huge boulders.

The trail traverses easy, flat terrain along the side of the lake, then connects with the 1/3-mile Loop Trail (white blazes) back to the Nature Center, where you can take the æ-mile Elwell Trail (red blazes) loop back to the lake, explore a marsh habitat, then head back to the Nature Center through old-growth forest. The Nature Center features exhibits and interactive environmental puzzles and games the whole family can enjoy.

West Rattlesnake Bridle Path Trail, Sandwich

The summit of West Rattlesnake Bridle Path Trail lies within the Armstrong Natural Area, owned by the University of New Hampshire. The Armstrong Natural Area is named in memory of Mary Alice Armstrong (1864-1958) and Margaret Armstrong (1891-1971), environmentalists called the "ladies of the lake."

Information
Squam Lakes Association, Pinehurst Rd., Sandwich, 603/968-7336.
Squam Lakes Conservation Society, 603/279-1309.
University of New Hampshire, 603/862-3951.

Getting There
Take I-93 north to exit 24, U.S. Rte. 3 east, to Rte. 113. The trailhead is on the right side, 6.1 miles before Sandwich. Parking is just beyond on the left.

First Steps
Squam Lakes Association maintains the trail. No trail maps are available but the path is easily discernable and well traveled.

West Rattlesnake Bridle Path Trail. A private picnic at the top of the world is the reward bestowed for persevering up the steady but gradual incline to the summit of West Rattlesnake. The 1-mile path is four feet wide but littered with exposed rocks and roots, an erosional handicap overcome with good hiking boots. As you make your way up the mountain, an easy climb by anyone's standards, you'll be lulled into thinking this is just another lovely walk in the woods, for, though heavily forested, the shady canopy inhibits growth of any unusual flora.

This ho-hum illusion blows sky high, however, the moment you reach the summit at 1,231 feet. The forest simply ends in a virtual parking lot of pink granite, which covers the peak of West Rattlesnake like a skullcap. From every direction, you'll see New Hampshire's Lakes Region spread before you like a Persian carpet.

Consume the awesome panorama: Squam Lake, the prototype for the movie, "On Golden Pond," nestles in a cocoon of encompassing pines immediately below. Beyond, Lake Winnipesaukee dominates the landscape, peppered with islands and surrounded by an orbit of watery satellites—ponds, bays, fingers, and baby lakes. Then, like a halo, peak after peak of New Hampshire mountains burn the horizon in prismatic silhouette.

Loon Center and Markus Sanctuary, Moultonborough

Since 1975 the Loon Preservation Committee has sought to reverse the decline in the loon population in New Hampshire. The success of their mission is witnessed by the increase in both adult loons and nesting pairs on Lake Winnipesaukee, which have more than doubled in two decades. The 200-acre Markus Sanctuary includes 5,000 feet of undeveloped shoreline on the lake.

Information
The Loon Preservation Committee, Lees Mills Rd., P.O. Box 604, Moultonborough, NH 03254, 603/476-5666.

Getting There
Take I-93 to exit 23, Rte. 104 east, to Rte. 25. From Rte. 25, between Center Harbor and Moultonborough, turn on Blake Rd., at the Moultonborough Central School (look for Loon Center sign). Go 1 mile and turn right on Lee's Mills Rd. Center is on the left.

First Steps
Stop at the Loon Center and pick up a trail guide to Markus Wildlife

Sanctuary. No admission fee is charged. Guided tours are occasionally available. Call the Center for times and dates.

The Loon Center and Markus Sanctuary. From the Loon Center, take the flat, 1æ-mile Loon Nest Trail (yellow blazes), which initially traverses a second-growth forest, along a fern-banked creek. After 0.25 mile you'll encounter a wildlife viewing station, a raised platform that looks out over a logged wetland area. Follow the log footbridges over the wetlands. As you re-enter the forest, look for two white pines whose trunks have grown together over the years while the canopies grow in two different directions.

The forest becomes very dense and is littered with massive glacial erratics, one of which towers over the path like a lean-to, forcing you to bend over and wiggle through. A prolific bird habitat, the forest is alive with a profusion of melodic bird songs. As the forest thins somewhat, dappled light filters through trees. All the boulders here are covered with green moss, creating a very surreal atmosphere.

When the trail forks, stay to the left. This loop will take you to the two loon nesting spots, which have lookout platforms over the rushes and cattails. The trail continues to the shores of Lake Winnipesaukee and then once again returns to the fork. Retrace your steps heading back toward the Loon Center. Divert to the right onto the Forest Walk, a short loop through a mixed forest filled with warblers and wildflowers.

Back at the Loon Center, stop in to view the informational video on the efforts of the Loon Preservation Committee and check out the bulletin board, which posts the latest births among nesting loons.

Rainy Day Options

Castle in the Clouds Estate encompasses more than 5,200 acres in the Ossipee Mountains overlooking Lake Winnipesaukee. Now home of Castle Springs Water and Castle Springs Brewing Co., which makes the microbrew Lucknow Lager, the estate was the rugged home of a wealthy, retired eccentric, Thomas G. Plant, who built his own golf course on the property, then brought in a flock of sheep to maintain it. Well-marked mountain trails crisscross the estate's woodland and meadows. You can tour the granite mansion, Castle in the Clouds, which was built in 1913, as well as the spring water bottling facility and the microbrewery (complimentary tastings offered at both). You can also take a tram ride up a tree-covered mountain lane to the site where the pure spring site water naturally rises to the surface. *(Contact: Castle in the Clouds on the Castle Springs Estate, P.O. Box 9, Lincoln, NH 03251, 603/745-2135, www.castlesprings.com. Open weekends and holiday beginning in early May, then daily from early June through Oct. An admission fee is charged.)*

Quilters from all over the United States regard **Keepsake Quilting** as a shopping nirvana. Most stitchers must be content to order from Keepsake's extensive catalog. But when in New Hampshire, the bountiful Keepsake Quilting store is a must-visit, even if you don't sew a stitch. You may be inspired here to become a quilter. *(Contact: Keepsake Quilting, Rte. 25B, P.O. Box 1618, Centre Harbor, 603/253-8346, 800/865-9458.)*

Lodging

For more options, consult the New England-wide accommodations websites and reservation services listed in "How to Use This Book" or check out www.visitnh.gov.

Quiet, understated elegance and attention to guest comfort distinguish **The Trumbull House** ($+, 40 Etna Rd., Hanover, 603/643-2370, www.valley.net/~trumbull.bnb). Built in 1919 as the private residence of Hancock builder Harry Trumbull, this five-guest-room bed-and-breakfast sits on 16 wooded acres. The property, only 4 miles from Dartmouth College, is laced with walking trails and features a swimming pond and a wildflower-filled meadow.

With a candle in every window, the casual, cozy, charming, **Rosewood Country Inn** ($+, 67 Pleasant View Rd., Bradford, 603/938-5253, www.bbonline.com/nh/rosewood) creates an aura of rural romance. Even the aristocratic breakfast is served by candlelight. The pristine 12-guestroom Victorian sits on 12 acres surrounded by gardens.

Warm and welcoming, **Candlelite Inn Bed and Breakfast** ($, 5 Greenhouse Lane, Bradford, 603/938-5571, 888/812-5571, www.virtualcities.com-/ons/nh/y/nhyb601.htm) exudes the homey hospitality of its owners

Marilyn and Les Gordon. Built in 1897, the six-guestroom Victorian has always been an inn.

All but three of the 10- guestrooms of **Goddard Mansion Bed and Breakfast** ($, 25 Hillstead Rd., Claremont, 603/543-0603, 800/736-0603, www.goddardmansion.com) have private baths. The interior of this 1905 Victorian mansion features original cotton tapestry on the dining room walls, walnut paneling, a mahogany fireplace, and is chock-a-block with interesting antiques.

A virtual landmark at Dartmouth College, **The Hanover Inn** ($$, Main St., Hanover, 603/643-4300, 800/443-7024, www.HanoverInn.com) has sheltered dignitaries and visitors to the famed Ivy League university for centuries. Located aside the village Green, this full service hotel sits in the middle of collegiate action.

Chock full of authentic antiques and memorabilia, like a turn-of-the-last-century museum, **Glynn House Victorian Inn** ($+, 59 Highland St., Ashland, 603/968-3775, 800/637-9599, www.new-hamp-shire-lodging.com) straddles the White Mountain and Lake regions. The nine guest rooms in the main house and three fireplace/Jacuzzi suites in the carriage house offer 21st century creature comforts and Old World charm.

Three classic hotels and a marketplace mall make up the **Inns at Mill Falls** ($-$$$, Rte. 3, Meredith, 603/279-7006, 800/622-6455, www.millfalls-baypoint.com), at the tip of Lake Winnipesaukee. The Inn at Mill Falls offers 54 rooms within an historic old mill, complete with a waterfall and covered bridge. The Inn at Bay Point sits directly on the lake. All rooms have private balconies, fireplaces, and whirlpool tubs. The newest lodging is Chase House, 23 rooms and suites on a hill overlooking the water.

Offering commanding views of Squam Lake (location for movie "On Golden Pond"), **The Manor on Golden Pond** ($$+, Rte, 3, Holderness, 603/968-3348, 800/545-2141, www.manorongoldenpond.com) ignites visions of life in an English manor house. An Editor's Pick by *Yankee Magazine*, the Manor's restaurant has also won an Award of Excellence by *Wine Spectator*.

Inn at Valley Farms ($+, Wentworth Rd., Walpole, 603/756-2855, 877/327-2855, www.innatvalleyfarms.com), a 1774 Colonial filled with antiques and vintage memorabilia, sits on 105 acres of organic farmland in the Connecticut River Valley. Offering three guest rooms as well as three-bedroom family cottages, the Inn utilizes its fresh organic eggs and produce in its hearty morning breakfasts.

An original Shaker dwelling built between 1837 and 1841, the **Shaker Inn at the Great Stone Dwelling** ($+, 447 Rte. 4A, Enfield, 603/632-7810, 888/707-4257, www.theshakerinn.com) re-creates the Shaker experience, complete with historically correct Shaker-style furnishings. A part of the Enfield Shaker Museum and deemed "dazzlingly simple without being at all spartan," by *Travel & Leisure*, the Shaker Inn is one of a kind.

Food and Drink

For more dining options, consult www.visitnh.gov.

The food is eclectic and tasty at **Daniel's Restaurant and Pub** ($+, Main St., Henniker, 603/428-7621), but the view is sublime. Most every table looks out over the rapids of the Contoocook River.

The Pan Asian cuisine and high-tech décor of **Monsoon Asian Bistro and Satay Bar** ($$, 18 Centerra Pkwy., Centerra Marketplace off Rte. 120, Lebanon, 603/643-9227) are more New York than New Hampshire, and local folks drive as long as an hour to dine here. The food is that good. You will be wise to call for a reservation.

A quintessential college-town Irish pub, **Murphy's On The Green** ($, 11 South Main St., Hanover, 603/643-4075) offers traditional casual tavern fare in a convivial atmosphere.

Dine in luxury at the **Daniel Webster Room** ($$$) or in the sleek, modern Zins winebistro ($$) (The Hanover Inn, Main St., Hanover, 603/643-4300, 800/443-7024, www.HanoverInn.com). Either way, you'll experience fine New American cuisine crafted with innovative interpretations of classic New Hampshire ingredients.

Cute signs, old copies of *Saturday Evening Post* and *Life Magazine* on sale, a paint bucket that goes up and down on a pulley every time the front door opens. There is nothing common about **The Common Man** ($$, Main St., Ashland, 603/968-7030), including the food. From the complimentary cheese and crackers to the white chocolate chunks delivered with your bill, you'll find the cuisine as imaginative as the surroundings.

Exuding the rustic ambiance of a New Hampshire cabin, **Camp** ($, Chase House, Rte. 3, Meredith, 603/279-3003) offers a cozy little menu that includes burgers, camp cakes, and campfire steak. Eating here is tasty fun.

Offering a five-course prixe fixe dinner Wednesdays through Sundays, the **Inn at Pleasant Lake** ($$$$, 125 Pleasant St., New London, 603/526-6271, 800/626-4927, www.innatpleasantlake.com) offers a taste bud extravaganza. Winner of First Place Chocolate Truffles and Best of Show at Chocolatefest '99—need I say more?

For intimate dining in an 1825 former residence, **Mame's** ($$, 8 Plymouth St., Meredith, 603/279-4631) offers interesting renditions of New American cuisine. Dine in one of six small rooms, which feature wide-plank pine flooring, hand-hewn beams, and brick walls.

Great seafood, great mixed grille, great view. **The Boathouse Grill** ($$, Rte. 25, Meredith, 603/279-2253), in the Inn at Bay Point, sits right on the edge of Lake Winnipesaukee.

Red Hill Inn ($$, Rte. 25B & College Rd., Centre Harbor, 603/279-7001, 800/5733-4455, www.redhillinn.com), situated in a 100-year-old brick mansion overlooking Squam Lake, offers consistently fine dining. The chef utilizes fresh herbs from his kitchen garden to augment the flavors of his stellar cuisine.

White Mountains

Forested mountains and rugged landscape with rock ledges and river gorges comprise the White Mountains region, which makes up the northern tier of New Hampshire. The White Mountains National Forest, 714,336 acres of hardwood and alpine forest, dominates the area. Established in 1911 by Congress as a remedy for excessive logging, erosion, and forest fires, the national forest is a little larger than the state of Rhode Island. The national forest designation means that unlike a national park, the forest is managed for multiple uses that include timber, water, recreation, and wildlife. This area boasts 1,200 miles of hiking trails, 45 lakes and ponds, and 650 miles of fishing streams. The crown jewel of the mountain ranges is Mount Washington, at 6,288 feet the highest peak in the Northeast. The other ranges are also named for U.S. presidents: Adams, Eisenhower, Garfield, Jefferson, Lincoln, Madison, Monroe, and Pierce.

Regional Information

White Mountain National Forest Information Headquarters, 719 North Main St., Laconia, 603/528-8721.
White Mountains Attractions, P.O. Box 10, N. Woodstock, NH 03262; 800/346-3687; www.visitwhitemountains.com.

Getting There

Take I-93 north, then specified state and county roads.

Black Fly Season

Black flies are prevalent in the White Mountains of New Hampshire and the Green Mountains of Vermont from late spring to early summer. They are at their worst from mid May to mid June. Most have disappeared by early July. Dates vary from year to year depending upon the weather. Some insect repellents work, especially those with a high deet factor. Insects are worse in wet, swampy places. John Josselyn said in 1672 in New England Rarities Discovered: "The black flies are so numerous that a man cannot draw his breath but he will suck some of them in."

Lost River Gorge, Kinsman's Notch

Lost River tumbles down Mount Moosilauke, through a boulder-filled gorge and disappears among rocks, potholes, and caves. Local legend portends that two boys, Royal and Lyman Jackman, discovered the river. They were fishing when Lyman suddenly vanished into the earth. He dropped 12 feet through a hole into a waist-deep pool. Royal retrieved his brother, scared but unhurt. Royal supposedly returned to North Woodstock as an old man, blazed a trail through the woods, and found "Cave of the Shadows" where his brother had discovered Lost River.

Information
Lost River Gorge, Rte. 112, North Woodstock, 03262, 603/745-8031; www.FindLostRiver.com.

Getting There
Take I-93 to exit 32, Rte. 112 west, and continue for 6 miles past North Woodstock.

First Steps
Pick up a "Pocket Map and Guide to Lost River" when you pay your admission fee. Lost River is preserved by the Society for the Protection of New Hampshire Forests and is operated by the White Mountains Attractions Association. It is open from mid May to Mid Oct. Wear sturdy shoes and bring a flashlight if you plan to explore the caves.

Lost River Gorge. Lost River Gorge is simply a gift from the gods. Water, wind, weather, and time contributed to the formation of this natural phenomenon. As the glacier receded more than 10,000 years ago, melt-waters carved a 50-foot-deep gorge in the Lost River Valley. The river appears and disappears through caverns, crevasses, and caves and between unusual rock formations made of Kinsman quartz and monzonite, a type of granite.

You'll initially descend for 300 feet down wooden steps, where a 0.75-mile trail of paths and boardwalk leads you along the river's sinuous hidden path. Should you be agile enough (and even I was!) you can negotiate the tight rocky passages—on foot, on hands and knees, sometimes even on your belly—for a true insiders view of the erosion process. Alternately, stay on the boardwalk, for a safe, interesting—if less adventurous—excursion. Along the way, interpretive signs describe the caves and places of interest.

The lower gorge was opened to the public in 1984. Early explorers to the area named the caves after gods of Norse mythology and legends. The first cave you will encounter is the Sun Altar, one of the few caves which ever sees the sunshine. Trees here grow out horizontally from the gorge, then reach to the sky in search of light. All along this path you'll encounter the dark, sometimes damp caves, which you are invited to explore—Cave of Odin, Thor's Cauldron, Devil's Kitchen, Parallel Rocks, Bear Crawl, Judgment Hall of Pluto, and more. Signs detail specific instructions you should follow to explore the crevasses. Lit candles illuminate the interiors slightly, which, nevertheless, still seem dark as death. The Lemon Squeezer is the most difficult encounter in the gorge. Only the most agile should attempt this one. You have to fit through the "squeezer gauge" to enter the cave. If you cannot make it through the gauge, you will not be permitted to attempt the Lemon Squeezer, because you will get stuck within!

A photographer's dream, fantastic waterfalls and whirlpools abound all throughout this walk. Once you exit the Lost River Gorge trail, the path leads through a lovely nature garden before climbing back up to the visitor center.

The Flume, Franconia Notch State Park

Considered the flagship of the New Hampshire Park System, Franconia Notch State Park showcases astounding natural wonders, none more beautiful than the Flume, a narrow natural gorge that extends 800 feet at the base of Mount Liberty. The Flume's Conway-granite walls rise 70 to 90 feet, 12 to 20 feet apart. A boulder dislodged in the avalanche of 1883 is said to have deepened the watercourse and created the waterfalls. Ninety-three-year-old Aunt Jess Guernsey is credited with discovering this awesome gorge while she was fishing for brook trout in 1808.

Information
Franconia Notch State Park, U.S. Rte. 3, Franconia, NH 03580; 603/745-8391, 603/823-5563, www.whitemtn.org/franconia.

Getting There
Take I-93 north to Franconia Notch Parkway exit 1, U.S. Rte. 3.

First Steps
You'll receive a guide to the Flume when you pay your admission fee at the Gilman Visitor Center. Then view the 15-minute introductory video before you start out on the trail. This is a very popular spot, especially in

the summer season. Come early in the morning to beat the crowds and maximize your commune with nature. The Flume is open daily from early May through Oct.

The Flume. Begin your 2-mile walk with the 0.7-mile section from the Visitor Center to the Flume (in the summer, a shuttle bus takes those who want a less energetic excursion to the Flume). You'll pass a gigantic 300-ton boulder, a glacial erratic deposited more than 25,000 years ago, and cross a covered bridge over the Pemigewasset River, which is full of eddies swirling over slabs of pink granite. The trees are labeled along this portion of the trail.

Follow Flume Path to Table Rock—500 feet long, 75 feet wide—a "table" of pink granite that has been exposed by the rushing waters of Flume Brook. Continue along Flume Brook, which tumbles downhill in a tumult of small waterfalls. The trail changes to a series of steps and wooden boardwalks that lead uphill within the Flume. Trees hang over the gorge above, and moss and lichens grow on the 90-foot perpendicular granite walls, creating the illusion of a natural cavern. The only sound is that of rushing, crashing water.

> **Waterfall Phenomenon**
>
> As you encounter waterfalls on some of your walks in the White Mountains, you may notice tan-colored foam at the base of falls. This is a natural byproduct of the forest caused by the vegetation of the area. Rain dissolves the natural foaming agents from the organic residue of decaying leaves and vegetation on the forest floor. These foaming agents are carried to the river after a rain and coat the air bubbles caused by total saturation of air in the water. As this mixture is carried over the falls it is agitated, the air escapes leaving behind the shells of the bubbles, which coagulate to form the unusual foam you see.

Steps lead steeply to the top of the gorge and Avalanche Falls. At intervals you'll see pictures of the Flume in the 1800s, and you can compare then and now, viewing the changes erosion has caused in the two hundred years. Fungi and algae, hundreds of years old, grow side by side on the granite walls, dependent on each other for survival. The plants obtain food and water from the air and thrive in the moist conditions of the gorge. Avalanche Falls is the centerpiece of the Flume. The crashing 45-foot waterfall creates an almost orange glow as it cascades over the pink granite walls.

As you leave the gorge, follow the Downhill Ridge Path, a gravel road traversing heavy woods, and head to Liberty Gorge and Cascades (look for a 100-foot turnoff leading to an overlook). Waters of Cascade Brook tumble into the narrow valley of Liberty Gorge, creating a singularly beautiful panorama. Continue on, taking the footbridge across Cascade Brook to the Pool, a deep basin formed at the end of the Ice Age by a silt-laden stream flowing from the glacier. Cliffs surrounding the pool are 80 feet high. The Pool is 150 feet in diameter and 40 feet deep.

Cross Sentinel Pine Covered Bridge, named for a sentinel pine that was uprooted in the Hurricane of 1938. It was said to be 175 feet high and 16 feet in circumference. Its trunk forms the base of the bridge. Continue on the Wildwood Path, where you can see Mount Liberty (4,460 feet), Mount Flume (4,327 feet), and Mount Osceola (3,640) in the distance. Birch tree roots along this trail are amazing: One looks like a big ostrich sitting on the edge of a rock, with his two big legs crossed and hanging over the side; another looks like the giant talons of a prehistoric raptor grabbing a rock. Continue along the path, returning to the Visitor Center.

Mount Cannon Summit Loop, Franconia Notch State Park

A deep valley between the peaks of Franconia and Kinsman Mountains, Franconia State Park encompasses 6,440 acres of scenic wonder. The region is known as Franconia because of resemblance to the Franconian Alps in Germany. An enclosed aerial tramway cable car, which carries 80 passengers, ascends 2,200 feet for more than a mile, to the summit of Mount Cannon. Visible from Rte. 3 at the base of Mount Cannon is the internationally known Old Man and the Mountain, or Profile Mountain, immortalized by Daniel Webster and Nathaniel Hawthorne and recognized as the unofficial symbol of New Hampshire. A natural granite profile formed by five separate ledges, the profile measures 40 feet from chin to forehead.

Information
Franconia Notch State Park, U.S. Rte. 3, Franconia, NH 03580; 603/745-8391, 603/823-5563, www.whitemtn.org/franconia.
Cannon Mountain, I-93, Franconia Notch, NH 03580; 603/823-8800, www.cannonmt.com.

Getting There
Take I-93 north to Franconia Notch State Parkway exit 2.

First Steps
Take the aerial tramway to the top of Mount Cannon (fee charged). The tramway operates from the end of May to mid Oct., every 15 minutes, weather permitting.

Mount Cannon Summit Loop. Take the 7-minute tramway ride to the summit of Mount Cannon, which treats you to a spectacular vista on a clear day: Old Man and the Mountain, the Basin, the Flume, Echo Lake, Eagle Cliffs, Franconia Ridge, and more. Follow the 0.5-mile summit loop, which leads from the tramway station to the observation tower and back, around the perimeter of the mountaintop. Though short, this walk along the Rim Trail clings to the precipice of Kinsman Ridge, netting fantastic views of the surrounding valleys and mountains.

The first thing you'll notice is that your olfactories will be assaulted with the exquisite odor of "Christmas," an overpowering balsam scent that pervades the entire summit. The narrow trail winds through this arbor of red spruce and balsam fir, with dizzying panoramic views from every clearing. About 2/3 of the way around the loop you'll encounter an observation tower, which you can climb for an even loftier view of Franconia Notch State Park. Follow the trail back to the tramway, where the trip back down the mountain yields more enchanting vistas.

Around the Lake Trail, Crawford Notch

Legend has it that Europeans discovered Crawford Notch in 1771, when Captain Timothy Nash became lost while following a moose through the dense forest. Climbing a tree to get his bearings, he supposedly saw a gigantic cleft in the mountains. The notch was named for Abel Crawford, who constructed a trail through the Notch, making it accessible from other areas.

Information
Crawford Notch State Park, Rte. 302, Harts Location, 603/374-2272.

Getting There
Take I-93 to exit 36, U.S. Rte. 3, to U.S. Rte. 302. Park at the Appalachian Mountain Club's Visitor Center at the head of Crawford Notch.

First Steps
Walk north on the service road between the Appalachian Mountain Club's hostel on your right and a field on your left. At the flagpole, look for the sign for the Around the Lake Trail.

Around the Lake Trail. Bear left at the first two forks as you head through a forest of red spruce, balsam fir, and paper birch to Ammonoosuc Lake. This 1.75-mile loop path (marked with white AMC signs and yellow blazes) continues to bear left, over a footbridge to Merrill Spring, which is marked by a stone outcropping (don't drink this water). Walk quietly on the path around tiny Ammonoosuc Lake, for moose sightings are reportedly quite common here, especially at dawn and dusk. Look into the shallows for bullfrogs and feeding blue herons and wood ducks.

Bear left on the side trail to Red Bench Overlook. Ford the stream over the sometimes slippery boulders, carefully cross an active railroad track, and continue along the trail, shadowing a small creek and gradually gaining elevation. At the end of the trail is a strategically placed red bench, from which you can see the smoke of the cog railway as it climbs to the tower atop Mount Washington. You can also spot Mounts Clay, Jefferson, and Eisenhower.

Retrace your steps from the Red Bench and bear left around Lake Ammonoosuc. Cross a concrete dam, augmented by the work of several beavers. (This is a good place for a swim.) Take the grassy path to a gravel road and cross a footbridge over a run-off stream. When the loop ends, retrace your steps back to Crawford Depot.

Ripley Falls, Crawford Notch State Park

Crawford Notch encompasses six miles of rugged unspoiled beauty in a scenic mountain pass. Ripley Falls is named after Henry Wheelock Ripley, an old fisherman who discovered the lower falls in 1858. Born in 1828,

Ripley visited the White Mountains for 53 consecutive years, climbing Mount Washington 85 times by 1889.

Information
Crawford Notch State Park, Rte. 302, Harts Location, 603/374-2272.

Getting There
Take I-93 to exit 36, U.S. Rte. 3, to U.S. Rte. 302. About 0.5 mile beyond Willey House (a good place to pick up sandwiches for a picnic at the falls), look for the Ripley Falls sign. The parking area is about 0.2 mile up this turnoff at the site of the old Willey House Station.

First Steps
No trail guides are available here, but trails are well marked with blue blazes.

Ripley Falls Trail. Cross the old Marine Central railroad tracks and head up the Ethan Pond Trail (part of the Appalachian Trail) and the 1-mile Ripley Falls Trail, both of which leave from the trailhead. The first part of the trail is the steepest—a slow, steady uphill climb. Most of the forest is made up of northern hardwoods, but some of the birch trees along this trail measure a foot or more in diameter and are hundreds of feet high.

At 0.3 mile Ripley Falls Trail (called Arethusa-Ripley Falls Trail) diverts to the left and evens out for a short while. The path is narrow and has a steep fall-away. The trail continues uphill above Avalanche Brook, until, at about 0.75 mile, you'll be able to hear the falls. Scramble and fanny slide down the steep bank to the brook and falls.

Ripley Falls, 100 feet high, spectacularly cascades over a granite face to the Avalanche Brook below. You'll find lots of granite boulders upon which to sit and drink in the dramatic view. (If you want a more intensive workout, continue on the 3.8-mile Arethusa-Ripley Trail, which continues past Ripley Falls to Frankenstein Cliffs and Arethusa Falls, at 200 feet the highest waterfall in New Hampshire.) Or, scramble back up the hill from Ripley Falls and retrace your steps back down the trail to the parking area.

Sabbaday Falls, Kancamagus Highway

The 34.5-mile Kancamagus Highway is the only federally designated Scenic Highway in New England. It stretches from the Pemigewasset River at Lincoln to the Saco River at Conway. The highway climbs to an elevation of nearly 3,000 feet. The scenic byway was named for Kancamagus, an Indian chief who tried to keep peace between the Native Americans and the white pioneers in the late 1600s. Many hiking trails begin from points along the highway. The name Sabbaday was given by early explorers during their travels to Passaconaway Valley. Reaching the falls on a Sunday, they decided to return home. Years later the falls became a favorite Sabbath Day journey.

Information
White Mountains Attractions, P.O. Box 10, N. Woodstock, NH 03262; 800/346-3687; www.visitwhitemountains.com.

Getting There
Take I-93 to Rte 112 east (Kancamagus Hwy.), midway between Lincoln and Conway. The trailhead for Sabbaday Falls is on the south side of Kancamagus Highway.

First Steps
This 1.5-mile round-trip walk is graded and suitable for walkers of all ability levels. No map is needed for this walk, but detailed trail maps for all Kancamagus Highway trails may be purchased at the Saco Ranger Station Visitor Center in Conway or at the Information Center in Lincoln. If you want a more intensivee hike, try the 3.5-mile Boulder Loop Trail or the 4-mile Greeley Ponds Trail, both found along the Kancamagus Highway.

Sabbaday Falls. Follow the wide, level path under a high forest canopy along the 30-foot-wide Sabbaday Brook, which cascades down over big granite boulders and small rocks. The well-maintained walkway follows a gentle incline at first, but then becomes steeper, uphill all the way. Take the well-marked fork to Sabbaday Falls.

Sabbaday Falls began over 10,000 years ago, when large volumes of water from the last melting glacier, carrying loads of sand, gravel and boulders, carved out the main gorge. Signs along the path explain the important geological features. You'll begin to hear the roar of the falls at the Lower Pool, formed thousands of years ago by the scouring action of falling water and rock. As time passed, the scouring rocks retreated to their present location leaving a narrow gorge or flume. Take the steps up to the flume and follow the gorge, where you'll encounter three amazing waterfalls.

Walk out onto the exposed rocks. Serious volumes of water are crashing down here over a huge granite ledge. The flume makes a right angle. Take the steps to the top of second waterfall. Whirlpool action of the Upper Pool has carved and smoothed the rock at the base of the waterfall into a pink-granite Jacuzzi. The third waterfall, at the uppermost point, cascades from a granite shoot.

Scramble up the bank and rejoin the Sabbaday Brook Trail, which now becomes narrow and rocky and is covered with tree roots. The path heads upstream, following the rushing water to its source. (Most people take only the short path to the waterfalls, so you will be pretty much alone.) You'll find lots of places to scramble down to the rushing brook, sit on a boulder, and dangle your feet in the water. The tranquility of the moment is mesmerizing. At the point when the brook splits into three narrow tributaries, the trail ends. (The distance you'll be able to continue upstream on the Sabbaday Brook Trail is entirely dependent upon how high the water table is.) Retrace your steps back to the parking lot.

Lost Pond Trail to Ellis River (Glen Ellis Falls), Pinkham Notch

The Presidential Range dominates the landscape of the Pinkham Notch region, which is noted for its large bowl-shaped ravines. The scenery here is ruggedly beautiful and includes a profusion of waterfalls and ponds amid the forest.

Information

White Mountains Attractions, P.O. Box 10, N. Woodstock, NH 03262; 800/346-3687; www.visitwhitemountains.com.

Getting There

Take I-93 north to exit 32, Rte. 112 east (Kancamagus Hwy.), to Rte. 16

north to the Appalachian Mountain Club Pinkham Notch Visitor Center.

First Steps
Trail leaves across the road from the AMC Pinkham Notch Visitor Center
on Rte. 16. AMC maintains trail, which is well marked white blazes.

Lost Pond Trail to Ellis River (Glen Ellis Falls). Cross the wooden plank
bridge over the Ellis River and take the Lost Pond Trail into the forest.
The trail shadows the river, whose water is so crystal clear that you can
count the stones in the bottom. Monster trees wrap around rocks here,
their roots gripping the boulders like the talons of prehistoric birds. After
some uphill rock scrambling, you'll come to Lost Pond, about 0.5 mile into
this walk. Lost Pond is a pretty little body of water with marshy edges and
lily pads, surrounded by pines and deciduous forest. The trail skirts the
pond.

Beyond the pond, footing becomes precarious, as the path becomes a
stand of boulders over which you must climb. At the T-fork signpost, turn
to the right on Wildcat Ridge Trail for a short distance, to Ellis River.
Here you will be faced with two alternatives. If the water is high, turn
around and retrace your steps back to the beginning, a 2.25-mile round
trip. But, if water is low enough, a steeping stone bridge emerges, over
which you can ford Ellis River.

If you can successfully ford Ellis River, turn left on the other side and
follow the trail for 0.6 miles to Glen Ellis Falls, a 64-foot waterfall on the
Ellis River. The dramatic waterfalls were created when avalanches blocked
the flow of the Ellis River and forced the water to cascade over a glacially
carved bowl in the side of the mountain. (If the river is too high to ford,
you can access Glen Ellis Falls on the west side of Rte. 16, about 0.7 mile
south of the Visitors Center. The walk to the falls from there borders the
highway for a 1.2-mile roundtrip.

Thompson's Falls Trail, Pinkham Notch

Thompson's Falls are named for Colonel J.M. Thompson, who once
owned Glen House at the base of Mount Washington Auto Road.

Information
White Mountains Attractions, P.O. Box 10, N. Woodstock, NH 03262; 800/346-3687; www.visitwhitemountains.com.

Getting There
Take I-93 north to exit 32, Rte. 112 east (Kancamagus Hwy.), to Rte. 16 north, to the Wildcat Mountain Ski Area.

First Steps
Park in the ski area lot. Walk past the Wildcat Mountain Visitor Center, cross a footbridge, and follow signs to the Way of the Wildcat Nature Trail. Pick up a trail guide for the nature trail at the Wildcat Mountain Visitor Center.

Thompson's Falls Trail. Follow the Wildcat Nature Trail, which follows the Peabody River with 16 numbered stops. After about 1/4 mile, bear left on the Thompson's Falls Trail (blazed yellow). Ford a small stream by walking across the rocks (this may be difficult during springtime water run-offs). Cross a service road. After about 0.5 mile you will come to Thompson's Falls. The water of Thompson's Falls cascades over a giant granite outcropping creating an idyllic pool at the base. It appears that you could probably swim right up to the falls here.

Now you will begin a steep rock scramble to the second falls, which is somewhat smaller. Continue scrambling up the steep banks of pine needles and tree roots to finally reach the spot where Thompson's Brook begins its cascades. A barrage of waterfalls constantly cascades on your left. Rock-step over the stream and continue your steep climb. (The waterfalls will now be on your right.) You'll probably need to take frequent rest stops, but even if you don't, pause, sit down and look around. Waterfalls are everywhere here, sparkling in the sunlight like a fairy tale. At the end of the trail you can walk out on the granite slab that tops Thompson Falls. Below, you will see the multi-level cascades of water, created by the falling Thompson's Brook. You'll garner a great view of Mount Washington to the right. Retrace your steps to the Wildcat Nature Trail, bear right, and note the remaining numbered nature stops on this trail. The round-trip to Thompson's Falls is 1.8 miles.

Lodging

The White Mountains are peppered with distinctive inns and resort hotels. For more options, consult the New England-wide accommodations websites and reservation services listed in "How to Use This Book" or check out www.visitnh.gov.

Three buildings make up the 21-guest-room **Woodstock Inn** ($+, Main St., N. Woodstock, 800/321-3985, www.WoodstockInnNH.com)—the Main House, a 100-year-old Victorian, Deachman House, and Riverside. Like visiting grandma's house, the rooms are clean, comfortable, and reasonably priced. Some have shared baths; be sure to inquire.

The Jefferson Inn ($+, U.S. Rte. 2, Jefferson, 603/586-7998, 800/729-7908, www.jeffersoninn.com), a Victorian farmhouse with sweeping views of the Northern Presidential Range and Mt. Washington, offers 11 guest rooms and comfortable common rooms decorated to reflect the life and times of our third President. Each immaculate room is designed around a unique theme. Wood floors are buffed to a high sheen. The tower room in the turret is popular with honeymooners.

Given by Frank Hogan as a wedding gift to his only daughter in 1927, **Adair Country Inn** ($$+, 80 Guider Lane, Bethlehem, 603/444-2600, 888/444-2600, www.adairinn.com) wears its elegant grace like a fine ball gown. The grand and gracious country home cum inn leaves no detail to chance. Two hundred wooded acres surround exquisite gardens, which were designed by the famed Olmstead Brothers. The granite taproom invites cozying up to the fire or a game of billiards. And ooooh the romantic rooms . . . sublime.

The Notchland Inn ($$+, Rte. 302, Hart's Location, 603/374-6131, 800/866-6131, www.Notchland.com) carries a colorful history within its granite walls, dating to 18th-century N.H. pioneer Abel Crawford—for which the nearby notch is named. The exquisitely appointed inn, a mansion built in 1880, sits on 100 acres at the base of Mount Bemis. Walking trails crisscross the property, which sports two swimming holes. A wood-fired hot tub sits in an outdoor gazebo. Guest rooms have wood-burning fireplaces.

The jewel in the crown of the White Mountains, **The Inn at Thorn Hill** ($$$$, Thorn Hill Rd., Jackson Village, 603/383-4242, 800/289-8990, www.innatthornhill.com) has been named "one of 10 most romantic inns in North America" by the *Washington Post*. A vision both inside and out, the inn offers stunning views of Mount Washington and the Presidential Range. Décor and amenities of common rooms, guest rooms, and suites defy superlatives. The tariff is steep, but The Inn at Thorn Hill more than makes the grade.

Set on a mind-boggling 15,000 acres, way up in Dixville Notch, **The Balsams** ($$$$, Rte. 26, Dixville Notch, 603/255-3400, 800/255-0600, www.thebalsams.com) has reigned as the grand dame of resort hotels since 1866. Their tariff an all-inclusive American plan, the resort offers 27 holes of golf, tennis, swimming, boating, and fishing, in addition to miles of annotated walking and hiking trails. Guests are treated to superb dining and live entertainment. You'll get drunk on the spectacular scenery and pampered to the max.

A holdover from a bygone era, **The Mount Washington Hotel & Resort** ($$$+, Rte. 302, Bretton Woods, 603/278-1000, 800/258-0330, www.mtwashington.com) sits at the base of the Presidential Range. This full-scale grand resort is a White Mountain classic, offering myriad diversions in a phenomenally gorgeous setting and boasts a whopping seven restaurants.

The Main Inn, c.1786, and the Salt Box, c.1778, of Christmas Farm Inn ($$+, Rte. 16B, Jackson, 603/383-4313, 800/443-5837, www.christmasfarminn.com) offer Colonial ambiance with modern day comforts. Other inn lodgings include those in the sugarhouse, carriage house, and log cabin, as well as individual cottages.

Built in 1834 and operated by the Philbrook family since 1861, **Philbrook Farm Inn** ($+, 881 North Rd., Shelburne, 603/466-3831, www.innbook.com/inns/phil/) offers simple, genuine, rural hospitality. Surrounded by mountains in the Androscoggin River Valley, the inn sits on 900 acres. Home-cooked meals and tea by a crackling fire add to the ambiance.

Bungay Jar ($+, Easton Valley Rd., Rte. 116, Franconia, 603/444-0100, 800/421-0701, www.bungayjar.com), a charming bed-and-breakfast in a former 18th-century barn, looks out over the Kinsman Range. The former hayloft is now the two-story living room, and other nooks and crannies abound in the uniquely decorated guest rooms. English gardens surround the property to complete the illusion.

Food and Drink

Villages and towns are few and far between in the White Mountains. Many of the historic inns also offer wonderful meals. For more dining options, consult www.visitnh.gov.

Originally **Woodstock Station** ($, The Woodstock Inn, Main St., N. Woodstock, www.WoodstockInnNH.com) was the Lincoln Railroad Station, built in the late 1800s. Cut in half in 1984 and moved to its present location along with the Stock Room in '86 and the Porter's Room in '93, and the Brew Pub in '95, this popular gathering place offers yummy tavern fare, great beer, and some crazy cocktails.

Although the classic country New Hampshire dinners are reliably tasty, breakfast at the **Clement Room Grille** ($+, Woodstock Inn, Main St., N. Woodstock, www.WoodstockInnNH.com) is their pièce de résistance. You'll find eight Benedict Arnolds, Wonderful Wizard's eight waffle creations, 15 omelet selections, even womlettes (a puffy omelet on a malted waffle). This meal could hold you all day.

Small and exquisite, **Tim-bir Alley** ($$, Adair Country Inn, 80 Guider Lane, Bethlehem, 603/444-2600, 888/444-2600, www.adairinn.com) serves cuisine from two intimate dining rooms at Adair during the summer season. A cloth Chinese temple scene covers the walls, cream-colored swags accent the windows, and black linen tops tables, upon which flicker tiny candles. And the food? Otherworldly.

The Notchland Inn ($$$$, Hart's Location, 603/374-6131, 800/866-6131, www.Notchland.com) presents a gourmet five-course meal on Tuesday through Sunday evenings at 7pm, served by firelight in their window-encased dining room, which looks out over a pond and rambling gardens. Each day the chef creates a new menu featuring inventive New American cuisine. If you are not a guest at the inn, be sure to call for a reservation.

You'll dine like royalty—by firelight—at **The Inn at Thorn Hill** ($$$$, Thorn Hill Rd., Jackson Village, 603/383-4242, 800/289-8990, www.innatthornhill.com). The "good" china, silver, and crystal adorn linen-topped tables, which are festooned with flickering hurricane lamps and fresh flowers. The wine cellar overflows with superb vintages, service is prompt and unobtrusive, and the chef hits a home run night after night with innovative combinations of classic country ingredients.

Still using the recipes of Great Grammie Govoni, **Govoni's Italian Restaurant** ($$, Rte. 112, North Woodstock, 603/745-8042) brings authentic Italian fare to the White Mountains. The vista here is as great as the food. Located at the foot of Mount Moosilauke, Govoni's perches aside the waterfall and caverns of Agassiz Basin.

Gaze at the White Mountains and chow down a mountain breakfast at **Polly's Pancake Parlor** (Hildex Farm, Rte. 117, Sugar Hill, 603/823-5575). *Bon Appétit* said it "can't be beat."

Be sure to get a reservation for dinner at **Sugar Hill Inn** (Rte. 117, Franconia, 603/823-5621, 800/548-4748, www.sugarhillinn.com), because this is a perennially popular place. The wine and food pairings rival the great mountain views from the dining room.

The Bernerhof Inn (Rte. 302, Glen, 603/383-9132, 800/548-8007, www.bernerhofinn.com) showcases Middle European classics as well as more contemporary seasonal offerings in their dining room, elegantly appointed with linens and crystal, etched glass, and rich paneling. "A Taste of the Mountains Cooking School" also operates here, with classes in all but the summer season for novice and professional alike.

Locals know the best spots to eat and **The Wildcat Inn & Tavern** (Rte. 16A, Jackson Village, 603/383-4245, www.wildcatinnandtavern.com) consistently packs them in. Everyone knows the food here is always good and a great value as well. The dining room serves gourmet cuisine and boasts a temperature-controlled wine storage area with over 100 select wines. The tavern has a ten-tap system direct draw with local microbreweries and specializes in pub fare.

Maine

Introduction

Maine triggers visions of lobsters, moose, and quaint seacoast towns. Quite rightly so, because the state harvests 40-million pounds of lobster annually; can boast of more moose per square mile than any other state or province in North America, including Alaska; and has 3,478 miles of shoreline peppered with charming villages. But add the coast to the densely wooded, sparsely populated inland areas, and Maine becomes almost as large as the other five New England states combined. Its 67,200 square miles sport 6,000 lakes, 32,000 miles of rivers, more than 2,000 islands, as well as Acadia National Park on Mount Desert Island, the second most visited national park in the U.S.

During the Ice Age, glaciers formed what is geologically known as Maine's drowned coastline. The weight of the glaciers caused the land that is now the coast to sink. As glaciers melted and oceans rose over the land, bays were created in former river valleys, and the peaks of hills drowned to mere islets. Waves battered the granite coastline, causing peninsular fingers and fjordlike coves. Some say a typical Maine beach is "a little coarse sand and a great many stones."

Maine—named by French trappers after a homeland province—has been a logging state since colonial times, and most of its cities developed as lumber-shipping ports. In 1677, Massachusetts purchased Maine, which finally declared independence in 1820 and became our nation's 23rd state. Residents still call themselves "State of Mainers," proud of their eventual statehood.

By mid 19th century Maine was the sailing and shipbuilding capital of the United States and an international port of call. "Downeast," a term commonly used when referring to Maine, originated with these commercial sailing vessels, which utilized the prevailing winds from the southwest. Ships would sail from Atlantic ports to ports in Maine by running with the wind behind them, or "downwind to the east." Sea captains' mansions and more than 60 lighthouses still abound. (Portland Head Light was commissioned by George Washington.)

Fog is a phenomenon ubiquitous to the Maine coast. Warm moisture-laden air riding north over the Gulf Stream hits the cold water coming down on the Labrador Current, causing water vapor in the air to condense into a thick fogbank that stands off the coast. When the fog is blown offshore, skies are clear and sparkling blue, but the fog creeps in if the wind changes, obliterating the coastal islands and bathing Maine's shoreline in an eerie mist. Fog blankets Bar Harbor and Portland 50 to 60 days a year.

Southcoast Maine

Southcoast Maine flaunts a seductive mix of sprawling beaches, picturesque villages and a rich seafaring past. A visit here applies the breaks to the hustle-bustle 21st-century existence so taken for granted these days. Peppered along coastal U.S. Route 1 on the Atlantic, Kennebunkport, Portland, Ogunquit and Wells offer charm without kitsch, luxury without pretension and great exploration opportunities on foot.

Regional Information
Maine Tourism Association, 325B Water St., Hallowell, ME 04347; 207/623-0363; www.mainetourism.com.
Maine Publicity Bureau, Inc., www.visitmaine.com
Maine Resource Guide, www.maineguide.com

Getting There
By Air: Most major airlines offer service to Portland Airport.
By Automobile: I-95 north

Kennebunkport— Dock Square and Parson's Way Shore Walk

Kennebunkport tops the list of quaint and picturesque Maine villages. Its craggy coastline, sandy beaches and famous summer residents elevate the tiny enclave to must-visit-when-in-Maine status. Bound to the sea since it was settled in the 1800s, Kennebunkport's shipping trade boomed in the 19th century, then gave way to a thriving fishing and lobstering industry. The unparalleled combination of sun, sand and surf attracted wealthy city folk, who built mansion "cottages" along Ocean Avenue. Today, you'll see as many yachts as dories gracing the harbor (the largest to date was 140 feet long), but Maine lobster still reigns supreme here.

Information
Kennebunk/Kennebunkport Chamber of Commerce, 17 Western Ave., Kennebunk, ME 04043; 207/967-0857; www.kkcc.maine.org.

Getting There
Take I-95 north to exit 3, Rte. 35 east. Follow signs to Kennebunkport.

First Steps
Park behind Town Hall, 30 North St. or at the Consolidated School lot
on School St. Begin and end your 4.8-mile roundtrip walk at Dock Square.
The Brick Store Museum, 117 Main St., Kennebunk (207/985-4802) offers
seasonal guided walks of the Kennebunk National Register Historic
District.

Dock Square and Parson's Way Shore Walk. The Parson's Way Shore
Walk leads from the center of Kennebunkport at Dock Square—the
village's compact commercial center for more than 200 years—to Walker's
Point, the family compound of George and Barbara Bush. Begin your walk
at the memorial to "our soldiers and sailors," which stands in the middle
of Dock Square. Follow Ocean Drive along the Kennebunk River, a 1.5-
mile stretch peppered with galleries, boutiques, specialty shops and
restaurants, many of which are tucked down narrow alleys in restored
18th- and 19th-century sea shanties.

As you round the corner at Colony Beach, the ocean unfurls to your right,
while to your left, summer "cottage" mansions built at the turn of the last
century line Ocean Drive. Drink in the salt air and glimmering water as
you walk the paved path along the sea wall. Opposite Spouting Avenue,
look for Spouting Rock and, just after you round Cape Arundel, Blowing
Cave. These two natural water-show phenomena are best spotted during
high or rising tides.

Continue along Ocean Avenue to the iron gates and guardhouse at the
entrance to Walker's Point, whose gracious main house and cottage
outbuildings occupy a primo piece of oceanfront. Generations of Bushes
gather here every summer. In 1999 they marked the occasion by flying the
state flags of Florida (Governor Jeb) and Texas (Governor George W).
Sightings of the famous family in the Dock Square shops and restaurants
are common occurrences. One shopkeeper advises: "If you see a portly
woman who resembles Barbara Bush, with disheveled gray hair, wearing
frumpy knock-around clothes, look again, it is Barbara Bush!"

Retrace your steps back along Ocean Drive to Dock Square. Amazingly, the
ocean vista appears quite different on the return trip. Explore the bounty
of the village. The restored warehouses of Dock Square, once overflowing
with merchandise to be shipped abroad or with supplies for local
shipbuilders, now house an eclectic upmarket assortment of baubles,

fashions, and maritime memorabilia aimed at Kennebunkport's primary 21st-century industry—tourism.

Historic Portland

Founded as Falmouth Neck in 1632 by English settlers attracted to its sheltered harbor, Portland endured a fiery history. Indians massacred the settlement during the Indian War of 1690; the English navy blasted the village in 1775; and on July 4, 1866, the "Great Fire" destroyed most of the downtown. The city rebuilt after the fire—started by an errant firecracker—using a predominance of red brick. Today Portland, which was renamed by its residents in 1786, remains one of the best-preserved, most vibrant cities in Maine.

Information
Chamber of Commerce of the Greater Portland Region, 60 Pearl St., Portland, ME 04101; 207/772-2811.
Convention and Visitors Bureau of Greater Portland, 305 Commercial St., Portland, ME 04101; 207/772-5800; www.visitportland.com.
Portland's Downtown District, 207/772-6828; www.portlandmaine.com.

Getting There
Take I-295 to exit 7, Franklin St., to Congress St. (Arts District), or Middle St. (Old Port area), or Commercial St. (Waterfront area). The METRO provides local bus service.

First Steps
Stop at the Visitors Bureau, 305 Commercial St., to pick up the "Discover Historic Portland on Foot" walking tour brochures. Also, look for the Downtown Guides, who are dressed in white outback hats and purple shirts. During the summer season they act as "walking information booths," dispensing free information, maps and directions.

Historic Portland. Together, the Greater Portland Landmarks, Inc. and the Chamber of Commerce of the Greater Portland Region have devised, mapped, and documented four detailed walks of the historic areas of Portland: Old Port Exchange, State Street, Congress Street, and the Western Promenade. Walk all four historical treks for a complete capsule of Portland's interesting past.

Portland thrived as a shipping port in its early years, first exporting lumber to the West Indies in exchange for molasses used in the manufacture of rum. The Embargo Act of 1807, the War of 1812, and the "Great Fire" of 1866 dealt serious blows to the city's commerce. But Portland revived after each disaster and became a major commercial center by the late 1800s, a bustling railroad terminus and shipping port that exported—in addition to lumber—grain, livestock and manufactured goods. Commercial Street, 100-feet wide and 1-mile long, was constructed between 1850 and 1852 to service the waterfront. Today, Portland is a major port for export of oil to Canada. Many of this walk's 25 historic buildings—massive brick warehouses and mercantile offices—which were built in the late 1800s after the fire, have been reincarnated as galleries, shops, restaurants and offices.

State Street Historic District began as a tony neighborhood of Federal-style mansions, first developed in the early 1800s when Portland was booming as a center for shipping and commerce. The Embargo Act, which curtailed trade with England, plunged Portland into an economic depression, and homes subsequently built in the area were much more modest. By the 1830s, the city's economy rebounded and Greek Revival and Italianate structures proliferated. This walk begins at the Longfellow Monument and visits 32 buildings, including the Park Street Church, circa 1828.

The Western Promenade was developed in 1836 as a public walkway and carriage path that enjoyed commanding views of the undeveloped countryside. The neighborhood that spread behind the Promenade in the middle of the 19th century (and which adopted its name) grew with the prospering wealth of Portland's sea and rail trade industries. After the "Great Fire," when much of Portland burned, construction in the Western Promenade burgeoned. This walk encompasses 37 historic landmarks and residences, which include High Victorian Gothic, Colonial Revival, Italianate, Queen Anne, Shingle and Second Renaissance Revival architectural styles.

Much of the Congress Street Historic District also burned in the "Great Fire." Redevelopment centered on commercial ventures—which moved up from the waterfront—rather than residences, which were built in the Western Promenade. Today, this area still is the commercial backbone of Portland. This walk focuses on 17 structures varying from the Colonial Wadsworth-Longfellow House, c.1785, to the Romanesque Revival-style

Portland Public Library, c.1888, to the modern Portland Museum of Art, c.1979.

Back Bay Cove Loop, Portland

A favorite exercise loop for locals-in-the-know, Back Bay Cove Loop is an oasis of nature in the middle of Portland's urban center.

Information

Convention and Visitors Bureau of Greater Portland, 305 Commercial St., Portland, ME 04101; 207/772-5800; www.visitportland.com.

Getting There

Take I-295 to High St., to the Baxter Blvd. parking lot.

First Steps

No map needed for the free, easy walk around Back Bay Cove. You'll find no refreshments or restroom facilities along this route.

Back Bay Cove Loop. This 3-mile in-town walk loops around Back Bay Cove. Low tide exposes acres of mud flats, which attract herons and shorebirds in the summer, waterfowl and gulls year round. High tide creates a glimmering saltwater lake. Most of the loop follows a paved path that runs close to the water beneath the shade of a leafy parklike canopy. You will have to cross Tukey's Bridge, about halfway around, however, which is teeming with traffic from I-295. This destroys the peaceful waters-edge atmosphere for a while, but Back Bay Cove remains popular with locals and fitness buffs.

Marginal Way, Ogunquit

The tiny, quaint seaside village of Ogunquit long has attracted artists wishing to paint its spectacular scenery, becoming a bona fide art colony by the end of the century. Today, the village's three miles of white sand beaches, thriving galleries and summer theatre lure visitors to its shores. Ogunquit's most popular attraction, the Marginal Way, begins at Perkins Cove, a former fishing community now loaded with upscale boutiques, maritime memorabilia shops and seafood restaurants.

Information
Ogunquit Chamber of Commerce, Rte. 1 South, Ogunquit, ME 03907; 207/646-2939; www.ogunquit.org.

Getting There
Take I-95 to exit 4 (Ogunquit/York). Turn left on Rte. 1 and go north for 7.5 miles. Turn right on Bourne's Lane, then right on Shore Road to Perkin's Cove.

First Steps
Park at the metered parking lot in Perkins Cove. Cost is $1 per 30 minutes with a 2-hour maximum and is closely monitored by local law enforcement.

Marginal Way. Originally an Indian trail, Marginal Way runs for 1.25 mile along craggy ocean-side cliffs, beginning from the parking lot at Perkins Cove. Modest summerhouses with fabulous cutting gardens line the left flank of the narrow paved walk, while rugosa roses cascade down the cliff side, and the Atlantic's breakers crash against the shore. The village has placed park benches at thoughtful intervals and stocked the path with lots of trash cans—which are labeled with homilies referring to such attributes as generosity and kindness—in an attempt to control littering. At spots, huge granite boulders climb like stair steps from the sea. You can scramble over them to water's edge if you're sure-footed.

Marginal Way teems with tourists during the summer months, interrupting the serene commune with the sea that can be experienced during the rest of the year. But if you do choose to walk the Way in June, July or August, a footpath at the path's terminus leads down to an expansive beach. Join the other sun-worshipers littering the sand.

Wells National Estuarine Research Reserve

Here at Laudholm Farm, a historic saltwater farm, the Little and Webhannet Rivers meet the Atlantic Ocean, creating a diverse number of habitats called home by myriad wildlife, such as arethusa orchids, blue flag iris, piping plovers, peregrine falcons and least terns. The Reserve is situated in the Atlantic Coast Bird Migration Corridor, where diverse species stop to feed, rest and nest.

Information
Wells National Estuarine Research Reserve, 342 Laudholm Farm Rd., Wells ME 04090; 207/646-1555; www.wellsreserve.org.
Wells Chamber of Commerce, Rte. 1, Wells, ME 04090; 207/646-2451.

Getting There
From Wells take Rte. 1 north for 1.5 miles to Laudholm Farm Road and follow signs.

First Steps
Pick up a "Trails and Habitats" map from the Visitor Center. Check the Visitor Center for dates and times of the occasionally offered nature walks, wildflower walks, and nocturnal wildlife walks. The York County Audubon Society also leads birding walks.

Wells National Estuarine Research Reserve. Five walks encompassing 7 miles of trails take you on an interpretive junket through portions of the 1600 acres of estuarine waters, marshland, shoreland and uplands protected by the Laudholm Trust since 1982.

The Salt Marsh Loop (1.3 miles) overlooks freshwater uplands and brackish marsh with good views of Webhannet estuary. The salt marsh is filled with Spartina grass, which extracts salt from the twice-daily tidal flow. Webhannet Overlook Loop (.9 mile) explores an abandoned apple orchard. Barrier Beach Walk (1.4 miles) features all the Reserve's habitats and is the best trail to take if you have limited time. The dunes serve as a barrier to the salt marshes behind. Little River Loop (1.8 miles) emerges at Little River Outlook, where you may be able to spot Canada geese or ducks. Salt Hay Walk (1.6 miles) follows Pilger Trail along the foot of a glacial moraine across open fields to a brackish marsh, where you'll see muskrats and otters.

Native Americans prowled this area, foraging for food until European settlers established Laudholm Farm in 1643. Only four families have lived here since; the farmhouse now houses the Reserve's Visitor Center. The Reserve conducts ongoing research—soft-shell clam enhancement, salt marsh restoration and estuarine water quality analysis—in the farm outbuildings.

Rainy Day Options

The Center for Maine History commingles three historic buildings on a 1-acre campus to showcase Maine's fascinating history. The Wadsworth-Longfellow House—built in 1785 by the poet's grandfather—sheltered young Henry W. during his childhood years. The home, furnished with belongings of the Wadworths and Longfellows, is open for tours. Adjacent to the house, the Maine Historical Society Library contains a multitude of the state's historical and genealogical books and manuscripts. The Maine History Gallery displays changing exhibitions of historical Maine. *(Contact: The Center for Maine History, 485-489 Congress St., Portland, 207/774-1822, www.post@mainehistory.org.)*

A lavish representation of 1858 Italianate architecture, **Victoria Mansion** was the summer home of New Orleans hotelier Ruggles Sylvester Morse and his wife Olivia. Built of brownstone over brick, the interiors feature extensive frescoes, intricate carvings and stained glass windows. The restored mansion—now a museum open to the public seasonally—exhibits more than 300 items owned by the Morses. *(Contact: Victoria Mansion, 109 Danforth St., Portland, 207/772-4841, www.portlandarts.com/-victoriamansion.)*

Lodging

For more lodging options, consult the New England-wide lodging websites and reservations services listed in "How to Use This Book" or contact the Maine Innkeepers Association, 207/773-7670.

Secreted in a carriage barn built of red brick and stone at the turn of the last century, **Old Fort Inn** ($$-$$$$, Old Fort Ave., Kennebunkport, 207/967-5353, www.oldfortinn.com) provides high-end amenities, even in standard rooms. You'll enjoy down duvets, lace canopied beds, modern baths and antique furnishings, even a heaping plate of chocolate chip cookies. The memorabilia-filled common room showcases an amazing collection of walking sticks, bed warmers, telescopes, sleds, primitives and Shaker boxes.

Mile-high four-poster beds, flickering gas fireplaces, heated tile floors in updated bathrooms, and lavish bed coverings sewn by the innkeeper herself set apart **The Captain Lord Mansion** ($$-$$$$, 207/967-3141, www.captainlord.com) from also-rans in Kennebunkport. Bricks dedicated to guests who have stayed at the inn 10 times or more encircle a fountain in the Memory Garden. The Federalist-Colonial offers 16 guestrooms; four units are next door at Phoebe's Fantasy.

A stay at the **Yachtsman Lodge and Marina** ($+, Ocean Ave., Kennebunkport, 207/967-2511, www.kport.com/yachtsman) is like an overnight in the forward cabin of a luxury yacht. Once a 1950s motel on the Kennebunk River, the 30 guestrooms were totally redesigned in a nautical theme in 1999 to the standards enjoyed by its tony sister property, the White Barn Inn. You can utilize complimentary bikes and canoes during your visit. And angler alert: an Orvis guide will pick you up at your door if you like.

If your wallet is flush and romance is high on your list, the **White Barn Inn** ($$$+, Beach St., Kennebunkport, 207/967-2321, www.whitebarn-inn.com) will pamper you with amenities usually afforded only the European landed gentry. Every detail of this circa 1850 homestead exudes luxury. A Relais & Chateau property, White Barn Inn showcases a negative-edge swimming pool nestled in a wooded hermitage.

A restored 1869 Victorian in the Western Promenade Historic District, **Inn on Carleton** ($$, 46 Carleton St., Portland, 207/775-1910, 800/639-1779, www.innoncarleton.com) features trompe l'oeil painted by Charles Schumaker, a noted 19th-century New England artist. The six guestrooms showcase faux finished walls and authentic 19th-century antique bedroom sets. The inn was formerly part of a two-home mansion known as the Granville Chase Block.

A Victorian jewel, **The Maine Stay Inn & Cottages** ($, 34 Maine St., Kennebunkport, 207/967-2117, 800/950-2117, www.mainestayinn.com) features a suspended spiral staircase, sunburst crystal-glass windows, a cupola and a wrap-around porch peppered with white wicker rockers. Exquisitely furnished with period furnishings, wall coverings and fabrics, this inn offers a gracious step back in time.

Small and special, the **Pomegranate Inn** ($$, 49 Neal St., Portland, 207/772-1006, 800-356-0408, www.pomegranateinn.com), an 1884 Italianate-style mansion, retains the elegance of its historic beginnings in Portland's tony Western Promenade. The eight unusually decorated guestrooms showcase art works and antiques, and some have working fireplaces.

Built as the home of silversmith Joseph Holt Ingraham in 1823, **The Danforth** ($$, 163 Danforth St., Portland, 207/879-8755, 800/991-6557, www.danforth@maine.com), restored in the late 1990s to its former luster as a grand mansion, the bed-and-breakfast features 12 fireplaces, a classic billiard room and a cupola widow's watch. Antiques and hospitality abound here.

Captain Jefferds was a seafaring man, so it is fitting that the owners of **The Captain Jefferds Inn** ($$, 5 Pearl St., Portland, 207/967-2311, 800/839-6844, www.captainjefferdsinn.com) named the 16 renovated guestrooms of the Federal-style mansion for their favorite places around the world. Constructed in 1805, the inn combines top-drawer creature comforts with homespun hospitality.

Just baby steps from the Marginal Way, **Rockmere Lodge** ($-$$, 40 Stearns Rd., Ogunquit, 207/646-2985, www.rockmere.com), enjoys an uninterrupted view of the Atlantic. The eight-guestroom, shingle-style bed-and-breakfast provides comfort at a good value, even supplying beach towels, chairs and umbrellas.

Food and Drink

Lobster reigns supreme in Maine, but other seafood offerings provide stiff competition. For more options, log on to www.mainerestaurant.com.

Consistently garnering "best of . . ." awards, the **White Barn Inn** ($$$$, Beach St., Kennebunkport, 207/967-2321) presents an otherworldly dining experience. The restaurant's setting is as sparkling as its cuisine. Three-story windows, fore and aft, illuminate the converted barn's rustic beams and antique-filled loft. Exquisite creature sculptures—birds, animals, fish—made in France from sterling silver flatware, adorn each table. And, between courses you'll be served sorbet in a glass hibiscus. Magic!

Hugging the water's edge at the tip of Cape Porpoise, **Seascapes** ($$$, Pier Rd., Cape Porpoise, 207/967-8500) augments its picturesque setting with shining fusion cuisine that borrows secrets from the Pacific Rim and the Mediterranean. Awash in tropical colors, with live music playing softly in the background, this oasis of gourmet dining offers a romantic seaside interlude, just minutes from Kennebunkport.

Perfetto's ($$, 28 Exchange St., Portland, 207/828-1001) offers upmarket seafood-studded cuisine with a decidedly Mediterranean touch. Situated in an historic building in Portland's Old Port district, the two long narrow dining areas reveal the building's original brick walls and a ceiling that spans almost two stories. The chefs create their magic from an open kitchen.

A bastion of the Portland waterfront, the cavernous, floating **DiMillo's** ($$, Long Wharf, Portland, 207/772-2216) offers the best harbor seat on the wharf. Commissioned "The Richmond" in 1941, this former car ferry provides a seafaring ambiance and a large selection of simply prepared American fare.

Watch ships entering Portland Harbor and lobstermen bring in their catch from **Two Lights Lobster Shack** ($, 225 Two Lights Rd., Cape Elizabeth, 207/799-1677), which nestles below the lighthouse and next to the foghorn. You'll not find a more picturesque spot from which to eat lobster-in-the-rough than here.

Perched on the Atlantic at the beginning of Marginal Way, **Oarweed** ($, Perkins Cove, Ogunquit, 207/646-4022) rolls out seafood like the crashing breakers below. Perfect for lunch or dinner after walking the Way, Oarweed's known for great lobsters and yummy Maine blueberry pie.

If you're looking for a fun place for a beer and a bite, try **Three Dollar Dewey's** ($, 241 Commercial St., Portland, 207-772-3310, www.3dollar-deweys.com). How did this pub get its unusual name? Seems that back in the Yukon, if a guy got lonely he visited a house of pleasure, which advertised: $1, Lookie; $2, Feelie; $3, Dewey.

Packed with vendors and every conceivable nosh the senses could desire, **Portland Public Market** ($, 25 Preble St., Portland, 207-228-2000, www.portlandmarket.com) should not be missed, even if you're not hungry. The first Portland public indoor market was established in the early 1800s. This late-1990s reincarnation will push your taste buds to the limit.

Touted as having the "best steamers in Maine," **J's Oyster Bar** ($, 5 Portland Pier, Portland, 207/772-4828) also is renowned for their freshly shucked oysters and a potpourri of innovative seafood.

Arrows ($$$$, Berwick Rd., Ogunquit, 207-361-1100) secrets itself in a remote farmhouse outside Ogunquit, an unlikely spot to find such exquisite cuisine. Innovatively prepared with accents from the Pacific Rim, Arrows' offerings win rave reviews.

Mid-Coast Maine

Life in Midcoast Maine always has revolved around the sea—shipping and trading, fishing, shipbuilding, and finally tourism. The rocky islands, craggy inlets and sheltered harbors of the area's sunken coastline beckon today's visitors like they attracted European explorers of yesteryear. Nature's bounty spills out of the waters and tidal pools of the Atlantic, joining a rich history to ricochet throughout the picturesque villages that line the coast.

Regional Information
Maine Publicity Bureau, 800/533-9595.
Bath-Brunswick Chamber of Commerce, 59 Pleasant St., Brunswick ME 04011; (207) 725-8797; www.midcoastmaine.com.
Camden-Rockport-Lincolnville Chamber of Commerce, Public Landing, Camden, ME 04843; 207/236-4404; 800/223-5459; www.camdenme.-org.

Getting There
By Air: Major airlines offer service to Portland International Jetport or Bangor International Airport.
By Auto: I-95 to Rte. 1.

Historic Brunswick

Settled by Thomas Purchase in 1628 on the banks of the Androscoggin River and incorporated in 1739, Brunswick quickly grew to prominence as a lumbering center. Named for the British house of Brunswick, whose standard bearer became King George I, Brunswick became one of three railroad hubs in Maine by the middle of the 1800s. Founded in 1794, Bowdoin College impacted the growth and character of Brunswick for all time, becoming the centerpiece of the town. Federal and Greek Revival-style sea captain's mansions line the city streets, and fascinating museums pepper the college campus.

Information
Pejepscot Historical Society, 159 Park Row, Brunswick, ME 04011; 207/729-6606; www.curtislibrary.com/pejepscot.
Bath-Brunswick Chamber of Commerce, 59 Pleasant St., Brunswick, ME 04011; 207/725-8797; www.midcoastmaine.com.

Getting There
Take Maine Turnpike to exit 9, then I-95 to exit 22 (Brunswick, Rte.1), to Maine Street. Turn right.

First Steps
The Bath-Brunswick Branch of the American Association of University Women has detailed an in-town walking tour (and country driving tour) of historic Brunswick: "From the Falls to the Bay—A Tour of Historic Brunswick, Maine." Pick up a copy at the Historical Society office on Park Row before you begin your walk.

Historic Brunswick. This route allows you to explore the high spots of historic Brunswick, a unique blend of architecturally interesting residences, college buildings, churches and museums. The AAUW tour brochure will provide architectural details of the buildings you'll pass along the way. Begin at the First Parish Church (1), the dominant landmark between the village center and Bowdoin College. Built in 1846 as a "board and batten cruciform church" designed by John Updike, First Parish's pulpit has been graced by the likes of Henry Wadsworth Longfellow, President William Howard Taft, Edna St. Vincent Millay, Eleanor Roosevelt and Martin Luther King.

Walk to the corner of Maine and Potter to the Joshua Chamberlain House Museum (2). Chamberlain—Civil War hero, former governor of Maine and president of Bowdoin College—bought the c.1825 house in 1859, moved it from Potter Street to the corner, raised it 11 feet, then built a Victorian-Gothic/Italianate first floor underneath and added intricate detailing throughout. The home is partially restored and features exhibits highlighting Chamberlain's long and varied career.

Cross Maine Street to the central green of Bowdoin College. The liberal arts college was named for James Bowdoin of Boston, who generously gave both land and money. Four of the college's buildings rate particular merit and exploration. Visit the Walker Art Building, c.1892, to explore the offerings of the Bowdoin College Museum of Art (3). Don't miss the rotunda murals of Athens, Rome, Florence and Venice, the cities revered by Victorian educators. Hubbard Hall—a massive limestone, brick and granite structure with a battlement built in 1902—houses the Peary-MacMillan Arctic Museum (4), a collection of memorabilia from the polar explorations of Admiral Robert M. Peary (class of 1877) and Admiral

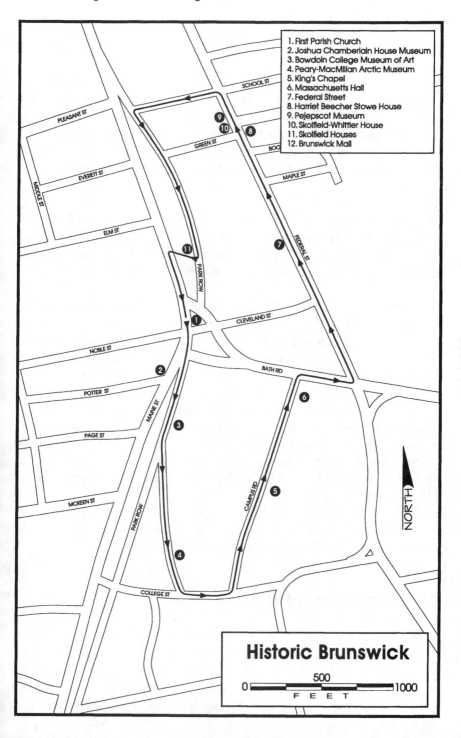

1. First Parish Church
2. Joshua Chamberlain House Museum
3. Bowdoin College Museum of Art
4. Peary-MacMillan Arctic Museum
5. King's Chapel
6. Massachusetts Hall
7. Federal Street
8. Harriet Beecher Stowe House
9. Pejepscot Museum
10. Skolfield-Whittier House
11. Skolfield Houses
12. Brunswick Mall

Historic Brunswick

NORTH

0   500   1000
F E E T

Donald B. Macmillan (class of 1898). A portrait gallery graces the third floor.

The King's Chapel (5) resembles a 12th-century English church and features an old-world seating design with pews arranged along the edges of the walls facing a center aisle. Frescoes adorn the walls. Federal-style Massachusetts Hall (6), the first building built at Bowdoin in 1802, once housed the entire college. Legend has it that college president Joseph McKeen hit his cane against the staircase to announce the change of classes.

From the college, turn right on Bath Road, then left on Federal Street (7). Well-preserved 19th-century residences line this thoroughfare. Number 63 (8) is of special interest because Calvin and Harriet Beecher Stowe lived there from 1850 to 1852, when Ms. Stowe wrote *Uncle Tom's Cabin*.

Turn left on School Street, then left on Park Row. Open year round, the Pejepscot Museum (9), #159, dedicates its changing exhibitions to the local history of Brunswick and surrounding areas. Home of the Pejepscot Historical Society (founded in 1888), the museum features more than 20,000 photographs in its archives and 50,000 artifacts in its collection. The Skolfield-Whittier House (10) at #161 is a 17-room mansion that was preserved—locked and unoccupied—for more than 50 years. Furnishings, dÈcor, even receipts and spices remain intact—a time capsule loaded with three generations of memorabilia. George Skolfield had the two homes constructed for his two seafaring sons and their wives. Captain Samuel Skolfield, who lived at #159, traded with India; his brother, Captain Alfred, shipped cotton and molasses aboard.

Fronting the horseshoe-shaped Park Row is the Brunswick Mall (12), the village green still used for town gatherings. Here you can terminate your tour or explore the shops that line Maine Street.

Bath Architectural Walking Tour

Long the center of Maine's largest industry—shipbuilding—Bath, the "city of ships," has been constructing vessels since the early 18th century. Shipyards lined the Kennebec River, and wooden vessels built here sailed the world over. Modern tankers, warships and merchant vessels are still built in Bath. But the heart of this old seafaring town, incorporated in

1791, rests in a 19th-century time warp, proudly wearing its history like an architectural mantle.

Information
Sagadahoc Preservation, Inc., P.O. Box 322, Bath, ME 04530; 207/871-4099.
Bath-Brunswick Chamber of Commerce, 45 Front Street, Bath, ME 04530; 207/443-9751; www.visitbath.com.

Getting There
Take the Maine Turnpike to exit 9. Then take I-95 to exit 22 and follow Rte. 1 through Brunswick to the Historic District exit in Bath.

First Steps
Pick up walking brochures from the Chamber office at 45 Front Street: "An Historical Walking Tour Through Downtown Bath, Maine" and "Architectural Tours—Self-Guided Walking and Driving Tours of the City of Bath." Magical History Tours offers guided walks, which leave from the Chocolate Church Arts Center, 804 Washington St. on Tues. and Thurs., weather permitting, from June through early Sept. (207/442-8455).

Bath Architectural Walking Tour. Sagadahoc Preservation, Inc. has surveyed all architecturally significant buildings built in Bath before 1920 and has detailed a walking (and driving) tour of the Bath National Historic District. The brochure illustrates and describes the 12 major architectural styles you'll encounter, from the early 1700s Cape style to the Georgian-Colonial Revivals seen between 1890 and 1930. In addition, the 1996 seventh-grade class at Bath Middle School produced a very credible historic place walking tour of the downtown area, which features photographs and a wealth of historic detail.

Follow this route to combine the highlights of both walking tours (refer to the Sagadahoc guide for architectural details of the private residences you'll pass along the way). Begin at the Patten Free Library and Columbia Park (1), the grassy green encompassed by Summer, Washington, Linden and Front Streets. Galen Moses donated $10,000 for the library's construction in 1889, whose cornerstone honors Bath shipbuilders John and George Patten. Exhibits in the library include a model of the *Wyoming*, a six-masted schooner that was built in Bath. A British warship cannon perches at the northeast corner of the park.

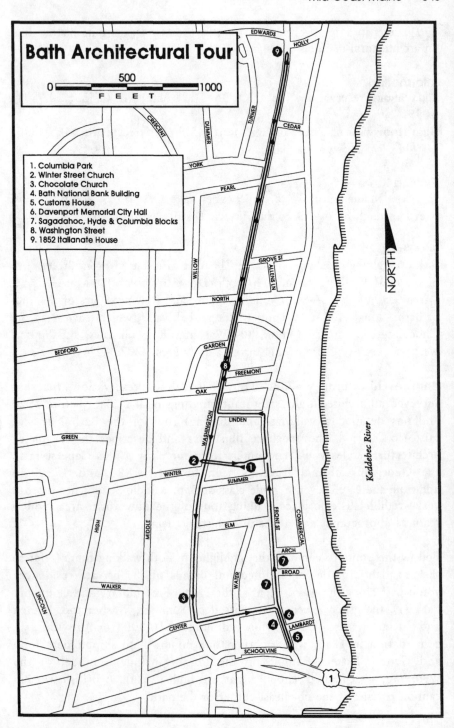

Bath Architectural Tour

500
0 ——————— 1000
F E E T

1. Columbia Park
2. Winter Street Church
3. Chocolate Church
4. Bath National Bank Building
5. Customs House
6. Davenport Memorial City Hall
7. Sagadahoc, Hyde & Columbia Blocks
8. Washington Street
9. 1852 Italianate House

NORTH

Kennebec River

Across Washington Street from the library, Winter Street Church (2) was designed by Anthony Coombs Raymond and built in 1843. John Calvin Stevens designed interior alterations to the Gothic Revival structure at the turn of the last century, and Frances Fassett designed the Italianate parish hall in 1860. All three men were prominent architects in Bath in the later part of the 19th century. On this tour you'll encounter many of the buildings they designed.

Continue down Washington, past the historically dated homes, to the Chocolate Church (3). Now a performing arts center named for its brown color, the structure was built in 1847 as Central Church. The church accommodated the congregation of the Old South Church after a mob of "Know Nothings," rioting in an outburst of anti-Catholic bias, burned the church to the ground.

Turn left on Centre Street to Front Street. Turn right for a short distance, where you'll see the Lincoln Block, Church Block and Bath National Bank Building (4), three massive 19th-century brick structures. President Harrison (1889) and Democratic Presidential candidate William Jennings Bryan (1896) both spoke from the steps of the Customs House (5) across the street, which was built in 1858.

Retrace your steps to the Centre Street intersection and continue north on Front Street along the brick sidewalk to the Davenport Memorial City Hall (6), c.1928, which is topped by a weathervane that is a replica of the *Roanoke*, built in Bath in 1892. A Paul Revere bell, sold to the city of Bath in 1805, resides in the belfry. Brick building "Blocks" (7)—Sagadahoc, Hyde, and Columbia—occupy both sides of Front Street, now showcasing boutiques, antique shops and restaurants. Grand hotels, theaters and churches once occupied the Block sites, but fell victim to fire by the middle of the 19th century.

At Linden Street turn left and follow the edge of Library Park to Washington Street (8). Turn right and walk north on Washington, examining the fine architectural specimens that line the street. (Details are highlighted in the Sagadahoc Preservation brochure.) Cross at #1080 (9)—a c.1852 Italianate home that features fabulous moldings and diamond-shaped windows—then retrace your steps down the other side of the street until you get back to Library Park where you began.

Salt Bay Preserve Heritage Trail and Middens

The Damariscotta River is a 16-mile-long tidal estuary that connects the Atlantic Ocean with Great Salt Bay. The tides, which can rise as much as 10 feet, mingle with freshwater streams that flow into the bay, creating 2 square miles of eel grass meadows, salt marsh and intertidal mudflats that support a fertile habitat rich in wildlife.

Information
Damariscotta River Association, P.O. Box 333, Belvedere Rd., Damariscotta, ME 04543; 297/563-1393.

Getting There
Take Rte. 1 to Rte. 215 north (Mills Road) in Newcastle. The Lincoln County Publishing Company has granted permission for walkers to use their parking lot. They ask that you park at the far end of the lot and be careful not to block trucks or other vehicles.

First Steps
The trailhead starts across the street from the parking lot, where you can pick up a trail map. Orange plastic arrows on stakes mark the 3-mile trail. You could get wet feet in some sections during spring runoff or tidal fluctuations, so wear appropriate walking gear. Also, you're sure to encounter mosquitoes in this habitat, so generously apply insect repellent before you set off.

Salt Bay Preserve Heritage Trail and Middens. Shortly after entering the trail, you will cross a tidal salt marsh on a heavy plank boardwalk. Once over the marsh, you'll plunge into waist-high grass. The marsh habitat is littered with remains of horseshoe crabs (Great Salt Bay is one of the northernmost breeding sites for horseshoe crabs) and unusually shaped driftwood. Huge butterflies work the grasses.

The trail leaves the marsh and leads into the woods. You'll come out to water's edge again shortly to cross over a small inlet of Great Salt Bay, which is teeming with minnows. (A high-water crossing option circles back in the woods, if necessary.) Still following the edge of Great Salt Bay, the pine-needle path leads back into the old growth forest, which is sprinkled with ferns and small plants, punctuated with glacial erratics and scented with balsam.

Walk under Rte. 1 through a low-ceilinged culvert tunnel (be prepared to bend over as you walk). Fork left to the oyster middens on the shore of the Damariscotta River at Glidden Point. These shell mounds, known as Glidden Middens, are reportedly more than 2,000 years old, the result of 1,500 years of American Indian feasts. Look for river otters, which live near the shore and in the woods along the trail and sometimes can be spotted fishing for eels or shellfish.

Retrace your steps to the main path. The birding along the Salt Bay Heritage Trail is excellent—keep your eyes pealed for a bald eagle. As you approach the tidal salt marsh on this return loop, look for ospreys, herons, ducks or even snowy egrets, all of which often summer in Maine. Cattails border the brackish water here. The path winds through chest-high weeds, grasses, raspberries and beach plums.

The trail terminates at a small fresh water pond filled with lily pads. You'll have to cross Rte. 1 and walk a short distance back to the parking lot where you began. (The only drawback to this walk is its proximity to the automobile traffic noises of the highway, which mars the solitude of such an incredibly rich habitat and occasionally destroys the ambiance of your commune with nature. Earplugs?)

Rockland Breakwater

The tiny village of Rockland bills itself as the Lobster Capital of the World, hosting a lobster festival every summer. Shipbuilding, commercial fishing and granite quarrying figured in its economic history over the years. The bustling lobster industry is still very much in evidence in Rockland harbor, but, as with other Mid-Coast villages, tourism now takes center stage here.

Information
Rockland-Thomaston Chamber of Commerce, Harbor Park, Rockland, ME 04856; 207/596-0376; www.midcoast.com/~rtacc.

Getting There
Take Rte. 1 to Waldo Ave., then turn right and follow Samoset Rd. for 0.5 mile to the public parking area at the end of the street.

First Steps
Stop at the Public Landing on Rte. 73 to pick up a "Mid-Coast Maine" guide from the Information Center.

Rockland Breakwater. Picturesque to the max, the Rockland Breakwater extends for almost a mile into Penobscot Bay. Built in the 1880s of Vinalhaven granite, the breakwater guards Rockland Harbor from the devastating effects of Maine's ever-occurring Nor'easters. Engineers and laborers toiled 18 years to finish the stone structure, on whose terminus were placed lanterns hung from wooden beams, then a small portable light station. Considered a stop-gap measure at best, the light station was replaced with a stone light tower and keeper's house between 1900 and 1902.

Begin your walk on the path at the end of Jameson Point, where the banks are covered with wildflowers. The breakwater is comprised of slabs of granite that are mostly level, but sizeable spaces separate some of the blocks, requiring careful attention to footing. Be sure to wear good walking shoes or hiking boots. This walk is magic on a sunny summer day: A rainbow of lobster-trap buoys litters the watery landscape. The throaty motors of the lobster boats sing as the lobstermen work the harbor, putting from buoy to buoy,

Lobster Tales

Perhaps the most famous Maine resident is the lobster, although, truth be told, the yummy crustacean is harvested along the entire New England seacoast. Now a pricey delicacy, the lofty lobster has experienced a humble past. Lobster was a staple of the coastal Penobscot tribe, so plentiful they could be picked up by hand at low tide. Usual size of a lobster in those days was 6 pounds! The Native Americans used crushed lobster shells for fertilizer and made pipes from the claws. They taught the white settlers the fine art of the New England clambake—steaming seaweed-covered lobsters and shellfish in a sandpit lined with red-hot wooden charcoal. Lobsters remained so plentiful and inexpensive that, believe it or not, in Bar Harbor's Golden Age in the mid-19th century, it was considered poor man's food or rations for prisoners. Sometimes it even was fed to the cattle. Servants regularly were fed lobster, while the gentry couldn't stand the sight of it.

Commercial lobstering began in the 1700s and by 1840 was a very profitable business. Today, colorful lobster buoys litter Maine's coastal waters like billiard balls. Whistles moan and engines hum ubiquitously as lobstermen, two by two, putter by boat to their buoys, whose combination of colors must be registered with the state. Daily, they haul up their traps by winch, check their catch, and re-bait the traps. Only legal-size lobsters are kept; the rest are returned to the ocean. Lobsters are six to seven years old by the time they reach legal size. And now for a lobster tale: The largest known lobster caught in Maine measured 36 inches from its back to the end of its tail.

harvesting the catch and re-baiting traps. Cormorants splash and dive in the water, while gulls buzz overhead, chasing any bait that might fall errant from the lobster boats.

The view from the end of the breakwater will take your breath away, and a heavenly sea breeze caresses your face like an embrace. Panoramic green mountains shadow the harbor. Outlines of nearby islands lurk on the horizon. Penobscot Bay sparkles with a peppering of schooners, sailboats, ferries, commercial fishing vessels and even the patrolling U.S. Coast Guard.

The lighthouse is locked and abandoned, but you can walk around its ground floor and peak in the windows. (The Friends of Rockland Breakwater Lighthouse are raising funds to restore and preserve the lighthouse, and eventually plan to open it to the public.) Rockland Breakwater rates as a quintessential Maine encounter. Don't miss it.

Camden Village

Named for the 18th-century English Earl of Camden, the village of Camden nestles in the shadow of 900-foot Mount Battie, aside a protected harbor in Penobscot Bay. Fishing, farming and shipbuilding supported early settlers, then the village became a mill town for a time. By the early 1900s and continuing into the 21st-century, tourists flocked to this quintessential seaport village like birds to the Atlantic flyway. Yachts and schooners pepper its picturesque harbor. No wonder Hollywood chose to film "Peyton Place," "Captains Courageous" and Stephen King's "Thinner" here.

Information
Camden-Rockport-Lincolnville Chamber of Commerce, Public Landing, Camden, ME 04843; 207/236-4404; 800/223-5459; www.camdenme.-org.
Camden-Rockport Historical Society, Rte. 1, Camden, ME 04843; 207/236-2257.

Getting There
Take I-95 north (Maine Turnpike) to exit 9 (still I-95, but no longer the turnpike). Then take exit 22, coastal Rte. 1 north to Camden.

First Steps
Pick up a copy of "A Visitor's Tour" from the historical society in the Conway House, Rte. 1, just south of the IGA store.

Camden Village. The Camden-Rockport Historical Society has compiled a walking tour that encompasses three architecturally significant areas in the village: Downtown Camden, High Street and Chestnut Street. The tour brochure details the history of these buildings, most of which are private residences. The walking order is not spelled out for you, however, so follow the 3-mile route outlined below and refer to the architectural walking tour brochure for the skinny on what once went on behind the closed doors.

Begin your exploration of Downtown Camden at the Village Green (1). Visit the Romanesque Revival-style Camden Opera House (2) at Elm and Washington Streets, then walk up Elm Street (3), where you'll see the First Congregational Church, c.1834, historic residences and the Conway Boulder as described in the Historical Society brochure.

Referring to your architectural walking guide, backtrack down Elm and take a right on Union Street (4). Cross Belmont Avenue to Pleasant Street (5). Turn right on Wood Street (6), then turn right on Chestnut Street (7). Stroll up the right side of the street as far as the Simeon Howe House, c.1830, then cross Chestnut and retrace your steps. Take particular note of the U.S. Post Office, c.1913—a time capsule of 1913 artifacts is buried under the cornerstone.

Back at the Village Green, walk to the waterfront at Camden Public Landing (8), then proceed up Main Street (9) past the shops and boutiques. After the Great Fire of 1892, Camden rebuilt its downtown district in brick. If you look down Bayview Street toward the water, you'll see Camden Yacht Club (10), c.1912. Frederick Olmstead designed the landscaping in 1947. At the corner of Main and Atlantic Streets you'll find Bok Amphitheatre and Harbor Park (11), c.1929, where Camden stages many special events. The park features memorials to the Civil and Spanish-American wars, as well as a statue of Edna St. Vincent Millay, who spent time in Camden. Across from the park, the Camden Public Library (12), c.1928, showcases its unique 1996 underground addition.

Continue up Main Street to High Street (13), which is lined with Victorian-era Greek Revival-style residences that are detailed in the walking tour brochure. Take special note of the Whitehall Inn (c.1903). Edna St. Vincent Millay stayed here in 1912 as a young girl. Continue on to catch a glimpse of the imposing stone castle, Norumbega (1886), now an upmarket hotel.

Retrace your steps back to the center of town. Walk down lower Washington to the Camden Fire Station (14), where you'll see an 1892 steam-powered, horse-drawn fire pumper displayed. Conclude your tour on Lower Mechanic Street (15) aside the Megunticook River, which once was the manufacturing center of Camden. Two former mills have been converted as the Highland Mill Mall and the MBNA New England complex. This trek will no doubt trigger quite a thirst, so stop in at the neighboring Sea Dog Brewing Company to recharge your batteries.

Camden Hills State Park

Many trails at Camden Hills State Park reward you with fantastic vistas of Lake Megunticook, Camden village, and the scattered islands of Penobscot Bay.

Information
Camden Hills State Park, Rte. 1, Camden, ME 04843; 207/236-3109. Camden-Rockport-Lincolnville Chamber of Commerce, Public Landing, Camden, ME 04843; 207/236-4404; 800/223-5459; www.camdenme.-org.

Getting There
Take Rte. 1 north from Camden. Park entrance is on your right. The trail system is accessed across the road.

First Steps
Pick up a map of the trails at the park entrance on Rte. 1 or at the Chamber of Commerce office at Public Landing in Camden. The park is open seasonally, from May to October.

Camden Hills State Park. Nineteen trails at the 5,500-acre Camden Hills State Park offer good day hiking for all ability levels. One of the most popular moderate trails, Maiden's Cliff (2-mile return), climbs to the top of rugged 800-foot cliffs for a good view over Lake Megunticook. A tall medal cross marks the spot where a young girl fell to her death in 1862.

The Mount Battie Trail (1 mile return), also moderate, climbs to the summit of the mountain, ending at the Mount Battie Tower. This monument to World War II veterans was constructed of stones from an old hotel that used to stand on the site. Carriages brought people to the top of Mount Battie, where they stayed in the hotel for $1 per night. After a scramble up this trail, Edna St. Vincent Millay was inspired to write her poem "Renascence," where she referred to "three islands in a bay," derived from the view she saw from the summit. (If you aren't up to the climb, you can drive to the top of Mount Battie.) All the trails involve climbing and most interconnect so that you can devise a hike that meets your time allotment and ability level.

Blueberries

Maine grows more wild low-bush blueberries than any state in the country. A Native American legend portends that during a time of starvation the Great Spirit sent "star berries" down from heaven to relieve tribal hunger. The star referred to the five-pointed calyx from the berry's flower. Indians ate the berries fresh, dried them for use as seasoning in soups, made blueberry tea as a cure for spasms, and cooked blueberry syrup to treat coughs. Early white settlers learned about the sweet wild berries from the Indians and mimicked their uses.

Maine's wild blueberries are smaller, bluer, and more intensely flavored than cultivated varieties. The blueberries grow in barrens, which are large burned out areas cleared of brush and trees. (You'll be able to see wild blueberries growing along the side of U.S. Hwy. 1; stop and pick yourself a sweet treat.) Most often blueberries are harvested by hand. Pickers use rakes said to look "like dustpans with teeth," and comb the berries off the low bushes. Late summer finds the coveted Maine wild blueberries marketed all over New England in grocery stores and farm stands. The town of Machias sponsors a Blueberry Festival the third week of August every year. For more information contact the Wild Blueberry Association of American, 800/233-8453.

Merryspring Horticultural Nature Park

The brainchild of Mary Ellen Ross in 1973, Merryspring is a blooming work in progress.

Information

Merryspring Horticultural Nature Park, Conway Rd., Camden, ME

04843; 207/236-2239.

Getting There
Take Rte. 1 south from Camden. Turn right on Conway Rd.

First Steps
Stop at the park office for a map and guide. Admission here is free.

Merryspring Horticultural Nature Park. A network of intermingled trails connects Merryspring Horticultural Park's acres of gardens, fields and arboretum. The Ross Center, the park's office and education facility, anchors the park and looks out over a series of formal gardens that are punctuated with bursts of flowering annuals. The gardens include a myriad of herbs divided by their usage; hybrids, floribundas and old garden roses; a continuously blooming perennial border; 60 varieties of hosta; 30 varieties of heather, even a children's garden.

The Perimeter Trail encircles the entire property, offering the most rugged terrain of the 10 path options, including some exposed ledges. Within this boundary you can divert on any of the other well-marked trails. You'll encounter crickets, butterflies, songbirds and scolding squirrels along the trails, but rarely another human in this solitary hermitage. The 10-acre Kitty Todd Arboretum showcases 75 species of trees, which are labeled for easy identification.

Fort Knox State Historic Site Park

Fort Knox was named for America's first Secretary of War, Major General Henry Knox, who lived in Thomaston, Maine, during his retirement (Fort Knox, Kentucky, was also named after him).

Information
Fort Knox State Historic Site, RR 1, Box 1316, Stockton Springs, ME 04981; 207/469-7719.
Bureau of Parks and Lands, 22 State House Station, Augusta, ME 04333; 207/287-3821.

Getting There
Take the Maine Turnpike to exit 9. Then take I-95 to exit 22 and follow

coastal Rte. 1 north to Rte. 174. (The park is across the river from Bucksport.)

First Steps

You'll receive a Fort Knox brochure and map from the park ranger's station as you enter the parking lot and pay a nominal admission fee. The fort's steps may be wet or uneven so wear good walking shoes. Flashlights are needed in parts of the fort.

Fort Knox. A fascinating historic exploration on foot, Fort Knox was the first granite fort built in Maine. Remarkably intact, the large military complex intricately unfolds like the ultimate maze, beckoning you in contradictory directions as you devise your own route.

Construction on Fort Knox began in 1844, after the U.S. became alarmed that Great Britain might try to take control of the Penobscot River and lumber-rich Bangor after a border dispute between Maine and New Brunswick. The fort was designed to protect the Penobscot River Valley from a British naval attack. "A" Battery was completed by 1845, but building continued on the granite block fortress until 1869. No battles were ever consummated at Fort Knox, although troops were garrisoned here during both the Civil War and the Spanish-American War.

The main structure of the fort, built from granite quarried at Mt. Waldo, 5 miles upriver, is shaped like a polygon with three landward sides and a bastion facing the river. A dry moat ditch was defended on each side by walls pierced with musket ports. Begin your tour here. Enter Long Alley, where the narrow, black-as-death corridors (you'll need a flashlight here) snake around the lower perimeter, opening at intervals to reveal the inner workings of the fortress.

After the first turn, you'll begin gradually walking downhill. (The footing here is dark and rather uneven, so exercise caution.) Serpentine alleys traverse the perimeter of the fort, opening onto stone chambers used as ordnance storerooms, powder magazines or casemates. Two-Step Alley leads into the bowels of the fort with two steps every 10 feet or so. This long, narrow chamber has gun barrel-sized windows about 4 inches wide and 2-feet tall. Short staircases lead to the interior parade ground, which is flanked by the officer's and men's quarters, the bakery, a large cistern and underground food storage bins. A spiral staircase leads to the roof, where cannon mounts pepper the fortress. From this vantage point, the view of the Penobscot River is unobstructed to this day.

If you exit the main gates of the fort facing the river, you can examine the "A" and "B" Batteries, upon which multiple cannons were mounted. Each had a hot-shot furnace, which heated the cannonballs so hot that when they hit a ship, the vessel would begin to burn. (Once ships were made of iron, hot-shot furnaces became obsolete.) Hugging the cliffs of the river, Fort Knox looms impenetrable. A trek through its interiors releases the engineering and construction techniques utilized in later Maine forts, as well as freeing the ghosts of our country's military past.

Rainy Day Options

In their compound of exhibition buildings, The **Maine Maritime Museum** examines the enduring relationships between the people of Maine and the sea. Artifacts, memorabilia, videos, dioramas and hands-on interactive exhibits illustrate the many maritime occupations enjoyed here over the ages. The Percy & Small shipyard interprets the process of building a ship. (Ships were actually constructed in the five buildings here from 1894 to 1920.) In the lobstering exhibit, interpreters stage the preparation of lobster meat in a reproduction canning room. The *Sherman Zwicker*, a Grand Banks fishing schooner, moors at the waterfront dock. And an excursion boat cruises up the Kennebec River, passing Bath Iron Works, which still builds ships today. *(Contact: The Maine Maritime Museum, 243 Washington St., Bath, 207/443-1316, www.bathmaine.com.)*

The campus of the **Farnsworth Art Museum and Wyeth Center** encompasses five buildings that display more than 6000 works of art created over three centuries. The museum also features a substantial collection of American Impressionist art. Opened in 1998, the Wyeth Center showcases works of three generations of this "First Family of American Art"—N.C. Wyeth, Andrew Wyeth and James Wyeth. These fascinating dual museums tell the Maine story pictorially. *(Contact: Farnsworth Art Museum and Wyeth Center, 356 Main St., Rockland, 207/596-6457; www.farnsworthmuseum.org; www.wyethcenter.com.)*

Lodging

For more options, consult the New England-wide lodging websites and reservations services listed in "How to Use This Book" or contact the Maine Innkeepers Association, 207/773-7670.

Built for the captain and his family in 1819, the Federal-style **Captain Daniel Stone House** ($$+, 10 Water St., Brunswick, 207/725-9898) combines antiquity with modern comfort and convenience. Rooms in the original building feature marble fireplaces and period wall coverings and furnishings, but even the new sections exude Colonial ambiance.

Faintly evocative of the old television show, "Dark Shadows," **The Galen C. Moses House** ($, 1009 Washington St., Bath, 888/442-8771, www.galenmoses.com) offers guests the opportunity to overnight in a turn-of-the-last-century home in Bath's historic district. A headless lady mannequin with feather boa, which the owner introduces as Mrs. Bates, greets guests at the top of the grand staircase. The B&B showcases fantastic architectural detailing and Victorian furnishings and trappings with museumlike authenticity.

With ocean vistas on three sides, the **Rock Gardens Inn & Cottages** ($, Rte. 217, Sebasco Estates, 207/389-1339, www.rockgardeninn.com) makes the off-the-beaten-track journey from Bath worthwhile. Besides enjoying spectacular views, prolific gardens, fascinating coves and cozy cottages with woodburning fireplaces, you can join in one of the five multi-day art workshops offered every summer.

Situated across the Megunticook River footbridge in the converted mill area of Lower Mechanic Street, **Camden Riverhouse Hotel** ($$, 11 Tannery Lane, Camden, www.camdenmaine.com), a Best Western facility, offers modern amenities with the ambiance of Colonial Camden. Clean and comfortable, Riverhouse is minutes from the action.

A mainstay on Camden's High Street historic district as well as on the must-stop list of discerning travelers, **Maine Stay Inn** ($+, 22 High St., Camden, 207/236-9636) consistently wins raves for its gracious hospitality. Four guestrooms in the 1802 Greek Revival-style inn shelter visitors, who are cosseted by a fireplace in the parlor and treated to a hearty country breakfast each morning.

Norumbega ($$$$, 61 High St., Camden, 207/236-4646, www.norumbegainn.com) means "city of gold," and opulent it surely is. Joseph Stearns built this castle in 1886, after a year of touring the castles of Europe. He incorporated his favorite features in Norumbega, which perches high above Sherman's Cove overlooking Penobscot Bay. No detail has been missed here. Expect to be treated like royalty.

Constructed as a Greek Revival-style home in 1854 by wealthy Camden shipbuilder Elijah Glover, **The Camden Windward House** ($$, Six High St., Camden, 207/236-9656, www.windwardhouse.com) offers eight exquisite guestrooms that are decorated with antiques and reproductions. Featherbeds sit atop polished hardwood floors and period wall coverings mingle with intricate chair rails and moldings.

The six guestrooms of the main house and four quarters of the carriage house offer guests of **The Hawthorn Inn** ($+, 9 High St., Camden, 207/236-8842, www.camdeninn.com) the ambiance of High's Street's opulence of yesteryear. Accommodations feature whirlpool tubs, fireplaces and private decks.

Another of the historic houses on High Street, **Abigail's** ($+, 8 High St., Camden, 207/236-2501, www.midcoast.com/~abigails) coddles your psyche with a fireside tea, soothes aching muscles in a whirlpool tub and then beds you in a queen-size four poster. Originally built for U.S. Representative E.K. Smart in 1847, the Greek Revival frequently hosted Jefferson Davis as an overnight guest.

Embosomed at the base of Mount Battie, **Swan House** ($, 49 Mountain St., Camden, 207/236-8275, 800/207-8275, www.swanhouse.com) offers six quiet, cozy guestrooms, whimsically named after—you guessed it—different types of swans. Built in 1870 as a private family home, Swan House creates an away-from-the-fray, country-casual getaway.

Food and Drink

Be sure to try lobster-in-the-rough, preferably while sitting outside by the sea. For more options, log on to www.mainerestaurant.com.

When you're hankerin' for lobster, head to **Cook's Lobster House** ($$, Rte. 24, Brunswick, 207/833-2818, www.cookslobster.com), on Bailey's

Island, for a Down Easter shore dinner. You'll face a dilemma here: "Which is better, the food or the picturesque view of the vessel-filled harbor?" This is a popular spot, so come early if you want to dine on the outside deck. After dinner, walk to the point to look at the Cribstone Bridge, a historic landmark built in 1927, then visit the wharf to see the working fishing fleet.

Stick with the basics at **J.R. Maxwell & Co.** ($+, 122 Front St., Bath, 207/443-2014), where you'll find an extensive menu of traditionally prepared fish and seafood, meat and pasta. The restaurant occupies an 1840 brick building that formerly was an elegant hotel called The Elliot House. This is a good place to take the kids.

T-shirts at **Beale Street Barbeque & Grill** ($, 215 Water St., Bath, 207/442-9514) state "Because it's a long way from Memphis," the reason, no doubt, that this small grill is Maine's answer to barbecue. Blues music plays in the background and Elvis icons grace the walls. How's the barbecue? Great, even by southern standards. Ribs, chicken, pulled pork, BBQ beef—the choice is yours.

Smack, dab in the middle of Camden's four corners, **Cappy's** ($+, One Main St., Camden, 207/236-2254) percolates with good food, good ale and good cheer, all day long. Lunch or dinner, you'll have a great time here. Cappy's Bakery, around the corner, guarantees something sweetly decadent to top off your chowder.

Travelers have enjoyed good food and libation at **Peter Ott's** ($$, 16 Bay View St., Camden, 207/236-4032) since the German native first opened his home to friends and visitors in the early 1770s. And though Ott himself has long rested in the Mountain View Cemetery, this popular meeting place bears witness to Camden's evolving history, as well as a stellar selection of great seafood, Black Angus beef and a well-packed salad bar.

Seafood with a decidedly Pacific Rim approach marks the **Atlantica Gallery & Grille** ($$, One Bay View Landing, Camden, 207/236-6011) for culinary distinction. The menu of this harborside bistro positively shines with creativity and innovation. If your taste buds crave unusual ingredient combinations with an Asian flare, this is the place for you.

The name says it all at **Waterfront Restaurant,** ($$, Bay View St., Camden, 207/236-3747) because you can't get closer to the water than this. With its outside dining deck all but hanging over Camden Harbor, Waterfront punctuates its seafood-studded menu with some interesting vegetarian dishes. For lunch, don't miss the lobster rolls here.

For a burger and a brew, the **Sea Dog Brewing Co.** ($, 43 Mechanic St., Camden, 207/236-6863) knows how to serve it up. This popular watering hole just happens to be located near the final stop on your Camden village walking tour.

Overlooking Rockport Harbor, the **Sail Loft Restaurant** ($+, Public Landing, Rockport, 207/236-2330) has been a popular local mainstay for more than 30 years.

For an unforgettable view, try a cozy pub on the beach. **The Whale's Tooth Pub & Restaurant** ($+, Rte. 1, Lincolnville Beach, 207/789-5200) serves up lobsters, seafood, and prime rib with quintessential Maine atmosphere.

Downeast Maine

This area of Maine—East Penobscot Bay, Mount Desert and up the coast to the Canadian border—earned its down east moniker because prevailing winds blow from the southwest and, since yesteryear, have pushed sailing schooners downwind toward the east. The economy of downeast Maine has always been tied to the sea—boat building, fishing, shipping—forging a strong maritime tradition that persists today.

Regional Information
Mount Desert Regional Chamber of Commerce, P.O. Box 675, Bar Harbor, ME 04609; 207/288-3411.
Ellsworth Area Chamber of Commerce, P.O. Box 276, Ellsworth, ME 04605; 207/667-5584; www.eacc@downeast.net.

Getting There
By Air: Major airlines offer service to Bangor International Airport (207/947-0384).
By Automobile: Take I-95 to exit 45, I-395, then Rte. 15 south to Rte. 1.

East Penobscot Bay Region

Narrow fingers of land cascade into East Penobscot Bay like a rap singer's dreadlocks, creating a plentitude of peaceful coves and fine harbors and secreting tiny quaint villages that carry on with life as it used to be . . . or at least like it should be. Peaceful, unhurried and tranquil, Castine, Blue Hill and Deer Isle offer a spectacular combination of sea, sun and solitude.

Castine History Tour

Castine has endured a turbulent history. First established as a trading post by Plymouth Pilgrims and fought over until after the War of 1812 by the English, French and Dutch because of its prize location on Penobscot Bay, Castine was named for French trader Jean St. Castin. Castine has had to grow with the flow, and like other downeast villages, livelihoods ran the gamut from farming and fishing to trading and shipbuilding, all of which declined with the advent of the railroad. Wealthy summer visitors, called "rusticators," breathed new life into the area when they began building beautiful Georgian- and Federalist-style homes here at the turn of the last century.

Information
Castine Historical Society, Abbott School, Town Common, ME 04421; 207/326-4118.

Getting There
Take Rte. 1 to Rte. 175 south, to Rte.166A. Cross the bridge over the British Canal (dug by the British in the 18th century to avert an American invasion) into Castine.

First Steps
Pick up a copy of "A Walking Tour of Castine" at the Castine Historical Society, Abbott School on the Town Common, Court St.

Castine History Tour. Castine's quaint seaside wharf and rich maritime history continues to attract 21st-century visitors. The Castine Historical Society has compiled a comprehensive walking tour of this tiny, picturesque village. Follow the guide to the 50 numbered locations, which include architecturally significant homes, churches, and landmarks. As you follow the prescribed route, a series of historical markers recount Castine's fascinating story and trace its colorful past.

The walking tour begins on Water Street, then winds up Perkins Street to the Dyces Head Lighthouse (a footpath here leads down the cliff to water's edge). Of particular note on Perkins Street is the Wilson Museum, which houses prehistoric and local maritime memorabilia in addition to a blacksmith shop and a hearse house. Fort Madison, built by the U.S. in 1811 and re-fortified later in the century, perches on a cliff between two formerly grand Victorian summer "cottages."

From the lighthouse, the tour leads you down Battle Avenue, where the history of the bloody 1779 battle between the English and Americans is told on a series of historical site markers. The ruins of Fort George are open to the public. The British built Fort George, the last spot surrendered by the colonies at the end of the Revolution. (The first hanging in Hancock County happened here, and legend claims that every August the ghost of a young boy can be heard drumming.)

From Battle Street you'll pass the Maine Maritime Academy on Main Street and finish your history tour at the Town Common on Court Street. Of special interest here are the beautiful Bulfinch steeple and Revere bell of the Unitarian Church, c.1790. Before you leave Castine, however, walk to Sea Street and explore the fascinating wharf, where you can tour the Maritime Academy training ship, *Maine*, when it is in port.

Osgood Summit Trail, Blue Hill

Like other coastal downeast villages, Blue Hill historically relied on shipbuilding, shipping and fishing to support its residents, but, in the late 1800s, the town also began mining and shipping copper. After the mines closed at the end of the century, Blue Hill quarried granite until that market also dissipated in the 20th century. Now a haven for summer visitors, the village nestles between Blue Hill Bay and the small mountain from which it got its name—Blue Hill.

Information
Ellsworth Area Chamber of Commerce, P.O. Box 276, Ellsworth, ME 04605; 207/667-5584; www.eacc@downeast.net

Getting There
Take Rte. 15 (Pleasant St.) to Mountain Rd. Continue on Mountain Rd. for 0.4 mile to the trailhead.

First Steps
The trailhead is on the left. No trail maps are available and the trail is not blazed, but the path to the summit is well trodden.

Osgood Summit Trail. Begin your 1-mile hike to the summit through a level, fern-laden mixed growth forest. The trail is named for the Osgood family, early settlers of Blue Hill. Quickly you will begin a moderately strenuous rock-scramble ascent. Look for pileated woodpeckers, which nest in the top of some of the dead pines. When you reach the bald granite top of Blue Hill, you'll be rewarded with a panoramic view of Blue Hill Harbor and the scattered islands in East Penobscot Bay. You can even see Mount Desert Island and Acadia National Park in the distance. Low bush blueberries pepper the mountaintop. The intensely flavored, small berries inspired the name of the hill.

Retrace your steps to Mountain Road. (The path also continues down the other side of the mountain, terminating at Rte. 172 across from the Blue Hill Fairgrounds. You will need to park cars at both Mountain Road and Rte. 172 trailheads to ascend and descend the two different trails.)

Deer Isle

Reached by a high suspension bridge over Eggemoggin Reach from Sedgwick on the mainland, Deer Isle has two small villages—Deer Isle in the northern two-thirds and Stonington, the ferry terminus to Isle au Haut. Fishing has long been the mainstay of these communities, but they harbor fabulous walks within their rocky borders, three of which are featured below. This picturesque area also is home to the Haystack Mountain School of Crafts.

Information
Deer Isle/Stonington Chamber of Commerce, Rte. 15, Deer Isle, ME 04627; 207/348-6124 (summer), www.acadia.net/deerisle.
Island Heritage Trust, P.O. Box 42, Deer Isle, ME 04627.
Walking Trails Group, 207/367-2448.

Getting There
Take Rte. 1 east, to Rte. 175 south, to Rte. 15.

First Steps
Stop at the Visitors Center on Rte. 15 to pick up a "Natural Areas" brochure.

Edgar M. Tennis Preserve, Deer Isle

Since 1972, Edgar M. Tennis and his family have given 145 acres to the State of Maine to be preserved for use as a public walking trail.

Getting There
Take Rte. 15 through Deer Isle Village. After the white church and gas station turn left on Sunshine Rd. Take Sunshine for 2.4 miles, bearing right at the fork, to Fire Rte. 523. Trailhead is 0.3 miles on the left.

First Steps

Pick up a trail map in the blue box at the trailhead. Limited parking is up the road about 100 feet on the right. The 3-mile trail is blazed yellow; a double-yellow blaze indicates a right turn.

Edgar M. Tennis Preserve. Begin your walk along a pine-needle path that follows Pickering Cove. The balsam-scented forest smells like a bow-filled Yuletide mantle. The azure water shimmers in the sunlight, punctuated with small granite-cropped islands and a smattering of fishing gulls. Coves cut into the shoreline, offering private nooks from which to swim. Mussel shells sparkle like jewels in the crystal clear water.

The trail cuts away from the water and leads inland to an ancient family burial ground. Here lie the Billings and the Toothakers, who died in the late 1800s. The trail winds through the shady old-growth forest, dead branches spiraling up the trees in a futile search for the sun. Gray-green reindeer lichen blooms on the rocky outcrops.

Cross the fire road and continue through the forest to the cove at Southeast Harbor. The forest sounds like it is filled with ghosts, as the ancient pines eerily creak in the wind. (When you encounter an enormous outcropping of granite, it will appear you've lost the blaze system. Actually, the blaze is a small triangular pile of stones—called a cairn—placed atop the granite, so

The Islands of Maine

Islands are such a dominant feature of the Maine coast that the state's name itself seems to distinguish the mainland—the main—from the offshore islands. More than 200 islands pepper Penobscot Bay alone—former mainland hills drowned by the melting waters of the last glacier about 11,000 years ago. Some of the islands are easily accessible for day trips; a few offering limited lodging opportunities. Distinguished by sculpted granite shores, thick spruce forests, highlands, and great ocean views, the islands offer a potpourri of picturesque hiking trails.

Among the most popular islands are Matinicus Island and Vinalhaven, accessible by ferry from Rockland Ferry Terminal on Rte. 1, and Isleboro, accessible by a 20-minute car ferry ride from Lincolnville Beach on Rte. 1. Some of the best scenery in Maine can be seen on Monhegan Island, where artist Jamie Wyeth painted the island's dramatic cliffs. Monhegan is accessible by mailboat out of Port Clyde, just south of Rockland on Rte 131. Orr's and Bailey Islands are two of the most visited of the 45 Harpswell Islands of Casco Bay. The two islands can be reached via a granite "honeycomb" bridge, said to be the only crib-stone bridge left in the world. More than half of Isle au Haut is preserved as part of Acadia National Park. The island's lighthouse has been converted into an inn, The Keeper's House (207/367-2261), open seasonally. Isle au Haut is accessible by mailboat from Stonington. Ferries in Bass Harbor, on Mount Desert Island, take passengers to Swans Island and Frenchboro. For more information on the islands of Maine, contact www.visitmaine.com.

make a 90-degree turn, walk over the granite expanse past the blaze, scramble down the other side of the rock and look for the double-yellow blaze that will indicate the trail.)

The path traverses huge root systems of the old-growth forest for a distance, then leads past the foundations of the old Davis Farm and apple orchard. Jog right at the double-yellow blaze and walk through tall grass as the trail follows Great Brook back to the trailhead. This is a great walk on which to bring a picnic and a swimsuit.

Barred Island Preserve—Deer Isle

Barred Island was owned at the turn of the last century by the famed New England landscape architect, Frederick Law Olmstead. His grandniece gave the island to The Nature Conservancy in 1969. George Pavlov, owner of Goose Cove Lodge, contributed 48 acres of maritime boreal fog-forest, providing access to the island by land.

Getting There
Take Rte. 15 to Deer Isle Village, then 15A to Goose Hill Rd. Follow Goose Hill Rd. (becomes a washboard dirt road about halfway) to parking area (six cars only) on the right.

First Steps
Pick up a trail map at the trailhead. Check posted tidal chart before setting off for Barred Island, which is accessible for 3 hours on either side of dead-low tide. This 2.5-mile moderately difficult trail demands careful attention to footing over giant tree roots or flat boulders. Wear hiking boots. The trail is blazed white. Choose a warm, sunny day for this walk if you can, so that you can fully engage all your senses.

Barred Island Preserve. This must be the forest primeval. Pine needle paths wind through an incredible bunchberry-punctuated carpet of reindeer lichen and "old man's beard," which clings to the granite surfaces. Condensation over the Gulf of Maine bestows bountiful precipitation on the forest, fostering the growth of these lichens and mosses. Giant red spruce and balsam fir reach for the sun, which only penetrates the canopy in dapples. Some trees even grow atop granite boulders.

At the fork, follow the sign to Barred Island. You'll emerge from the shady forest through a thicket of wild raspberries to an overlook showcasing the sparkling waters of Goose Cove and Penobscot Bay. Follow the trail down the hill. As you near the water you'll go through a very dense coniferous forest, where you'll feel a noticeable drop in temperature. Everywhere, you are reminded you are in Maine because of the huge granite outcroppings and the constant throaty hum of lobster boats in the distance.

You'll come out of the forest at a granite point, where wild roses cascade down to the water and an isthmus of sand emerges at low tide. Cross the pebble-sand causeway, which is littered with mussel shells and dismembered blue crabs, the remains of the seagulls' day. Moving counterclockwise around the island, scramble over the giant pastel granite boulders—ribboned with pink alpite—that emerge from the water. (The amount of time you can spend on Barred Island is totally dependent upon the time remaining in your tidal opportunity window.)

This is heaven, Maine style. A 360-degree watery panorama, sprinkled with islands and peppered with boats, sparkles like a sea of diamonds. Sea breezes kiss the cheeks and tickle the olfactories like freshly laundered sheets. Geese, ducks, cormorants and gulls take off and land like planes on a jetway, working the water in search of a meal. Ship to shore radios of the working lobster fleet echo like gunshots in a canyon.

You can only walk halfway around Barred Island, because the rest of the shoreline is a bird sanctuary for nesting ospreys. Retrace your steps across the boulders, then traverse the sandbar to the shore. Return through the forest following the Shore Loop Trail.

Settlement Quarry—Stonington

Stonington granite forms the bedrock of the southern part of Deer Isle, created 360 million years ago when Maine was geologically active. Settlement Quarry employed hundreds of men in the early 1900s, when Stonington granite was quarried for use in the Williamsburg and Manhattan Bridges in New York City, the New York County Courthouse and the Boston Museum of Fine Arts. Most active in the 1920s, Stonington Quarry was quarried briefly in the 1960s, when it provided granite for the John F. Kennedy Memorial in Arlington National Cemetery. The quarry closed permanently about 1980.

Getting There
Take Rte. 15 through Deer Isle Village and continue on until you see signs to Oceanville (Ron's Mobil is on the corner). Turn left on Oceanville Rd. for .9 mile. Quarry is on the right.

First Steps
Pick up a Settlement Quarry map/brochure at the kiosk in the parking lot. The Glacial Erratic Trail is blazed orange and Grout Pile Trail, blue.

Settlement Quarry. Begin your 1-mile exploration of Settlement Quarry by walking through the canopied forest along the Glacial Erratic Trail. The ground is covered with bunchberries—six-leafed low plants that sport springtime white flowers and red berries in the summer. A huge boulder sits in the middle of the path. This glacial erratic—not granite like the surrounding outcroppings—was deposited here by a melting glacier. Cross a huge "carpet" of granite to the viewing platform. Here you'll enjoy a panoramic view of Webb Cove, Isle au Haut and Camden Hills.

The quarry, which is shaped like an amphitheater with flat benches and vertical faces, falls away steeply to the south. To quarry the granite, a line of vertical holes was drilled behind an exposed rock face; then the slabs were broken free by splitting the holes open with a winch or an explosive charge. A fine-grained pink rock called aplite cuts through the main sheets of granite in long, thin sheets of rock called dikes. Aplite is made up of the same minerals as granite but the individual grains are much smaller.

From the quarry, follow the Grout Pile Trail past the huge waste rock piles (called grout). (These hills are unstable, so do not attempt to climb them.) Then follow the old quarry road back to the parking area where you began.

Mount Desert Island

History credits French explorer Samuel Champlain with the discovery and christening of Mount Desert Island as *isle des monts deserts* or island of barren mountains. Although the bald peak of Cadillac Mountain tops the island, Mount Desert is anything but barren—a treasure trove of 17 mountains and four lakes. Aeons ago, glaciers carved through an east-west ridge of granite, forming mountains that rise from sea and catching lakes in their valleys. The ocean encircles the island, wedging a tidal zone between sea and mountains, where tidal pools—pockets of seawater stranded in rock basins—trap a city of fascinating marine organisms.

Acadia National Park

The oldest national park on the East Coast, established in 1916, Acadia National Park encompasses 41,000 acres on Mount Desert Island, a portion of Schoodic Peninsula and a peppering of offshore islands. Rugged and breathtakingly beautiful, Acadia features more than 120 miles of trails, from level strolls near the water's edge, to moderate walks along a system of carriage roads, to hardy hikes up steep elevations such as Precipice Trail. You also can drive to the summit of Cadillac Mountain, 1,530 feet, where a 0.25-mile level foot trail circumvents the peak.

Information
Acadia National Park, P.O. Box 177 (Rte. 233), Bar Harbor, ME 04609; 207/288-3338; www.nps.gov/acad/anp. The Park offers ranger-led walks during the summer season.

Getting There
Take I-95 to exit 45A, I-395, to Rte. 1A through Ellsworth, to Rte. 3 south.

First Steps
Stop at Hulls Cove Visitor Center on Rte. 3 to purchase "The Complete Map and Guide of Acadia National Park on Mount Desert Island and Bar Harbor," which features all hiking trails on Mount Desert Island. In addition to mapped trails, this publication rates the walks and hikes by ability level and gives complete directions to each trailhead. Also pick up the Acadia Carriage Road User's Map, which is free. Two representative walks in the easy-to-moderate range—Jordan Pond Walk (park in the Jordan Pond lot, not the Jordan Pond House lot.) and Witch Hole Pond Carriage Loop Trail—are highlighted below.

Jordan Pond Walk. This moderate, scenic 3.3-mile walking loop begins at the end of the boat ramp behind Jordan Pond House. The Jordan family built the original farmhouse here, which the Tibbetts family turned into a restaurant in the 1880s. A popular teahouse by the 1900s known for its popovers, Jordan Pond House's reservation list has included Rockefeller, Ford, Astor, Carnegie, Pulitzer and President Taft.

When you get to the water's edge, turn right and follow the path around Jordan Pond. (Be sure to wear sturdy walking shoes, not sneakers.) Surrounding the pond you'll see Jordan Ridge, Sargent Mountain, Pemetic Mountain and the Bubbles. The Bubbles are twin peaks that were rounded into knobs as the glacier traveled over them. The glacier scooped out a basin at the foot of the Bubbles and melted, forming Jordan Pond, actually the size of a small lake.

Keep the pond on your left as you follow the path, which is flat and even in the beginning. Because this is a watershed area, waters are gin clear here. You'll walk through pine forests, the water rippling and lapping at the shore. And while you may scare up an occasional pileated woodpecker, the Jordan Pond walk is serene and bucolic, especially in the spring and autumn before the peak tourist season.

About 2/3-mile into the walk, the terrain, while still flat, becomes more challenging. The path becomes a minefield of roots and flat pink-granite boulders that are punctuated by rough-hewn log boardwalks. Stop and look behind you every so often to drink in the view because it is easy to keep looking down at your precarious footing and thereby miss the wonders of this glorious pond.

Witch Hole Pond Carriage Loop Trail. From 1913 to 1941, John D. Rockefeller, Jr., a skilled horseman, financed and built 57 miles of carriage roads throughout Mount Desert. This network of woodland roads was kept free of motor vehicles for enjoyment by hikers, bicyclists, horseback riders and carriages. The 16-foot-wide broken-stone carriage roads cut through the hillside and are connected by 17 hand-cut stone bridges made of island granite. The near-road landscape is naturalized with low bush blueberries and ferns.

(To find the entrance for Witch Hole Pond Carriage Road, drive 2.5 miles west of Bar Harbor on Rte. 233. At .8 mile beyond where Park Loop Road joins Rte. 233, turn right on an unnamed road for 1.1 mile to Duck

Brook Bridge. Park along the road.) Begin your 3.3-mile walk of Witch Hole Pond Carriage Trail by crossing the triple-arched, stone Duck Brook Bridge and turning right.

This peaceful wooded walk traverses a flat, fine-gravel path and loops around Witch Hole Pond (on your left) and then Halfmoon Pond (on your right), both of which are filled with white water lilies and flowering purple water plants. (This road is maintained to accommodate wheelchairs and strollers.) You have the option of diverting up the Paradise Hill loop for an extra 1.5-mile roundtrip hiking loop, where, on a clear day, you'll be rewarded with a fine view of Hulls Cove and Frenchman's Bay. If you visit in late July, you'll find ripe low-bush blueberries bordering the carriage road.

Bar Harbor—Shore Path and Bar Island

Named after Englishman Sir Richard Eden, the village that is now Bar Harbor was incorporated as Eden in 1796. Farming, lumbering, shipbuilding and fishing supported the townsfolk over the next century. By the 1850s, a regular steamboat run attracted Hudson Valley School artists and wealthy "rusticators," as they were called, from New York and Boston, who built large summer mansions that rivaled Newport, Rhode Island. The village changed its name to Bar Harbor in 1918 and continued to flourish as a tourist destination until a disastrous fire in 1947—started in a cranberry bog—which destroyed the entire town. The village re-emerged from the ashes, however, to become a popular summer tourist mecca once again.

Information
Bar Harbor Chamber of Commerce, 93 Cottage St., Bar Harbor, ME 04609; 207/288-5103; www.barharborinfo.com.
Bar Harbor Historical Society, 33 Ledgelawn Ave., Bar Harbor, ME 04609; 207/288-3807.

Getting There
Take I-95 to exit 45A, I-395, to Rte. 1A through Ellsworth, to Rte. 3 south.

First Steps

Stop at the Chamber of Commerce office on Cottage Street to purchase a "Bar Harbor Map and Guide." Both portions of this walk begin and end at Town Pier. You can do them in either order, but be sure you time the Bar Island portion by the tidal restrictions noted below. The Shore Path is a 1-mile walking loop over even terrain. Bar Island is a 2-mile return trip jaunt over uneven terrain with easy elevations.

Bar Harbor Shore Path and Bar Island. Begin at Town Pier at the corner of Main and West Streets where commercial fishermen and lobstermen bring in their daily catch. Whale-watching cruises depart from this wharf, and visiting sailboats and motor yachts are moored in the adjacent harbor. Agamont Park overlooks the pier, a leafy green peppered with park benches and a fountain.

Walk up Main Street, a quaint-looking thoroughfare lined with boutiques, restaurants and specialty shops. (Divert down Cottage or Mount Desert Streets if you need a larger shopping "fix." Pass the Village Green, long the center for Bar Harbor summer festivals and concerts. When you get to Wayman Lane turn left and proceed to the ocean. Turn left and enter the Shore Path, a century-old path open to the public through the generosity of the abutting landowners and the Village Improvement Association.

The view of the ocean from this elevated path is spectacular. Frenchman's Bay is on your right, some of Bar Harbor's 20th-century mansion "cottages" and grand hotels on your left. During a receding tide you'll see large pastel granite boulders littering the shore. Just before Grant Park, a glacial erratic—Balanced Rock—hangs precariously. Follow Shore Path back to Town Pier.

You must time the Bar Island portion of this walk to coincide with low tide, because the sandbar that leads from Bridge Street to the island is under water at other times. Set off from Town Pier about 1.5 hours before dead-low tide. Walk down West Street to Bridge Street, then turn right and walk across the emerging causeway to the island. A path leads to the summit of Bar Island, which offers a panoramic view of Bar Harbor and the Porcupine Islands. Retrace your steps back to the mainland before the tide starts coming in again and return to Town Pier.

Rainy Day Options

You won't find a front door at the **Colonel Black Mansion** because this brick, Georgian-style home, c.1828, sports triple-track windows instead. Once the two lower panes are raised, you literally will walk through a window into another era, because three generations of Blacks lived here at "Woodlawn" for more than 100 years. (John Black earned his title "Colonel" in the War of 1812.) The house, which was willed to the county in 1928 as a museum by the last surviving family member, is preserved intact. Furniture, carpeting, tapestries, needlepoint coverings, rope beds and English antiques dating to the 1600s adorn the rooms. Three miles of trails wind throughout the 180-acre property. (Several generations of Blacks are buried in the tomb at the end of the carriage trail.) Trails are open year round; guided tours of the mansion, from June 1 to October 15. *(Take Main St. west from downtown Ellsworth. Cross Union River Bridge and take the left fork onto Surrey Road, Rte. 172. Entrance is .2 miles on the right at the "Woodlawn" sign. Contact: Colonel Black Mansion, Rte. 172, Ellsworth, 207/667-8671.)*

Lodging

For more options, consult the New England-wide lodging websites and reservations services listed in the "How to Use This Book" or contact the Maine Innkeepers Association, 207/773-7670, for more options.

Built in 1898,the late Victorian Italianate-style **Castine Inn** ($, Main St. Castine, 207/326-4365, www.castineinn.com) is an oasis of culture and fine dining in the midst of Castine's historic district, one block from the harbor. Each summer, three free eventide concerts play from the inn's wraparound porch; listeners soak up the music from perches in the surrounding English gardens. The inn's guestrooms, a bit tired, are being given facelifts, but you'll find the common room a virtual art gallery, the pub cozy, and the dining room superb (See Food and Drink).

An operating inn since 1840, **The Blue Hill Inn** ($+, Union St., Blue Hill, 207/374-2844, www.bluehillinn.com) entertains guests with the gracious hospitality afforded a welcome family friend. Nineteenth-century period furniture adorns the 11 guestrooms, suites and common rooms, soft classical music fills the background, and a roomful of Maine guidebooks help you plan your stay. Architectural details of the c.1830 Colonial include wide-plank pumpkin pine flooring, six-over-six windows and a 20-candle French chandelier. Enjoy the complimentary hors d'oeuvres hour from 6 to 7 PM.

Elizabeth Cush Haskill began operating her ancestral home as a guesthouse in 1890. Today, everything about this 1793 Colonial, now **Pilgrim's Inn** (\$\$, P.O. Box 69, Deer Isle, 207/348-66150, www.pilgrimsinn.com), is magic. You'll be enveloped in the warm and personal yet unobtrusive hospitality here. The country-style guestrooms are comfy, but head outdoors and grab an Adirondack chair at the edge of the tranquil tidal pond. A legendary complimentary hors d'oeuvres hour foreshadows a phenomenal multi-course gourmet daily repast (rates here are MAP). All senses become sated in no time.

The Ledgelawn Inn (\$\$, 66 Mt. Desert St., Bar Harbor, 207/288-4596, 800/274-5334, www.barharborvacations.com) exudes its understated elegance like a lady of "good breeding." The 33 guestrooms of this 1904 restored summer "cottage" and adjacent carriage house are furnished with Lexington antique reproductions, period-inspired fabrics and wall coverings, and antique photographs. A sweeping staircase dominates the parlor, a reminder of the grand gatherings the "rusticators" enjoyed here at the turn of the last century.

You can't sleep closer to the ocean that this. **The Balance Rock Inn** (\$\$\$+, 21 Albert Meadow, Bar Harbor, 207/288-2610, 800/753-0494, www.barharborvacations.com), a 1903 shingle-style summer mansion "cottage" cum elegant inn, sits directly on the Atlantic overlooking the historic Shore Path. With views from here to eternity from nearly every room, a gracious salon complete with baby grand piano, and an ocean-side verandah, pool and copious gardens, Balance Rock re-creates the luxury of a forgotten era.

If you like to be smack-dab in the center of the action, with the harbor at your fingertips, you'll like **The Golden Anchor** (\$+, 55 West St., Bar Harbor, 207/288-5033, 800/328-5033, www.goldenanchorinn.com). The motel-style rooms vary in cost based on the view of the water. Water-view accommodations open onto balconies that afford sweeping views of the harbor vessel traffic and great people watching on the adjacent granite pier.

Castine Harbor Lodge ($+, Perkins St., Castine, 207/326-4335, www.castinemaine.com) hugs a primo perch above Castine Harbor with fabulous views over Penobscot Bay. This 1893 stick-style mansion was built for a wealthy New Yorker and showcases 250 feet of porches, all of which face the ocean. Each of the 16 guestrooms has great views as well.

Standing at the site of Deer Isle's only link to the mainland—the ferry—until a bridge was built across Eggemoggin Reach in 1939, **The Inn at Ferry Landing** ($+, R.R. 1, Deer Isle, 207/348-7760, www.ferry-landing.com) now offers guests a private, watery hermitage. All four guestrooms of the restored 1840s farmhouse have great water views. The two-room family annex is popular because young children are welcome there.

Tucked in a secluded cove on Frenchman's Bay, **The Inn at Canoe Point** ($$, Eden St., Rte. 3, Bar Harbor, 207/288-9511, www.innatcanoepoint.com) is a Tudor-style "cottage" built in 1889. Nestled in tall pines, this intimate bed and breakfast offers five guestrooms, two of which are suites. Everywhere you look here, you are afforded magnificent vistas of the open water.

Once a stagecoach stop and rural tavern, the **Coach Stop Inn** ($, Rte. 3, Bar Harbor, 207/288-9886, www.coachstopinn.com) still cossets guests with warm hospitality. Built as a Cape Cod-style Colonial in 1804, the bed and breakfast showcases original-issue wide-plank pine floors and hand-hewn pegged beams. Out of the way and away from the fray, Coach Stop Inn offers five cheerful guestrooms and good value.

Food and Drink

Lobster pounds abound in downeast Maine and most restaurants offer an extensive selection of fresh local seafood as well. For more options, log on to www.mainerestaurant.com.

A former sail and rigging loft in the 1880s, **Dennett's Wharf** ($$, Sea Street, Castine, 207/326-9045) serves good basic poultry, meat and seafood with a natty, maritime flair. Nautical flags hang from its dollar bill-peppered vaulted ceiling and a polished pine bar runs the length of the restaurant. An outside deck hangs over the harbor, affording a gull's eye view of the seafaring action. Don't miss the mussels here.

Maine's natural wonders attracted Chef Tom Gutow to the **Castine Inn** ($$+, Main St. Castine, 207/326-4365, www.castineinn.com), and his innovative cuisine will lure you here, too. Choose between the cozy pub and the dimly lit, mural-lined dining room. Either ambiance ensures an elegant setting for a sumptuous meal. The menu reads like culinary prose and tastes like pure poetry. And, like all good works of art, desserts are worthy of the Louvre.

Dedicated to a philosophy of fresh local ingredients used in inventive combinations, **Pilgrim's Inn** ($$$$, P.O. Box 69, Deer Isle, 207/348-66150, www.pilgrimsinn.com) offers a dining adventure every evening. From the hour-long hors d'oeuvres extravaganza in the rustic common room to the multiple courses that follow in the country-style glass-enclosed dining room, an evening here is worth the prix fixe tariff. (Reservations for diners not staying at the inn are limited so call well in advance for a reservation.)

Its white-clothed tables adorned with fresh flowers, **Jonathan's** ($$, Main St., Blue Hill, 207/374-5226) sets the stage for upscale, eclectic, inventive cuisine. Culinary offerings and corresponding prices are divided by plate size—small, medium, large—so mix and match as your appetite and pocketbook advises, but whatever the combination, you won't be disappointed.

Secreting a colorful past, the building now hosting **Galyn's** (17 Main St., Bar Harbor, 207/288-9706) was a boarding house for local seamen in the 1890s and a speakeasy during prohibition with a gambling casino in the back room. Galyn's retained the pressed-tin ceiling and native birch floor from yesteryear and rewrote history with its imaginative seafood-studded menu. The only true decadence at Galyn's now is dessert.

Freddie's Route 66 ($+, 21 Cottage St., Bar Harbor, 207/288-3708) is a treasure trove of fun. Chockful of memorabilia from the ë50s, this trip down Memory Lane will fire up your imagination along with your taste buds. From the classic Fonzie burger—you ëgotta be cool' to eat it—to the 1957 Chevy Special—a hot brownie with ice cream and the trimmings served in a pink '57 Chevy convertible that you can take home with you—you'll get your kicks at Route 66.

Good service, great sauces, large portions and white-napkin bistro elegance mark **Anthony's Cucina Italiana** ($-$$, 191 Main St., Bar Harbor, 207/288-3377) for distinction. Classic Italian renditions utilize predominantly Bar Harbor's fresh local seafood, but you'll also find "it-tastes-like-Italy" quality pasta dishes and gourmet pizzas. The line is out the door in the summer season; call ahead for reservations.

Sit atop a granite pier that juts into the harbor and savor a freshly boiled Maine lobster while sightseeing vessels, sloops and lobster boats putter around the port. A summer afternoon doesn't get any better than this. **The Pier** ($, 55 West St., Bar Harbor, 207/288-5033) offers indoor seating as well, with equally wonderful views of the harbor.

Although the menu certainly offers more options, **The Docksider Restaurant Too** ($, 131 Cottage St, Bar Harbor, 207/288-9093) is the place to go for great "chowdah," sweet lobster rolls and down-home Maine blueberry pie. A second restaurant, The Docksider, is on Sea Street in Northeast Harbor (207/276-3965).

For fresh-off-the-boat lobster and shellfish, stop at Beal's Lobster Pound ($+, **Beal's Lobster Pier**, Clark Point Rd., Southwest Harbor, 207/244-3022). You'll eat at picnic tables right on the pier in the midst of Beal's commercial lobstering operation. Open from Memorial Day to Labor Day, this is the place to go on a fine, sunny day.

Index